BURT FRANKLIN: RESEARCH & SOURCE WORKS SERIES 518
American Classics in History & Social Science 134

THE WRITINGS OF
COLONEL WILLIAM BYRD
OF WESTOVER IN VIRGINIA ESQ^R.

Colonel William Byrd.

THE WRITINGS OF
COLONEL WILLIAM BYRD

OF WESTOVER IN VIRGINIA ESQ^R.

EDITED BY

JOHN SPENCER BASSETT

ILLUSTRATED

BURT FRANKLIN
NEW YORK

911.755
B995ω

Published by BURT FRANKLIN
235 East 44th St., New York, N.Y. 10017
Originally Published: 1901
Reprinted: 1970
Printed in the U.S.A.

S.B.N. 04427
Library of Congress Card Catalog No.: 76-125631
Burt Franklin: Research and Source Works Series 518
American Classics in History and Social Science 134

PREFACE

THE present edition of the writings of Colonel William Byrd II of Westover has been planned to include all the really important matter from his pen which has come down to us. The editor has omitted the numerous irrelevant papers which are included in the old vellum-bound volume which is preserved by the family at Brandon. These papers were printed in the Wynne edition of 1866, because it was the intention of Wynne to make that an exact reprint of the manuscript. The editor has ventured to omit the " Essay on Bulk Tobacco " on the ground that Byrd did not write it. Although the title of the "Essay" declares that the piece was written by Byrd in 1692, this must have been a mistake, because at that time Byrd was only eighteen years old and had been for over eight years a resident of Europe. Moreover, the "Essay" itself professes to have been written by London merchants. Its presence in Byrd's manuscript volume was probably due to the error of a copyist. On the other hand, the editor has been able to include in the present edition some samples of Byrd's letters. He had expected to reprint extensively from this source, but on investigation he learned that the Virginia Historical Society had secured copies of these letters and was about to publish them serially in its "Magazine," and he did not feel that he had a right to forestall so laudable an undertaking. In two appendices have been included the catalogue of the Byrd library and a genealogy of the immediate Byrd family. The former will interest those who are curious to know the contents of the largest private library in the

English colonies, and the latter has a personal value to many Virginia families.

The sketch of the Byrd family, which is given as the Introduction, has been taken almost wholly from manuscript sources. It is based : (1) on the abstracts of the Virginia papers in the British Public Records Office made by Mr. W. Noël Sainsbury and preserved in the State Library at Richmond under the title of "Sainsbury Papers"; (2) on the Council Minutes, two volumes of which — those for 1705–1721 and 1721–1734 — are in the State Library in Richmond, and one volume — that for 1698–1700 — is in the Congressional Library; (3) on the letters of William Byrd[I] and William Byrd[II], which are preserved, in original form or in copies, by the Virginia Historical Society; and (4) on other documents of a miscellaneous nature to which due reference has been made in the foot-notes. This sketch is submitted to the public with a little hesitation. Where so little territory previously has been explored it is difficult to be entirely sure of one's course.

The editor has received assistance in his work from many sources. His thanks are due especially to Mr. W. G. Stannard, secretary of the Virginia Historical Society, and to his assistant, Mrs. Sally Nelson Robins, for putting at his disposal the valuable documents in the possession of the society. They gave, moreover, much personal information without which the editor's previous unfamiliarity with Virginia genealogies must have been a serious inconvenience. His thanks are also due for many courtesies to Messrs. R. A. Brock, W. W. Scott, and F. P. Brent, and to Dr. J. A. C. Chandler, of Richmond; to Mr. William Byrd and to the authorities of the Columbia University Library, of New York; to Messrs. M. O. Sherrill and Marshall De L. Haywood, of Raleigh, N. C.; and to Mr. J. F. Rowe, treasurer of the Middle Temple, London.

JOHN SPENCER BASSETT.

Trinity College, Durham, N. C.,
    October 8, 1901.

CONTENTS

LIST OF PLATES

INTRODUCTION

THE BYRD FAMILY IN VIRGINIA

T HE aristocratic form of Virginia society was fixed
soon after the Restoration of the Stuarts. It proceeded from economic, social, and political causes. On its
economic side it was supported by land and servitude; on
its social side it was sustained by the ideals, and somewhat
by the blood, of the English country gentlemen; on its
political side it was fostered by a system of appointments
to office which left the least room for a democracy. In
the century which preceded the Revolution it was in its
greatest vigor. Like all aristocracies which are not
frequently renewed from outside sources, it at length went
into decay; but in the century of its vigor it produced a
type of leadership which few other communities have
equaled. These leaders of men have won the admiration
of numerous people by their conservative progress, by their
political integrity, and, most of all, by their force of
character. It is the purpose of this introductory sketch
to show how two of the most eminent of these leaders, a
father and his son, acquired their industrial, social, and
political positions, and how they used them. If we understand this development we shall better know how such a
man as Washington was made possible.

The holding of land and of slaves in Virginia took the
form of vastness during the century of which I speak.
Before that time land grants had been kept more or less
within the original compass of fifty acres for each person
actually imported. When the colony had become thor-

oughly settled there was a demand for much larger holdings. The importation rights became valuable,—in fact,
they took a market value,—and in 1699 the Council threw
aside the old custom, and ordered that any one who paid
five shillings sterling should have the right to take up
fifty acres of land in lieu of an importation right.[1] The
effect was to throw land freely on the market, and the
action could have been taken only in response to a strong
popular demand. It did not create the custom of large
holdings, for they had existed to a considerable extent before, but it relieved purchasers of the necessity of evad-
ing the importation clause. If that clause had been
steadily enforced, the population of the colony must have
been much greater than it was. The views we get from
the Council journals of the land grants in this period show
that the average land grant was very large. For instance,
on June 14, 1726, there were granted, in twenty-seven
grants, 48,284 acres, an average of 1788 acres to a grant.
These, it must be remembered, included no extraordinary
grants. Of the latter there were not a few, as when Spotswood in one night signed various grants for 10,000, 20,000,
and 40,000 acres each, and managed it so that 86,650
acres were for himself.[2] When we remember that most of
the grants made in 1726 were to persons who already
owned land, it will be seen how much the tendency to build
large estates was developed. It would, perhaps, not be
too much to say that the average well-to-do Virginian of
the period owned as much as three thousand acres of land,
while there were in every community a few people who
owned much more.

The extension of slavery proceeded in direct ratio with
this extension of land grants. There had been no great
numbers of slaves in the colony before the close of the
century, but they now were imported in great numbers.

[1] Council Minutes, June 21,
1699.
[2] Drysdale to the Board
of Trade, Sainsbury Papers,
1720–30, entry for June 6,
1724.

They were necessary to the great estates. The colonists
had tried white labor for over a half-century, and it
proved unreliable. It was possible to hold it till the
terms of indenture were expired, but after that such servants were quickly converted into landholders on their
own account. They took up land and settled in the
colony, or, after the aristocratic tendency had become so
marked, they filed off to North Carolina, where conditions
were more equal. If the Virginians could have repro-
duced the English country estate worked by a body of
white tenants they would gladly have done it. The slow-
ness with which they turned to African slavery shows this
conclusively. But in America such estates were not possible. They did the next best thing, as it seemed to people of the age : they developed slaveholding estates.

This industrial development was affected by, and in
turn affected, the social conditions of the colony. The
most striking phase of the social life of the period is the
arrival of the Cavaliers. These people were no more all
earls and dukes than the royal army was composed of
earls and dukes. Many of them had noble blood in their
veins, without doubt, but in the royal army they had been
among the minor officers, and most of them had lost their
property. They came to Virginia from economic as well
as social reasons. They were received by the people with
warmth. Governor Berkeley gave them lands and appointed them to offices. If we may believe Governor
Nicholson, they married most of the desirable heiresses
and widows among the colonists. They were not numerous, as compared with the older population, but they had
an influence out of proportion to their numbers. They
gave manners a warmer tone ; they emphasized the ideal
of country life ; they gave Virginians their passion for
handsome houses and fast horses ; and they gave public life
something more than it had before of the English notion
that offices should be held for the benefit of the gentry.
Their intermarriage with the colonists soon made Vir-

ginians of them. By the time Berkeley was thrown from power, in 1677, they may be said to have become absorbed into the population.

From that time colonial society of tide-water Virginia was fixed. If there had ever come in England another social upheaval which would drive out a large number of the gentry, there might have come a new stream of immigration to this section. But such an upheaval was not to be. The poorer people with fortunes to make, who are always the vast majority of immigrants, passed on to North Carolina. Thither went also the indented servants after the expiration of their terms of service, and sometimes before, for lands were cheap there and life democratic. Thus there developed a difference of social structure between the two colonies which produced an unfortunate lack of sympathy which is not yet entirely outlived.[1]

Lieutenant-Governor Nicholson, who had seen something of life in other colonies, described the condition in Virginia in 1701. "There is little or no encouragement," said he. "for men of any tolerable parts to come hither. Formerly there was good convenient land to be taken up and there widows had pretty good fortunes which were encouragements for men of parts to come. But now all or most of the good lands are taken up, and if there be any widows or maids of any fortune, the natives for the most part get them; for they begin to have a sort of aversion to others, calling them strangers. In the Civil War sev-

---

[1] In 1708 the Board of Trade asked why so many people left Virginia to settle elsewhere. The Virginia Council replied that people left Virginia to settle in North Carolina: (1) because the good land in Virginia was taken up; (2) because land was cheap and the terms of taking it up easy in North Carolina; (3) because, although Virginia debts were pleadable, it was almost impossible to win a suit there against one who had run away from his debts in Virginia, and this was due both to a popular sympathy for such debtors and to the unsettled condition of the country. (See Council Minutes, vol. for 1705–21, entry for Oct. 19, 1708.)

eral gentlemen of quality fled hither, and others of good
parts, but they are all dead ; and I hope in God there will
never be such a cause to make them come in again." [1]
Nicholson regretted this state of affairs, especially because
it produced so few men capable of filling the offices ; but
to him the Board of Trade made the very pertinent observation that it ought to be his aim under the circumstances to develop out of the Virginians men who were
capable of office. [2] This observation indicates just what
did happen. Virginia society had taken to itself its own
direction. Except for the small number of persons who
arrived from time to time in some official capacity, the
life of the colony had received its last external impression
till the arrival of the great stream of Scotch-Irish in the
upper districts shortly after 1730.

The political conditions during the century before the
Revolution had great influence on the development of life
in Virginia. Public life at the time was the least bit
democratic. The only election in the colony was held for
the members of the Assembly. The county officers were
appointed, either by the governor, or by the governor and
Council, or by some other officer to whom the right of appointment had been given. The Council, the members of
which were appointed by the king on the recommendation
of the governor, was the upper house of the Assembly, and
could therefore check legislation. How this body always
maintained a remarkable degree of independence of the
governor, and, in fact, constituted the chief ruling force in
the colony during the administration of most of the colonial governors, will be shown later. Here it is enough to
say that it, in common with the local government, worked
steadily to aid the industrial and social forces which have
been pointed out in the process of building up in every
county men of strong personality who were able to speak
for the action of their respective counties in public affairs.

[1] The Sainsbury Papers, Vol. II. Part II. (1625–1715), p. 291.
[2] Ibid., p. 378.

These men had the political traditions of the English country gentlemen, and they were strong enough in their own state, and in conjunction with the trading interests of other states they were strong enough in the nation, to restrain that extreme republican feeling which, while a prime motive force in the Revolution, was a serious danger in the formation of the Constitution.

The period of which I have spoken is almost exactly covered by the lives of the three men who made the name of Byrd famous in the history of Virginia. The first William Byrd came to America about 1670; the third William Byrd died in 1777. The history of these three men of the same name is closely interwoven with every phase of the economic, social, and political history of the colony for that period. The two first of them represented the very flower of Virginia life, both strong men, and wealthy men, and intelligent men, and the second especially brilliant. The other, the last of the succession, represents the decay of the family, wealthy, and in the beginning influential, cultured, perhaps, but less strong in character, and less able to hold in his hands either his property or his passions. His own children, who were many, although men and women of personal worth, were less wealthy and less influential than he, and took their places quite naturally among the people who make up society without being able to direct its course.

William Byrd[I], whose good fortune it was to arrive in Virginia when the society there was just beginning to fix itself, was the grandson on his mother's side of that Captain Thomas Stegg, or Stegge, who was sent by Parliament to America in 1651 as one of the commissioners to reduce the colonies of Virginia and Maryland to obedience. His good success in that enterprise was perhaps partly due to the fact that he had been for some years a resident of the former colony. As early as 1637 we find that he was a merchant trading in James River. His home was near Westover, in Charles City County. He was a member of the

Assembly, and of enough influence to be elected Speaker
in 1643, and in 1644 he was a member of the Council. He
was a Parliamentarian at this time, and on that side had in
the same year letters of marque by virtue of which he
seized a Bristol ship in Boston harbor. In 1651, after receiving the submission of the colony, he embarked on a
ship from Virginia for England, and was lost on the passage.[1] He left his estate in Virginia to his son, Thomas
Stegg, and his houses in London to his daughter, Grace
Byrd. The son sold his lands in Charles City, and settled
in 1661 at the falls of the James, in Henrico, where he
died without heirs in 1671. He was a man of influence in
his county. In 1663 he was, with Henry Randolph, col-
lector of quit-rents for Henrico and Charles City counties,[2]
and he was successively captain and colonel [3] of the militia,
member of the Council,[4] and auditor-general.[5] His estate
in land and stock he left to his nephew, William Byrd[I].

William Byrd[I] was descended on his father's side from a
family of Brexton, or Broxton, which is traced in Holms's
"Heraldic Collection for Cheshire" to the family of the same
name which was living at Charlton as early as the middle
of the twelfth century. John Byrd, or Bird,[6] as it was
then spelled, was a goldsmith in London. He was an honest tradesman of means, but the glimpses of his family
which we get from the letters of his eldest son indicate
that he was neither rich nor influential. He married
Grace, the daughter of Captain Thomas Stegg, and had
several children, the oldest of whom was William Byrd[I].

The will of Thomas Stegg was dated March 31, 1670,

[1] Neil, Virginia Carolorum,
pp. 135, 136, 167, 179, 218, 219.
In 1650 Charles II, then in
Breda, appointed him a councilor in Virginia, but evidently
he did not lean to the Stuart
king. (See Cal. of Eng. Col.
State Papers, Vol. I.)

[2] Va. Histl. Mag., III. 43.

[3] See his will in the Byrd Title-
book.

[4] Neil, Virginia Carolorum,
317.

[5] Va. Histl. Mag., VI. 300.

[6] It is thus in Stegg's will. It
was perhaps changed later to
conform with the spelling of the
Brexton family.

when William Byrd[1], who was born in 1652, was only eighteen years of age. It was proved May 15, 1671. It contained much good advice for the young man, cautioning him " not to be led away by the evil instructions he shall receive from others, but to be governed by the prudent and provident advice he shall receive from his aunt, the testator's loving wife." The absence of any words in the will to show that Byrd was at this time living in London would seem to imply that he was then in Virginia,[1] perhaps brought over by Stegg with the view of making him his heir.

The social position of Stegg was the best, and Byrd at once succeeded to it. The former had had for his close friend Governor Berkeley himself, to whom he left fifty pounds in token of the many favors that gentleman had shown him. Another friend, who was also remembered in the will, was Thomas Ludwell, the secretary of the colony. Him he urged "for the Dear Friendship that we have so long mutually enjoyed " to show the same kindness to Byrd which he had shown to the testator.

Rich through the favor of his uncle, and well introduced, William Byrd[1] did not fail to press rapidly into the foremost ranks of colonial life. He married as early as 1673, which was the year he became of age, Mary, the daughter of Warham Horsemanden. The latter was an officer in the royal army who had found the triumph of the Puritans so disagreeable that he had come to live in Virginia, where he settled in Charles City County. He was either a close friend or a relative of that Dame Frances who married, first, Samuel Stephens, governor of the Albemarle settlement, and secondly, William Berkeley, governor of Virginia, and thirdly, Philip Ludwell, governor of Carolina ; for at her

---

[1] For example, when William Byrd[1] died in 1704, his will provided that if his son should be out of the colony at the time, certain persons should be trustees to act till the son's return. There is nothing like this in Stegg's will. Byrd took up land at the falls of the James in 1673. (See Byrd Title-book.)

first marriage he was one of the trustees to whom Stephens conveyed the lady's marriage settlement before marriage, to be conveyed to her after the ceremony had been performed. He was in the colony as late as December 11, 1673, when he released all legal claim he might be supposed to have to the said estate.[1] Afterward, however, he went to England, and many of the letters which William Byrd[I] wrote to England were written to him at Purleigh, in Essex. In these letters Byrd often gives his correspondent news of " my Lady Berkeley." Before he went he perhaps held in his arms his grandson, William Byrd[I], for that young gentleman was born in Virginia, March 28, 1674.[2]

The estate which Stegg left to Byrd comprised lands at the falls of the James, on both sides of the river. As one stands now on some tall building in Richmond, he will notice that the land on the north side of the river lies hilly and uninviting to the agriculturalist, while on the south side, a little below the town of Manchester, the river makes a curve around a large tract of level ground which slopes gently down to the James. It was the fertility of that piece of land which attracted the notice of Stegg. Here he had his residence, a stout stone house with a large stone chimney in the center.[3] This tract embraced eighteen hundred acres, more or less, beginning at the falls on the west, that is, at a place near the present Southern Railway bridge, and stretching away eastward as far as Goode's Creek, the boundary of the ancient estate of "Whitby."

Thomas Stegg the elder had been a merchant in Charles City, and it is not improbable that his son was one also at

[1] Henning's Statutes, II. 323.

[2] When Byrd[I] applied for the position of secretary of Virginia in 1702, the Board of Trade spoke of him as a native of Virginia. (See Sainsbury Papers, Vol. II. Part I., 1625–1715, p. 301.)

I am told by Mr. R. A. Brock that Warham Horsemanden was buried in Charles City County, Virginia.— EDITOR.

[3] A rude drawing of it is shown on a plat in the Byrd Title-book.

the falls. At any rate, the earliest view we get of Byrd
from his own letters shows that he was both a country
merchant and an Indian trader.   His location was excellent for the latter business, although from the sparsely settled condition of the back country it was not so favorable
for the former.   South of the river began the trail which
before the middle of the century had already penetrated
into the interior more than four hundred miles.[1]   Along
it his own traders were sent, carrying on their pack-
horses his goods as far as the Catawbas and the Cherokees.   On this trail they sometimes came to untimely ends
at the hands of the Indians, as we see they did in 1684,
when five traders were killed thirty miles beyond the Occo-
neechees, and again in 1686, when two more were killed
about four hundred miles from the falls, probably among
the Catawbas.

William Byrd[1] describes at length the route of this
trade. The Trading Path, says he, crossed the Roanoke at
Moniseep Ford, which was about one mile above where the
dividing-line crossed that river.   If it ran in a straight
line it traversed Granville County, North Carolina, near
the town of Oxford, crossed Tar River eight miles to the
southwest, and cut Flat, Little, and Eno rivers from five
to ten miles above where they unite to form the Neuse.
Leaving what is now University Station a mile to the
north, it ran westerly through the Haw Old Fields, where
Byrd says there were fifty thousand acres of the richest
highland to be found in one tract in that part of the world,
then across Haw and Alamance rivers not far above the
point at which they unite, and onward to the Deep River
at a distance of forty miles, and then as much farther, till
at length it crossed the Yadkin. Here the traders rested
their horses, stopping to let them crop for some days the
rich canes which grew on the banks of the river.   Finally
the path passed through the counties of Stanley, Cabar-
rus, and Mecklenburg, and reached the rich low grounds

[1] Byrd to Lane and Perry, May 10, 1686.

of the Catawba, on which the Indians of the same name lived. Along this route, in the days of William Byrd[I], the traders went in caravans of fifteen or more, escorting a hundred pack-horses. But after South Carolina was settled the Charleston traders absorbed so much of the trade that when William Byrd[II] wrote his "History of the Dividing Line,"[1] not more than half that many persons went in a caravan.

In the country trade Byrd dealt in all the miscellaneous English goods which would be demanded by a rural community. He ordered duffles and cotton goods, window-glass, with lead and solder, and "ten boxes of Lockyer's Pills." But most especially he ordered servants. "If you could send me," said he, "six, eight, or ten servants (men or lusty boys) by the first ship, and the procurement might not be too dear, they would much assist in purchasing some of the best crops they seldom being to bee bought without servants. If you could help me to a Carpenter, Bricklayer, or Mason, I would willingly pay somewhat Extraordinary."[2] These were white servants, but from Barbadoes he ordered 4 negroes, 1200 gallons of rum, 3000 pounds of "muscovado sugar," 1 barrel (200 pounds) of white sugar, 3 tons of molasses, 1 cask of lime-juice, and 2 hundredweight of ginger.

William Byrd[I]'s progress in public life also was rapid. As early as 1676,[3] when he was twenty-four years old, he was a captain in the county militia, and only four years later he was called "Colonel Byrd" in the Charles City court records.[4] In the same year we have evidence that he was escheator of Henrico County.[5] Within this period he is said to have been more than once a member of the House of Burgesses. In 1680 he was appointed by Culpeper, shortly after the arrival of that gentleman in the

---

[1] 1738, or a little later.
[2] Maxwell, Va. Histl. Reg., Vol. I. p. 63.
[3] Henning's Statutes, II. 328; also Va. Histl. Mag., IV. 121–124.
[4] Va. Histl. Mag., III. 158.
[5] Byrd Title-book.

government, a member of the Council in the place of Colonel Swanne, deceased. Culpeper did not report the appointment to the Board of Trade till December 12, 1681, and five days later that body recommended that the nomination be confirmed.[1] Thus Byrd's rank in the Council dates from 1682, after Ralph Wormley and Richard Lee; but it seems certain that he sat from the time of his temporary appointment, which was some time between May 3 and August 11, 1680.

In Bacon's Rebellion Byrd appears in the beginning as one of the principal supporters of Bacon. This outbreak of popular indignation was due to Berkeley's Indian policy. Byrd himself was an Indian trader. Just before that time the savages had been giving the frontier settlers much trouble. Their irregular depredations had undoubtedly interfered with trade. Moreover, in 1676 Berkeley had got his servile Assembly to pass a law which forbade the trade to all former traders.[2] The ostensible purpose of this was to remove all cause of ill feeling between the two races. But the same act provided that Indians should buy goods from no others than from five men whom the governor should appoint in each county. This might well bring to bear against the governor all the influence of the dispossessed traders. In the spring of the same year there ran through the upper counties the report that the Indians were coming down on the whites. The people flew to arms to protect their homes. A body of the militia had assembled at Jordan's Point, near the falls of the James. On the opposite side of the river Captain James Crews, Henry Isham, Sr., and Captain William Byrd[1] were together, in company with Nathaniel Bacon, Jr. The conversation fell naturally upon the sad state of the country. It was recounted that the Susquehannas had come down to within twelve miles of the falls of the James, and committed many murders there, one of which had been on

[1] Sainsbury Papers, vol. for 1679–82, pp. 125, 127, 135.
[2] Henning's Statutes, II. 336.

Bacon's overseer. Excited by this and by the drink which had been indulged in, Bacon was persuaded by the others to go across the river to the militia and to take them some rum. The militia themselves were without a leader, and were easily persuaded to follow so eloquent a leader as Bacon. He, however, hesitated on account of the responsibility, fearing to go against the Indians without a commission; but his three friends urged him on, and promised that they would follow him, commission or no commission,[1] and so he undertook the task. As long as Bacon's operations were confined to the Indians, Byrd was true to this promise, and led a portion of Bacon's troops; but when the passionate young leader went beyond that and proposed to reform the Constitution of the colony, he drew back and made his peace with the governor. He was too practical a man for a revolution. Had Bacon followed him, instead of giving himself up to the schemes of political theorizers, he would have dispersed his troops after the defeat of the Indians and have trusted to the support of the country for his personal safety.

Byrd's connection with Bacon did not impair his popularity. He was so well intrenched in the good will of the burgesses that in 1679 a bill passed giving him a special jurisdiction over a tract of land at the falls of the James, lying five miles on each side of the river and extending into the interior one mile on the south side and two miles on the north side. The grant really created a manor, with Byrd at the head of it. The condition on which it was made was that he should settle there a garrison of fifty armed men, ready at short notice to repel an attack, but that he should not bring more than two hundred and fifty other persons to the place. This was deemed too great a privilege by the authorities in England, and the scheme failed for lack of their approval.

Not discouraged by this rebuff, Byrd proposed four years

[1] See the report of Berry and Moryson, Va. Histl. Mag.,
IV. 121–124.

later a more daring scheme. The frontier, in spite of the
severe punishment Bacon had inflicted on the Indians, was
not entirely safe. In the winter of 1679–80 there had
been some trouble, for which Byrd quickly took vengeance,
much to the regret of the secretary, Nicholas Spencer.[1]
Three years later he proposed to Governor Culpeper that
if he were given the monopoly of the Indian trade he
would compose all the differences between the Indians and
the whites, see that the king's annual tribute was duly paid,
explore the country west of the mountains as soon as peace
should be made with the Senecas, and pay to his Majesty
£100 a year, provided he were allowed to transport his
Indian commodities to England.[2] Culpeper, in transmit-
ting this proposition to the Board of Trade, said[3] that,
while he would not advise what should be done in this
case, yet his maxim was for free trade, and that he had followed that course continually, "though to my owne great
losse." The board did not favor the proposition, and nothing more was heard of it. In this connection it is interesting to note that in 1716 William Byrd[II] was most
active before the same body, the Board of Trade, to secure
the disallowance of a law giving the same kind of a monopoly to Spotswood and some of Spotswood's friends.

Byrd had thus tried two schemes to make money through
his political connections. He now came to a third, which
was destined to be more successful than the others. He
applied for the office of auditor, which was, in fact, the
office of colonial treasurer. It was held at that time by
Nathaniel Bacon, uncle of the revolutionary leader, but
he was old and quite willing to give up the office. Byrd,
as soon as he had made proper arrangements in Virginia, set out in the spring of 1687 for London, where he
found but little difficulty in his way. The gift of the
auditorship was in the hands of William Blathwayt, who
was auditor-general for all the colonies, and whose deputy

[1] Sainsbury Papers, vol. for   [2] Ibid., entry for Feb., 1683.
1679–82, entry for March 18, 1680.   [3] Va. Histl. Mag., III. 236.

was the Virginia auditor. The appointment of deputy
auditor seems to have carried that of receiver-general along
with it. Lord Howard of Effingham, then governor of
Virginia, gave Byrd his support, and it seems that Byrd
found means of interesting Blathwayt in his behalf. On
December 4, 1687, he received the appointment, and lost
no time in returning to Virginia, where he arrived on
February 24, 1688. He found no trouble about his office
there, so he wrote to "Father Horsemanden," except that
Bacon wanted the perquisites for the year about to end.[1]
But from another quarter there was coming a controversy,
the relation of which throws much light upon political life
at that time.

Although Bacon had been given his office in 1675, on
the death of Edward Digges, yet in 1677 the king had
granted the office for life to Robert Ayleway, intending, as
it seems, either to supersede Bacon or to give Ayleway the
opportunity to make some arrangement with him by which
Bacon might execute the office in Virginia, while the
other remained in England as his absent superior.[2] But
almost immediately Ayleway was sent to Ireland to be
clerk of the office of ordnance there, and Bacon remained
in office. The appointment of Byrd aroused the interest
of Ayleway, and in May, 1689, he petitioned the king, setting forth the above facts, and praying that as he had the
legal title to the office he might also have the fruits of it.
The king referred the petition to the Board of Trade, who
in turn referred it to Lord Howard of Effingham, who was
then in England. He, who was committed to Byrd in the
matter, could not deny that Ayleway had the legal title to
the office, but he added that the office ought to be executed

---

[1] Letter-book. To "Father
Horsemanden," April 16, 1688.
The king's order to put Byrd
into the office of "Auditor of
the public accounts of Virginia"
is preserved in the Sainsbury
Papers, vol. for 1625–1715, p. 118.

[2] The Virginia Assembly declared in 1680 that Ayleway's
grant was surreptitiously obtained and that they were
glad it was not allowed. (Sainsbury Papers, vol. for 1679–82,
p. 91.)

by some one on the spot. The board adopted this view of the matter, and the king finally gave judgment that Ayleway should be put into possession of the office if he would execute it in person in Virginia; otherwise he was told that he might seek his redress in the courts.[1] That he was not willing to do, and Byrd was able to make an arrangement by which he became Ayleway's deputy for two years, he agreeing to pay his superior one half of the profits of the office.[2]

The whole affair gave rise to considerable manœuvering. Ayleway said in his petition to the king that Byrd was "a creature of the late Lord Chancellor's," who was no other than the corrupt Lord Jeffreys. Byrd himself said, a year before this charge was made, in a letter to his uncle, that while he was in England he was often a suitor on the Lord Chancellor, but that he could have no discourse with him.[3] It is not impossible that Byrd used money with those from whom he was seeking an office which he valued chiefly for its salary. When the English politicians were themselves so corrupt, it would be a strange thing if their dependents in Virginia should have remained uncontaminated.

The limiting of the period of agreement between Byrd and Ayleway to two years did not suit the former. He wanted the office entirely and was willing to purchase it outright. In doing that he brought to his assistance Blathwayt, John Povey, and Micajah Perry. As the first, however, was clerk of the privy council, Byrd wrote that he would rely on the efforts of the two others for active solicitation. To Povey he gave £20 a year for his good offices. All of the three, however, and Effingham also, sent him word that they would do what they could to get the place for him. Thus encouraged, he was able to write to "Father Horsemanden," July 25, 1690, that "with ye help of some more potent Gold" he hoped soon to have the

---

[1] Sainsbury Papers, vol. for 1640–91, pp. 226, 236, 240, 243.
[2] Letter-book. To Perry and Lane, July 19, 1690.
[3] Letter-book, April 16, 1688.

affair in good shape.   The potency of his gold had lessened, however, for in 1688 he had offered Ayleway 100 guineas, but now he was constrained to tell Perry that he might go so far as £300, although he hoped the office could be had for less.   Ayleway had tried to bring Philip Ludwell to bid for the office, but there was too much of official courtesy among the Virginia councilors to allow them to bid against one another in such an affair, and Ludwell said promptly that he was not an applicant.   To " Father Horsemanden " he wrote that it was true that Ayleway had the right to the office, but that " as long as I can keep an uninterrupted possession thereof I shall not much value it ; but I hope to buy him out."   To Perry he said that he thought Blathwayt's and Povey's influence was enough to conclude the affair " without incurring any danger of the Law against purchasing offices."   The Letter-book, from which I have drawn freely, fails us after June 9, 1691, but we know that Byrd got the office without restriction and held it till his death.   One of the last letters in the Letter-book contains an injunction to Perry to bring the matter to a close, so that Byrd might not " lye open to every one that will bid money for itt." [1]

As auditor and receiver-general it was Byrd's duty to receive and care for, and make a proper report on, all the money collected in the colony by the authority of the king. This money was derived from quit-rents, from a tax of two shillings a hogshead collected on all the tobacco exported from the country and from other funds, as fines and escheats.   The duty of two shillings a hogshead was settled for the expenses of the government, as the salaries of governor and others, and the rest was to be accounted for with the crown.   The collection of quit-rents was the most considerable as it was the most troublesome part of his duty. Quit-rents were paid at the rate of two shillings for each hundred acres of land held in the colony.   They were actually collected by the several sheriffs, who paid them

[1] Letter-book, Aug. 8, 1690, July 19, 1690, and June 3, 1691.

into the hands of the receiver-general. The king had
granted that they might be paid at the discretion of the
payer in tobacco at the rate of one penny a pound. The
result was that when tobacco was below one penny a pound
people would tender that instead of money for their quit-
rents. Another effect of this concession was that the
poorer tobacco would be tendered for quit-rents, just as it
was given for the parsons' salaries. Had it been necessary
for Byrd to have received and stored all this tobacco in
barns, his office would have been a laborious one ; but there
was authorized by law a system of public warehouses to
which persons were allowed to take their tobacco, receiving
in exchange certificates which were receivable for public
dues. In these the quit-rents were paid. It was, therefore, Byrd's business to take these certificates as they were
handed in, and at the end of the season to sell the large
amount of tobacco corresponding to them to the best advantage of the revenues. The king preferred that this
tobacco should be sold at auction, and more than once
instructed the governor to that effect ; but the Council
favored a sale by private arrangement, and that method
was generally followed during the incumbency of Byrd[1].
In the controversy of Byrd[II] with Spotswood this was a
point of prime importance, as we shall see later, but now
it occasioned no trouble. It did, indeed, bring out a
protest from the faction which was opposed to Governor
Andros, but the point was not pressed very strongly.
Blair, Hartwell, and Chilton, who were in England in
1697, and who, at the request of the Board of Trade,
wrote an account of affairs in Virginia which at last found
its way into print, testified to the board as to the abuse
which grew out of this kind of a sale. It was the custom,
said Chilton,[1] for Mr. Auditor Byrd to dispose of the quit-
rents to the members of the Council. The price of tobacco
in Virginia, he added, was generally in that year twenty

[1] Sainsbury Papers, vol. for 1691–97, p. 351. Chilton was
corroborated by Hartwell, ibid., 345.

shillings a hundredweight, but the quit-rent tobacco had sold from four to six shillings a hundredweight.[1] It would be unwise to introduce here the arguments on this point, since they were gone over in a more complete manner in the controversy with Spotswood. It is enough to say that on the evidence of such men as Blair, Chilton, and Hartwell, for their association together in the matter in hand would make them jointly responsible for matters of fact to which one of them testified, it is evident that the Council was doing what most of the English officials were doing, using their offices for purposes of their own prosperity.

As to irregularity in the keeping of his accounts, there was none of it. It is true that when Blair, Ludwell, and others appeared in England in 1704 to secure the removal of Nicholson, there was an intimation that all was not right with Byrd's books. The Board of Trade called young Byrd before it and asked him to explain the matter. He filed his reply in due time, and Blair said, when he saw it, that his party "did not insist in their complaints upon having the Auditor and Receiver General's Places in two distinct Offices if the accounts of the Revenue were regularly audited before the council, as usual." [2] The complaint grew, evidently, out of the general fact that the two

---

[1] This method of collecting quit-rents led to the farming of them at times. October 19, 1699, Byrd was given authority by the Council to sell the quit-rents of any county to anybody who would pay for them in money at the rate specified in the patents, that is, at one penny a pound of tobacco, and who would allow the sheriffs their ten per cent. for collecting. As soon as this was enacted by the Council, Byrd reported that he had already made arrangements to sell the quit-rents of all the counties except Princess Anne.

He was instructed to collect the rents in tobacco in that county and to sell it at auction. The advantage to him who farmed the quit-rents was in the possibility that tobacco might be sold for more than one penny a pound. In Princess Anne it was of inferior quality, and that is why the quit-rents were not farmed out there. (See Council Minutes for date given.)

[2] Sainsbury Papers, vol. for 1625-1715 (Vol. II. Part I.), entries for May 24, 29, 30, and 31, 1704.

offices had been allowed to be in one man, and not out of
any personal failing of the incumbent. It was perhaps
accentuated by the fact that Byrd, who was always a practical man, did not choose to join with those members of the
Council who had asked for the removal of the lieutenant-
governor.[1] Nicholson then said that Byrd's accounts were
all right. After he had been removed he cast some impu-
tations on them, and the Lord High Treasurer wrote the
Virginia Council to have the said accounts thoroughly
examined. The Council complied. They found that there
was indeed an amount unpaid at the time of Byrd's death,
but that it was fully protected by his bond, and it was in
due time paid into the treasury.[2] It was evidently money
Byrd had collected during the season in which he died
and for which he held the tobacco unsold. It was paid by
Byrd[II] as his father's executor, who was the only person
who could have paid it.

In his later years Byrd was a man of great importance.
For several years before he died he was third in rank in the
Council, being preceded by Ralph Wormley and Richard
Lee. But in 1699 Lee resigned on account of ill health,[3]
and in 1703 Wormley died,[4] so that Byrd was for the year
before his death president of the Council. He retained till
his death his position as colonel and commander-in-chief
of the militia of Henrico County, with William Randolph
lieutenant-colonel.[5] He was appointed a member of the
committee to build William and Mary College, and had
the contract to erect the building called the Chapel.[6] All
of these places he filled satisfactorily. Moreover, he was all
the time accumulating property. He is described shortly
before his death as one of the richest men in Virginia.

[1] Sainsbury Papers, vol. for
1625–1715, June 7, 1704.

[2] Council Minutes, 1705–21, pp.
19, 29, and entries for Aug. 29
and 30, 1706.

[3] Ibid., 1698–1700, Oct. 27, 1699.

[4] Dec. 5, 1703. (See Wm. and
Mary Quarterly, VI. 152, note;
but Vol. VII. 69, note, says he
died 1701.)

[5] Council Minutes, 1698–1700,
June 3, 1699.

[6] Meade, Old Churches and
Families, I. 318, note.

While all this political progress had been coming, Byrd
was steadily advancing in social importance.   When he
was first married he had, no doubt, lived in Stegg's stone
house, on the south of the James at the falls.   But after a
while he bought the property on the north side of the
river, and there built a handsome house which he called
"Belvidere."   It was situated on what is now called Belvidere Street, to the west of Gamble's Hill.   It must have
been near to the river, for Byrd said in 1685 [1] that there
had just been a great flood in the river, so that the water
stood two feet in his parlor.   Anburey, who slept there
for a night in 1779, spoke of the place as "an elegant villa,"[2]
and indicates that it was at that time outside of the town
limits.   A plat accompanying an old deed which has been
preserved in Richmond contains a rude drawing of the
house, evidently as a landmark.   It shows a substantial
house, the center two stories and a dormer, and the two
wings one story and a dormer.[3]   The house was long an
interesting spot in Richmond, and survived the march of
improvements till the middle of the nineteenth century,
long after it ceased to be the seat of its former magnificence.[4]

After becoming auditor Byrd found the place at the falls
too remote from the center of the political life of the colony.
To this inconvenience there was added a positive danger
from the Indians.   This was not so much from those who
lived in the neighborhood, as from Northern and Southern
tribes who, in their frequent wars one on the other, crossed
the frontier of Virginia not far above the falls.   As late as
1689 they came down on his settlement, and killed one and
carried off two of his people.[5]   For Mrs. Byrd the place had
always been lonely, and now that her husband was so fre-

[1] June 5.   To "Father Horsemanden."

[2] Interior Travels through
America, II. 328.

[3] This information is from Mr.
W. G. Stannard of Richmond,
who has seen the old deed in

possession of Mr. Peyton Car-
rington of the same place.

[4] Mordecai, Richmond in By-
gone Days (edition of 1860),
p. 89.

[5] To " Father Horsemanden,"
July 25, 1690.

quently absent on public business it was doubly so. It held no society for her except that of servants and negroes. How much it was distasteful may be seen from her urging that her children should be sent away to England for their training. All of these considerations moved Byrd to look for another place of residence.

The place selected was the estate which he and his son made famous under the name of "Westover." It is more than twenty miles from the falls by country road, though much farther by the river. Adjoining it on the west was Berkeley Hundred; on the opposite side of the river were Upper and Lower Brandon; while on the east, not far off, was Green Springs. The place lies in a beautiful situation on the north side of the James, and to this day draws the attention of the passengers on the river, as much by its natural beauty as by its historical interest. Byrd bought it in 1688. Its history before that time is worth recounting as an illustration of the growth of a famous colonial property. It early attracted the attention of the settlers on account of its fertility, and was patented in 1638 by Captain Thomas Pawlett, a kinsman of Sir William Berkeley, in a grant which included 2000 acres. It was as early as this that it got its name of "Westover," or "Westopher." [1] When the patentee died a few years later it went to his brother, Sir John Pawlett, in England. He conveyed part of it, how much does not appear, to Otho Soutcoat, and the rest he sold, in 1665, to Theodorick Bland for £170. After Bland's death his part passed to his two sons, Theodorick and Richard, and it was they who sold it in 1688 to William Byrd[1] for £300 sterling and 10,000 pounds of tobacco, a sum equal, perhaps, in our own money, to $7000. The deed was for 1200 acres, but on

[1] The latter spelling is the earlier and was used continually by Byrd[1]. The name may have come from that of the parish. The locality was settled by the brothers West. There is in England a riding and a tithing in Southampton County of the same name; but I am unable to connect the two localities.—EDITOR.

actual survey the amount was found to be much less.
There was in the midst of the tract a piece containing 200
acres, belonging to James Minge.   This Byrd also bought;
and in 1731, when the old church was moved from its first
location in the midst of the estate[1] to a more convenient
one, William Byrd[II] increased his estate by the eight acres
which had belonged to it.   These transfers completed
the estate.[2]   The Westover community was an old one,
and held many families of influence.   It was, said William
Byrd[I], "two miles above where the great ships ride."[3]
This fact, perhaps, made it a favorable trading-place in the
early years of the colony.   Here Stegg the elder had
his headquarters.   Here, too, or near here, Horsemanden
had settled.   Here at Westover Byrd[I] built a house in
1690.   It was not the pretentious brick mansion which has
become historic, for that was built by the son.   It was
more likely a wooden building.   But it was well furnished,
as we may see from Byrd's orders to his agent in Rotterdam for bedsteads, curtains, looking-glasses, etc., "to be
handsome and neat, but cheap," and for one dozen best
Russia-leather chairs and three tables.[4]   Late in 1691 he
made the removal to his new quarters.

Byrd's political promotion had also brought him to indulge in greater display of life.   It made it necessary for
him to have apartments in Jamestown, a "chamber," he
called it.   He ordered for that place a secretary and "Inke-
Glasses," to be "left att Gaulers att Towne,"[5] and also a
hogshead of claret, "with some more in bottles."   He goes
on to say that this much claret he must certainly have (it
seems to have been a political drink), but if claret were
high, on account of the French war, he would take the rest of
his order for wine in port or "Barabar."   The latter was per-

---

[1] This lends credulity to the
notion that the estate took its
name from the parish.

[2] These facts are from the
Byrd Title-book, pp. 1–45.   (See

also Wm. and Mary Quarterly,
IV. 151.)

[3] Letter-book.   To Hutchins,
Aug. 1, 1690.

[4] To Senserfe, Aug., 1690.

[5] Letter-book, June 10, 1689.

haps for the trade.   He was also commissioned by the other
members of the Council to order the wine which they used.
At the very end of the letter he adds in his thrifty way :
"I have by Tonner sent my long Periweg wch I desire you
to get made into a compagne one & send mee." It was
at the same time that he sent back to England his old
silver-hilted sword, to be exchanged for a new silver-hilted
rapier.[1]

Byrd was now willing to bring home his two daughters,
Susan and Ursula, who had been at school at Hackney, in
England.   He felt a pride, no doubt, in the prospect of the
superior position they would assume among the colonial-
trained maidens.   He ordered that they should be taken
from school ; but on account of the war between England
and France, he did not think it prudent that they should
run the risk of capture on a voyage across the ocean, and
he did not think London a proper place for them.   In this
dilemma he turned to his brother-in-law, Daniel Horsemanden, who had recently married a lady of fine social
position, and who lived in good style in the country.   To
him Byrd wrote, requesting that he take the girls till
the opportunity for their return came, and offering to re-
pay to his brother-in-law whatever they should cost him.
The latter complied, but was soon sorry of it.   He wrote
to Byrd complaining of the conduct of the girls, but in
what particular does not appear.   The letter aroused a
storm in the home on the bank of the James, and to it
Byrd sent the following outspoken reply :[2]

VIRGINIA June ye 2d, 1691.

SR.   I recd one from you this year, and am glad to hear of yours
& your Ladys good health, which I heartily wish you may both
long injoy & may See a numerous progeny who may live happy
in the World without troubling their relations.   I am sorry my
Children have been so troublesome to others, chargeable I hope
not Since I paid whatever was charged on mee, though (had the

---

[1] Letter-book.   To Perry and Lane, June 10, 1690, and to
A. North, same date.   [2] See Letter-book.

money left by Sr Ed^w Fillmer been fairly accounted for) there might have been no occasion for thatt. Hereafter I shall indeavor to provide otherways for them ; & as soon as the War is over, remove them far enough. I am sorry I had occasion for this ; & that reflections have past wch might deserve more. However on all occasions I shall bee ever ready to express my Selfe,

Dear S^r

Yo^r Obliged Humble Servt

W. B.

On the day after this letter was written he wrote to Perry and Lane to " put out the Girls for their most advantage without any unnecessary charge." When they came home is not known. Perhaps Susan did not come at all ; for she married John Brayne of London, whom she must have met about this time. Ursula returned to Virginia, and all the rest we know of her is from her epitaph and from her father's will. By the former we learn that she was the wife of Robert Beverley, the historian, and that she died October 31, 1698, aged sixteen years and eleven months and two days ; from the latter that she left one son.

William Byrd's general prosperity led him to the usual course of large landed investments. This was a natural thing in the society of the day. There might be room for an increase of capital in trade up to a certain point, but beyond that it was impossible to go. Then, as much later in the South, the only very profitable investment for accumulated capital was land and negroes. It was thus that Byrd began at an early day to buy land and kept it up till his death. The process was typical of the colony, and a list of his purchases is introduced here for the purpose of illustration.

We have already seen that he received from his uncle 1800 acres on the south side of the James. The titles of three small portions of this tract were disputed, but Byrd eventually bought up the claims and held all of the estate as the nucleus of his property. In 1688, the same year in which he bought Westover, which contained nearly 1400 acres, he made a much larger acquisition near his first

holding. " Foreseeing that he should want Timber and
being willing to have Elbow Room," says the Title-book,
he took out a patent for 3313 acres, lying back from the
river and adjoining on that side his other property. This
action illustrates a second phase of the taking up of land
in the Southern colonies generally. The first land taken
was the rich river-banks, and then, when this was somewhat cultivated, the next thing to do was to secure the best
portions of the adjacent highlands. This grant of Byrd's
in 1688, however, was not cultivated according to the re-
quirements of the law, and lapsed. Byrd was not concerned on account of that. He was a member of the Council, and the Council must approve all land grants, and he
was, moreover, escheator, through whom land must be
legally declared to be lapsed. He let the matter lie as it
was till 1701, when Nathaniel Harrison, acting collu-
sively for his friend and near neighbor, got a new patent
for the land and transferred it to the former owner. This
was cheaper than paying quit-rents. Byrd, however, in
1687, had patented on Falling Creek a tract which, after
he had sold an undesired corner, amounted to 1521 acres.
In 1696 he took up 5644 acres adjoining his other land on
Falling Creek, his reason for so doing being that he wished
to reopen some iron-mines on the former tract and would
need this tract for fuel. The last acquisition lapsed, but
his friend Richard Bland petitioned for it, and the petition, after lying unnoticed for two or three years (which
saved quit-rents), was granted in 1706, and the land was
transferred to Byrd's son and heir. In 1700 he bought
269 acres in the Falling Creek neighborhood. In 1704
he patented 4171 acres between Powhite and Poakashock
creeks, ten miles from his other lands, the temptation
being the discovery of iron on it. All of these lands were
on the south side of the river. On the north he had others.
On this side Stegg had taken up 1280 acres on both sides
of " Shacco Creek, formerly called Chippiack Creek." A
plat of this tract shows near the mouth of the creek the

"Cabins of the Powite Indians."   Stegg allowed this patent
to lapse, but in 1673 it was reissued to Byrd.   "At the
Head of these 1280 Acres," says the Title-book, "lay a
great body of Level High Land which was for the most
part very good, which tempted Capt. Byrd to encrease the
quantity to 7351 acres," and to the temptation he yielded
in 1676.   In 1687 he got some more land below Shacco
Creek, probably as much as 500 acres.   In 1704 he took up
344 acres more near Manakin Town, the "temptation"
being coal.   The sum total of all these holdings is 26,231
acres, more or less.[1]   And yet Byrd was not by any means
the largest landholder in Virginia.[2]

From Byrd's business letters it is possible to get a view
of the conditions of a merchant's life in the colony.   There
must have been large profits on both the goods imported
and the tobacco exported ; but they were not got without
much trouble.   The letters show that the merchant was
continually at odds with his London and Barbadian cor-
respondents.   From the former he received all kinds of
goods and almost as many kinds of injuries.   His accounts
were often delayed in their statement for two years, and
then showed a balance on the wrong side.   The goods sent
were often of inferior quality or at very high prices.   The
tobacco was sold at unexpectedly low rates, and unexpected charges for handling or selling or storage were added,
on one pretext or another.   All these abuses Byrd paid off
in good round railings ; but his pocket was none the fatter
for his strong words.   He might change his agent, as he
sometimes did, but the old complaints were soon found
charged up against the new agent.   There was no other thing
to do but to endure and make it up in the profits of the

[1] In 1704 Byrd took up an
escheated patent for 4250 acres
above Bermuda Hundred formerly granted to John Zouch.
On it a large number of smaller
holders were seated without
valid title.   Byrd made them
deeds to the land, which, says
the Title-book, was "much to the
credit of his humanity." (p. 113.)
[2] All the above grants are
mentioned in full in the Title-
book, and plats are given of
most of the land.

trade, and it is not unlikely that Byrd knew how to do this. Most of his dealings, like those of his son in the first half of his career, were with the long-continuing house of Perry and Lane. If the books of that commercial firm have been preserved they ought to be a most valuable source of the economic history of Virginia.

Much of the inconvenience felt by the trader in Virginia was on account of transportation. Both of the Byrds complain loudly of this. The transportation facilities were in the hands, for the most part, of those London merchants who had regular customers in Virginia. They would send each fall ships of their own, or such as they had chartered, to Virginia, with instructions to bring back tobacco from their customers. The captains of these ships would arrive in the fall or early winter. They would make engagements to fill their ships, giving the preference to their regular customers. If it happened that a man had more tobacco to ship than he had been able to foresee some time ahead, it might be very hard for him to find a ship which had the room for it. This was especially true in years of large crops. In fact, the planters, with a view of keeping prices up, were not very careful to inform the London people how large the crop was likely to be. The Londoners, anxious not to send to the colony more ships than necessary, often failed to send all that were needed. Thus it was more frequent to find competition among the Virginians to get shipping facilities than among the ships to get freight. The evil would have been remedied, of course, if Virginia had had one or more large trading ports by which it sent the tobacco to England through the hands of exporters. Such exporters would have had a regular fleet carrying the tobacco on quick trips and steadily throughout the year. They would have bought the tobacco from the people for bills of exchange or for money, and it would have been a natural thing for a large importing business to have grown up. Such a general development would have come if Virginia trade had depended on the small planter. But the large

planter was opposed to it, for it gave too much of the
year's crop to the middlemen. He was enough of a factor
in the industrial situation to control it. To him the merchant found it profitable to continue sending the ships to
bring home his valuable consignments of tobacco, and to send
back to him his equally valuable invoices of European commodities. Thus it happened that when, in 1691, a law was
passed, with the support of the English merchants, to encourage the establishment of towns, it raised so great a
storm in Virginia that it was finally repealed.

The existing method of shipping tobacco made freights
high. As it was, a ship must be in Virginia long enough to
make her engagements, or, so far as she knew till she arrived,
there might be no tobacco for her. This meant that she
arrived by the beginning of the winter. She stayed in the
rivers, awaiting her load till the early spring, perhaps till
June. There was comparatively little freight from England to Virginia, and so it was necessary to make the
return trip pay most of the expenses of the long voyage.
Moreover, the fact that a large majority of ships went
chartered to take tobacco from certain planters to certain
merchants gave enough uncertainty to the shipping trade
to keep out independent, unchartered ships.

Byrd received much tobacco on account of his trade.
He bought a great deal, also, from the smaller planters, as
a matter of speculation. It is likely that many planters
who were not merchants were in the same ventures. He
shipped as much as five hundred hogsheads a season. He
accordingly suffered all the inconveniences to which I have
referred. He suggested to Perry and Lane that some small
Bristol or Liverpool ships be hired and sent to Virginia,[1]
but nothing seems to have come of the suggestion. These
ships could load quickly and hurry home so as to get the
tobacco on the market before the bulk of the crop was
there to glut it. If tobacco were high in London the
Virginia agents of the merchants had instructions to buy

[1] Letter-book, July 21, 1690.

largely in Virginia, where there was little fluctuation in price. Even the sailors caught the spirit of speculation and bought tobacco in such times. All this meant little opportunity for freight to the Virginia trader. Byrd was moved on account of it to protest "that we may not ever be instanced as wee are, to Lade the Ships when Tobo. is worth nothing, but when there's an Hope of profitt, then wee must be last Served, & take itt as a great favo[r] if we may have a little after ye owners, master and sailors are served, but enough of this. I wish itt may learne us more witt." [1]

The manifestation of "witt" to which it led Byrd was to write to John Carey, a London merchant, in the following year, to suggest that Carey send to the Upper James River a ship holding from four to six hundred hogsheads to load tobacco for England. He himself would send half that much in her, and he would guarantee to load her, even if she carried eight hundred hogsheads. But the scheme showed its weakness in that he was obliged to add that he would trust the tobacco to Carey to be sold; for that was, it is seen, but the old plan, and there was no guaranty that in thus transferring his business to Carey he was not building up with a new man all the evils he had found with others. What came of this scheme is not known.

Byrd's letters show also some interesting traits of character. Now and again he orders a book of his agent. Sometimes it is a book of entertainment, and sometimes it is a book of information, as, for example, when he ordered a work on minerals in order to know the possibilities of certain iron ores. But books do not appear in his orders often enough to make it probable that he bought any considerable portion of the large library which later on was at Westover. His letters, too, show that he was very religious. His advice to his son is expressed in a tone which the good Bishop Meade would have found as commendable

[1] Letter-book, July 21, 1690.

as he found the religious attitude of the second Byrd objectionable. Among his friends he was a good companion and doubtless a good liver. In the earlier letters, when his recollections of London were fresh, he speaks often of certain "tokens" sent to and from Virginia by mutual friends. These "tokens" were presents of wine, or, if the sender were in Virginia, of tobacco to be invested in wine. In Virginia they were usually left at Captain William Randolph's, on the James, and there drunk to the health of friends in England. To his brother-in-law he wrote: "Capt. Randolph & I & some other friends seldom meet but we remember you."

But to Byrd, the prosperous trader, planter, and politician, the closing years of the century brought accumulating sorrows. His brilliant son was in London, shining, unquestionably, as the father desired, but leaving him lonely. Then, in October, 1698, the daughter, Ursula Beverley, died, a mother at less than seventeen. On November 9, 1699,[1] his wife, Mary Horsemanden, died also. Her high-strung Cavalier spirit had never failed him, or her, in all the difficulties of the life at the falls. There she had borne his children—one of them while he was absent on a political errand in Albany. She had lived resolutely alone while three of her children went back to England to learn to be gentlemen and ladies for their own good. She was a type of a worthy race, who won homes out of the forests while their husbands, with the aid of black hands, took fortunes out of the soil. Of the children other than William and Ursula, Susan was, as I have said, married in London; Warham was dead; and Mary, who was alive in 1700, when her father's will was written, was not with him in 1704, when he died. Where she was, or what became of her, is not known.

The Title-book contains a full account of the death of William Byrd[1]. He was at the time alone at Westover,

[1] At this time (Nov. 16) the Council, desiring the presence of the auditor, held its meeting at Westover. (See Minutes.)

with only his housekeeper, Joanna Jarratt, and Jean Marat, his man. He had been ill for some time, being so "very lame of the gout" in 1700 that he was excused from attendance at Council meetings.[1] On December 3, 1704, when he believed that death was upon him, he sent a boat for Lieutenant-Colonel William Randolph, who came at once, although the weather was bad. To him Byrd gave some instructions in regard to his will, and early the next morning he died. He was buried at Westover. His epitaph, perhaps written by his learned son, runs : *Hic reconduntur cineres Gulielmi Byrd Armigeri et regii huj Provinciae Quaestoris qui hanc Vitam cum Eternitate commutavit 4to Die Decembris 1704 postquam vixisset 52 annos.*[2]

Byrd's will was a short one. To his youngest daughter, Mary, he gave £300; to "Mrs. Susan Brayne," £100; to William Beverley, son of Ursula, £50; and to Mrs. Joanna Jarratt, his housekeeper, a small bequest, added just before he died. All the rest of his fortune was left to his son William, who was to be executor. But if William should be out of the country at the time, William Randolph and two other friends were to be executors until the son should return. As William Byrd II was out of Virginia when his father died, Randolph and the two others qualified as temporary executors, and proved the will on February 3, 1705.[3]

WILLIAM BYRD II, the second of the name in Virginia, who succeeded to his father's large estate in 1704, was born in Virginia, March 28, 1674. His epitaph, written by some warm admirer, and perhaps a long time after his death, is

---

[1] Council Minutes, April 24, 1700.

[2] Wm. and Mary Quarterly, IV. 144. Here the date of his death is quoted as 1701. If there is not an error in the quotation the epitaph contains one, for 1704 as the date of his death is established by both the reports of the governor to England and by the Title-book.

[3] See Title-book, p. 114.

often quoted as the best epitome of the story of his life.
It reads :

being born to one of the amplest fortunes in this country,
he was early sent to England for his education,
where under the care and direction of Sir Robert Southwell,
and ever favoured with his particular instructions,
he made a happy proficiency in polite and varied learning.
By the means of the same noble friend,
he was introduced to the acquaintance of many of the first
persons of the age
for knowledge, wit, virtue, birth, or high station,
and particularly contracted a most intimate and bosom
friendship
with the learned and illustrious Charles Boyle, Earl of Orrery.
He was called to the bar in the Middle Temple,
studied for some time in the Low Countries,
visited the Court of France,
and was chosen Fellow of the Royal Society.
Thus eminently fitted for the service and ornament of his
country,
he was made Receiver-General of his majesty's revenues here,
was thrice appointed public agent to the court and ministry of
England,
and, being thirty-seven years a member,
at last became President, of the Council of this Colony.
To all this were added a great elegance of taste and life,
the well-bred gentleman and polite companion,
the splendid economist and prudent father of a family,
with the constant enemy of all exorbitant power,
and hearty friend to the liberties of his country.[1]

William Byrd [II] differed from his father in many respects.
The latter was always the man of business, shrewd, practical, and skilful in the management of men. The former
was always something of a man of pleasure. He had
crossed with the blood of the London goldsmith the Cavalier blood of his mother. He went before he was ten years

[1] The use of the word " colony " indicates that this epitaph
was written before the full establishment of statehood. The
reference to the " liberties of his
country " indicates that it was
written after the beginning of
the quarrel with England.

old to England for his education, and was thrown entirely among his mother's people. He returned to Virginia with a greater amount of social training than his father, but with less business capacity. Yet neither was lacking in each quality. It would not be far wrong to say that the elder had a great deal of business capacity and somewhat less of social capacity, while the younger had a great deal of social capacity and somewhat less of business capacity. This does not mean the latter was an unfortunate business manager, for he died a wealthy man. But he was not the "splendid economist" his epitaph proclaimed him. He did some rash things for which his affairs suffered. For example, he assumed for a consideration all of Colonel Parke's debts, without knowing exactly how much they amounted to; and while he was badly involved on this account he remained in England at a heavy expense, and his old age was vexed sorely with the clamors of his creditors. It is certain his father never did a thing like this.

Our first glimpses of the younger Byrd are in his father's letters, which begin to be preserved early in 1684. The boy was then at school in England under the supervision of his grandfather Horsemanden, who lived at Purleigh in Essex. The name of his teacher was Christopher Glassock,[1] who sent the father good reports of the progress of the pupil. To the latter, whom he always called Will, Byrd wrote, March 31, 1685: "I received your letter and am glad to hear you are with so good a Master who I hope will see you improve your time, & that you be careful to serve God as you ought, without which you cannot expect to do well here or hereafter."[2]

The impetus to the English education for her children seems to have come mostly from Mrs. Byrd. Already two of them, Will and Susan, were in England, and in 1685 the father wrote to his "Father Horsemanden":

---

[1] Byrd wrote a letter to him, March 31, 1685. See Maxwell, Va. Histl. Reg., I. 80.   [2] Ibid., I. 81.

"My wife hath all this year urged me to send little Nutty home to you, to which I have at last condescended, & hope you'll be pleased to excuse the trouble. I must confess she could learne nothing good here in a great family of Negroes. She comes in the Ship Culpepper where the master promised she shall want nothing that's necessary for her. I writ to Mr. North & Mr. Coe to supply her with what necessary's she wants. I pray God send her safe to you."

When we next hear of Will he is in Holland, where he had been studying. He was, no doubt, sent here to imbibe some of the fine business sense of the Dutch. It must have been at this early date that he came under the supervision of Sir Robert Southwell,[1] as the epitaph declares. Now, Sir Robert had a son, Edward, three years older than Will, and him he was educating himself, with the assistance of Sir William Petty.[2] It is not improbable, therefore, that Byrd, either directly or indirectly, was put through many of the forms of education which recommended themselves to Petty,[3] and, with Petty's admiration for Holland, he might well have been responsible for the period of study there. At that early age, however, the boy could not have learned much about Dutch society.[4] He seems there to have been in touch with Mr. Senserfe, a merchant of Rotterdam, for Byrd wrote in 1690, thanking him for his civilities to the boy.

Will Byrd himself grew tired of Holland, and asked to be taken away. To him his father wrote, July 25, 1690, as

[1] The elder Byrd had close business relations with Blathwayt and Povey, who were half-brothers-in-law of each other. Perhaps they had some relation with Sir Robert Southwell as early as this. At any rate, the latter's son afterward married a daughter of Blathwayt. This may give us an idea of how Byrd came to meet Sir Robert.

[2] See Sir Robert Southwell in Nat. Dict. of Biog.

[3] There was a copy of The Political Arithmetick in the Byrd library.

[4] This view is supported by the fact that most of the Dutch books in the Byrd library were text-books.

follows: "According to your desire, I have wrote to Messrs. Perry and Lane to send for you to London, there to learne what may be farther fitting for you, and also to imploy you about Business, wherein I hope you will indeavour to acquaint yourselfe that you may be no Stranger to itt when necessity will require you to attend to itt. But above all be mindful of your duty to Heaven, & then you may be assured that God will bless you in all your undertakings." [1] To Perry and Lane he wrote: "I desire you to send for my son to London, and put him into business, or if he wants anything to accomplish him I desire he might learn it there." [2]

Soon after his arrival in London the boy was entered as a student of law in the Middle Temple.[3] At that time the regulations of the Inns of Court provided that a student must have read at least three years before he was called to the bar,[4] but the usual course was for him to take at least five years. As Byrd was duly called to the bar, it is probable that he was a law student till late in 1695 or early in 1696. His course must have been a thorough one, for in the catalogue of the Byrd books are most of the great legal classics, both Roman, English, and Continental. His life was made pleasant here by companionship with Benjamin Lynde, afterwards chief justice of Massachusetts. In a letter to Lynde, February 20, 1736, he recalls the time when they were both strangers together in a strange place; and he gives a spicy picture of what they did to relieve their loneliness. "If I could persuade our captain of the Guard ship," says he, "to take a cruise to Boston at a

[1] See under the date in William Byrd's Letter-book.

[2] Ibid., July 25, 1690.

[3] In the catalogue of the Byrd library is inserted a piece of paper, seemingly the fly-leaf of a book, on which is written in Byrd's hand: "W. Byrd, E. Societate M. Templi, 1692." A letter received since the above was in print from Mr. J. F. Rowe, treasurer of the Middle Temple, contains the information that William Byrd became a member of that inn April 25, 1692, but that nothing appears to show that he was of Virginia.

[4] See Pearce, Guide to the Inns of Court, pp. 305, 397.

proper season, I woud come and beat up your quarters at Salem. I want to see what alteration forty years have wrought in you since we used to intrigue together in the Temple. But Matrimony has atoned Sufficiently for such Back slidings, and now I suppose you have so little fellow feeling left for the naughty Jades, that you can order them a good whipping without any relenting. But tho I should be mistaken, yet at least I hope your conscience, with the aid of three score and ten, has gained a complete victory over your constitution, which is almost the case of Sir yours etc."

Byrd was back in Virginia by the middle of 1696. His father's influence introduced him at once into public life, and he was a member of the Assembly which met first in September of that year. He represented Henrico County; but in the second session, which met in October, 1697,[1] he was out of the country and another man was returned in his place.[2] He seems to have gone to England early in 1697, for in April of that year the Council wrote that he, in conjunction with John Povey, would lay before the Board of Trade an address from the Assembly.[3] In December of the same year he appeared with Povey again to represent Andros in the Lambeth Conference. Here he was pitted against Commissary Blair, for whose trained Scotch mind his young powers were no match. He was outclassed at every point, if the proceedings are correctly reported, and Blair's victory was easy.[4] In October, 1698, he was nominated by the Council as agent of the colony in London.[5] His salary in this capacity was, perhaps, £100.[6] During this immediate period there is no evidence that he

---

[1] Henning's Statues, III. 137, note, and 166, note.

[2] Va. Histl. Soc. Mag., III. 425.

[3] Sainsbury Papers, vol. for 1691–97, p. 309.

[4] See Perry, Historical Collections of the Colonial Church in Virginia, I. 36.

[5] Sainsbury Papers, vol. for 1625–1715 (Vol. II. Part I.), p. 89.

[6] This is on the supposition that the "Solicitor" mentioned in the Council Minutes in the summer of 1699 was the agent.

solicited, in England, any other colony affairs than the reference to him in 1697 indicates. In September of that year he was living in Lincoln's Inn, and had in his possession a copy of the laws of Virginia, which the Board of Trade found it convenient to borrow.[1] His companions were congenial, and by his own confession he found the life pleasant, while his father had influence enough to keep him in office. When Nicholson and the people came into violent opposition because the latter refused to vote £900 to defend the frontiers of New York, the burgesses and the Council elected Byrd their agent, and through him sent an address to the British government in defense of their position. This was in December, 1701. In March, 1702, he was before the Board of Trade on this affair, and was also before the privy council. The board, which was in sympathy with Nicholson, took exception at Byrd's agency, and declared that sending a petition through any hands but those of a governor was irregular and a bad precedent, and that they hoped the king would so inform the Virginians.[2] This request was complied with and the Council was rebuked. That body, of which Byrd[1] was a prominent member, replied submissively that they did not know that the king would receive no address except through the governor, and that they would not in the future use their own agent.[3] After that Byrd's agency ceases. It was just at this time that he applied for the office of secretary, to succeed Wormley. He had a favorable recommendation from the Board of Trade, but the king gave the office to Jennings, who had been assistant of the former incumbent.[4] The words in which the Board of Trade recommended

[1] Sainsbury Papers, 1691–97, pp. 349, 375. William Fitzhugh perhaps refers to the same collection of laws. (See Va. Histl. Soc. Mag., V. 297.)

[2] Sainsbury Papers, Vol. II. Part I. (1625–1715), pp. 278, 330, 338, 352, 360.

[3] Council Minutes, entered without date, but between November 11, 1702, and April 24, 1703.

[4] Sainsbury Papers, Vol. II. Part I. (1625–1715), pp. 258, 274, 301.

Byrd to the king were (following the abstract) : "Bird is a native of Virginia, son of one of the most eminent of his Majesty's subjects in those parts, is a person of good character, unblamable conduct & known loyalty to His Majesty & his Government & has had the advantage of a liberal education & knowledge in the laws of England & may be very fit to serve his Majesty as he desires."

If Byrd's life during this period was socially gay it was not a profitless one. His friendship with Sir Robert Southwell, as the epitaph states, led him to make many acquaintances among people of good standing. From this same source we know that one of these was Charles Boyle, Earl of Orrery, with whom Byrd maintained a warm friendship till the death of the former in 1731. This gentleman was a popular literary man of the day, and waged a furious war in behalf of a party in London known as the Christ Church men, a contest which is the more interesting to us because it led Swift to write " The Battle of the Books." It was at this time, perhaps, that Byrd was elected a fellow of the Royal Society. The honor undoubtedly came through Sir Robert Southwell, who was president of that body from 1690 till 1695, and who till his death in 1702 never ceased to be greatly interested in its work. So far as the published " Transactions " show, Byrd's connection with the society did not lead to much. He is represented there by only one paper, a very short one communicated in 1697. It was "An Account of a Negro Boy that is dappled in Several Places of his Body with White Spots. By Will. Byrd, Esq. F. R. S.," and was published in the issue for December, 1697, p. 781.[1] Byrd, however, did not undervalue his connection with the Royal Society. His library catalogue shows that he got and kept the published

[1] Other Virginians of this period reported papers to the society. In August, 1697, there was published an account of a storm in Virginia in 1694, received from Mr. Scarburgh of Accomac, and communicated by Sir Robert Southwell. Some observations on insects made by John Banister in Virginia in 1680 also were published in 1699.

" Transactions." In 1741 he wrote to Sir Hans Sloane,[1] who was himself, in that year, president of the society : "I take it a little unkindly Sir that my name is left out of the yearly List of the Royal Society, of which I have the honour of being one of its ancientest members. I suppose my long absence has made your Secretarys rank me in the number of the Dead ; but pray let them know I am alive, and by the help of Ginsing hope to survive Some years longer."

At the time of the death of his father, December 4, 1704, young Byrd was still in London. As soon as he had news of the event he sailed for America. He arrived in the following spring. By his father's will he was sole heir of the large estate in Virginia, with the exception of some small legacies. He at once took possession of the estate, for he was named executor, and then he turned his attention to securing the political offices his father had held. Lieutenant-Governor Nott readily put him temporarily in charge of the office of auditor and receiver-general, subject to the approval of the queen.[2] Blackiston, who had just been made Virginia agent in London, also was complaisant enough to ask that he be given the seat at the Council board which had been held by his father.[3] The latter request was not granted. The Board of Trade, to whom the application had been made, replied that they had a very good opinion of Mr. Byrd, but that Messrs. John Smith and John Lewis, who had been previously recommended, had better claims to the vacancies then in sight.[4] Byrd thus had to wait, as it happened, till 1708. But in that year, on August 18, the queen, acting on the recommendations of the absentee Governor Hunter, and of Micajah Perry, the influential London merchant, was pleased to

[1] Byrd Letters, April 10, 1741.
[2] Sainsbury Papers, Vol. V. Part II. (1705–07), p. 354. This was in September, 1705. Since the death of Byrd the office had been filled by Gov. Nicholson. Also see Council Minutes, vol. for 1705–21, pp. 3, 5.
[3] Ibid., p. 316. The date was Dec. 24, 1705.
[4] Ibid., p. 377.

order that William Byrd[II] should be of the Council of Virginia in the room of John Lightfoot, deceased.[1] On September 12, 1709, he took the prescribed oaths, and was duly admitted to membership.[2] It was the most honorable appointment ever given him. As his father had worn it, so he wore it, with dignity and with influence. He held the position till his death in 1744, and in the last year of his life he was, by virtue of being the longest in office, President of the Council. This high dignity he would have had longer had he not been preceded by Commissary Blair, whose tough Scotch constitution enabled him to round out a life of eighty-seven years.

As for the auditorship, Byrd was more fortunate. He was confirmed in that at once—in fact, before he arrived in Virginia.[3] But it was soon to be robbed of half of its importance. In response to a demand several times made by those who had criticized the ordinary method of keeping the accounts, it was now decided to have the offices of auditor and receiver-general in the hands of different men. This was regardless of the fact that the Virginia Council, to whom the Board of Trade had referred the matter for an opinion, said that the salary attached to the office was too small for two men, and that they approved the old way of uniting the offices, and requiring the accounts to be examined by the Council before they were sent to England.[4] Byrd was given the office of receiver-general, while Dudley Digges was made auditor. Both men presented their commissions to the Council early in 1706, Byrd's dated October 17, and Digges's dated October 10, 1705.[5] Byrd's salary was to be three per cent. of the receipts, but later he got it raised

---

[1] Ibid., vol. for 1706–14, under dates Aug. 10, 13, 18, 1708.

[2] Council Minutes, vol. for 1705–21, entry for Sept. 12, 1709.

[3] His commission from the queen, dated April 2, 1705, is preserved in the back of the Council Minutes, vol. for 1705–1721.

[4] Council Minutes, vol. for 1705–21, entry for Sept. 4, 1705.

[5] Ibid., pp. 26, 33. The two commissions are preserved in the back of this volume.

to five per cent.,[1] and since it remained the same under his successor, it is safe to assume that it continued five per cent. throughout Byrd's incumbency.

Settled now in the colony, Byrd took up the responsibilities of the life of a country gentleman in good earnest. In 1706 he married Lucy, youngest daughter of General Daniel Parke.[2] Her father was that sparkish gentleman who had forcibly tried to eject the wife of Parson Blair from a pew in the Jamestown church during the administration of Andros. He had married a daughter of Philip Ludwell, Sr., by whom he had two children, both girls. About the time Andros left Virginia, Parke appeared in London. His handsome face recommended him to the Marlboroughs, and he was made an aide to the duke in the campaign in the Low Countries. To him was given the favor of bearing to the queen the tidings of the victory of Blenheim. As a reward for this, it is said, he was made governor of the Leeward Islands, where he was unpopular from the time of his arrival till he was killed in 1710 in a riot in Antigua. His murder occurred just at the time of the fall of the Marlborough party, and the succeeding party did not trouble itself to avenge the dead man.

Frances, the elder daughter of Parke, had married John Custis of Virginia. Now, when Parke died, as Byrd says in the Title-book, " a Will was produced and proved which he had made not long before his Death. By that will he left all his Estate in England and Virginia to his Eldest Daughter Mrs. Custis, and his Estate in the West Indies (which was of twice the Value of all the rest) to Lucy Chester, which he had too much Reason to believe his own Daughter, altho' her mother was at that time a

---

[1] This is taken from the commissions. In 1715 the joint salary of the auditor and receiver-general was raised to ten per cent. by order obtained from the treasury, whereas before October 20, 1712, it had been only seven and a half per cent. (See Sainsbury Papers, vol. for 1715–20, p. 463.)

[2] Parke's mother was Jane, or Rebecca, Evelyn, daughter of George Evelyn of Surrey County, England.

marry'd woman.   And as for Mrs. Byrd (who never had
offended her Father, but was marry'd not only with his
consent but at his earnest desire) she was fobb'd off with
One Thousand pounds." [1]   Moreover, all his debts and the
legacies were charged against the Virginia and English
property, and Custis was named executor in matters relating to that property.   Byrd, whose family pride was not
small, was unwilling that the land should go into the hands
of strangers.   He accordingly came to an agreement with
Custis by which he bought enough of the Virginia lands,
and the English property also, as it seems, to pay the obli-
gations against the estate.   It is a singular illustration of
business affairs in the colony that they proceeded without
the use of either money or bills of exchange.   Custis transferred the lands to Byrd,[2] and Byrd assumed the debts and
legacies.   Like so many other Virginians, Parke was in debt
to Micajah Perry, who had been his London agent.   By a
schedule of the debts which Perry sent to Byrd, it appeared that the estate owed £6280, besides £400 due to the
queen as interest on Parke's bond.   The latter Byrd tried
to get remitted.   Parke had an estate at Whitechurch, in
England, which Perry said was worth £4000, but which
was charged with a mortgage of £2230.   Byrd trusted to
Perry's schedule.   He had much cause to regret it.   He
said in 1723,[3] twelve years after the agreement was made,
that he had then paid £1000 more than the schedule, on
account of debts hitherto unheard of.

In 1710, the very year in which Parke died, there came
to Virginia a man who was destined to make things uncomfortable for more than one man there, and for Byrd
among the others.   This was Colonel Alexander Spotswood, who came as lieutenant-governor under the Earl of

[1] See the Byrd Title-book in
connection with the land which
Byrd now received from Custis,
p. 195.

[2] The Virginia lands were en-
tailed, and an act of Assembly
was necessary to sell them. (See
Henning's Statutes, III. 29.)

[3] Letter to John Custis, July
29, 1723.   It is preserved among
the MSS. of the Va. Histl. Soc.,
File VII.

Orkney, the absentee governor-in-chief. He was a strong-willed Scotchman, who believed with proverbial Scotch insistency in maintaining the prerogative and the dignity of the crown. Spotswood found soon after he arrived in the country what kind of a thing a Virginia Council was.

As a matter of fact, the Council was an oligarchy, jealous of its rights, and powerfully established through personal relations, which many of its members had, with prominent men in London. Its members were men of towering personality, as the Ludwells, " King" Carter, the Lees, and Ralph Wormley. Moreover, they had been used for a long time to the largest share in the control of the government. Since the days of Sir William Berkeley there had been no governor who had been completely the head of his own administration. Culpeper and Effingham were too much bent on advancing their own interests to contend with the Council. Both Andros and Nicholson had ideas of their own dignity, but their tempers were ill suited to the task of disestablishing the authority of the Council. Spotswood declared that it was the intention of the Council to control affairs which had caused the troubles in both of those administrations, which, being translated into a saner form, means that these two governors had resented the authority of the Council, and through their testy tempers fallen into disgraceful quarrels with most of the councilors. Nott, who followed these two governors, was confessedly a weak-spirited man, approved of by Blair before he was appointed, and, had he not so soon ended his life, would hardly have disputed the rule of the leaders. Then came the long interregnum during which no governor came to Virginia, and the administration was left formally to the Council. Thus it had happened that for the space of a generation— from the fall of Berkeley till the arrival of Spotswood, the Council was a chief force in government. It was to be the principal effort of the latter governor to bring it to that subserviency which existed in some of the Northern colonies. Spotswood's attempt, though outwardly success-

ful, was inwardly a failure. He was watched quietly by
the party he had opposed, till at last he was taken at a disadvantage and his removal was secured. He was succeeded
by Drysdale, and after him by Gooch, neither of whom ventured to raise the questions which loomed so large in the
time of Spotswood. In fact, till the time of the Revolution
the dignity of the Council was unabated.[1]

It is not possible to refrain from pointing out the remarkably fortunate effect this had upon the political
aspect of the Revolutionary period. Instead of throwing
the councilors, who through abilities and position were
the natural leaders of the community, into an inane es-
pousal of the rights of the crown, it developed in them a
strong colony sense. They felt that they were Virginians
first of all. They did not go with the ministry in their
taxation schemes. They did not, perhaps, feel the fullest
sympathy with the lurid popular agitation for liberty, but
they gave to that agitation the blessings of an experienced
conservatism, holding back the movement till the proper

[1] The following is the oath of
a councilor on taking his place
in the Council: "You shall
swear to be a true and faithful
servant unto the King's Majesty as one of his Council of
State and to be aiding and assisting to his Excellency his
Majesties Lieutenant Governor
of Virginia; You shall in all
things to be moved treated
and debated in the Council
faithfully to declare your Mind
and opinion, according to your
heart and Conscience, and shall
keep secret all matters committed and revealed unto you
according to the same, and that
be treated Secretly in the
Council, until such times as by
the Consent of His Majesties
Lieutenant and Governour Gen-
erall and the full consent of the
Council of State there Resident
or the major part of them, Pub-
lication shall be made thereof;
You shall to your utmost bear
faith and Allegiance to the
King's Majesty his heirs and
lawful Successors, and shall assist and defend all Jurisdiccons,
proheminoncos and authorities
granted unto His Majesty and
annext unto the Crown against
all fforeign Princes Persons Pre-
lates and Potentates whatsoever
and Generally you shall act and
doe in all things as a faithfull
and true subject ought to doe
to his Majesty — So help you
God." (From the Council Minutes, 1721–34, among some miscellaneous papers entered in the
back of the book.)

time, and setting it forth, when it did come, with a dignity and an ability which won for it at once the respect of the world.

An illustration of how far this independence of the Council had gone in Virginia in 1706 is seen from a statement by the Rev. James Blair, who, from opposing the power of the Council, came at last to participate in it. In this year he joined Hartwell, Chilton, and Benjamin Harrison in a memorial to the Board of Trade against the Council's acquisition of such great powers. He was then in England, and being called before the board, testified that there were " several in the government who have been for years endeavoring to have all power invested in the Council, and by degrees they try to lessen the prerogative and to render the Queen's Governor little better than a cypher, and in truth they have in effect gained their point." [1] Then Blair went on to give instances to prove his point ; but they have not been included in the abstracts. Were this not from one of the most upright men in Virginia it might be discounted as the vaporings of a disappointed politician. But the character of the president of the college and the commissary of the Bishop of London is too good to be disposed of so lightly.

The basis of the power of the councilors, aside from their political influence, was in their large landed estates. They were not, it is true, the only large landowners in the colony, but they were very large ones. Whatever irregularity in granting or holding land might redound to the profit of the holder they found it to their own advantage to wink at. Thus it seems to have been the universal habit to give very generous measure in laying out patents, and to conceal the amount of land subject to quit-rents. Now the Council, as the representatives of the king, ought to have been the first to see that these irregularities were not practised ; but their interests as large landowners made

[1] Sainsbury Papers, Vol. V. Part II. (1705–15), p. 467 ; the quotation is from the abstract.

it a temptation to them to let the law be violated. That they did this is the only way to account for the abuses in the issuing of importation rights, and in the loose way of construing the law of the seating of land. Certainly, had they actively engaged themselves to reform these evils they would have succeeded.[1]

When Lieutenant-Governor Alexander Spotswood arrived in 1710, he found this state of affairs fully developed. He had possibly had some intimations of it before he left England. At any rate, he made a conscience of bringing the prerogative, and the lieutenant-governor as the representative of it, into the fullest vigor. His first step was to get through the Assembly a law to provide better for the seating of land. The old law had stipulated that on every tract of land, within three years after it was granted, a house must be built, and one acre cultivated; otherwise it lapsed. Thus it was possible to hold a large tract for a very small outlay. The new law provided that failure to pay quit-rents for three years should cause the grant to lapse.[2] This law he got through without arousing the opposition of the Council. Then came the troubles in North Carolina, in which he was twice called on for assistance, and he had not time for controversies at home. But in 1713 the coast was clear, and he began to turn his attention to the quit-rents.

It was at this point that Spotswood came into opposition to Byrd. He had made up his mind that the interest of the king's revenue demanded more businesslike methods of collecting the quit-rents and of selling the tobacco in which they had been paid. His proposition did not openly

[1] Edward Chilton testified in 1697 that he knew of a tract of 27,017 acres on which the improvements consisted of a house that did not cost ten shillings and a few hogs turned loose in the woods. It was a notorious fact, he said, that some years ago Colonel Ludwell raised a patent for 2000 acres to 20,000 by the addition of a cipher and that his influence in the Council was such that nothing was said of it. (Sainsbury Papers, 1691–97, p. 350.)

[2] Spotswood Letters, I. 50–52, 60–61.

assail Byrd's integrity, but it did imply that the old method had been singularly faulty. The elder Byrd, under the circumstance, would have bowed to the power of the Council and maintained the office while he took the salary in making the new scheme work. The younger Byrd had more of the Cavalier pride about him. He considered himself attacked in his honor, and he prepared for a fight.

The farming of the quit-rents, which was practised in 1699, had not been maintained. When Spotswood arrived they were collected by the sheriffs of the counties through their deputies. The sheriffs settled with the receiver-general, who was Byrd. It was admitted on both sides that the sheriffs did not properly collect, and the implication was that by passing through so many hands the quit-rents became very much, and often very unwarrantably, lessened.

Spotswood, perhaps, gave some inkling of his dissatisfaction with the existing system as early as 1713; for in that year Byrd prepared and offered to the lieutenant-governor a new scheme for collecting the quit-rents. Its features were: (1) the quit-rents to be collected by four deputy receivers; (2) those who paid in tobacco-notes to do so before the last of March; and (3) deputy receivers to account to the receiver-general, and make sworn returns of their accounts to the auditor. This plan, said Byrd, in the bitterness of his controversy, Spotswood received with the scorn with which he received all proposals which "hath not the advantage of his own contrivance."[1] Spotswood's scorn may have been due to a suspicion that the scheme would only create more officials to build up the strength of the party already too strong.

This much had been done privately. But in July, 1714, Spotswood asked Byrd and Ludwell to propose a better scheme for collecting the quit-rents. Byrd proposed the scheme he had already once submitted. In November Spotswood, ignoring Byrd's scheme, announced to the Council that he would submit a scheme, which he at once

[1] From Byrd's defense. Preserved in MS. by the Va. Histl. Soc.

proceeded to do. The chief features of his scheme were: 1. The sheriffs to collect quit-rents at places appointed by the county court, and not on the land, as formerly. 2. If the quit-rents were brought to them they were to receive only five per cent. for their commission, and the payer was to have five per cent. discount. 3. Those who paid the receiver-general in person were to have eight per cent. discount. 4. Sheriffs to settle directly with the receiver-general in Williamsburg, and to file copies of their accounts with the auditor and the clerks of the respective county courts. 5. Quit-rents to be paid in sterling money, or, if in foreign coins, to be rated with Mexican silver at three and a half pennyweights for a shilling, or with Peruvian silver at nineteen pennyweights for five shillings, or in tobacco-notes on any warehouse in Virginia. 6. On a given day there should be posted in the general court-house at Williamsburg a list of all the quit-rent tobacco by parcels, and buyers must enter their bids opposite the parcels; and at the end of ten days the tobacco would be sold to the highest bidder. The purpose of the scheme was to secure economy in collecting and more competition in selling the quit-rent tobacco. Spotswood asked the Council to think over the proposition. The various features of the scheme were voted on separately. They all passed, Byrd and Ludwell voting against all that were material to the purpose of the scheme. On the third proposal Byrd first voted "yea," thinking it would increase the revenue, and it was passed by a vote of four to five. But on the following morning, before the minutes of the preceding day were read in the Council, he announced that he wanted to change his vote. Spotswood refused to allow this, and declared the proposal adopted.

Byrd's objections to Spotswood's scheme were summarized in his defense[1] as follows: 1. Sheriffs were not the

---

[1] His defense is preserved among the MSS. of the Va. Histl. Soc. It was submitted to the Board of Trade, Sept. 27, 1716. (Sainsbury Papers, vol. for 1715–20, p. 563.)

proper persons to collect quit-rents, because they were
changed too often; and if they did poorly at ten-per-cent.
commissions, they would do no better at five per cent.
2. The giving of the payer five per cent. in the second proposal was granting away the king's money, and that they
had no right to do. 3. To give eight per cent. discount
to those who paid directly to the receiver-general reduced
the reward of the sheriff so that the office would not be
worth his while.   Besides, it increased greatly the expenses
of the receiver-general.   When Byrd wrote his defense the
scheme had been working two years.   He said that when
tobacco was high rich persons bought the quit-rent tobacco
from the smaller farmers and sent the money with long
lists of names to the receiver-general, and that the bringer
had to be entertained till his accounts could be settled.
Thus there was a large additional expense, both for entertainment of messengers and for clerk-hire; but that, he
thought, was very agreeable to Spotswood.   4. To the
fourth proposal Byrd made no objection.   5. Spotswood's
rating of foreign coins reduced the amount of money the
king received from the quit-rents, and taking tobacco-
notes from any county induced men to buy up the tobacco
raised in unfavorable counties with which to pay their
quit-rents.   He did not know why Spotswood had proposed this unless it was because he had lately become a
large landowner.   6. The old method of selling quit-rents
by private sale had long been approved by the Council
and governors.   No fault was found with it till after the
removal of Nicholson.   The new method would not work
because the buyers would agree among themselves not to
bid against one another.   How they should be less apt to
agree to this same thing in a private sale he does not
say.

  Against this let us put Spotswood's statement.[1] There was,
he said, in the collection of the quit-rents in Virginia "the
grossest Mismanagements and most fraudulent Collections

[1] Spotswood Letters, II. 86.

that ever was known in a Revenue," and he offered to prove it. The sheriffs, indeed, were the "Gent. of the Country," but their deputies were those who would give most to be deputies. The latter did the actual collecting, and rendered their accounts to their superiors. At the end of the year the high sheriff would go before the auditor and swear that his accounts were true, to the best of his knowledge. As these accounts did not specify the several tracts of land on which the quit-rents were paid, it was very difficult to discover an error or a fraud.

It is notable that these charges, in which Spotswood had no hesitancy to be severe enough, did not reach the moral integrity of either Byrd or Ludwell. The receiver-general and the auditor had nothing to do with the collecting or with the appointment of the sheriffs and the deputy sheriffs. They could neither one do more than receive the accounts that were submitted to them. The fraud, as appears by the statement of the lieutenant-governor, was with the sheriffs and their deputies. Byrd and Ludwell both admitted this. The essential difference between their scheme and Spotswood's was that the former wanted to reform affairs by creating special collectors, while the latter wanted to use the existing machinery, and throw more of the strain on its central point, the receiver-general; for, as he said to the board, he did not conceive that it was his Majesty's intention that the receiver-general should be no more than a formal officer whose work was all done by others. Byrd's scheme was born of the spirit of the then existing English office-holding; Spotswood's was the product of thrifty Scotch management, which contemplated no sinecures. The latter scheme was the more businesslike. After one annual collection had been made under it, Spotswood declared: "One-third of the Crown lands in this Colony has this year yielded a greater Revenue than the whole did formerly." [1]

Late in 1713 Byrd had asked for leave of absence for a

[1] Spotswood Letters, II. 117.

year to go to England on private business.[1] He may have
desired this in connection with the debts of Parke, or he
may have had an inkling of the coming quarrel with Spotswood. Early in 1715 he departed,[2] leaving Nathaniel
Harrison as his deputy. He carried with him a strong
feeling of resentment against Spotswood. In London he
was received with consideration. On July 15 and 26,
1715, he was called before the Board of Trade to give information in regard to the Indian war in South Carolina.[3]
On August 11 he presented a memorial that the Virginia
quit-rents should not be taken over into the English treasury. The latter matter caused much concern in the
colony. The new sovereign contemplated converting this
revenue into the royal treasury as soon as it was collected.
The old way had been to leave it in the colony till it
reached a considerable sum, subject to the orders of the
king. Occasionally some of it had been used to repair de-
ficiencies in the ordinary fund of two shillings a hogshead.
Alarmed at the prospect of having permanently diverted
to king's use a fund which had always offered them a sure
recourse in times of unexpected outlay, the colonists now
sent up a cry that the quit-rents should be held for the
use of the colony. Byrd, as receiver-general, was in the
center of the commotion, and went actively to work for
the colonists. He was several times before the Board
of Trade, giving them information. To them he said that
the two-shilling duty yielded ordinarily £3000 a year,
and the quit-rents from £1200 to £1500, and that the expenses of the government were about £3500 a year. Spotswood could not be so indifferent to the interests of the
colony as not to desire that the quit-rents should not be
diverted from its use ; but he said, when delivering his

[1] Sainsbury Papers, vol. for
1706–14, entry for Jan. 25, 1714.

[2] He last attended the Council
meeting on Feb. 23. The next
meeting, at which his prolonged

absence begins, was April 25.
(See Council Minutes.)

[3] Sainsbury Papers, vol. for
1715–20, under the dates mentioned.

opinion to the board, that he hoped they would do what
he asked as in response to his request and not as in response to the address of the Assembly, which had been
forwarded.[1] After due deliberation it was decided that
the quit-rents should be spent as formerly, but that the
colony was not to take this as a warrant for extravagant
expenditures.[2]

The success of this affair was gratifying to Byrd, and it
tended to increase his influence in Virginia. He next proceeded to move for the repeal of two laws which Spotswood had got passed in 1714. One of these was a law to
provide for the payment of debts in tobacco, and the other
created a company to which was given a monopoly of the
Indian trade. Byrd thought both of these laws injurious
to the colony, and he set out actively to get them disal-
lowed. He made strong arguments before the Board of
Trade, especially against the latter law. Spotswood defended himself by saying that the Indian trading company
had been established to prevent the abuses committed in
the trade by indiscriminate traders, and that the scheme
did not injure the old traders, since all of them except
Byrd, who was about to leave the country when the law
was proposed, had been asked to take stock in the company.
He added that since the trade was concentrated at Christiana, where his Indian school was, and since the company
agreed to contribute a sum to the support of this school,
the scheme held out great promise of the solution of the
Indian question. But Byrd had on his side the Englishman's hatred of monopoly, and on July 31, 1717, the king,

[1] Sainsbury Papers, vol. for
1715–20, p. 478. This address
was perhaps the one forwarded
by the hands of Byrd when he
went to England, and referred to
in a letter to the Board of Trade,
an undated copy of which is
preserved in the collection of
the Virginia Historical Society.

[2] Byrd gave as one of the reasons why he had once favored
having distinct justices of the
General Court that it would
create more offices and thus
keep a part of the quit-rent
revenue in the colony. (See
his letter to Ludwell, Sept. 24,
1717.)

on the recommendation of the Board of Trade, ordered both the laws to be repealed.[1]

In the meantime in Virginia the war had become acute. Spotswood had come to an open breach with Ludwell, because Ludwell resented his quit-rent policy and would not submit his books to Spotswood, and the upshot of the matter was that the lieutenant-governor suspended him till the case could be tried in England. To Blathwayt, who, as auditor-general, was Ludwell's superior, Spotswood sent an account of his action, and regretted that it had been necessary. To the Board of Trade he sent his charges against the deputy auditor. Now he gradually came to feel as much resentment against Byrd as against Ludwell. He charged both with obstructing the execution of his quit-rent policy, but said that inasmuch as Byrd was out of the country he did not like to proceed definitely against Harrison, who was only a deputy to Byrd. The affair would have gone through a long and tedious investigation, no doubt, had not Blathwayt anticipated Spotswood. Before he received Spotswood's charges against Ludwell he had removed the latter gentleman from office.[2] But neither Ludwell nor Byrd were satisfied to leave the matter as it was. They both prepared stated defenses, which were submitted to the Board of Trade, and to which Spotswood was allowed to make reply. Byrd wrote both defenses. All of his, though partly illegible, and a fragment of Ludwell's, are preserved among the manuscripts in the possession of the Virginia Historical Society. They were able instruments, clear and cutting, and not without the biting sarcasm which renders Byrd's less strenuous writings so delightful.

[1] Sainsbury Papers, vol. for 1715–20, pp. 549, 616, 630.

[2] Blathwayt's view of this dispute is worth noting. In announcing the removal of Ludwell he said: "In the main it is perhaps more agreeable to Col. Spotswood to have the management of the revenues in his own or creature's hands by which means there might be no control over him or his friends being Commander in Chief. This I conceive to be the truth of the matter." (Ibid., 560.)

They were a worthy offset to Spotswood's strong and serviceable arguments, so that the reader is left in doubt as to which side handled its weapons more skilfully.

Byrd was better able to wage this war from having relieved himself of his office; for as a servant of the king it did not become him to oppose the king's representative, except in the spirit of official humility, and of that spirit Byrd had none. On October 2, 1716, he wrote to John Custis saying that he had sold his place of receiver-general for £500 to James Roscowe,[1] the first person he met who was willing to pay his price. This was not because he feared that he would be removed, but because the office was a burden under existing conditions. To hold it gave Spotswood the opportunity to charge him with misconduct, and to get thereby the credit of being zealous in the interest of the king; so that the holder "must either be a slave to his [Spotswood's] humour, must fawn upon him, jump over a stick whenever he was bid, or else he must have so much trouble loaded on him as to make his place uneasy. In short, such a man must be either the governor's dog or his ass; neither of which stations suit in the least with my constitution." Now, he added, he could give himself entirely to opposing Spotswood's arbitrary and unjust designs.[2] A year later he again wrote that he was laboring with all his might "to hinder so great a power from being lodged in any bashaw."

Byrd's defense took up Spotswood's charges in order: 1. To the statement that Byrd kept the quit-rent accounts intermixed with his private affairs, and for four years had refused to give an itemized account of them, he replied that Spotswood had not complained about the accounts before 1714, as the Council minutes would show, that these

---

[1] Roscowe was admitted to the office of receiver-general by the Council on Jan. 22, 1717, but his commission was dated March 26, 1716. (See Council Minutes.)

[2] This letter is printed in Lossing's Edition of G. W. P. Custis's Recollections of Washington, in the Memoir of Custis by Mrs. Lee, p. 29.

accounts had always been kept in separate books, and that he had submitted those books to the board just after he arrived in England. 2. To the charge that he would not make a rent-roll he replied that every governor had been ordered to make a rent-roll, but that it was not a duty put on the receiver-general; that it was a difficult matter and had long engaged the attention of the Council, and that some of the sheriffs "return'd uncouth medleys instead of Rentrolls," they being very ignorant. 3. To the complaint that sheriffs received bad tobacco he answered that the sheriffs were appointed by the governor. 4. To the complaint that abuses had occurred in the sale of importation rights he replied that this was true, but he was in no way responsible for it, and that he had heartily supported the reforms which had been made in regard to the same. 5. To the charge that he received Spanish silver at nineteen pennyweights for five shillings, which was exorbitant, and paid it out for sixteen pennyweights for five shillings, he replied that it was the custom of the country in small purchases, and he introduced witnesses to prove the point.[1]   In his reply for Ludwell he said that if the king got what was due him he did not see how there could be complaint about the kind of money in which the receiver-general had dealt. 6. To the charge that his method of keeping the accounts was "dark & idle" he replied that they had been in use for years, and had been approved by the Board of Trade and by the former governors, and that Spotswood himself had not objected to them till the expiration of Nicholson's commission in 1714.[2] 7. To the charge that he had always opposed Spotswood he said that he had opposed him only when the king's interests seemed to him to demand it, and that such was his sworn

---

[1] Byrd in his own reply refers for this to Ludwell's defense. He introduced his witnesses before the Board of Trade, Nov. 2, 1716. (See Sainsbury Papers, vol. for 1715–20, pp. 568–571.

[2] To what commission he referred I am unable to guess.— EDITOR.

duty ; that he had not tried to excite popular feeling against Spotswood, and that the popular discontent was rather due to Spotswood's temper and to his habit of thinking that all opposition was insolent. 8. As to the complaint against certain words which Ludwell had used to Spotswood, he owned that they were improper, but called attention to the fact that they were not spoken in Council or in a court of justice, but at a muster-field, where the lieutenant-governor had no business to be. 9. This article referred to the quit-rent scheme, which has already been mentioned. 10. As to the charge that the majority of the Council were related to Ludwell and Byrd, he replied with a list of the councilors, showing how each was related to the two ; and by his own showing four of them were related by blood or marriage to Ludwell, and two of these four to Byrd ; and these four, with Byrd, who was himself related to Ludwell by marriage, would give six or half of the Council of one family connection.

With Ludwell's defense we are not directly concerned, but there is one point in it which illustrates so strikingly his relation to Spotswood that it will be well to mention it. This is the personal controversy referred to by Byrd in the eighth article above, the story of which is as follows : In the days of Governor Berkeley the colony had set aside 3000 acres of land near Jamestown for the use of the governor, and Berkeley had lived on it for many years, during which time he took up in his own name 2090 acres adjoining the same tract. He also had confirmed to himself personally several leases of parts of the former tract. Soon after his arrival in Virginia, Spotswood had the governor's tract surveyed, and found that it contained little more than 2000 acres. He believed that the encroachment had been from Berkeley's side. Berkeley's property had come, through the marriage of Dame Frances, his widow, to Philip Ludwell, into the hands of the second Philip Ludwell. On this disputed land were the fine house and grounds of "Green Springs," which Berkeley had built. Spotswood was anxious to recover this land, and Ludwell says it was because he wanted to get the fire-wood on it. He made a proposition to Ludwell to exchange it for other lands of the government near Jamestown, and other proposals were made, but nothing came of any of them. Finally, in the winter of 1715–16 it came time to procession lands in the neighborhood. By law, if a piece of land were peacefully processioned for the third time, its title was irrevocably fixed in the holder.[1] Spotswood, therefore, filed a caveat against Ludwell's processioning the disputed tract. He realized that if he did not act now he would lose all chance of recovery. This step brought about a lawsuit.[2]

As to what next happened Spotswood gives no particulars. Ludwell, however, describes it as follows : "I should be too tedious to enumerate the extraordinary methods & the indefatigable pains that were taken by the Governor & others appointed by him for carrying on this Law-suit, but in short a jury met on the land to lay out the bounds at which the Governor appeared in person & by his severe & hasty way of examining the witnesses I brought to prove the ancient bounds & his angry countenance they were so Terryfyed they hardly knew how to answer any thing that was asked them. Insomuch that I lost the benefit of one of my Witnesses entirely ; at last the Jury having heard the Witnesses viewed the Grounds, received all papers that were offered them & heard all the arguments on both sides retired to consult among themselves & having agreed what they would do called for the surveyor to goe about it, but out of Respect to the Governor they thought fitt to informe him of their resolutions, which being disagreeable to him he rated them very Severely in order to make them alter their resolutions, representing them as Ignorant obstinate fellows. Among other things he called them by way of derision a Chickahominy Jury, told them they acted unfairly & partially, that they would not do their sovereign

[1] Henning's Statutes, III. 325.
[2] Spotswood Letters, II. 155.

justice (for the Suit was made in the King's name & is to
be at the King's charge tho' if the King should gain the
cause he will loose twelve pence a year for every fifty acres
the Governor should recover) & that their names Should
all be sent to England &c.   I being vexed to see my cause
in so much danger by the Jurys being thus run down & so
much disheartened by this unfair practice and haveing been
provoked a little before by the Governor representing my
Uncle who had been formerly Secretary & my father who
had been formerly clerk of the Secretarys office & Deputy
secretary, as Destroyers of Records, I did at last say these
words, I think that this is very hard that my witnesses
must be brow-beaten & the Jury hectored out of their
Senses & not Suffered to proceed upon their own resolutions.   But I protest I had not the least thought of dis-
honouring his majesty. . . . Certainly it must be very hard
to be put under the delemma of keeping silence & loosing
my house, or Speaking to defend it & loosing my office." [1]

Spotswood's only testimony is that at the trial he was
treated "with more rudeness & ill-manners than I believe
any Governor ever was treated."   Ludwell's relations
urged him not to think of the matter, and said that Ludwell would apologize for it as soon as his anger cooled, but
no apology was offered.   Of the Board of Trade Spotswood
asked "a Suitable Reparation for a Affront done to me in
my public Capacity, which I should not have acquiesced
under, had it been offered to me as a private person.   I
shall only add this observation, that since the Lands now
in dispute came into the hands of Mr. Ludwells Father,
that Family have never suffered any Governor to be at
ease after he once begun to enquire into their Title, as y'r
Lo'ps, by looking into the plantation affairs, will find that
all the Clamours rais'd against Colo. Jeffreys, L'd Effingham, S'r Edmund Andrews[2] and Colo. Nicholson have been
fomented and Carryed on either by the Father or the

---

[1] This jury trial was in March, 1716.
The quotation is from Ludwell's defense.   [2] Andros.

Son."[1]   After all due allowances are made for the exaggeration of persons highly indignant, here is an instructive picture of the inner political life of an American colony.

These two papers were submitted to the Board of Trade in 1716.[2]   Neither man was in office, and there was no encouragement to thresh over straw which held no grain, and so the matter was allowed to lie.

But there had already arisen in Virginia another quarrel with Spotswood. This was one that brought almost the whole Council down upon him. The highest court in the colony was the General Court. A law of 1705, following a former law, enacted that it should be held by the governor and Council;[3] but Spotswood, in 1710, got a law passed providing that the former law should not abridge the king's prerogative to erect special courts of oyer and terminer.[4] Spotswood saw plainly enough that holding the highest court in the colony gave the Council a vast deal of power, and this he proposed to lessen by extending the privilege of holding special oyer and terminer courts. He proposed to appoint to hold the court some councilors and some who were not councilors. He justified himself chiefly on the ground that since six members of the Council were of one family, and since they must all retire from the bench when a case involving a member of that family was to be tried, it was important to have the court constituted differently. There was much truth in Spotswood's assertion, but there was a weakness in his position, due to the fact that his proposition would give the appointment of the judges to the governor; and if there was any good reason that the advisory part of the executive should not engross the judicial function, there was better reason that the presiding part of it should not do so. What the colony

---

[1] Spotswood Letters, II. 156.

[2] Byrd's defense was submitted Sept. 27, 1716. I have not found when Ludwell's was submitted.

[3] Henning's   Statutes,   III. 288.

[4] Ibid., III. 489, and Spotswood Letters, II. 224.

did need was a Supreme Court, distinct from all other departments of government.

In December, 1712, a man was to be tried for his life, and Spotswood joined the Speaker and two leading burgesses with the Council to hold the court of oyer and terminer that tried him. It is noticeable that he thus began to bind to himself the most influential members of the House of Burgesses. The councilors, however, objected to the innovation, and the matter was dropped for a time. In referring the matter to the Board of Trade, he insisted that he had the right which he had claimed, and that he thought it should occasionally be exercised, if for no other reason, to establish a respect for the king's prerogative.[1] On June 1, 1716, the Board of Trade, returning to this subject, wrote that he had the right to appoint such courts, unless there were a colonial law to the contrary.[2] There was no such law, as the act of 1710, already referred to, clearly shows. This decision pleased Spotswood, and as there were some criminal cases to be tried, he appointed a special court of oyer and terminer, consisting of five councilors and four other persons. Only one of the councilors was willing to serve. He was perhaps William Cocke, whom Byrd pronounced "a devoted Creature to the Lieut Governor." There was such an ominous look on the face of the affair that Spotswood hurriedly sent to England an explanation of his proceeding, lest the other side might send over a secret remonstrance "to private Agents, to be used for concealed Designs," in which he unquestionably alluded to Byrd.[3]

The Council, in fact, which had hitherto been mostly for Spotswood, regardless of the affair of Byrd and Ludwell, were much aroused. They saw in the present step the beginning of a formidable attack on one of their strongest positions. They sent a petition against the lieutenant-

[1] Spotswood Letters, II. 25.
[2] Sainsbury Papers, vol. for 1715–20, p. 524.
[3] Spotswood Letters, II. 260.

governor's scheme to the Board of Trade, to which eight of
them had set their hands.   Byrd heard the news joyfully.
"I am glad to find," he wrote, "that the Council is fairly
ingaged with the Lieut-Governour.   They have a good
cause & I hope I shall be able to procure justice to be done
to them."[1]   It was true, he added, as if to put himself thoroughly into touch with his brethren, that he had once proposed to make a Supreme Court in the colony, differentiated
from the Council, but he had shown the plan to nobody
but the Lord Justice, who had approved of it.   His only
purpose had been to obviate the absurdity of having men
who knew no law, as the councilors were, sitting on law
cases, and he had proposed to leave the Council the chancery jurisdiction, which would enable them to retain their
salary of £350 a year.   He had thought, too, that it would
be good to have the quit-rents paid out in salaries to the
judges, who would spend it in Virginia, and that it would
also be a good thing because it would encourage the Virginians to bring up their sons to be lawyers.   These were
his reasons, "and not the mean prospect of being one of the
Judges myself."   But, he said, since the Council was opposed to the plan he should certainly not urge it again.

Up to this time Byrd had had free access to the Board of
Trade, but that body, influenced, no doubt, by Spotswood's
allusion to "private Agents," now objected to receiving
addresses through him.   He insisted that as a member of
the Council he should be heard in this matter which affected the Council so much, and on this ground they told
him he might appear.   But he wrote to Ludwell that the
Assembly ought to have an agent of its own, since Blackiston, the agent appointed by the Council, was in the influence of Spotswood.   In Virginia the Assembly was in
opposition to the lieutenant-governor.   Spotswood declared
that it was composed mostly of relatives and dependents of
the disaffected councilors.   It met in April, 1718, and

[1] To Ludwell, Sept. 24, 1717.   In the possession of the
Virginia Historical Society.

elected Byrd its agent in England. Spotswood vetoed the bill, but the burgesses resolved that they would pay the salary of the agent,[1] and Byrd proceeded to discharge the duties of the office.[2]

Byrd was diligent enough in the meantime. "We have nothing to fear if we miscarry," he said to Ludwell, "for he cant be more our adversary than he is already."[3] Before the board he was very active, but he could make but little impression. That body was from the beginning on Spotswood's side. They took the opinion of the attorney-general, who declared that Spotswood had the right he claimed, but that it would be impolitic for him to use it except on extraordinary occasions. This decision they sent to Spotswood, saying that they hoped he would use the power thus assured to him very discreetly.[4] Byrd then appealed to the king. He did not now doubt, he said, the legality of the lieutenant-governor's action, but he submitted that it gave him a privilege dangerous to the liberties of his Majesty's subjects. The king called on the Board of Trade for an account of the whole case, which they sent, evidently tired of the affair, with the opinion that it was not the people of Virginia who were disturbed, but only "those persons who would engross the priviliges of being sole Judges in all criminal cases." Against this strong opinion Byrd could make no headway, and the appeal to the king came to naught.[5]

In the meantime Spotswood was pressing hotly on the councilors in Virginia. He had learned that in the address which eight of them had sent to England he had been charged with introducing into the government "new mea-

[1] Spotswood Letters, II. 278.

[2] Ibid., II. 304, 307. Byrd's instructions from the Assembly were dated May 30, 1718. (See Sainsbury Papers, vol. for 1715–1720, p. 710.)

[3] Letter of Sept. 24, 1717.

[4] Sainsbury Papers, vol. for 1715–20, pp. 656, 662, 669, 671, 675, 677, 686.

[5] Ibid., p. 691. Byrd's defense of the Council in regard to courts of oyer and terminer is preserved among the MSS. in possession of the Virginia Historical Society.

sures " of dangerous consequences. On March 12, 1718, when five of the eight subscribers were present, he brought this statement to their notice, and demanded that they should point out what "new measures" he had proposed. The confused councilors asked that the matter be postponed till the next meeting, when all of the eight subscribers would be present. Spotswood replied that he would have thought an hour long enough to remember one of these very dangerous "new measures," but that he would give them the time they desired.[1]   March 31 seven of the subscribers were present,[2] and they gave for their answer that it was not proper "to meddle with that Letter without directions from their Lordships," especially since negotiations for peace between the two factions were in progress. Spotswood replied that he knew proposals of peace had been proposed, but that they were not accepted, and he ordered it entered in the minutes that he had called on his opponents for specifications of their charges and had got none, and that he concluded they could give none.

But Spotswood was to have one more chance to humble the pride of his opponents.   On May 14, 1718, he appeared in Council with the opinion of the attorney-general in regard to the holding of courts of oyer and terminer. "Then," say the minutes, "the Governor asked those Gentn of the Council who have hitherto disputed the right of the Governor to nominate the Judges of the Courts of Oyer and Terminer whether they now acquiesced that the Governor has a Power of constituting the Judges of these courts with or exclusive of the Council, upon which the said Gentn said that they acquiesced in the Determination of the Lords Commissioners of Trade."   When he next appointed a court of oyer and terminer, however, he announced that he should name councilors only, but that each member must publicly

[1] Council Minutes.
[2] They were Robert Carter, James Blair, Philip Ludwell, John Smith, William Bassett, Nathaniel Harrison, and Edmund Berkeley. John Lewis was absent.

acknowledge that he held by virtue of Spotswood's appointment and not because he was a councilor ; and in this the Council acquiesced.[1] Thus passed the oyer and terminer controversy.

If this were Spotswood's story, it would be profitable to look at all the charges against him ; but enough has been told to show how the general affair affected Byrd, who was Spotswood's most active opponent. Let us now turn to Byrd.

The statement made in the Council on March 31, that peace negotiations were on foot, was true. They had been started by Nathaniel Harrison at the suggestion of Spotswood. Harrison was already veering around from Ludwell and Byrd. A letter of his to Ludwell shows that Byrd's influence was waning. "I consider," said he, "the consequences if Colo Byrd should ever obtain his end and Come here Governor and we should be so unfortunate as to Differ with him. Now that Colo Byrd will come here in that Station I have much reason to think and therefore we should act so as not to give him any advantage against us by which he might keep us in awe."[2] It is doubtful whether or not Byrd was really popular in Virginia. He was so much of the fine gentleman, with highly cultivated tastes, that it would have been natural enough for him to have stood aloof from the real life around him.

As soon as Spotswood was sure of his victory in the oyer and terminer matter he moved straight on his enemy. On July 1, 1718, he proposed to Orkney, his superior, to have Byrd, Ludwell, and Blair removed from their seats in the Council.[3] August 19 Orkney was before the Board of Trade, and said that inasmuch as amicable arrangements of the difficulty had failed, he should now request the board to hold an investigation, and to dismiss the party who should be found guilty.[4] The board postponed the matter ;

[1] Council Minutes, Dec. 9, 1718.
[2] Letter, May 15, 1719. It is in the possession of the Virginia Historical Society.
[3] Sainsbury Papers, vol. for 1715–20, p. 712.
[4] Ibid., p. 725.

but in the meantime Spotswood wrote them to urge the removal of Byrd from the Council on account of his long absence.[1] This move gave Byrd serious concern. He asked the
Board of Trade to do nothing in regard to it till the three
gentlemen affected were heard from. But in February,
1719, Spotswood again urged the removal of "that implacable gentleman Byrd," who called always on his friends for
complaints, whether true or false, in hopes of worrying the
Council at last into the removal of Spotswood. The board
did not need this urging. On February 24 they recommended the king to appoint Mr. Cole Digges a councilor in
the place of Byrd, who had been absent from the colony for
three and a half years.[2] Then Byrd humbled himself, as is
shown in the following abstract in the Sainsbury Papers : [3]
"William Byrd to the Lords of Trade—To convince their
Lordships that he is sincerely inclined to peace, he promises
to employ all the credit he has with the Council to dispose
them to a sincere pacification upon the terms of the Lieut.
Governors own plan but to do this good work effectually
begs their Lordships to prepare the way by writing letters
both to the Lieut. Governor & to the Council on the several points which he especially refers to " ; and if this were
done he thought harmony would be restored. Orkney
seconded this request,[4] and the board yielded so much
that on April 8 they recommended Digges to be of the
Council in the room of Edmund Berkeley, deceased ; and
as if to keep Byrd still in awe, they recommended that
Peter Beverley be appointed in Byrd's place.[5] On June
25 the question of removing Byrd came up in the privy
council. He sent them his reasons for his long absence,
and asked that he might stay in England a year longer.
The petition was sent back to the board, with orders for a
full report,[6] perhaps to kill time while Byrd proved the

[1] Spotswood Letters, II. 304.
[2] Sainsbury Papers, vol. for
1715–20. See entry under Feb.
24, 1719.
[3] Ibid., March 24, 1719.
[4] Ibid., p. 760.
[5] Ibid., p. 766.
[6] Ibid., p. 788.

sincerity of his professions of a desire for peace. Byrd at last got orders from the king continuing him in the Council, and arrived with them in Virginia about February 1, 1720. But since he had not been suspended they were unnecessary, and he resumed his seat in Council with his former rank. On April 29 he fulfilled his promise as to the reconciliation of the factions. The minutes for the day record: "Whereas divers Disputes and Controversys have heretofore arisen between his Majesty's Lt Governor, and some of the Council, occasioned by a difference in opinion in matters relating to the Administration of the Government, Both Parties heartily inclining to put a Period, as well to all past Contentions as to prevent any future discords wch may happen of the like nature, have this day mutually agreed that all past controversys of what kind soever between the Governor and any of the Council, be forever buried in Oblivion, and that there may be hereafter no other contention than who shall most promote the King's Service and the public benefit of the Colony." It was agreed that all future disputes should be referred to England for adjustment. As to the dispute which had arisen in regard to collation to ecclesiastical benefices, it was agreed that it should be referred to the General Court, with right of appeal to England if the decision there was not satisfactory.[1]

This difficulty left no hard feelings between Byrd and Spotswood. The latter had not hesitated to say of the former's defense that it was full of lies, but when in 1732 Byrd made a visit to Germanna in his "Progress to the Mines" they met one another with the warmth of old friends.

During the five strenuous years of his stay in England sad changes had come into Byrd's domestic life. He had formerly lived happily with his family at Westover, quite forgetting London gaieties. His irrepressible good nature fitted itself into the quiet country life, as is shown in

[1] Council Minutes.

the following letter to Custis, his brother-in-law, written October 9, 1709:

I have lately been favored with an unusual pleasure from Antigua, from which I find we have not altogether been forgotten. Our Father Parke says his time was very short and he could not write to you *then*, but is much in charity with us all. I give you joy on the blessing you have had of a daughter, and hope she will be an ornament to the sex, and a happiness to her parents. Our son sends you his dutiful respects, and I may venture to say, as much for Miss Evelyn, who has grown a great romp, and enjoys very robust health. How is Madam Dunn? for there goes a prophecy about, that in the eastern parts of Virginia a parson's wife will, in the year of our Lord, 1710, have four children at a birth, one of which will be an admiral, and another Archbishop of Canterbury. What the other two will prove, the sybil cannot positively say, but doubtless they will be something extraordinary.[1]

The change from these rural delights to London was sudden, and he wrote that he found the town, which formerly had so many charms, tasteless enough now. In fact, his heart was with his family at Westover. To his wife he was warmly attached. Two of his children, both boys, had died before he left his home. One other, the famous Evelyn, he had left there with her mother; and now came the news of another one, the little Wilhelmina, who was born November 6, 1715. But when he realized that his stay would be long, he sent for his wife, who arrived in the summer or fall of 1716. The trip was ill fated for her. In December she died of smallpox. Byrd sent an account of her death to Custis in the following letter, dated December 13, 1716 [2]:

When I wrote last I little expected that I should be forced to tell you the very melancholy news of my dear Lucy's death, by the very same, cruel distemper that destroyed her sister. She was taken with an insupportable pain in her head. The doctor soon discovered the ailment to be the small-pox, and we thought it best

[1] Parke, Recollections of Washington, p. 27 (Lossing's Edition).
[2] Custis, Recollections of Washington, p. 32 (Lossing's Edition).

to tell her the danger. She received the news without the least fright, and was persuaded she would live until the day she died, which happened in 12 hours from the time She was taken. Gracious God what pains did she take to make a voyage hither to seek a grave. No stranger ever met with more respect in a strange country than she had done here, from many persons of distinction, who all pronounced her an honour to Virginia. Alas! how proud was I of her, and how severely am I punished for it. But I can dwell no longer on so afflicting a subject, much less can I think of any thing else, therefore, I can only recommend myself to your pity, and am, as much as anyone can be, dear brother, your most affectionate and humble servant,   W. BYRD.

In September, 1717, Evelyn arrived in London. Perhaps Wilhelmina was there already. Much of Byrd's energy was spent in the education of these girls. Evelyn grew up into a famous wit and beauty. The story is that she was very popular in London society, and that she loved the Earl of Peterborough, but that Byrd objected to the match, and prevented it. She returned to Virginia, and died unmarried November 13, 1737. Her portrait, showing a beautiful face, has been preserved, and an interest more than normal has centered around her fate. Wilhelmina married Thomas Chamberlayne of King William County, Virginia, and from the union has come a large and worthy Virginia family.

Byrd's prolonged stay in London had served to form a new circle of friends there. The Assembly of the fall of 1720 passed an address to the king, the nature of which is not known, and appointed Byrd to deliver it.[1] Thus for the third time he was made agent in England.[2] His resi-

[1] Sainsbury Papers, vol. for 1720–30. The volume is not paged, and the entry referred to is put out of its regular order after that of Aug. 17, 1724. See also the entry for March 6, 1721, by which it appears that Spotswood objected to the appointment of an agent by the Assembly.

[2] In 1722, when Blackiston was just dead, Spotswood suggested to the Council that either Byrd or John Carter would be a good successor; but the Council chose Carter. Carter, however, served but a short time, and the office was then given to Peter Le Heup, although Byrd's name was again sug-

dence there lasted till 1726.   Within that period, probably
in 1724, he married Maria, daughter of Thomas Taylor of
Kensington.[1]   To this union a daughter, Anne, was born
on February 5, 1725.   The prospect of a family seems to
have turned his thoughts back to Virginia.   He arrived in
the colony early in 1726, and resumed his seat in the Council on April 28.   At Westover he spent the rest of his life,
devoting himself to the dignified and courteous pursuits of
a cultivated English country gentleman.   This later period
was the best of his life.   In it he wrote his " History of the
Dividing Line," "The Journey to the Land of Eden," and
"The Progress to the Mines," which undoubtedly gave him
place as the sprightliest and most genial native American
writer before Franklin.

In 1727 the long dispute over the North-Carolina-
Virginia boundary was ready to be settled, and in September of that year Byrd and Nathaniel Harrison were
appointed commissioners for that purpose on the part of
Virginia.   In December of the same year Harrison died,
and William Fitzwilliams and William Dandridge were
put into his place.   On February 13, 1728, the commissioners received their instructions.   By them they were
empowered to run the line independently, if the North
Carolina commissioners refused or failed to coöperate with
them ; and if the people of North Carolina should resist,
they were authorized to call out the militia of the southern
counties of Virginia in their defense.   How these commissioners executed their task is seen in Byrd's "History of
the Dividing Line."   This line was run in 1728 and not in
1729, as Byrd indicates in the dates in the margins of his
manuscript.

gested to the Council.   Byrd's
agencies had not been very successful.   He was perhaps too
little of a sycophant for the
office. (See Council Minutes,
vol. for 1721–34, p. 31, and entry for April 1, 1723 ; also Sainsbury Papers, 1720–30, entry for
June 23, 1722.)

[1] Maria Taylor's sister married Francis Otway, who became
a colonel in the English army.
Many of Byrd's letters are to
him.

The "History of the Dividing Line" was written from the rough journal Byrd made in the woods. This journal was sent to England.[1] It was but a skeleton of the later work. But Peter Collison, in England, heard of it, and asked to see a copy of the history of the expedition. Byrd wrote him in 1736 that he could not show him the history till it was finished, but that he would send him the journal, but cautioned him not to let it go out of his hands unless Sir Charles Wager wanted to see it. Somehow Mark Catesby saw it and complimented Byrd upon it. To him Byrd wrote in 1737 : "I am obliged to you for the compliment you are pleased to make to my poor Performances. 'Tis a sign you never saw them, that you judge so favourably. . . . It will seem like a joke when I tell you that I have not time to finish that work. But tis very [certain] I have not, for I am always engaged on some project for improvement of our Infant Colony. The present scheme is to found a city at the falls of James River, and plant a colony of Switzers on my Land upon Roanoke." To Collison he wrote, July 5, 1737, that he expected to finish the history during the coming winter, and that as he expected to describe some of the wild animals of Virginia, he should take it kindly if Collison would make arrangements for some cuts. The latter statement shows that he intended to have the book printed. When it was written does not appear.[2]

Byrd's literary style is characterized by the word "sprightly." It runs on smoothly and clearly, and now and then there is some droll phrase or witty comparison

[1] The journal and the surveyors' notes are published in full in the North Carolina Colonial Records, Vol. II. 750, 799.

[2] The original copy of the Byrd MSS. is preserved at Brandon. It is a handsome old volume bound in white vellum, and contains an inscription which shows that it was given by Mrs. Mary Willing Byrd to her daughter, Evelyn Taylor Harrison. The inscription states also that it was intended to pass to the latter's son, George Evelyn Harrison, who died in 1839, leaving two children, George E. and Isabella Harrison of Brandon.

which sets our minds to tingling. It is impossible to read him without interest. It would be hard to find before Franklin a better master of the art of writing clear, forceful, and charming English. His pages abound in the free and easy speeches which were allowed in the English literature of the day, but no man ever used them with more telling force, or with more of that refinement of touch which makes them wit instead of gross awkwardness.

Byrd's last appointment to a prominent official duty was to be first of the commission to survey the bounds of the Northern Neck. This task was performed in 1736, but yielded no entertaining history, as that of 1728. Of his assignment to this arduous duty, Byrd said in December, 1735, in a letter to Spotswood : "I suspect the Council has done me this honour with the wicked design of wearing the Oldest out first, & making a vacancy near the chair. Yet they may happen to be bit, because so much exercise and change of Air may probably renew my Age, and enable me to hold out with the most Vigorous of them except your old friend the Commissary." On this expedition Byrd and his associates visited Germanna, where, as he said, "Colo Spotswood received us very courteously. And lest we should have forgot the memorable Battles of the Duke of Marlborough, he fought them all over again to us the nine and fortieth time."

Of Byrd's later life at Westover we have a suggestion in the following extract from a letter to a London friend : "We that are Banished from those Polite Pleasures, are forct to take up with rural Entertainments. A Library, a Garden, a Grove, and a Purling Stream are the Innocent Scenes that divert our Leizure." [1] In this spirit he gave his never-tiring energies to the life around him. He experimented with new varieties of fruits ; he gave himself to the study of the curative qualities of the wild herbs of the country ; he sent advice to his sick friends about their dis-

[1] To Mrs. Armiger, 1729.

orders, and acquired much skill as a neighborhood quack. More than all, he collected and used his great library. It is to this time that we are to refer most of his extant letters. They are to people of consequence in England, among them being letters to Sir Charles Wager, Sir Hans Sloane, Mark Catesby the botanist, Sir Jacob Acworth, Lord Isley, Peter Collison, General Oglethorpe, Lord Egmont, and Lord Carteret. With all of them he seems·to have been on terms of cordial friendship. These letters show that his London associates were thoughtful men of culture who belonged to the lower gentry or to the upper ranks of the untitled.

Much of Byrd's interest during this period centered in his estate of Westover. Here he lived in the fine old brick house which, although twice burned since that day, is at present in much the same style as that in which it was first erected.[1] This he adorned with the pictures of many of his London friends. Among them were pictures of Lord Orrery, Sir Wilfried Lawson, Lord Oxford, the Marquis of Halifax, the Duke of Argyle, Sir Robert Southwell, Lady Elizabeth Southwell, Lord Egmont, Sir Charles Wager, William Blathwayt, General Daniel Parke, Lady Betty Cromwell, and Mrs. Taylor, who was the "Cousin Taylor" of his letters.[2] Some of these portraits still exist.[3] There were also portraits of his children and of his two wives, and three of himself, but only one of the last survives. Byrd also

---

[1] It is usually said that Byrd built this house in 1737, on what grounds the editor has not discovered. In 1735 Byrd had a plat made of the grounds showing all the largest buildings. He had then finished his grounds. He would hardly have done this before he built. In 1737 he was too much embarrassed financially to build. It would seem more reasonable to say that he built shortly after his return from England. Moreover, in 1736 he was anxious to sell Westover on account of his debts. (See Letters to Pickford, Dec. 6, 1735, and to Capt. Parke, Feb., 1736.)

[2] Byrd refers to this portrait in a letter to her of Oct. 10, 1735.

[3] On the death of Mrs. Mary Willing Byrd in 1814 they were divided among the heirs. (See Mrs. Byrd's will, Va. Histl. Soc. Mag., Vol. VI. 346.)

adorned his home with handsome grounds, which were
long famous for their beauty. Anburey said of them in
1779 that they were laid out with great taste, and presented
a delightful view from the river.[1] The library which he
had here, when it was sold in 1778, numbered nearly four
thousand volumes. It was, no doubt, the largest private
library in the English-speaking colonies.[2] It was collected
chiefly by the second Byrd, and the character of the books
shows that his literary taste was the best.

Byrd had the ordinary Virginian's land hunger. The
Title-book, which he caused to be prepared, gives a list of
all his holdings. Besides the 26,231 acres he inherited
from his father, he acquired vast tracts on his own account.
The records show that he bought various small tracts before his departure for England in 1715: in 1707, in two
tracts, 1203 acres; in 1710, in two tracts, 618 acres; and in
1712, in four tracts, 3702 acres. But it was after the survey of the dividing line in 1728 that the fever for speculation seized him. The sight of vast tracts of fertile river-
bottoms in the west was too much for him. His first acquisition here was 20,000 acres, which he bought from the
North Carolina commissioners, to whom it was assigned in
payment for their services. It was located at the junction
of the Dan and Irvine rivers, near the ancient village of
the Saura Indians. It was so fertile that Byrd called it the
"Land of Eden." There was some criticism afterward
about the fairness of his method of acquisition, but it seems
to have been unfounded. It was to lay out this tract that
he took his Journey to the Land of Eden in 1733. But his
survey did not include the rich site of the abandoned

[1] Anburey's Travels through
Interior Parts of America, II. 329.

[2] Among the books in Byrd's
library were the two manuscript
volumes of the Southampton
Papers, copied for the earl of
that name when the Virginia
Company was dissolved. They
remained in possession of the
earl's family till after the death
of his son in 1667. At that time,
says Stith, "the late Col. Byrd's
Father, being then in England,
purchased them of his Executors, for sixty Guineas."
(Stith's Hist. of Va., p. vi.)

Saura Town, and in 1743 he took out from the North Carolina government a patent for 6000 acres, to include that delightful spot. But the long distance to those lands led him to desire some intermediate plantation for the convenience of going and coming. The site he hit upon was the rich bottoms and islands of the Roanoke at the point where it is formed by the Dan and the Staunton. Here in 1730 he patented 1550 acres on Bluestone Creek, in 1733 he bought 751 acres more, and in 1738 he patented in four tracts 2910 acres more, all at the forks of Roanoke. This speculation had got a decided hold on him, and in 1742 he surpassed all his other efforts by patenting 105,000 acres on both sides of the Dan at the point at which it is united with the Hico, and stretching from thence to the North Carolina line.[1] He then bought a small plantation of 429 acres on Meherrin River as a half-way house to the Roanoke lands. To these lands are to be added those he acquired from the Parke estate, which embraced 9710 acres, and 1336 acres which he had by will of Thomas Grendon. Thus Byrd owned when he died no less than 179,440 acres of the best land in Virginia. With the exception of his large grant on the Dan and Hico, these acquisitions were not extraordinary for the times, as one may see who will read the Council Minutes.

Of course Byrd did not expect to cultivate all these lands. He expected, perhaps, to sell much of each of the large tracts, and to hold the rest for cultivation at some future time. This is indicated by his buying land at the forks of Roanoke and on Meherrin for intermediate stages. But his expectations to sell were not realized. Among his

---

[1] This large grant was to be free if he should seat one hundred Protestant families on it by 1737. This he failed to do, and he had to pay for the land at the ordinary rates, which made it cost him £525. The deed is dated in 1742. He got the land assigned much sooner, as we see from his letters. Probably the patent was not issued formally till 1742, or reissued at that time. Byrd in 1740 wrote that he had already paid for this land. (See letter to Leaderger, Nov. 12, 1740.)

letters are several which relate to the scheme. One of them shows that he had expected a colony of Swiss, which were taken instead to South Carolina, where they suffered severely from the climate. He had at first held out for a sale in a large tract to a colony; but as that failed, he consented to sell to individuals, and for that purpose placed an agent on the land,[1] and gave him the most minute directions about his conduct there. Byrd died possessed of most of these lands; but they were valuable property, for the tide of southward immigration was just about to come to that region. It is likely that the third Byrd realized a good profit on his father's investment.

During most of the period covered by the existing correspondence Byrd was much embarrassed by the Perry debt, which had been incurred in 1711 on account of the Parke estate. He had paid the most importunate of the debtors in 1715, and funded the rest of the debts at five per cent. interest.[2] This was so easy that he did not concern himself to create a sinking fund. Early in the extant letters we find that he was hard pressed by " Alderman Perry " for the payment of the principal. The matter was galling to his independent spirit. July 2, 1736, he wrote : "My affairs are now a little mended with Alderman Perry. I am selling off Land and Negroes to stay the stomack of that hungry magistrate. I had much rather incommode my self a little than continue in the Gripe of that Usurer. I have already lessened my Debt near a Thousand Pounds, and I hope to wipe off the whole Score in a short time." He continued to pay as much as he could each year,—it was usually £500,—till in 1740 the amount due was £1000, and he was trying to borrow that to discharge the debt. This affair was all the more harassing because Perry expected to have Byrd's tobacco. The latter finally stopped sending

[1] To Wood, March 10, 1741.

[2] Custis, Recollections of Washington, p. 28 (Lossing's Edition). The interest was possibly six per cent. at first, but afterward reduced to five per cent. In 1736 the common rate was three per cent.

it to him because Perry gave him twenty-five per cent. less than others gave. This made the merchant more importunate than ever.[1] It is likely that the debt was finally discharged by 1744. So great had been Byrd's distress that in 1736 he was seeking to sell Westover in order "to emancipate myself from that slavery to which all debtors are subject."[2]

Byrd's long residence abroad and his reading of the best works developed breadth of view in regard to some important social and political affairs. Thus his position on slavery was ahead of his time. To Oglethorpe he wrote, July 12, 1736, to congratulate him on the exclusion of rum and negroes from Georgia; but he did not think that it would be possible to keep rum out, for the "Saints of New England" would find a way to import it. Their rum was called "Kill Devil" in Virginia. Nobody else could "slip through a penal statute" like the New-Englanders. "They import so many Negroes hither that I fear the Colony will some time or other be Confirmed by the name of New Guinea." Slavery, he said, made the white people proud and disdainful of work, and their resulting poverty gave them a tendency to pilfering. The presence of many negroes forced the whites to be severe with them. Virginia did not practise the cruelty on the negroes that the islands practised, but it was necessary to hold a "tort rein" on them, and that was repugnant to a good-natured man. He also feared that a servile war would come, and he urged that the British government should put a stop to the slave-trade.[3] In another letter he says: "Our negroes are not so numerous or so enterprising as to give us any apprehension, or uneasiness, nor indeed is their Labour any other than Gardening, & less by

[1] There must have been accumulated interest on this debt, for in 1736 Byrd said that if he had £2000 from his wife's estate he could stop Perry's cry for a while, and pay off the balance without inconvenience. Evidently to Otway.

[2] To Capt. Parke, Feb., 1736.

[3] This letter is reprinted in the American Historical Review, Vol. I.

far, than what the poor People undergo in other countrys. Nor are any crueltys exercised upon them, unless by great accident they happen to fall into the hands of a Brute, who always passes here for a Monster." When he wrote this letter he was trying to persuade his correspondent to move to Virginia, and under such circumstances nobody could better sing the praises of the colony.

In his old age Byrd had some hope of getting office. In 1736 [1] he wrote to ask a friend to use his influence with Sir Robert Walpole to get him an office. He wanted to be governor, and hinted that the office would be suitable to him, if Gooch were given something better. In 1737 he asked Sir Charles Wager to use his influence to get him the office of surveyor of the customs for the southern district of America. It was, he said, worth £500 a year, and that would "disentangle me from all my Difficultys and make me perfectly easy." But in each case his ambition was disappointed. The only honor that came to him was the presidency of the Council, to which he succeeded after the death of Commissary Blair in 1743. This was a place of much dignity but of little power. To Byrd it probably was a little disappointing that he should have been preceded in the Council by Blair, whose constitution held out till he was eighty-seven years old. Blair's mind remained acute till the last, but his hearing failed as early as 1741, and that made it necessary for Byrd to preside over the General Court.[2]

About Byrd's own death, which occurred August 26, 1744, little is known. He was buried in the garden at Westover which he had loved so much, and there is found to this day his monument with the epitaph which has been quoted. His will was proved by his wife, Maria Byrd, one of the executors, in March, 1744–45.[3]

---

[1] July 2. The name of the correspondent is not given.

[2] To Otway, Feb. 10, 1741.

[3] It has been supposed that this will would have been recorded in England, but a search made for the Editor at Somerset House, London, where the register of wills is kept, fails to find such a document,

The name of the second William Byrd has always been held in great esteem in Virginia. His portrait shows a highly refined if a somewhat haughty face. Under his management Westover was known throughout the colony for its elegance, its hospitality, and its good company. He has become the idol of his large family connections, and from his esthetic sense he has received from them the name of the "Black Swan" of the family. His own writings reveal to us a man possessed of great kindliness of heart and indefatigable energy. He seems to have been in his life as well as in his writings a man of sprightly mind and engaging personality. It is certain there were few men in all the colonies who were socially more delightful. His personality must be more and more known and enjoyed as Americans become more and more cultivated.

About William Byrd III, who succeeded to most of his father's estate, there is but little to be said. He was still a child when his father died, and his life shows the lack of the training he would have had from such a wise father. He married, April 14, 1748, Elizabeth Carter, the heiress of "Shirley." At the time he was perhaps nineteen, and she was only sixteen and a half. The marriage seems to have been an unhappy one. In 1760, within six months after the death of this wife, he married Mary Willing of Philadelphia, with whom he lived happily. He died by his own hand, January 1, 1777. He held prominent office in the colony. For some years he was a member of the Council, and was one of the judges in the famous "Parsons' case" of 1763, in which he voted on the side of the parsons. He was given command of the Second Virginia Regiment, raised after Braddock's defeat in 1755 to protect the frontiers against the French and Indians. Washington had command of the First, and it is no bad compliment to Byrd that he acquitted himself creditably, since his conduct was open to comparison with that of his distinguished colleague. He was afterward commissioner to the Cherokee Indians. His sympathy, however, in the Revolution was with England, and his oldest living son was a captain in the English army.[1]   Anburey says of him: "His great abilities and personal accomplishments were universally esteemed, but being infatuated with play, his affairs, at his death, were in a deranged state. The widow whom he left with eight children, has, by prudent management, preserved out of the wreck of his princely fortune, a beautiful home, at a place called Westover, upon James River, some personal property, a few plantations, and a number of slaves."[2] This quotation tells all we need to know about the squandering of the splendid property which the son of the goldsmith had built up, and which the elegant "Black Swan" had been able to preserve. With its departure went the influence of the family. The estate of Westover, the last of tne property, was sold after the death of Mrs. Mary Willing Byrd in 1814 for division among her children.[3] It has had the good fortune to be in the hands of people who have appreciated its historic importance, and to-day the massive colonial house, with its handsomely carved doorway and the fine old gateway, breathe a warm odor of the courtly life which once made it known on many another river than the James.

[1] But another son served with the Americans through the war.

[2] Travels in Interior America, II. 329.

[3] Westover was then purchased by William Carter, who lived there for four or five years; but becoming financially involved through indorsing for a friend, he sold it to a Mr. Douthat, who had gained $100,000 in a lottery. After his death it was sold to J. E. Harrison of Brandon. He found it so far from Brandon that it was inconvenient to keep it, and he sold it to John Selden, who at length sold it to Major Drewry. In 1901 it was bought from the Drewry estate by Mrs. William McC. Ramsay, who proposes to restore it in colonial style and make it her home. It was twice burnt, but each time was rebuilt in the old style by the Byrds. The last fire was on the occasion of the christening of that William Byrd who died at Caen in 1771. (See Genealogy, Appendix B.) The facts in this note are from notes made by Miss Elizabeth Byrd Nicholas of Washington City, and preserved by the Virginia Historical Society.

HISTORY OF
THE DIVIDING LINE

HISTORY OF
THE DIVIDING LINE:

Run in the Year 1728.

EFORE I enter upon the Journal of the Line between Virginia and North Carolina, it will be necessary to clear the way to it, by shewing how the other British Colonies on the Main have, one after the other, been carved out of Virginia, by Grants from his Majesty's Royal Predecessors. All that part of the Northern American Continent now under the Dominion of the King of Great Britain, and Stretching quite as far as the Cape of Florida, went *at first under the General Name of Virginia.*

The only Distinction, in those early Days, was, that all the Coast to the Southward of Chesapeake Bay was called South Virginia, and all to the Northward of it, North Virginia.

The first Settlement of this fine Country was

3

owing to that great Ornament of the British Nation, Sir Walter Raleigh, who obtained a Grant thereof from Queen Elizabeth of ever-glorious Memory, by Letters Patent, dated March the 25th, 1584.

But whether that Gentleman ever made a Voyage thither himself is uncertain; because those who have favour'd the Public with an Account of His Life mention nothing of it. However, thus much may be depended on, that Sir Walter invited sundry persons of Distinction to Share in his Charter, and join their Purses with his in the laudable project of fitting out a Colony to Virginia.

Accordingly, 2 Ships were Sent away that very Year, under the Command of his good Friends Amidas and Barlow, to take possession of the Country in the Name of his Roial Mistress, the Queen of England.

These worthy Commanders, for the advantage of the Trade Winds, shaped their Course first to the Charibbe Islands, thence stretching away by the Gulph of Florida, dropt Anchor not far from Roanoak Inlet. They ventured ashoar near that place upon an Island now called Colleton island, where they set up the Arms of England, and Claimed the Adjacent Country in Right of their Sovereign Lady, the Queen; and this Ceremony being duly performed, they kindly invited the neighbouring Indians to traffick with them.

These poor people at first approacht the English with great Caution, having heard much of the Treachery of the Spaniards, and not knowing but

these Strangers might be as treacherous as they.
But, at length, discovering a kind of good nature
in their looks, they ventured to draw near, and
barter their Skins and Furs, for the Bawbles and
Trinkets of the English.

These first Adventurers made a very profitable
Voyage, raising at least a Thousand per cent.
upon their Cargo. Amongst other Indian Commodities, they brought over Some of that bewitch-
ing Vegetable, Tobacco. And this being the first
that ever came to England, Sir Walter thought he
could do no less than make a present of Some of
the brightest of it to His Roial Mistress, for her
own Smoaking.

The Queen graciously accepted of it, but finding her Stomach sicken after two or three Whiffs,
it was presently whispered by the earl of Leices-
ter's Faction, that Sir Walter had certainly Poison'd Her. But Her Majesty soon recovering her
Disorder, obliged the Countess of Nottingham
and all her Maids to Smoak a whole Pipe out
amongst them.

As it happen'd some Ages before to be the fashion to Santer to the Holy Land, and go upon other
Quixot Adventures, so it was now grown the
Humour to take a Trip to America. The Spaniards had lately discovered Rich Mines in their
Part of the West Indies, which made their Maritime
Neighbours eager to do so too. This Modish Frenzy
being still more Inflam'd by the Charming Account
given of Virginia, by the first Adventurers, made
many fond of removeing to such a Paradise.

Happy was he, and still happier She, that cou'd get themselves transported, fondly expecting their Coarsest Utensils, in that happy place, would be of Massy Silver.

This made it easy for the Company to procure as many Volunteers as they wanted for their new Colony; but, like most other Undertakers who have no Assistance from the Public, they Starved the Design by too much Frugality; for, unwilling to Launch out at first into too much Expense, they Ship't off but few People at a Time, and Those but Scantily provided. The Adventurers were, besides, Idle and extravagant, and expected they might live without work in so plentiful a Country.

These Wretches were set Ashoar not far from Roanoak Inlet, but by some fatal disagreement, or Laziness, were either Starved or cut to Pieces by the Indians.

Several repeated Misadventures of this kind did, for some time, allay the Itch of Sailing to this New World; but the Distemper broke out again about the Year 1606. Then it happened that the Earl of Southampton and several other Persons, eminent for their Quality and Estates, were invited into the Company, who apply'd themselves once more to People the then almost abandon'd Colony. For this purpose they embarkt about an Hundred men, most of them Riprobates of good Familys, and related to some of the company, who were men of Quality and Fortune.

The Ships that carried them made a Shift to

find a more direct way to Virginia, and ventured
thro the Capes into the Bay of Chesapeak. The
same Night they came to an Anchor at the
Mouth of Powatan, the same as James River,
where they built a Small Fort at a Place call'd
Point Comfort.

This Settlement stood its ground from that time
forward in spite of all the Blunders and Disagreement of the first Adventurers, and the many
Calamitys that befel the Colony afterwards.

The six gentlemen who were first named of the
company by the crown, and who were empowered
to choose an annual President from among themselves, were always engaged in Factions and
Quarrels, while the rest detested Work more than
Famine. At this rate the Colony must have come
to nothing, had it not been for the vigilance and
Bravery of Capt. Smith, who struck a Terrour into
all the Indians round about. This Gentleman took
some pains to perswade the men to plant Indian
corn, but they lookt upon all Labor as a Curse.
They chose rather to depend upon the Musty Provisions that were sent from England: and when
they fail'd they were forct to take more pains to
Seek for Wild Fruits in the Woods, than they
would have taken in tilling the Ground. Besides,
this Exposd them to be knockt on the head by the
Indians, and gave them Fluxes into the Bargain,
which thind the Plantation very much. To Supply
this mortality, they were reinforct the year following with a greater number of People, amongst
which were fewer Gentlemen and more Labour-

ers, who, however, took care not to kill themselves
with Work.[1]

These found the First Adventurers in a very
starving condition, but relievd their wants with
the fresh Supply they brought with them.   From
Kiquotan they extended themselves as far as
James-Town, where like true Englishmen, they
built a Church that cost no more than Fifty
Pounds, and a Tavern that cost Five hundred.[2]

They had now made peace with the Indians, but
there was one thing wanting to make that peace
lasting.   The Natives coud, by no means, perswade themselves that the English were heartily
their Friends, so long as they disdained to intermarry with them.   And, in earnest, had the English consulted their own Security and the good of
the Colony — Had they intended either to Civilize
or Convert these Gentiles, they would have brought
their Stomachs to embrace this prudent Alliance.

The Indians are generally tall and well-propor-

[1] This paragraph appears in the manuscript as a note. It seems best to follow Wynne in placing it in the text.— EDITOR.

[2] The first place of worship in Jamestown was an old sail stretched between some trees. Next a tent was used. Then a rude wooden church was built which Smith describes as "a homely thing like a barn, set upon crotchets, covered with rafts, sedge and earth, so was also the walls." This building was burnt in 1608, but rebuilt at once. Lord Delaware, who ar-rived in 1610, renovated and beautified it. It was sixty by twenty-four feet, with chancel and pews of cedar and a com-munion-table of black walnut. "The church," says a contem-porary, "was so cast as to be very light within and the Lord Governor caused it to be kept passing sweet, trimmed up with divers flowers." On the con-trary, there was no tavern in the colony in 1623, as may be seen from the complaint of Na-thaniel Butler against the Com-pany and from the reply of the latter thereto.

tion'd, which may make full Amends for the Dark-
ness of their Complexions. Add to this, that they
are healthy & Strong, with Constitutions untainted
by Lewdness, and not enfeebled by Luxury. Besides, Morals and all considered, I cant think the
Indians were much greater Heathens than the first
Adventurers, who, had they been good Christians,
would have had the Charity to take this only
method of converting the Natives to Christianity.
For, after all that can be said, a sprightly Lover is
the most prevailing Missionary that can be sent
amongst these, or any other Infidels.

Besides, the poor Indians would have had less
reason to Complain that the English took away
their Land, if they had received it by way of Portion with their Daughters. Had such Affinities
been contracted in the Beginning, how much
Bloodshed had been prevented, and how populous
would the Country have been, and, consequently,
how considerable? Nor wou'd the Shade of the
Skin have been any reproach at this day; for if a
Moor may be washt white in 3 Generations, Surely
an Indian might have been blancht in two.

The French, for their Parts, have not been so
Squeamish in Canada, who upon Trial find abundance of Attraction in the Indians. Their late Grand
Monarch thought it not below even the Dignity of
a Frenchman to become one flesh with this People,
and therefore Ordered 100 Livres for any of his
Subjects, Man or Woman, that woud intermarry
with a Native.

By this piece of Policy we find the French Interest very much Strengthen'd amongst the Savages, and their Religion, such as it is, propagated just as far as their Love. And I heartily wish this well-concerted Scheme don't hereafter give the French an Advantage over his Majesty's good Subjects on the Northern Continent of America.

About the same time New England was pared off from Virginia by Letters Patent, bearing date April the 10th, 1608.[1] Several Gentlemen of the Town and Neighbourhood of Plymouth obtain'd this Grant, with the Ld Chief Justice Popham at their Head.

Their Bounds were Specified to Extend from 38 to 45 Degrees of Northern Latitude, with a Breadth of one Hundred Miles from the Sea Shore. The first 14 Years, this Company encounter'd many Difficulties, and lost many men, tho' far from being discouraged, they sent over Numerous Recruits of Presbyterians, every year, who for all that, had much ado to stand their Ground, with all their Fighting and Praying.

But about the year 1620, a Large Swarm of Dissenters fled thither from the Severities of their Stepmother, the Church. These Saints conceiving the same Aversion to the Copper Complexion of the Natives, with that of the first Adventurers to Virginia, would, on no Terms, contract Alliances with them, afraid perhaps, like the Jews of Old, lest they might be drawn into Idolatry by those Strange Women.

---

[1] The charters of the London and the Plymouth companies were both dated April 10, 1606.

Whatever disgusted them I cant say, but this false delicacy creating in the Indians a Jealousy that the English were ill affected towards them, was the Cause that many of them were cut off, and the rest Exposed to various Distresses.

This Reinforcement was landed not far from Cape Codd, where, for their greater Security they built a Fort, and near it a Small Town, which in Honour of the Proprietors, was call'd New Plymouth. But they Still had many discouragements to Struggle with, tho' by being well Supported from Home, they by Degrees Triumph't over them all.

Their Bretheren, after this, flockt over so fast, that in a few Years they extended the Settlement one hundred Miles along the Coast, including Rhode Island and Martha's Vineyard.

Thus the Colony throve apace, and was throng'd with large Detachments of Independents and Presbyterians, who thought themselves persecuted at home.

Tho' these People may be ridicul'd for some Pharisaical Particularitys in their Worship and Behaviour, yet they were very useful Subjects, as being Frugal and Industrious, giving no Scandal or bad Example, at least by any Open and Public Vices. By which excellent Qualities they had much the Advantage of the Southern Colony, who thought their being Members of the Establish't Church sufficient to Sanctifie very loose and Profligate Morals. For this Reason New England improved much faster than Virginia, and in Seven or Eight Years New Plimouth, like Switzerland, seemd too Narrow a Territory for its Inhabitants.

For this Reason, several Gentlemen of Fortune purchas'd of the Company that Canton of New England now called Massachuset colony. And King James confirm'd the Purchase by his Royal Charter, dated March the 4th, 1628. In less than 2 years after, above 1000 of the Puritanical Sect removed thither with considerable Effects, and these were followed by such Crowds, that a Proclamation was issued in England, forbidding any more of his Majesty's Subjects to be Shipt off. But this had the usual Effect of things forbidden, and serv'd only to make the Wilful Independents flock over the faster. And about this time it was that Messrs. Hampden and Pym, and (some say) Oliver Cromwell, to show how little they valued the King's Authority, took a Trip to New England.

In the Year 1630, the famous City of Boston was built, in a Commodious Situation for Trade and Navigation, the same being on a Peninsula at the Bottom of Massachuset Bay.

This Town is now the most considerable of any on the British Continent, containing at least 8,000 houses and 40,000 Inhabitants. The Trade it drives, is very great to Europe, and to every Part of the West Indies, having near 1,000 Ships and lesser Vessels belonging to it.

Altho the Extent of the Massachuset Colony reach't near one Hundred and Ten Miles in Length, and half as much in Breadth, yet many of its Inhabitants, thinking they wanted Elbow-room, quitted their Old Seats in the Year 1636, and formed 2 New Colonies: that of Connecticut and New Haven. These King Charles the 2d erected into one Government in 1664,[1] and gave them many Valuable Priviledges, and among the rest, that of chusing their own Governors. The Extent of these united Colonies may be about Seventy Miles long and fifty broad.

Besides these several Settlements, there Sprang up still another, a little more Northerly, called New Hampshire. But that consisting of no more than two Counties, and not being in condition to Support the Charge of a Distinct Government, was glad to be incorporated with that of Massachuset, but upon Condition, however, of being Named in all Public Acts, for fear of being quite lost and forgot in the Coalition.

In like manner New Plymouth joyn'd itself to Massachuset, except only Rhode Island, which, tho' of small Extent, got itself erected into a Separate government by a Charter from King Charles the 2d, soon after the Restoration, and continues so to this day.

These Governments all continued in Possession of their Respective Rights and Priviledges till the Year 1683,[2] when that of Massachuset was made Void in England by a Quo Warranto.

In Consequence of which the King was pleased to name Sir Edmund Andros His first Governor of that Colony. This Gentleman, it seems, ruled

[1] 1662.
[2] It was not till October 23, 1684, that judgment in this suit was finally entered.

them with a Rod of Iron till the Revolution, when they laid unhallowed Hands upon Him, and sent him Prisoner to England.

This undutiful proceeding met with an easy forgiveness at that happy Juncture. King William and his Royal Consort were not only pleasd to overlook this Indignity offered to their Governor, but being made sensible how unfairly their Charter had been taken away, most graciously granted them a new one.

By this some new Franchises were given them, as an Equivalent for those of Coining Money and Electing a governour, which were taken away. However, the other Colonies of Connecticut and Rhode Island had the luck to remain in Possession of their Original Charters, which to this Day have never been calld in Question.

The next Country dismembered from Virginia was New Scotland, claimd by the Crown of England in Virtue of the first Discovery by Sebastian Cabot. By Colour of this Title, King James the first granted it to Sir William Alexander by Patent, dated September the 10th, 1621.

But this Patentee never sending any Colony thither, and the French believing it very Convenient for them, obtained a Surrender of it from their good Friend and Ally, king Charles the 2d, by the Treaty of Breda. And, to show their gratitude, they stirred up the Indians soon after to annoy their Neighbours of New England. Murders happend continually to his Majesty's Subjects by their Means, till Sr William Phipps took their Town of Port Royal, in the year 1690. But as the English are better at taking than keeping Strong Places, the French retook it soon, and remaind Masters of it till 1710, when General Nicholson wrested it, once more, out of their Hands.

Afterwards the Queen of Great Britain's Right to it was recognized and confirmed by the treaty of Utrecht.

Another Limb lopt off from Virginia was New York, which the Dutch seized very unfairly, on pretence of having Purchasd it from Captain Hudson, the first Discoverer. Nor was their way of taking Possession of it a whit more justifiable than their pretended Title.

Their West India Company tamperd with some worthy English Skippers (who had contracted with a Swarm of English Dissenters to transport them to Hudson river) by no means to land them there, but to carry 'em some leagues more northerly.

This Dutch Finesse took Exactly, and gave the Company time soon after to seize the Hudson River for themselves. But Sr Samuel Argall, then governor of Virginia, understanding how the King's Subjects had been abused by these Republicans, marcht thither with a good Force, and obligd them to renounce all pretensions to that Country. The worst of it was, the Knight depended on their Parole to Ship themselves to Brasile, but took no measures to make this Slippery People as good as their Word.

No sooner was the good Governor retired, but the honest Dutch began to build Forts and

strengthen themselves in their ill-gotten Possessions; nor did any of the King's Liege People take
the trouble to drive these Intruders thence. The
Civil War in England, And the Confusions it
brought forth, allowed no Leisure to such distant
Considerations. Tho tis strange that the Protec-
tor, who neglected no Occasion to mortify the
Dutch, did not afterwards call them to Account
for this breach of Faith. However, after the Restoration, the King sent a Squadron of his Ships of
War, under the Command of Sir Robert Carr,[1] and
reduced that Province to his Obedience.

Some time after, His Majesty was Pleasd to
grant that Country to his Royal Highness, the
Duke of York, by Letters Patent, dated March
the 12th, 1664. But to shew the Modesty of the
Dutch to the Life, tho they had no Shaddow of
Right to New York, yet they demanded Surinam,
a more valuable Country, as an Equivalent for it,
and our able Ministers at that time had the Generosity to give it them.

But what wounded Virginia deepest was the
cutting off MARYLAND from it, by Charter from
King Charles the 1st, to sir George Calvert, afterwards Ld Baltimore, bearing date the 20th of
June, 1632. The Truth of it is, it begat much
Speculation in those days, how it came about that
a good Protestant King should bestow so bountiful a Grant upon a Zealous Roman catholic. But
'tis probable it was one fatal Instance amongst

---

[1] Carr was only one of the commanders of this expedition,
and Nicoll may be well regarded as chief commander.

many other of his Majesty's complaisance to the Queen.

However that happened, 'tis certain this Province afterwards provd a Commodious Retreat for Persons of that Communion. The Memory of the Gun-Powder-Treason-Plot was Still fresh in every body's mind, and made England too hot for Papists to live in, without danger of being burnt with the Pope, every 5th of November; for which reason Legions of them transplanted themselves to Maryland in Order to be Safe, as well from the Insolence of the Populace as the Rigour of the Government.

Not only the Gun-Powder-Treason, but every other Plot, both pretended and real, that has been trump't up in England ever Since, has helpt to People his Lordship's Propriety.

But what has provd most Serviceable to it was the Grand Rebellion against King Charles the 1st, when every thing that bore the least tokens of Popery was sure to be demolisht, and every man that Profest it was in Jeopardy of Suffering the same kind of Martyrdom the Romish Priests do in Sweden.

Soon after the Reduction of New York, the Duke was pleasd to grant out of it all that Tract of Land included between Hudson and Delaware Rivers, to the Lord Berkley and Sir George Carteret, by deed dated June the 24th, 1664. And when these Grantees came to make Partition of this Territory, His Lordp's Moiety was calld West Jersey, and that to Sir George, East Jersey.

But before the Date of this Grant, the Swedes began to gain Footing in part of that Country; tho, after they saw the Fate of New York, they were glad to Submit to the King of England, on the easy Terms of remaining in their Possessions, and rendering a Moderate Quit-rent. Their Posterity continue there to this Day, and think their Lot cast in a much fairer Land than Dalicarlia.[1]

The Proprietors of New Jersey, finding more Trouble than Profit in their new Dominions, made over their Right to several other Persons, who obtaind a fresh Grant from his Royal Highness, dated March 14th, 1682.

Several of the Grantees, being Quakers and Anababtists, faild not to encourage many of their own Perswasion to remove to this Peaceful Region. Amongst them were a Swarm of Scots Quakers, who were not tolerated to exercise the Gifts of the Spirit in their own Country.

Besides the hopes of being Safe from Persecution in this Retreat, the New Proprietors inveigled many over by this tempting Account of the Country: that it was a Place free from those 3 great Scourges of Mankind, Priests, Lawyers, and Physicians. Nor did they tell a Word of a Lye, for the People were yet too poor to maintain these Learned Gentlemen, who, every where, love to be paid well for what they do; and, like the Jews, cant breathe in a Climate where nothing is to be got.

The Jerseys continued under the Government

[1] Name of a former province of Sweden.

of these Proprietors till the Year 1702, when they made a formal Surrender of the Dominion to the Queen, reserving however the Property of the Soil to themselves. So soon as the Bounds of New Jersey came to be distinctly laid off, it appeared that there was still a Narrow Slipe of Land, lying betwixt that Colony and Maryland. Of this, William Penn, a Man of much Worldly Wisdom, and some Eminence among the Quakers, got early Notice, and, by the Credit he had with the Duke of York, obtain a Patent for it, Dated March the 4th, 1680.[1]

It was a little Surprising to some People how a Quaker should be so much in the good Graces of a Popish Prince; tho, after all, it may be pretty well Accounted for. This Ingenious Person had not been bred a Quaker; but, in his Earlier days, had been a Man of Pleasure about the Town. He had a beautiful form and very taking Address, which made him Successful with the Ladies, and Particularly with a Mistress of the Duke of Monmouth. By this Gentlewoman he had a Daughter, who had Beauty enough to raise her to be a Dutchess, and continued to be a Toast full 30 Years.[2]

But this Amour had like to have brought our Fine Gentleman in Danger of a Duell, had he not discreetly shelterd himself under this peaceable Perswasion. Besides, his Father having been a

[1] 1680–81.

[2] This piece of London gossip seems not to have been recorded by any other contemporary.

Penn's character and his declarations were entirely at variance with this report. See Clarkson's Life of Penn (1827), p. 44.

Flag-Officer in the Navy, while the Duke of York was Lord High Admiral, might recommend the Son to his Favour. This piece of secret History I thought proper to mention, to wipe off the Suspicion of his having been Popishly inclind.

This Gentleman's first Grant confind Him within pretty Narrow Bounds, giving him only that Portion of Land which contains Buckingham, Philadelphia and Chester Counties. But to get these Bounds a little extended, He pusht His Interest still further with His Royal Highness, and obtaind a fresh Grant of the three Lower Counties, called New-Castle, Kent and Sussex, which still remaind within the New York Patent, and had been luckily left out of the Grant of New Jersey.

The Six Counties being thus incorporated, the Proprietor dignifyd the whole with the Name of Pensilvania.

The Quakers flockt over to this Country in Shoals, being averse to go to Heaven the same way with the Bishops. Amongst them were not a few of good Substance, who went Vigorously upon every kind of Improvement; and thus much I may truly say in their Praise, that by Diligence and Frugality, For which this Harmless Sect is remarkable, and by haveing no Vices but such as are Private, they have in a few Years made Pensilvania a very fine Country.

The Truth is, they have observed exact Justice with all the Natives that border upon them; they have purchasd all their Lands from the Indians;

and tho they paid but a Trifle for them, it has procured them the Credit of being more righteous
than their Neighbours. They have likewise had
the Prudence to treat them kindly upon all Occasions, which has savd them from many Wars and
Massacres wherein the other Colonies have been
indiscreetly involved. The Truth of it is, a People whose Principles forbid them to draw the
Carnal Sword, were in the Right to give no
Provocation.

Both the French and the Spaniards had, in the
Name of their Respective Monarchs, long ago taken
Possession of that Part of the Northern Continent
that now goes by the Name of Carolina; but finding it Produced neither Gold nor Silver, as they
greedily expected, and meeting such returns from
the Indians as their own Cruelty and Treachery
deserved, they totally abandond it. In this deserted Condition that country lay for the Space of
90 Years, till King Charles the 2d, finding it a
DERELICT, granted it away to the Earl of Clarendon and others, by His Royal Charter, dated
March the 24th, 1663. The Boundary of that
Grant towards Virginia was a due West Line from
Luck-Island, (the same as Colleton Island,) lying
in 36 degrees N. Latitude, quite to the South Sea.
But afterwards Sir William Berkeley, who was
one of the Grantees and at that time Governour of
Virginia, finding a Territory of 31 Miles in Breadth
between the Inhabited Part of Virginia and the
above-mentioned Boundary of Carolina, advisd
the Lord Clarendon of it. And His Lordp had

Interest enough with the King to obtain a Second
Patent to include it, dated June the 30th, 1665.

This last Grant describes the Bounds between
Virginia and Carolina in these Words: "To run
from the North End of Corotuck-Inlet, due West
to Weyanoke Creek, lying within or about the
Degree of Thirty-Six and Thirty Minutes of North-
ern Latitude, and from thence West, in a direct
Line, as far as the South-Sea." [1]   Without question,
this Boundary was well known at the time the
Charter was Granted, but in a long Course of
years Weynoke Creek lost its name, so that it be-
came a Controversy where it lay.   Some Ancient
Persons in Virginia affirmd it was the same with
Wicocon, and others again in Carolina were as
Positive it was Nottoway River.

In the mean time, the People on the Frontiers
Enterd for Land, & took out Patents by Guess,
either from the King or the Lords Proprietors.
But the Crown was like to be the loser by this Incertainty, because the Terms both of taking up
and seating Land were easier much in Carolina.
The Yearly Taxes to the Public were likewise
there less burdensome, which laid Virginia under
a Plain disadvantage.

This Consideration put that Government upon
entering into Measures with North Carolina, to
terminate the Dispute, and settle a Certain Boundary between the two colonies.   All the Difficulty
was, to find out which was truly Weyanoke Creek.
The Difference was too Considerable to be given

---

[1] This quotation is materially but not literally correct.

The Mansion at Westover.

up by either side, there being a Territory of 15
Miles betwixt the two Streams in controversy.

However, till that Matter could be adjusted, it
was agreed on both sides, that no Lands at all
Should be granted within the disputed Bounds.
Virginia observed this Agreement punctually, but
I am sorry I cant say the Same of North-Carolina.
The great Officers of that Province were loath to
lose the Fees accrueing from the Grants of Land,
and so private Interest got the better of Public
Spirit; and I wish that were the only Place in the
World where such politicks are fashionable.

All the Steps that were taken afterwards in that
Affair, will best appear by the Report of the Virginia-Commissioners, recited in the Order of Council given at St. James's, March the 1st, 1710, set
down in the Appendix.

It must be owned, the Report of those Gentlemen was Severe upon the then commissioners of
North-Carolina, and particularly upon Mr. Moseley. I wont take upon me to say with how much
Justice they said so many hard things, tho it had
been fairer Play to have given the Parties accusd
a Copy of such Representations, that they might
have answerd what they could for themselves.

But since that was not done, I must beg leave
to say thus much in behalf of Mr. Moseley, that
he was not much in the Wrong to find fault with
the Quadrant produced by the Surveyors of Virginia, because that Instrument plact the Mouth of
Notoway River in the Latitude of 37 Degrees;
whereas, by an Accurate Observation made Since,

it Appears to lie in 36° 30′ ½′, so that there was an Error of near 30 minutes, either in the Instrument or in those who made use of it.

Besides, it is evident the Mouth of Notoway River agrees much better with the Latitude, wherein the Carolina Charter supposed Wyanoak Creek, (namely, in or about 36 Degrees and 30 minutes,) than it does with Wicocon Creek, which is about 15 Miles more Southerly.

This being manifest, the Intention of the King's Grant will be pretty exactly answered, by a due West Line drawn from Corotuck Inlet to the Mouth of Notaway River, for which reason tis probable that was formerly calld Wyanoak-Creek, and might change its Name when the Nottoway Indians came to live upon it, which was since the Date of the last Carolina Charter.

The Lievt Governor of Virginia, at that time Colo Spotswood, searching into the Bottom of this Affair, made very Equitable Proposals to Mr. Eden, at that time Governour of North Carolina, in Order to put an End to this Controversy. These, being formed into Preliminaries, were Signd by both Governours, and transmitted to England, where they had the Honour to be ratifyed by his late Majesty and assented to by the Lords Proprietors of Carolina.

Accordingly an Order was sent by the late King to Mr. Gooch, afterwards Lievt Governor of Virginia, to pursue those Preliminaries exactly. In Obedience thereunto, he was pleased to appoint Three of the Council of that colony to be Commissioners on the Part of Virginia, who, in Conjunction with others to be named by the Governor of North Carolina, were to settle the Boundary between the 2 Governments, upon the Plan of the above-mentiond Articles.

Two Experienct Surveyors were at the same time directed to wait upon the Commissioners, Mr. Mayo, who made the Accurate Mapp of Barbadoes, and Mr. Irvin, the Mathematick Professor of William and Mary Colledge. And because a good Number of Men were to go upon this Expedition, a Chaplain was appointed to attend them, and the rather because the People on the Frontiers of North-Carolina, who have no Minister near them, might have an Opportunity to get themselves and their Children baptizd.

Of these proceedings on our Part, immediate Notice was sent to Sir Richard Everard, Governor of North Carolina, who was desired to Name Commissioners for that Province, to meet those of Virginia at Corotuck-Inlet the Spring following. Accordingly he appointed Four Members of the Council of that Province to take Care of the Interests of the Lds Proprietors. Of these, Mr. Moseley was to serve in a Double Capacity, both as Commissioner and Surveyor. For that reason there was but one other Surveyor from thence, Mr. Swan. All the Persons being thus agreed upon, they settled the time of Meeting to be at Corotuck, March the 5th, 1728.

In the Mean time, the requisite Preparations were made for so long and tiresome a Journey;

and because there was much work to be done and some Danger from the Indians, in the uninhabited Part of the Country, it was necessary to provide a Competent Number of Men. Accordingly, Seventeen able Hands were listed on the Part of Virginia, who were most of them Indian Traders and expert Woodsmen.

27. These good Men were ordered to come armed with a Musquet and a Tomahack, or large Hatchet, and provided with a Sufficient Quantity of Ammunition.

They likewise brought Provisions of their own for ten days, after which time they were to be furnisht by the Government. Their March was appointed to be on the 27th of February, on which day one of the Commissioners met them at their Rendezvous, and proceeded with them as far as Colo Allen's. This Gentleman is a great oeconomist, and Skilld in all the Arts of living well at an easy expense.

28. They proceeded in good Order through Surry County, as far as the Widdow Allen's who had copied Solomon's complete housewife exactly. At this Gentlewoman's House, the other two Commissioners had appointed to join them, but were detained by some Accident at Williamsburg, longer than their appointment.

29. They pursued their March thro the Isle of Wight and observd a most dreadful Havock made by a late Hurricane, which happend in August, 1726. The Violence of it had not reachd above a Quarter of a Mile in Breadth, but within that Compass had

levelld all before it. Both Trees and Houses were
laid flat on the Ground, and several things hurld
to an incredible distance. Tis happy such violent
Gusts are confined to so narrow a Channel, because
they carry desolation wherever they go. In the
Evening they reacht Mr. Godwin's, on the South
Branch of Nansemond River, where they were
treated with abundance of Primitive Hospitality.

March 1. This Gentleman was so kind as to
shorten their Journey, by setting them over the
river. They coasted the N E Side of the Dismal
for several miles together, and found all the
Grounds bordering upon it very full of Sloughs.
The Trees that grew near it lookt very Reverend,
with the long Moss that hung dangling from their
Branches. Both cattle and Horses eat this Moss
greedily in Winter when other Provender is
Scarce, tho it is apt to scowr them at first.
In that moist Soil too grew abundance of that kind
of Myrtle which bears the Candle-Berries. There
was likewise, here and there, a Gall-bush, which is
a beautiful Evergreen, and may be cut into any
Shape. It derives its Name from its Berries turning Water black, like the Galls of an oak.

When this Shrub is transplanted into Gardens,
it will not thrive without frequent watering.

The two other commissioners came up with them
just at their Journey's end, and that evening they
arrivd all together at Mr. Craford's, who lives on
the South Branch of Elizabeth-River, over against
Norfolk. Here the Commissioners left the Men
with all the Horses and heavy Baggage, and

crosst the River with their Servants only, for fear
of making a Famine in the Town.

Norfolk has most the ayr of a Town of any in
Virginia. There were then near 20 Brigantines
and Sloops riding at the Wharves, and oftentimes
they have more. It has all the advantages of
Situation requisite for Trade and Navigation.
There is a Secure Harbour for a good Number of
Ships of any Burthen. Their River divides itself
into 3 Several Branches, which are all Navigable.
The Town is so near the sea, that its Vessels may
Sail in and out in a few Hours. Their Trade is
Chiefly to the West-Indies, whither they export
abundance of Beef, Pork, Flour and Lumber.
The worst of it is, they contribute much towards
debauching the Country by importing abundance
of Rum, which, like Ginn in Great Britain, breaks
the Constitution, Vitiates the Morals, and ruins
the Industry of most of the Poor people of this
Country.

This Place is the Mart for most of the Commodities producd in the Adjacent Parts of North
Carolina. They have a pretty deal of Lumber
from the Borderers on the Dismal, who make bold
with the King's Land there abouts, without the
least Ceremony. They not only maintain their
Stocks upon it, but get Boards, Shingles and other
Lumber out of it in great Abundance.

The Town is built on a level Spot of Ground
upon Elizabeth River, the Banks whereof are
neither so high as to make the landing of Goods
troublesome, or so low as to be in Danger of over-

flowing. The Streets are Straight, and adorned with several Good Houses, which Encrease every Day. It is not a Town of Ordinarys and Publick Houses, like most others in this Country, but the Inhabitants consist of Merchants, Ship-Carpenters and other useful Artisans, with Sailors enough to manage their Navigation. With all these Conveniences, it lies under the two great disadvantages that most of the Towns in Holland do, by having neither good Air nor good Water. The two Cardinal Vertues that make a Place thrive, Industry and Frugality, are seen here in Perfection; and so long as they can banish Luxury and Idleness, the Town will remain in a happy and flourishing Condition.

The Method of building Wharffs here is after the following Manner. They lay down long Pine Logs, that reach from the Shore to the Edge of the Channel. These are bound fast together by Cross-Pieces notcht into them, according to the Architecture of the Log-Houses in North Carolina. A wharff built thus will stand Several Years, in spight of the Worm, which bites here very much, but may be soon repaired in a Place where so many Pines grow in the Neighbourhood.

The Commissioners endeavourd, in this Town, to list Three more men to serve as Guides in that dirty Part of the Country, but found that these People knew just enough of that frightful Place to avoid it.

They had been told that those Netherlands were full of Bogs, of Marshes and Swamps, not fit for

Human Creatures to engage in, and this was Reason enough for them not to hazard their Persons. So they told us, flat and plain, that we might een daggle thro the mire by Our-Selves for them.

The worst of it was, we coud not learn from any body in this Town, what Rout to take to Coratuck Inlet; till at last we had the fortune to meet with a Borderer upon North Carolina, who made a rough Sketch of that Part of the Country. Thus, upon seeing how the Land lay, we determind to march directly to Prescot Landing upon N W River, and proceed from thence by Water to the Place where our Line was to begin.

4. In Pursuance of this Resolution we crosst the River this Morning to Powder-Point, where we all took Horse; and the Grandees of the Town, with great Courtesy, conducted us Ten Miles on our way, as far as the long Bridge built over the S Branch of the River. The Parson of the Parish, Mr. Marston, a painful Apostle from the Society,[1] made one in this Ceremonious Cavalcade.

At the Bridge, these Gentlemen, wishing us a good Deliverance, returnd, and then a Troop of Light Horse escorted us as far as Prescot-Landing, upon N W river. Care had been taken beforehand to provide 2 Periaugas to lie ready at that Place to transport us to Coratuck Inlet. Our Zeal was so great to get thither at the time appointed, that we hardly allowd ourselves leisure to eat, which in truth we had the less Stomach to, by reason the dinner was served up by the Land-

---

[1] The Society for the Propagation of the Gospel in Foreign Parts.

lord, whose Nose stood on such ticklish Terms, that it was in Danger of falling into the Dish. We therefore made our Repast very short, and then embarkt with only the Surveyors and Nine chosen Men, leaving the rest at Mr. W—n's to take Care of the Horses and Baggage. There we also left our Chaplain, with the Charitable Intent, that the Gentiles round about might have time and Opportunity, if they pleasd, of getting themselves and their children baptizd.

We rowd down N W River about 18 miles, as far as the Mouth of it, where it empties itself into Albemarle Sound. It was a really Delightful Sight, all the way, to see the Banks of the River adornd with Myrtle, Laurel and Bay-Trees, which preserve their Verdure the Year round, tho it must be ownd that these beautiful Plants, sacred to Venus and Appollo, grow commonly in very dirty Soil. The River is, in most Places, fifty or Sixty Yards wide, without spreading much wider at the Mouth. Tis remarkable it was never known to Ebb and flow till the year 1713, when a Violent Storm opend a new Inlet, about 5 Miles South of the old one; since which Convulsion, the Old Inlet is almost choakd up by the Shifting of the Sand, and grows both Narrower and Shoaller every day.

It was dark before we could reach the Mouth of the River, where our wayward Stars directed us to a Miserable Cottage. The Landlord was lately removed, Bag and Baggage, from Maryland, thro a Strong Antipathy he had to work and paying his Debts. For want of our Tent, we were obligd to

Shelter our Selves in this wretched Hovel, where we were almost devourd by Vermin of Various kinds.   However, we were above complaining, being all Philosophers enough to improve such Slender Distresses into Mirth and good Humour.

5. The Day being now come, on which we had agreed to meet the Commissioners of North Carolina, we embarkd very early, which we coud the easier do, having no Temptation to stay where we were.   We Shapt our Course along the South End of Knot's Island, there being no Passage open on the North.

Farther Still to the Southward of us, we discoverd two Smaller Islands, that go by the names of Bell's and Churche's Isles.   We also saw a small New England Sloop riding in the Sound, a little to the South of our Course.   She had come in at the New-Inlet, as all other Vessels have done since the opening of it.   This Navigation is a little difficult, and fit only for Vessels that draw no more than ten feet Water.

The Trade hither is engrosst by the Saints of New England, who carry off a great deal of Tobacco, without troubling themselves with paying that Impertinent Duty of a Penny a Pound.

It was just Noon before we arrivd at Coratuck Inlet, which is now so shallow that the Breakers fly over it with a horrible Sound, and at the same time afford a very wild Prospect.   On the North side of the Inlet, the High Land terminated in a Bluff Point, from which a Spit of Sand extended itself towards the South-East, full half a Mile.

The Inlet lies between that Spit and another on the South of it, leaving an Opening of not quite a Mile, which at this day is not practicable for any Vessel whatsoever.   And as shallow as it now is, it continues to fill up more and more, both the Wind and Waves rolling in the Sands from the Eastern Shoals.

About two a Clock in the Afternoon we were joind by two of the Carolina Commissioners, attended by Mr. S—n, their Surveyor.   The other two were not quite so punctual, which was the more unlucky for us, because there could be no sport till they came.   These Gentlemen, it seems, had the Carolina-Commission in their keeping, notwithstanding which they coud not forbear paying too much regard to a Proverb — fashionable in ther Country,— not to make more hast than good Speed.

However, that we who were punctual might not spend our precious time unprofitably, we took the Several bearings of the Coast.   We also surveyd part of the Adjacent High Land, which had scarcely any Trees growing upon it, but Cedars. Among the Shrubs, we were shewed here and there a Bush of Carolina-Tea calld Japon,[1] which is one Species of the Phylarrea.   This is an Evergreen, the Leaves whereof have some resemblance to Tea, but differ very widely both in Tast and Flavour.

We also found some few Plants of the Spired Leaf Silk grass, which is likewise an Evergreen, bearing on a lofty Stemm a large Cluster of

[1] Yaupon.

Flowers of a Pale Yellow.   Of the Leaves of this Plant the People thereabouts twist very strong Cordage.

A vertuoso might divert himself here very well, in picking up Shells of various Hue and Figure, and amongst the rest, that Species of Conque Shell which the Indian Peak is made of.   The Extremities of these Shells are Blue and the rest white, so that Peak of both these Colours are drilld out of one and the same Shell, Serving the Natives both for Ornament and Money, and are esteemd by them far beyond Gold and Silver.

The Cedars were of Singular use to us in the Absence of our Tent, which we had left with the rest of the Baggage for fear of overloading the Periaugas.   We made a Circular Hedge of the Branches of this Tree, Wrought so close together as to fence us against the Cold Winds.   We then kindled a rouseing fire in the Center of it, and lay round it, like so many Knights Templars.   But, as comfortable as this Lodging was, the Surveyors turnd out about 2 in the Morning to try the Variation by a Meridian taken from the North Star, and found it to be somewhat less than three degrees West.

The Commissioners of the Neighbouring Colony came better provided for the Belly than the Business.   They brought not above two men along with them that would put their Hands to any thing but the Kettle and the Frying-Pan.   These spent so much of their Industry that way, that they had as little Spirit as Inclination for Work.

6. At Noon, having a Perfect Observation, we found the Latitude of Coratuck Inlet to be 36 Degrees and 31 Minutes.

Whilst we were busied about these Necessary Matters, our Skipper row'd to an Oyster Bank just by, and loaded his Periauga with Oysters as Savoury and well-tasted as those from Colchester or Walfleet, and had the advantage of them, too, by being much larger and fatter.

About 3 in the Afternoon the two lagg Commissioners arriv'd, and after a few decent excuses for making us wait, told us they were ready to enter upon Business as soon as we pleas'd. The first Step was to produce our respective Powers, and the Commission from each Governor was distinctly read, and Copies of them interchangeably deliver'd.

It was observ'd by our Carolina Friends, that the Latter Part of the Virginia Commission had something in it a little too lordly and Positive. In answer to which we told them twas necessary to make it thus peremptory, lest the present Commissioners might go upon as fruitless an Errand as their Predecessors. The former Commissioners were ty'd down to Act in Exact Conjunction with those of Carolina, and so could not advance one Step farther, or one Jot faster, than they were pleas'd to permit them.

The Memory of that disappointment, therefore, induc'd the Government of Virginia to give fuller Powers to the present Commissioners, by Authorizing them to go on with the Work by Themselves, in Case those of Corolina should prove unreason-

able, and refuse to join with them in carrying the
business to Execution.   And all this was done lest
His Majesty's gracious Intention shoud be frus-
trated a Second time.

After both Commissions were considerd, the
first Question was, where the Dividing Line was to
begin.   This begat a Warm debate; the Virginia
Commissioners contending, with a great deal of
Reason, to begin at the End of the Spitt of Sand,
which was undoubtedly the North Shore of Coratuck Inlet.   But those of Carolina insisted Stren-
uously, that the Point of High Land ought rather
to be the Place of Beginning, because that was
fixt and certain, whereas the Spitt of Sand was
ever Shifting, and did actually run out farther now
than formerly.   The Contest lasted some Hours,
with great Vehemence, neither Party receding from
their Opinion that Night.   But next Morning, Mr.
M. . . . , to convince us he was not that Obstinate Person he had been represented, yielded to
our Reasons, and found Means to bring over his
Collegues.

Here we began already to reap the Benefit of
those Peremptory Words in our Commission, which
in truth added some Weight to our Reasons.
Nevertheless, because positive proof was made by
the Oaths of two Credible Witnesses, that the
Spitt of Sand had advancd 200 Yards towards the
Inlet since the Controversy first began, we were
willing for Peace-sake to make them that allowance.   Accordingly we fixed our Beginning about
that Distance North of the Inlet, and there Or-

dered a Cedar-Post to be driven deep into the Sand
for our beginning. While we continued here, we
were told that on the South Shore, not far from the
Inlet, dwelt a Marooner, that Modestly call'd himself a Hermit, tho' he forfeited that Name by Suffering a wanton Female to cohabit with Him.

His Habitation was a Bower, cover'd with Bark
after the Indian Fashion, which in that mild Situation protected him pretty well from the Weather.
Like the Ravens, he neither plow'd nor sow'd, but
Subsisted chiefly upon Oysters, which his Hand-
maid made a Shift to gather from the Adjacent
Rocks. Sometimes, too, for Change of Dyet, he
sent her to drive up the Neighbour's Cows, to
moisten their Mouths with a little Milk. But as
for raiment, he depended mostly upon his Length
of Beard, and She upon her Length of Hair, part
of which she brought decently forward, and the
rest dangled behind quite down to her Rump, like
one of Herodotus's East Indian Pigmies.

Thus did these Wretches live in a dirty State
of Nature, and were mere Adamites, Innocence
only excepted.

7. This Morning the Surveyors began to run the
Dividing line from the Cedar-Post we had driven
into the Sand, allowing near 3 Degrees for the
Variation. Without making this Just allowance,
we should not have obeyd his Majesty's order in
running a Due West Line. It seems the former
Commissioners had not been so exact, which gave
our Friends of Carolina but too just an Exception
to their Proceedings.

The Line cut Dosier's Island, consisting only of
a Flat Sand, with here and there an humble Shrub
growing upon it.   From thence it crost over a
narrow Arm of the Sound into Knot's Island, and
there Split a Plantation belonging to William
Harding.

The Day being far spent, we encampt in this
Man's Pasture, tho' it lay very low, and the Season now inclin'd People to Aguish Distempers.
He sufferd us to cut Cedar-Branches for our
Enclosure, and other Wood for Firing, to correct
the moist Air and drive away the Damps.   Our
Landlady, in the Days of her Youth, it seems, had
been a Laundress in the Temple, and talkt over
her Adventures in that Station, with as much
pleasure as an Old Soldier talks over his Battles
and Distempers, and I believe with as many Ad-
ditions to the Truth.

The Soil is good in many Places of this Island,
and the Extent of it pretty large.   It lyes in the
form of a Wedge: the South End of it is Several
Miles over, but towards the North it Sharpens into
a Point.   It is a Plentiful Place for Stock, by
reason of the wide Marshes adjacent to it, and
because of its warm Situation.   But the Inhabitants pay a little dear for this Convenience, by
losing as much Blood in the Summer Season by
the infinite Number of Mosquetas, as all their
Beef and Pork can recruit in the Winter.

The Sheep are as large as in Lincolnshire, because they are never pincht by cold or Hunger.
The whole Island was hitherto reckon'd to lye in

Virginia, but now our Line has given the greater
Part of it to Carolina.   The Principal Freeholder
here is Mr. White, who keeps open House for all
Travellers, that either Debt or Shipwreck happens
to cast in his way.

8. By break of Day we sent away our Largest
Periauga, with the Baggage, round the South end
of Knot's Island, with Orders to the Men to wait
for us in the Mouth of North River.   Soon after,
we embarkt ourselves on board the smaller Vessel,
with Intent, if possible, to find a Passage round
the North End of the Island.

We found this Navigation very difficult, by
reason of the Continued Shoals, and often stuck
fast aground; for tho' the Sound spreads many
miles, yet it is in most places extremely Shallow,
and requires a Skilful Pilot to Steer even a Canoe
safe over it.   It was almost as hard to keep our
Temper as to keep the Channel, in this provoking
Situation.   But the most impatient amongst us
strokt down their Choler and swallow'd their
curses, lest, if they suffer'd them to break out,
they might sound like Complaining, which was
expressly forbid, as the first Step to Sedition.

At a distance we descry'd Several Islands to
the Northward of us, the largest of which goes by
the Name of Cedar Island.   Our periauga stuck
so often that we had a fair chance to be benighted
in this wide Water, which must certainly have
been our Fate, had we not luckily spied a Canoe
that was giving a Fortune-teller a cast from Princess Anne County over to North Carolina. . But,

as conjurers are Sometimes mistaken, the Man
mistrusted we were Officers of Justice in pursuit
of a Young Wench he had carry'd off along with
him.   We gave the Canoe Chase for more than
an Hour and when we came up with her, threat-
end to make them all prisoners unless they would
direct us into the right Channel.

By the Pilotage of these People we row'd up
an Arm of the Sound, call'd the Back-Bay, till
we came to the Head of it.   There we were stoppt
by a miry Pocoson full half a Mile in Breadth,
thro' which we were oblig'd to daggle on foot,
plungeing now and then, tho' we pickt our Way,
up to the Knees in Mud.   At the End of this
Charming walk we gain'd the Terra Firma of
Princess Anne County.   In that Dirty Condition
we were afterwards oblig'd to foot it two Miles,
as far as John Heath's Plantation, where we expected to meet the Surveyors & the men who
waited upon them.

While we were performing this tedious Voyage,
they had carried the Line thro' the firm Land of
Knot's Island, where it was no more than half a
Mile wide.   After that they travers'd a large
Marsh, that was exceeding Miry, and extended to
an Arm of the Back-Bay.   They crosst that water
in a Canoe, which we had order'd round for that
Purpose, and then waded over another Marsh, that
reacht quite to the High Land of Princess Anne.
Both these Marshes together make a breadth of
five Miles, in which the Men frequently sunk up
to the Middle without muttering the least com-

plaint. On the contrary, they turn'd all these Disasters into Merriment.

It was discover'd, by this day's Work, that Knot's Island was improperly so call'd, being in Truth no more than a Peninsula. The N W Side of it is only divided from the Main by the great Marsh above-mentioned, which is seldom totally overflow'd. Instead of that, it might, by the Labour of a few Trenches, be drain'd into firm Meadow, capable of grazing as many cattle as Job, in his best Estate, was master of. In the Miry Condition it now lies, it feeds great Numbers in the Winter, tho', when the Weather grows warm, they are driven from thence by the Mighty Armies of Mosquetas, which are the Plague of the lower Part of Carolina, as much as the Flies were formerly of Egypt, and some Rabbis think those Flies were no other than Mosquetas.

All the People in the Neighbourhood flockt to John Heath's, to behold such Rarities as they fancied us to be. The Men left their belov'd Chimney Corners, the good women their Spinning Wheels, and some, of more Curiosity than Ordinary, rose out of their sick Beds, to come and stare at us. They lookt upon us as a Troop of Knight Errants, who were running this great Risque of our Lives, as they imagin'd, for the Public Weal; and some of the gravest of them question'd much whether we were not all Criminals, condemned to this dirty work for Offences against the State.

What puzzled them most was, what cou'd make

our men so very Light-hearted under such intolerable Drudgery. "Ye have little reason to be
merry, My Masters," said one of them, with a very
solemn Face, "I fancy the Pocoson you must
Struggle with to-morrow will make you change
your Note, and try what Metal you are made of.
Ye are, to be sure, the first of Human Race that
ever had the Boldness to attempt it, and I dare say
will be the last. If, therefore, you have any
Worldly Goods to dispose of, My Advice is that
you make your Wills this very Night, for fear you
die Intestate to-Morrow." But, alas! these frightfull Tales were so far from disheartening the men,
that they serv'd only to whet their Resolution.

9. The Surveyors enter'd Early upon their Business this Morning, and ran the Line thro' Mr.
Eyland's Plantation, as far as the Banks of North
River. They passt over it in the Periauga, and
landed in Gibbs' Marsh, which was a mile in
Breadth, and tolerably firm. They trudg'd thro'
this Marsh without much difficulty as far as the
High Land, which promis'd more Fertility than
any they had seen in these lower Parts. But this
firm Land lasted not long before they came upon
the dreadful Pocoson they had been threaten'd
with. Nor did they find it one Jot better than it
had been painted to them. The Beavers and Otters had render'd it quite impassable for any Creature but themselves.

Our poor Fellows had much ado to drag their
Legs after them in this Quagmire, but disdaining
to be baulkt, they cou'd hardly be persuaded from

pressing forward by the Surveyors, who found it absolutely Necessary to make a Traverse in the Deepest Place, to prevent their Sticking fast in the Mire, and becoming a Certain Prey to the Turkey-Buzzards.

This Horrible Day's Work Ended two Miles to the Northward of Mr. Merchant's Plantation, divided from N W River by a Narrow Swamp, which is causeway'd over. We took up our Quarters in the open Field, not far from the House, correcting, by a Fire as large as a Roman-Funeral-Pile, the Aguish Exhalations arising from the Sunken Grounds that Surrounded us.

The Neck of Land included betwixt N River and N-West River, with the adjacent Marsh, belong'd formerly to Governor Gibbs,[1] but since his Decease to Colonel Bladen, in right of his first Lady, who was Mr. Gibbs' Daughter. It would be a Valuable Tract of Land in any Country but North Carolina, where, for want of Navigation and Commerce, the best Estate affords little more than a coarse Subsistence.

[1] This was John Gibbs, who in 1690 was disputing Philip Ludwell's commission as governor of North Carolina. How he got his claim is not known. His fiery proclamation against Ludwell, in which he offered in defense of his claims to fight the latter "as long as my eyelidds shall wagg," has been preserved. (See Col. Recs. of N. C., I. 363.) It is known, also, that in 1690 he went to one of the precinct courts of Albemarle County and arrested and carried off two of the justices who would not recognize his commission. These prisoners he kept in his house surrounded by eighty of his followers. In August of the same year, we are informed that both Gibbs and Ludwell were about to go to England, presumably to lay their claims before the Lords Proprietors; and we hear no more of the controversy. (See the Sainsbury Papers in the State Library at Richmond, Va., vol. for 1640-91, pp. 297, 311; also Col. Recs. of N. C., I. 364, 366.)

10. The Sabbath happen'd very opportunely to give some ease to our jaded People, who rested religiously from every work, but that of cooking the Kettle. We observed very few corn-fields in our Walks, and those very small, which seem'd the Stranger to us, because we could see no other Tokens of Husbandry or Improvement. But, upon further Inquiry, we were given to understand People only made Corn for themselves and not for their Stocks, which know very well how to get their own Living.

Both Cattle and Hogs ramble in the Neighbouring Marshes and Swamps, where they maintain themselves the whole Winter long, and are not fetch'd home till the Spring. Thus these Indolent Wretches, during one half of the Year, lose the Advantage of the Milk of their cattle, as well as their Dung, and many of the poor Creatures perish in the Mire, into the Bargain, by this ill Management.

Some, who pique themselves more upon Industry than their Neighbours, will, now and then, in compliment to their Cattle, cut down a Tree whose Limbs are loaden with the Moss aforemention'd. The trouble wou'd be too great to Climb the Tree in order to gather this Provender, but the Shortest way (which in this Country is always counted the best) is to fell it, just like the Lazy Indians, who do the same by such Trees as bear fruit, and so make one Harvest for all. By this bad Husbandry Milk is so Scarce, in the Winter Season, that were a Big-belly'd Woman to long for it, She would lose her Longing. And, in truth, I believe this is often the Case, and at the same time a very good reason why so many People in this Province are markt with a Custard Complexion.

The only Business here is raising of Hogs, which is manag'd with the least Trouble, and affords the Diet they are most fond of. The Truth of it is, the Inhabitants of N Carolina devour so much Swine's flesh, that it fills them full of gross Humours. For want too of a constant Supply of Salt, they are commonly obliged to eat it Fresh, and that begets the highest taint of Scurvy. Thus, whenever a Severe Cold happens to Constitutions thus Vitiated, tis apt to improve into the Yaws, called there very justly the country-Distemper. This has all the Symptoms of the Pox, with this Aggravation, that no Preparation of Mercury will touch it. First it seizes the Throat, next the Palate, and lastly shews its spite to the poor Nose, of which tis apt in a small time treacherously to undermine the Foundation.

This Calamity is so common and familiar here, that it ceases to be a Scandal, and in the disputes that happen about Beauty, the Noses have in some Companies much ado to carry it. Nay, tis said that once, after three good Pork years, a Motion had like to have been made in the House of Burgesses, that a Man with a Nose shou'd be incapable of holding any Place of Profit in the Province; which Extraordinary Motion could never have been intended without Some Hopes of a Majority.

Thus, considering the foul and pernicious Ef-

fects of Eating Swine's Flesh in a hot Country, it
was wisely forbidden and made an Abomination to
the Jews, who liv'd much in the same Latitude
with Carolina.

11. We ordered the Surveyors early to their Business, who were blesst with pretty dry Grounds for
three Miles together.   But they paid dear for it in
the next two, consisting of one continued frightfull Pocoson, which no Creatures but those of the
amphibious kind ever had ventur'd into before.

This filthy Quagmire did in earnest put the
Men's Courage to a Tryal, and tho' I can't say
it made them lose their Patience, yet they lost
their Humour for Joking.   They kept their Gravity
like so many Spaniards, so that a Man might then
have taken his Opportunity to plunge up to the
Chin, without Danger of being laught at.   However, this unusual composure of countenance could
not fairly be call'd complaining.

Their Day's-Work ended at the Mouth of Northern's Creek, which empties itself into N W River;
tho' we chose to Quarter a little higher up the
River, near Mossy Point.   This we did for the
Convenience of an Old house to Shelter our Persons and Baggage from the rain, which threaten'd
us hard.   We judg'd the thing right, for there fell
an heavy shower in the Night, that drove the most
hardy of us into the House.   Tho' indeed, our case
was not much mended by retreating thither, because
that Tenement having not long before been us'd as
a Pork-Store, the Moisture of the Air dissolv'd the
Salt that lay Scatter'd on the Floor, and made it

as wet within Doors as without. However, the
Swamps and Marshes we were lately accustom'd
to had made such Beavers and Otters of us that
Nobody caught the least cold.

We had encampt so early, that we found time in
the Evening to walk near half a Mile into the
Woods.   There we came upon a Family of Mulat-
toes, that call'd themselvs free, tho' by the Shy-
ness of the Master of the House, who took care to
keep least in Sight, their Freedom seem'd a little
Doubtful.   It is certain many Slaves Shelter themselves in this Obscure Part of the World, nor will
any of their righteous Neighbours discover them.
On the Contrary, they find their Account in Settling
such Fugitives on some out-of-the-way-corner of
their Land, to raise Stocks for a mean and inconsiderable Share, well knowing their Condition makes
it necessary for them to Submit to any Terms.

Nor were these worthy Borderers content to
Shelter Runaway Slaves, but Debtors and Criminals have often met with the like Indulgence.   But
if the Government of North Carolina has encourag'd this unneighbourly Policy in order to increase their People, it is no more than what Ancient
Rome did before them, which was made a City of
Refuge for all Debtors and Fugitives, and from
that wretched Beginning grew up in time to be
Mistress of a great Part of the World.   And, considering how Fortune delights in bringing great
things out of Small, who knows but Carolina may,
one time or other, come to be the Seat of some
other great Empire?

12. Every thing had been so soakt with the Rain,
that we were oblig'd to lie by a good Part of the
Morning and dry them.   However, that time was
not lost, because it gave the Surveyors an Opportunity of Platting off their Work, and taking the
Course of the River.   It likewise helpt to recruit
the Spirits of the Men, who had been a little harass'd with Yesterday's March.   Notwithstanding
all this, we crosst the River before Noon, and advanc'd our Line 3 Miles.   It was not possible to
make more of it, by reason good Part of the
way was either Marsh or Pocoson.   The Line
cut two or three Plantations, leaving Part of them
in Virginia, and part of them in Carolina.   This
was a Case that happen'd frequently, to the great
Inconvenience of the Owners, who were therefore
oblig'd to take out two Patents and Pay for a new
Survey in each Government.

In the Evening we took up our Quarters in Mr.
Ballance's Pasture, a little above the Bridge built
over N W River.   There we discharg'd the two
Periaugas, which in truth had been very Servic-
able in transporting us over the Many Waters in
that Dirty and Difficult Part of our Business.

Our Landlord had a tolerable good House and
Clean Furniture, and yet we cou'd not be tempted
to lodge in it.   We chose rather to lye in the open
Field, for fear of growing too tender.   A clear
Sky, spangled with Stars, was our Canopy, which
being the last thing we saw before we fell asleep,
gave us Magnificent Dreams.   The Truth of it is,
we took so much pleasure in that natural kind of

Lodging, that I think at the foot of the Account Mankind are great Losers by the Luxury of Feather-Beds and warm apartments.

The curiosity of beholding so new and withal so Sweet a Method of encamping, brought one of the Senators of N Carolina to make us a Midnight Visit. But he was so very Clamorous in his Commendations of it, that the Centinel, not seeing his Quality, either thro' his habit or Behaviour, had like to have treated him roughly.

After excusing the Unseasonableness of his Visit, and letting us know he was a Parliament Man, he swore he was so taken with our Lodging, that he would set Fire to his House as soon as he got Home, and teach his Wife and Children to lie, like us, in the open field.

13. Early this Morning our Chaplain repair'd to us with the Men we had left at Mr. Wilson's. We had sent for them the Evening before to relieve those who had the Labour-Oar from Corotuck-Inlet. But to our great surprise, they petition'd not to be reliev'd, hoping to gain immortal Reputation by being the first of Mankind that Ventur'd thro' the great Dismal. But the rest being equally Ambitious of the same Honour, it was but fair to decide their Pretensions by Lot. After Fortune had declar'd herself, those which she had excluded offer'd Money to the Happy Persons to go in their Stead. But Hercules would have as soon sold the Glory of cleansing the Augean Stables, which was pretty near the same Sort of Work.

No sooner was the Controversy at an end, but we

sent them unfortunate Fellows back to their Quarters, whom Chance had Condemn'd to remain upon Firm Land and Sleep in a whole Skin.   In the mean while the Surveyors carry'd the Line 3 Miles, which was no Contemptible day's work, considering how cruelly they were entangled with Bryars and Gall Bushes.   The Leaf of this last Shrub bespeaks it to be of the Alaternus Family.

Our Work ended within a Quarter of a Mile of the Dismal above-mention'd, where the Ground began to be already full of Sunken Holes and Slashes, which had, here and there, some few Reeds growing in them.

Tis hardly credible how little the Bordering inhabitants were acquainted with this mighty Swamp, notwithstanding they had liv'd their whole lives within Smell of it.   Yet, as great Strangers as they were to it, they pretended to be very exact in their Account of its Dimensions, and were positive it could not be above 7 or 8 Miles wide, but knew no more of the Matter than Star-gazers know of the Distance of the Fixt Stars.   At the Same time, they were Simple enough to amuse our Men with Idle Stories of the Lyons, Panthers and Alligators, they were like to encounter in that dreadful Place.

In short, we saw plainly there was no Intelligence of this Terra Incognita to be got, but from our own Experience.   For that Reason it was resolv'd to make the requisite Dispositions to enter it next Morning.   We allotted every one of the Surveyors for this painful Enterprise, with 12 Men to

attend them. Fewer than that cou'd not be employ'd in clearing the way, carrying the Chain,
marking the Trees, and bearing the necessary Bedding and Provisions. Nor wou'd the Commissioners themselves have Spared their Persons on this
Occasion, but for fear of adding to the poor men's
Burthen, while they were certain they cou'd add
nothing to their Resolution.

We quarter'd with our Friend and Fellow Traveller, William Wilkins, who had been our faithful
Pilot to Coratuck, and liv'd about a mile from the
Place where the Line ended. Every thing lookt so
very clean, and the Furniture so neat, that we were
tempted to Lodge within Doors. But the Novelty
of being shut up so close quite spoil'd our rest, nor
did we breathe so free by abundance, as when we
lay in the open Air.

14. Before nine of the Clock this Morning, the
Provisions, Bedding and other Necessaries, were
made up into Packs for the Men to carry on their
Shoulders into the Dismal. They were victuall'd
for 8 days at full Allowance, Nobody doubting but
that wou'd be abundantly Sufficient to carry them
thro' that Inhospitable Place; nor Indeed was it
possible for the Poor Fellows to Stagger under
more. As it was, their Loads weigh'd from 60
to 70 Pounds, in just Proportion to the Strength
of those who were to bear them.

Twou'd have been unconscionable to have Sad-
dled them with Burthens heavier than that, when
they were to lugg them thro' a filthy Bogg, which
was hardly practicable with no Burthen at all.

Besides this Luggage at their Backs, they were oblig'd to measure the distance, mark the Trees, and clear the way for the Surveyors every Step they went. It was really a Pleasure to see with how much Cheerfulness they undertook, and with how much Spirit they went thro' all this Drudgery. For their Greater Safety, the Commissioners took care to furnish them with Peruvian-Bark,[1] Rhubarb and Hipocoacanah, in case they might happen, in that wet Journey, to be taken with fevers or Fluxes.

Altho' there was no need of Example to inflame Persons already so cheerful, yet to enter the People with better grace, the Author and two more of the Commissioners accompanied them half a Mile into the Dismal. The Skirts of it were thinly Planted with Dwarf Reeds and Gall-Bushes, but when we got into the Dismal itself, we found the Reeds grew there much taller and closer, and, to mend the matter was so interlac'd with bamboe-briars, that there was no scuffling thro' them without the help of Pioneers. At the same time, we found the Ground moist and trembling under our feet like a Quagmire, insomuch that it was an easy Matter to run a Ten-Foot-Pole up to the Head in it, without exerting any uncommon Strength to do it.

Two of the Men, whose Burthens were the least cumbersome, had orders to march before, with their Tomahawks, and clear the way, in order to make an Opening for the Surveyors. By their Assistance

1 Bark of the cinchona-tree.

we made a Shift to push the Line half a Mile in 3
Hours, and then reacht a small piece of firm Land,
about 100 Yards wide, Standing up above the rest
like an Island. Here the people were glad to lay
down their Loads and take a little refreshment,
while the happy man, whose lot it was to carry the
Jugg of Rum, began already, like Aesop's Bread-
Carriers, to find it grow a good deal lighter.

After reposing about an Hour, the Commissioners recommended Vigour and Constancy to their
Fellow-Travellers, by whom they were answer'd
with 3 Cheerful Huzzas, in Token of Obedience.
This Ceremony was no sooner over but they took
up their Burthens and attended the Motion of the
Surveyors, who, tho' they workt with all their
might, could reach but one Mile farther, the same
obstacles still attending them which they had met
with in the Morning.

However small this distance may seem to such as
are us'd to travel at their Ease, yet our Poor Men,
who were oblig'd to work with an unwieldy Load
at their Backs, had reason to think it a long way;
Especially in a Bogg where they had no firm Footing, but every Step made a deep Impression, which
was instantly fill'd with Water. At the same time
they were labouring with their Hands to cut down
the Reeds, which were Ten-feet high, their Legs
were hampered with the Bryars. Besides, the
Weather happen'd to be very warm, and the tall-
ness of the Reeds kept off every Friendly Breeze
from coming to refresh them. And, indeed, it was
a little provoking to hear the Wind whistling among

the Branches of the White Cedars, which grew
here and there amongst the Reeds, and at the same
time not have the Comfort to feel the least Breath
of it.

In the mean time the 3 Commissioners return'd
out of the Dismal the same way they went in, and,
having join'd their Brethren, proceeded that Night
as far as Mr. Wilson's.

This worthy Person lives within sight of the
Dismal, in the Skirts whereof his Stocks range and
Maintain themselves all the Winter, and yet he
knew as little of it as he did of Terra Australis
Incognita. He told us a Canterbury Tale of a North
Briton, whose Curiosity Spurr'd him a long way
into this great Desart, as he call'd it, near 20 Years
ago, but he having no Compass, nor seeing the Sun
for several Days Together, wander'd about till he
was almost famisht; but at last he bethought himself of a Secret his Countrymen make use of to
Pilot themselves in a Dark day.

He took a fat Louse out of his Collar, and expos'd it to the open day on a Piece of White
Paper, which he brought along with him for his
Journal. The poor Insect having no Eye-lids,
turn'd himself about till he found the Darkest Part
of the Heavens, and so made the best of his way
towards the North. By this Direction he Steer'd
himself Safe out, and gave such a frightful account
of the Monsters he saw, and the Distresses he
underwent, that no mortall Since has been hardy
enough to go upon the like dangerous Discovery.

15. The Surveyors pursued their work with all

Diligence, but Still found the Soil of the Dismal so
Spongy that the Water ouzed up into every foot-
step they took.   To their Sorrow, too, they found
the Reeds and Bryars more firmly interwoven than
they did the day before.   But the greatest Grievance was from large Cypresses, which the Wind
had blown down and heap'd upon one another.
On the Limbs of most of them grew Sharp Snags,
Pointing every way like so many Pikes, that requir'd much Pains and Caution to avoid.

These Trees being Evergreens, and Shooting
their Large Tops Very high, are easily overset by
every Gust of Wind, because there is no firm Earth
to Steddy their Roots.   Thus many of them were
laid prostrate to the great Encumbrance of the
way.   Such Variety of Difficulties made the Business go on heavily, insomuch that, from Morning
till Night, the Line could advance no further than
1 Mile and 31 Poles.   Never was Rum, that cordial of Life, found more necessary than it was in
this Dirty Place.   It did not only recruit the People's
Spirits, now almost Jaded with Fatigue, but serv'd
to correct the Badness of the Water, and at the
same time to resist the Malignity of the Air.   Whenever the Men wanted to drink, which was very often,
they had nothing more to do but to make a Hole,
and the Water bubbled up in a Moment.   But it
was far from being either clear or well tasted, and
had besides a Physical Effect, from the Tincture it
receiv'd from the Roots of the Shrubbs and Trees
that grew in the Neighbourhood.

While the Surveyors were thus painfully em-

ploy'd, the Commissioners discharged the long
Score they had with Mr. Wilson, for the Men and
Horses which had been quarter'd upon him during
our Expedition to Coratuck.   From thence we
march'd in good Order along the East Side of the
Dismal, and passt the long Bridge that lies over
the South Branch of Elizabeth River.   At the End
of 18 Miles we reacht Timothy Ivy's Plantation,
where we picht our Tent for the first Time, and
were furnisht with every thing the Place afforded.

We perceiv'd the happy Effects of Industry in
this Family, in which every one lookt tidy and
clean, and carri'd in their countenances the chearful Marks of Plenty.   We saw no Drones there,
which are but too Common, alas, in that Part of the
World.   Tho', in truth, the Distemper of Laziness
seizes the Men oftener much than the Women.
These last Spin, weave and knit, all with their
own Hands, while their Husbands, depending on
the Bounty of the Climate, are Sloathfull in every
thing but getting of Children, and in that only
Instance make themselves useful Members of an
Infant-Colony.

There is but little Wool in that Province, tho'
Cotton grows very kindly, and, so far South, is Seldom nippt by the Frost.   The Good Women mix
this with their Wool for their outer Garments;
tho', for want of Fulling, that kind of Manufacture
is Open and Sleazy.   Flax likewise thrives there
extreamly, being perhaps as fine as any in the
World, and I question not might, with a little care,
and pains, be brought to rival that of Egypt; and

yet the Men are here so intolerable Lazy, they seldom take the trouble to propagate it.

16. The Line was this day carry'd one Mile and
half and 16 Poles. The Soil continued soft and
Miry, but fuller of Trees, especially White cedars.
Many of these too were thrown down and piled in
Heaps, high enough for a good Muscovite Fortification. The worst of it was, the Poor Fellows began now to be troubled with Fluxes, occasion'd by
bad Water and moist Lodgings: but chewing of
Rhubarb kept that Malady within Bounds.

In the mean time the Commissioners decampt
early in the Morning, and made a March of 25
Miles, as far as Mr. Andrew Mead's, who lives upon
Nansimand River. They were no sooner got under
the Shelter of that Hospitable Roof, but it began to
rain hard, and continued so to do great part of the
Night. This gave them much Pain for their
Friends in the Dismal, whose sufferings spoilt their
Taste for the good Chear, wherewith they were
entertain'd themselves.

However, late that Evening, these poor Men had
the Fortune to come upon another Terra-firma,
which was the Luckyer for them, because the Lower
ground, by the rain that fell, was made a fitter
Lodging for Tadpoles than men.

In our Journey we remarkt that the North Side
of this great Swamp lies higher than either the
East or the West, nor were the approaches to it so
full of Sunken Grounds. We passt by no less than
two Quaker Meeting Houses, one of which had an
Awkward Ornament on the West End of it, that

seem'd to Ape a Steeple.   I must own I expected
no such Piece of Foppery from a Sect of so much
outside Simplicity.

That persuasion prevails much in the lower end
of Nansimond county, for want of Ministers to
Pilot the People a decenter way to Heaven.

The ill Reputation of Tobacco planted in those
lower Parishes makes the Clergy unwilling to accept of them, unless it be such whose abilities are
as mean as their Pay.   Thus, whether the Churches
be quite void or but indifferently filled, the Quakers
will have an Opportunity of gaining Proselytes.
Tis a wonder no Popish Missionaries are sent from
Maryland to labour in this Neglected Vineyard,
who we know have Zeal enough to traverse Sea
and Land on the Meritorious Errand of making
converts.

Nor is it less Strange that some Wolf in Sheep's
cloathing arrives not from New England to lead
astray a Flock that has no shepherd.   People un-
instructed in any Religion are ready to embrace
the first that offers.   Tis natural for helpless man
to adore his Maker in Some Form or other, and
were there any exception to this Rule, I should expect it to be among the Hottentots of the Cape of
Good Hope and of North Carolina.

There fell a great deal of Rain in the Night,
accompany'd with a Strong Wind.   The fellow-
feeling we had for the poor Dismalites, on Account of this unkind Weather, render'd the Down
we laid upon uneasy.   We fancy'd them half-
drown'd in their Wet Lodging, with the Trees

blowing down about their Ears. These Were the Gloomy Images our Fears Suggested; tho' twas so much uneasiness clear gain. They happen'd to come of much better, by being luckily encampt on the dry piece of Ground afore-mention'd.

17. They were, however, forct to keep the Sabbath in Spite of their Teeth, contrary to the Dispensation our good Chaplain had given them. Indeed, their Short allowance of Provision would have justify'd their making the best of their way, without Distinction of days. Twas certainly a Work both of Necessity and Self-preservation, to save themselves from Starving. Nevertheless, the hard Rain had made every thing so thoroughly wet, that it was quite impossible to do any Business. They therefore made a vertue of what they could not help, and contentedly rested in their dry Situation.

Since the Surveyors had enter'd the Dismal, they had laid Eyes on no living Creature: neither Bird nor Beast, Insect nor Reptile came in View. Doubtless, the Eternal Shade that broods over this mighty Bog, and hinders the sun-beams from blessing the Ground, makes it an uncomfortable Habitation for any thing that has life. Not so much as a Zealand Frog cou'd endure so Aguish a Situation.

It had one Beauty, however, that delighted the Eye, tho' at the Expense of all the other Senses: the Moisture of the Soil preserves a continual Verdure, and makes every Plant an Evergreen, but at the same time the foul Damps ascend with-

out ceasing, corrupt the Air, and render it unfit for
Respiration. Not even a Turkey-Buzzard will
venture to fly over it, no more than the Italian
Vultures will over the filthy Lake Avernus, or the
Birds in the Holy-Land over the Salt Sea, where
Sodom and Gomorrah formerly stood.[1]

In these sad Circumstances, the kindest thing we
cou'd do for our Suffering Friends was to give
them a place in the Litany. Our Chaplain, for his
Part, did his Office, and rubb'd us up with a Seasonable Sermon. This was quite a new thing to
our Brethren of North Carolina, who live in a
climate where no clergyman can Breathe, any more
than Spiders in Ireland.

/ For want of men in Holy Orders, both the Members of the Council and Justices of the Peace are
empower'd by the Laws of that Country to marry
all those who will not take One another's Word;
but for the ceremony of Christening their children,
they trust that to chance. If a Parson come in
their way, they will crave a Cast of his office, as
they call it, else they are content their Offspring
should remain as Arrant Pagans as themselves.

[1] Byrd's description of this
swamp is too unfavorable. The
place is not uninhabited at this
day. Persons who live in the
adjacent counties go thither to
hunt bears and deer as well
as wildcats. In the swamp is
Lake Drummond, a favorite
angling-ground for local sports-
men. The water, which from
its dark color might well seem
unwholesome to the observers,
is discolored by roots of the
juniper-trees, which abound
there. It is popularly called
"juniper water," and is held
in such high esteem as drinking
water that the inhabitants of
that whole region send for it
for many miles. I am assured,
also, that there are many snakes
in the swamp, and the only
reason Byrd's surveyors did not
encounter them is the early
season at which the expedition
was made. — EDITOR.

They account it among their greatest advantages that they are not Priest-ridden, not remembering that the Clergy is rarely guilty of Bestriding such as have the misfortune to be poor.[1]

One thing may be said for the Inhabitants of that Province, that they are not troubled with any Religious Fumes, and have the least Superstition of any People living. They do not know Sunday from any other day, any more than Robinson Crusoe did, which would give them a great Advantage were they given to be industrious. But they keep so many Sabbaths every week, that their disregard of the Seventh Day has no manner of cruelty in it, either to Servants or Cattle.)

It was with some difficulty we cou'd make our People quit the good chear they met with at this House, so it was late before we took our Departure; but to make us amends, our Landlord was so good as to conduct us Ten Miles on our Way, as far as the Cypress Swamp, which drains itself into the Dismal. Eight Miles beyond that we forded the Waters of Coropeak, which tend the same way as do many others on that side. In Six Miles more we reacht the Plantation of Mr. Thomas Spight, a Grandee of N Carolina. We found the good Man upon his Crutches, being crippled with the Gout in both his Knees. Here we flatter'd ourselves we should by this time meet with good Tydings of the Surveyors, but had reckon'd, alas!

---

[1] Governor Burrington in 1731 confirms this statement (Col. Recs. of N. C., III. 152-153). There were at that time a few Baptist and Quaker congregations in North Carolina.

without our Host: on the Contrary, we were told
the Dismal was at least Thirty Miles wide at that
Place.   However, as nobody could say this on his
own Knowledge, we Order'd Guns to be fired and
a Drum to be beaten, but receiv'd no Answer,
unless it was from that prating Nymph Echo, who,
like a loquacious Wife, will always have the last
Word, and Sometimes return three for one.

18. It was indeed no Wonder our Signal was not
heard at that time, by the People in the Dismal,
because, in Truth, they had not then penetrated
one Third of their way.   They had that Morning
fallen to work with great Vigour; and, finding the
Ground better than Ordinary, drove on the Line 2
Miles and 38 poles.   This was reckon'd an Her-
culean day's Work, and yet they would not have
Stopp'd there, had not an impenetrable cedar
Thicket chekt their Industry.   Our Landlord had
seated Himself on the Borders of this Dismal, for
the Advantage of the Green Food His Cattle find
there all Winter, and for the Rooting that Sup-
ports His Hogs.   This, I own, is some convenience
to his Purse, for which his whole Family pay dear
in their Persons, for they are devoured by mus-
ketas all the Summer, and have Agues every
Spring and Fall, which Corrupt all the Juices of
their Bodies, give them a cadaverous complexion,
and besides a lazy, creeping Habit, which they
never get rid of.

19. We Ordered Several Men to Patrole on the
Edge of the Dismal, both towards the North and
towards the South, and to fire Guns at proper Dis-

tances. This they perform'd very punctually, but cou'd hear nothing in return, nor gain any Sort of Intelligence. In the mean time whole Flocks of Women and Children flew hither to Stare at us, with as much curiosity as if we had lately Landed from Bantam or Morocco.

Some Borderers, too, had a great Mind to know where the Line wou'd come out, being for the most part Apprehensive lest their Lands Should be taken into Virginia. In that case they must have submitted to some Sort of Order and Government; whereas, in N Carolina, every One does what seems best in his own Eyes. There were some good Women that brought their children to be Baptiz'd, but brought no Capons along with them to make the solemnity cheerful. In the mean time it was Strange that none came to be marry'd in such a Multitude, if it had only been for the Novelty of having their Hands Joyn'd by one in Holy Orders. Yet so it was, that tho' our chaplain Christen'd above an Hundred, he did not marry so much as one Couple dureing the whole Expedition. But marriage is reckon'd a Lay contract in Carolina, as I said before, and a Country Justice can tie the fatal Knot there, as fast as an Arch-Bishop.

None of our Visiters could, however, tell us any News of the Surveyors, nor Indeed was it possible any of them shou'd at that time, They being still laboring in the Midst of the Dismal.

It seems they were able to carry the Line this Day no further than one mile and 61 Poles, and

that whole distance was thro' a Miry cedar Bogg,
where the ground trembled under their Feet most
frightfully.   In many places too their Passage was
retarded by a great number of fallen Trees, that
lay Horsing upon one Another.

Tho' many circumstances concurr'd to make
this an unwholesome Situation, yet the Poor men
had no time to be sick, nor can one conceive a
more Calamitous Case than it would have been to
be laid up in that uncomfortable Quagmire. Never
were Patients more tractable, or willing to take
Physick, than these honest Fellows; but it was
from a Dread of laying their Bones in a Bogg
that wou'd soon spew them up again.   That Consideration also put them upon more caution about
their Lodging.

They first cover'd the Ground with Square
Pieces of Cypress bark, which now, in the Spring,
they cou'd easily Slip off the Tree for that purpose.
On this they Spread their Bedding; but unhappily
the Weight and Warmth of their Bodies made the
Water rise up betwixt the Joints of the Bark, to
their great Inconvenience.   Thus they lay not
only moist, but also exceedingly cold, because
their Fires were continually going out.   For no
sooner was the Trash upon the Surface burnt
away, but immediately the Fire was extinguisht by
the Moisture of the Soil, Insomuch that it was
great part of the Centinel's Business to rekindle it
again in a Fresh Place, every Quarter of an Hour.
Nor cou'd they indeed do their duty better, because
Cold was the only Enemy they had to Guard

against in a miserable Morass, where nothing can inhabit.

20. We could get no Tidings yet of our Brave Adventurers, notwithstanding we despatcht men to the likeliest Stations to enquire after them. They were still Scuffling in the Mire, and could not Possibly forward the Line this whole day more than one Mile and 64 Chains. Every Step of this Day's Work was thro' a cedar Bog, where the Trees were somewhat Smaller and grew more into a Thicket. It was now a great Misfortune to the Men to find their Provisions grow less as their Labour grew greater; They were all forct to come to short Allowance, and consequently to work hard without filling their Bellies. Tho' this was very severe upon English Stomachs, yet the People were so far from being discomfited at it, that they still kept up their good Humour, and merrily told a young Fellow in the Company, who lookt very Plump and Wholesome, that he must expect to go first to Pot, if matters shou'd come to Extremity.

This was only said by way of Jest, yet it made Him thoughtful in earnest. However, for the Present he return'd them a very civil answer, letting them know that, dead or alive, he shou'd be glad to be useful to such worthy good Friends. But, after all, this Humorous Saying had one very good Effect, for that yonker, who before was a little enclin'd by his Constitution to be lazy, grew on a Sudden Extreamly Industrious, that so there might be less Occasion to carbonade him for the good of his Fellow-Travellers.

While our Friends were thus embarrasst in the
Dismal, the Commissioners began to ly under great
uneasiness for them.   They knew very well their
Provisions must by this time begin to fall Short,
nor cou'd they conceive any likely means of a
Supply.   At this time of the Year both the Cattle
and Hoggs had forsaken the Skirts of the Dismal,
invited by the Springing Grass on the firm Land.
All our hopes were that Providence wou'd cause
some Wild Game to fall in their way, or else direct
them to a wholesome Vegetable for Subsistence.
In Short they were haunted with so many Frights
on this Occasion, that they were in truth more
uneasy than the Persons whose Case they lamented.

We had several Visiters from Edenton, in the
Afternoon, that came with Mr. Gale, who had prudently left us at Corotuck, to Scuffle thro' that
dirty Country by our Selves.   These Gentlemen,
having good Noses, had smelt out, at 30 Miles
Distance, the Precious Liquor, with which the
Liberality of our good Friend Mr. Mead had just
before Supply'd us.   That generous Person had
judg'd very right, that we were now got out of the
Latitude of Drink proper for men in Affliction, and
therefore was so good as to send his Cart loaden
with all sorts of refreshments, for which the Commissioners return'd Him their Thanks, and the
Chaplain His Blessing.

21. The Surveyors and their Attendants began
now in good Earnest to be alarm'd with Apprehensions of Famine, nor could they forbear looking

with Some Sort of Appetite upon a dog that had been the faithful Companion of their Travels.

Their Provisions were now near exhausted. They had this Morning made the last Distribution, that so each might Husband his small Pittance as he pleas'd. Now it was that the fresh Colour'd Young Man began to tremble every Joint of Him, having dreamed, the Night before, that the Indians were about to Barbacue him over live coals.

The Prospect of Famine determin'd the People, at last, with one consent, to abandon the Line for the Present, which advanced but slowly, and make the best of their way to firm Land. Accordingly they sat off very early, and, by the help of the Compass which they carried along with them, Steer'd a direct Westwardly Course. They marcht from Morning till Night, and Computed their Journey to amount to about 4 Miles, which was a great way, considering the difficulties of the Ground. It was all along a Cedar-Swamp, so dirty and perplext, that if they had not travell'd for their Lives, they cou'd not have reacht so far.

On their way they espied a Turkey-Buzzard, that flew prodigiously high to get above the Noisome Exhalations that ascend from that filthy place. This they were willing to understand as a good Omen, according to the Superstitions of the Ancients, who had great Faith in the Flight of Vultures. However, after all this tedious Journey, they could yet discover no End of their toil, which made them very pensive, especially after they had eat the last Morsel of their Provisions. But to

their unspeakable comfort, when all was husht in
the Evening, they heard the Cattle low, and the
Dogs bark, very distinctly, which, to Men in that
distress, was more delightful Music than Faustina
or Farinelli cou'd have made. In the mean time
the Commissioners could get no News of them
from any of their Visiters, who assembled from
every Point of the Compass.

But the good Landlord had Visiters of another
kind while we were there, that is to say, some industrious Masters of Ships, that lay in Nansimond River.   These worthy Commanders came to
bespeak Tobacco from these Parts to make up their
Loadings, in Contempt of the Virginia Law, which
Positively forbad their taking in any made in
North Carolina.   Nor was this Restraint at all unreasonable; because they have no Law in Carolina,
either to mend the Quality or lessen the quantity
of Tobacco, or so much as to prevent the turning
out of Seconds, all which cases have been provided against by the Laws of Virginia.   Wher-
fore, there can be no reason why the Inhabitants of
that Province Shou'd have the same Advantage of
Shipping their Tobacco in our Parts, when they
will by no means submit to the same Restrictions
that we do.

22. Our Patrole happen'd not to go far enough to
the Northward this Morning, if they had, the People
in the Dismal might have heard the Report of their
Guns.   For this Reason they return'd without any
Tydings, which threw us into a great tho' unnecessary Perplexity.   This was now the Ninth day

since they enter'd into that inhospitable Swamp, and consequently we had reason to believe their Provisions were quite Spent.

We knew they workt hard, and therefore would eat heartily, so long as they had wherewithal to recruit their Spirits, not imagining the Swamp so wide as they found it. Had we been able to guess where the Line wou'd come out, we wou'd have sent men to meet them with a fresh Supply; but as we cou'd know nothing of that, and as we had neither Compass nor Surveyor to guide a Messenger on such an Errand, we were unwilling to expose him to no Purpose; Therefore, all we were able to do for them, in so great an Extremity, was to recommend them to a Merciful Providence.

However long we might think the time, yet we were cautious of Shewing our uneasiness, for fear of Mortifying our Landlord. He had Done his best for us, and therefore we were unwilling he should think us dissatisfy'd with our Entertainment. In the midst of our concern, we were most agreeably surpriz'd, just after Dinner, with the News that the Dismalites were all Safe. These blessed Tidings were brought to us by Mr. Swan, the Carolina-Surveyor, who came to us in a very tatter'd condition.

After very Short Salutations, we got about Him as if He had been a Hottentot, and began to Inquire into his Adventures. He gave us a Detail of their uncomfortable Voyage thro' the Dismal, and told us, particularly, they had pursued their Journey early that Morning, encouraged by the

good Omen of seeing the Crows fly over their
Heads; that, after an Hour's march over very
Rotten Ground, they, on a Sudden, began to find
themselves among tall Pines, that grew in the
Water, which in Many Places was Knee-deep.
This Pine Swamp, into which that of Coropeak
drain'd itself, extended near a Mile in Breadth;
and tho' it was exceedingly wet, yet it was
much harder at Bottom than the rest of the Swamp;
that about Ten in the Morning, they recovered
firm Land, which they embraced with as much
Pleasure as Shipwreckt Wretches do the shoar.

After these honest adventurers had congratulated each other's Deliverance, their first Inquiry
was for a good House, where they might Satisfy
the Importunity of their Stomachs.   Their good
Genius directed them to Mr. Brinkley's, who
dwells a little to the Southward of the Line.   This
Man began immediately to be very inquisitive, but
they declar'd they had no Spirits to answer Questions till after Dinner.

"But pray, Gentlemen," said he, "answer me
One Question at least: what shall we get for your
Dinner?"   To which they replied, "No Matter
what, provided it be but Enough."   He kindly
supply'd their Wants as soon as possible, and by
the Strength of that Refreshment they made a
Shift to come to us in the Evening, to tell their
own Story.   They all lookt very thin, and as
ragged as the Gibeonite Ambassadors did in the
days of Yore.   Our Surveyors told us they had
measur'd Ten Miles in the Dismal, and Computed

the Distance they had Marcht since to amount to about five more, So they made the whole Breadth to be 15 Miles in all.

23. It was very reasonable that the Surveyors, and the men who had been Sharers in their Fatigue, should now have a little Rest. They were all, except one, in good Health and good heart, blessed be God! notwithstanding the dreadful Hardships they had gone through. It was really a Pleasure to see the Chearfulness wherewith they receiv'd the Order to prepare to re-enter the Dismal on the Monday following, in order to continue the Line from the Place where they had left off measuring, that so we might have the Exact Breadth of that Dirty Place. There were no more than two of them that cou'd be perswaded to be reliev'd on this Occasion, or Suffer the other men to Share the Credit of that bold Undertaking, Neither wou'd these have Suffer'd it had not one of them been very lame, and the Other much Indispos'd.

By the Description the Surveyors gave of the Dismal, we were convinc'd that nothing but the Exceeding dry Season we had been bless'd with cou'd have made the passing of it practicable. It is the Source of no less than five Several Rivers which discharge themselves Southward into Albemarle Sound, and of two that run northerly into Virginia. From thence tis easy to imagine that the Soil must be thoroughly Soakt with Water, or else there must be plentiful Stores of it under Ground; to supply so many Rivers; especially since there is no Lake, or any considerable Body of that Element to be seen on the Surface. The Rivers that Head in it from Virginia are the South Branch of Nansimond, and the West Branch of Elizabeth; and those from Carolina are North-west River, North River, Pasquetank, Little River, and Pequimons.

There is one remarkable part of the Dismal, lying to the south of the Line, that has few or no Trees growing on it, but contains a large Tract of tall Reeds. These being green all the Year round, and waveing with every Wind, have procur'd it the Name of the Green Sea.

We are not yet acquainted with the precise Extent of the Dismal, the whole haveing never been Survey'd; but it may be Computed at a Medium to be about 30 Miles long and 10 Miles broad, tho' where the Line crost it, twas compleatly 15 Miles wide. But it seems to grow Narrower towards the North, or at least does so in many Places. The Exhalations that continually rise from this vast Body of mire and Nastiness infect the Air for many Miles round, and render it very unwholesome for the Bordering Inhabitants. It makes them liable to Agues, Pleurisies, and many other Distempers, that kill abundance of People, and make the rest look no better than Ghosts. It wou'd require a great Sum of Money to drain it, but the Publick Treasure cou'd not be better bestow'd, than to preserve the Lives of his Majesty's Liege People, and at the same time render so great a Tract of swamp very Profitable, besides the advantage of making a Channel to transport by water-carriage goods from Albemarle

Sound into Nansimond and Elizabeth Rivers, in Virginia.

24. This being Sunday, we had a Numerous congregation, which flockt to our Quarters from all the adjacent Country. The News that our Surveyors were come out of the Dismal, increas'd the Number very much, because it wou'd give them an Opportunity of guessing, at least, whereabouts the Line wou'd cut, whereby they might form Some Judgment whether they belong'd to Virginia or Carolina. Those who had taken up Land within the Disputed Bounds were in great pain lest it should be found to ly in Virginia; because this being done contrary to an Express Order of that government, the Patentees had great reason to fear they should in that case have lost their land. But their Apprehensions were now at an end, when they understood that all the Territory which had been controverted was like to be left in Carolina.

In the afternoon, those who were to re-enter the Dismal were furnisht with the Necessary Provisions, and Order'd to repair the Over-Night to their Landlord, Peter Brinkley's, that they might be ready to begin their Business early on Monday Morning. Mr. Irvin was excus'd from the Fatigue, in complement to his Lungs; but Mr. Mayo and Mr. Swan were Robust enough to return upon that painful Service, and, to do them Justice, they went with great Alacrity. The Truth was, they now knew the worst of it; and cou'd guess pretty near at the time when they might hope to return to Land again.

25. The Air was chill'd this Morning with a Smart North-west Wind, which favour'd the Dismalites in their Dirty March.   They return'd by the Path they had made in coming out, and with great Industry arriv'd in the Evening at the Spot where the Line had been discontinued.

After so long and laborious a Journey, they were glad to repose themselves on their couches of Cypress-bark, where their sleep was as sweet as it wou'd have been on a Bed of Finland Down.

In the mean time, we who stay'd behind had nothing to do, but to make the best observations we cou'd upon that Part of the Country.   The Soil of our Landlord's Plantation, tho' none of the best, seem'd more fertile than any thereabouts, where the Ground is near as Sandy as the Desarts of Affrica, and consequently barren.   The Road leading from thence to Edenton, being in distance about 27 Miles, lies upon a Ridge call'd Sandy-Ridge, which is so wretchedly Poor that it will not bring Potatoes.

The Pines in this Part of the country are of a different Species from those that grow in Virginia: their bearded Leaves are much longer and their Cones much larger.   Each Cell contains a Seed of the Size and Figure of a black-ey'd Pea, which, Shedding in November, is very good Mast for Hogs, and fattens them in a Short time.

[1] According to the Old Style the new year began on March 25, and in the manuscript the new year appears as 1729. This, however, is an error of the copyist, as the line was run in 1728. To repeat this error would be positively misleading, and the editor has ventured to deviate from the literal text in this single particular, so as to make the needed correction throughout the remainder of the History.

The Smallest of these Pines are full of Cones, which are 8 or 9 Inches long, and each affords commonly 60 or 70 Seeds. This Kind of Mast has the Advantage of all other, by being more constant, and less liable to be nippt by the Frost, or Eaten by the Caterpillars. The Trees also abound more with Turpentine, and consequently yield more Tarr, than either the Yellow or the White Pine; And for the same reason make more durable Timber for building. The Inhabitants hereabouts pick up Knots of Lightwood in Abundance, which they burn into tar, and then carry it to Norfolk or Nansimond for a Market. The Tar made in this method is the less Valuable, because it is said to burn the Cordage, tho' it is full as good for all other uses, as that made in Sweden and Muscovy.

Surely there is no place in the World where the Inhabitants live with less Labour than in N Carolina. It approaches nearer to the Description of Lubberland than any other, by the great felicity of the Climate, the easiness of raising Provisions, and the Slothfulness of the People.

Indian Corn is of so great increase, that a little Pains will Subsist a very large Family with Bread, and then they may have meat without any pains at all, by the Help of the Low Grounds, and the great Variety of Mast that grows on the High-land. The Men, for their Parts, just like the Indians, impose all the Work upon the poor Women. They make their Wives rise out of their Beds early in the Morning, at the same time that they lye and Snore, till the Sun has run one third of his course, and

disperst all the unwholesome Damps.   Then, after
Stretching and Yawning for half an Hour, they
light their Pipes, and, under the Protection of a
cloud of Smoak, venture out into the open Air;
tho', if it happens to be never so little cold, they
quickly return Shivering into the Chimney corner.
When the weather is mild, they stand leaning with
both their arms upon the corn-field fence, and
gravely consider whether they had best go and
take a Small Heat at the Hough: but generally
find reasons to put it off till another time.

Thus they loiter away their Lives, like Solomon's
Sluggard, with their Arms across, and at the
Winding up of the Year Scarcely have Bread to
Eat.

To speak the Truth, tis a thorough Aversion to
Labor that makes People file off to N Carolina,
where Plenty and a Warm Sun confirm them in
their Disposition to Laziness for their whole Lives.

26. Since we were like to be confin'd to this place,
till the People return'd out of the Dismal, twas
agreed that our Chaplain might Safely take a turn
to Edenton, to preach the Gospel to the Infidels
there, and Christen their Children. He was accompany'd thither by Mr. Little, One of the Carolina
Commissioners, who, to shew his regard for the
Church, offer'd to treat Him on the Road with a
Fricassee of Rum. They fry'd half a Dozen
Rashers of very fat Bacon in a Pint of Rum, both
which being disht up together, serv'd the Company
at once for meat and Drink.

Most of the Rum they get in this Country comes

from New England, and is so bad and unwholesome, that it is not improperly call'd "Kill-
Devil." It is distill'd there from forreign molosses,
which, if Skilfully manag'd, yields near Gallon
for Gallon. Their molosses comes from the same
country, and has the name of "Long Sugar" in
Carolina, I suppose from the Ropiness of it, and
Serves all the purposes of Sugar, both in their Eating and Drinking.

When they entertain their Friends bountifully,
they fail not to set before them a Capacious Bowl
of Bombo, so call'd from the Admiral of that name.
This is a Compound of Rum and Water in Equal
Parts, made palatable with the said long Sugar.
As good Humour begins to flow, and the Bowl to
Ebb, they take care to replenish it with Shear
Rum, of which there always is a Reserve under
the Table. But such Generous doings happen
only when that Balsam of life is plenty; for they
have often such Melancholy times, that neither
Land-graves nor Cassicks can procure one drop
for their Wives, when they ly in, or are troubled
with the Colick or Vapours. Very few in this Country have the Industry to plant Orchards, which, in
a Dearth of Rum, might supply them with much
better Liquor.

The Truth is, there is one Inconvenience that
easily discourages lazy People from making This
improvement: very often, in Autumn, when the
Apples begin to ripen, they are visited with Numerous Flights of paraqueets, that bite all the Fruit
to Pieces in a moment, for the sake of the Kernels.

The Havock they make is Sometimes so great, that
whole Orchards are laid waste in Spite of all the
Noises that can be made, or Mawkins that can be
dresst up, to fright 'em away.   These Ravenous
Birds visit North Carolina only during the warm
Season, and so soon as the Cold begins to come
on, retire back towards the Sun.   They rarely Venture so far North as Virginia, except in a very hot
Summer, when they visit the most Southern Parts
of it.   They are very Beautiful; but like some
other pretty Creatures, are apt to be loud and
mischievous.

27. Betwixt this and Edenton there are many
thuckleberry Slashes, which afford a convenient
Harbour for Wolves and Foxes.   The first of these
wild Beasts is not so large and fierce as they are
in other countries more Northerly.   He will not
attack a Man in the keenest of his Hunger, but run
away from him, as from an Animal more mischievous than himself.

The Foxes are much bolder, and will Sometimes
not only make a Stand, but likewise assault any
one that would balk them of their Prey.   The Inhabitants hereabouts take the trouble to dig abundance of Wolf-Pits, so deep and perpendicular, that
when a Wolf is once tempted into them, he can
no more Scramble out again, than a Husband who
has taken the Leap can Scramble out of Matrimony.

Most of the Houses in this Part of the Country
are Log-houses, covered with Pine or Cypress
Shingles, 3 feet long, and one broad.   They are
hung upon Laths with Peggs, and their doors too

turn upon Wooden Hinges, and have wooden Locks to Secure them, so that the Building is finisht without Nails or other Iron-Work. They also set up their Pales without any Nails at all, and indeed more Securely than those that are nail'd. There are 3 Rails mortised into the Posts, the lowest of which serves as a Sill with a Groove in the Middle, big enough to receive the End of the Pales: the middle Part of the Pale rests against the Inside of the Next Rail, and the Top of it is brought forward to the outside of the uppermost. Such Wreathing of the Pales in and out makes them stand firm, and much harder to unfix than when nail'd in the Ordinary way.[1]

Within 3 or 4 Miles of Edenton, the Soil appears to be a little more fertile, tho' it is much cut with Slashes, which seem all to have a tendency towards the Dismal.

This Town is Situate on the North side of Albemarle Sound, which is there about 5 miles over. A Dirty Slash runs all along the Back of it, which in the Summer is a foul annoyance, and furnishes abundance of that Carolina plague, musquetas. There may be 40 or 50 Houses, most of them Small, and built without Expense. A Citizen here is counted Extravagant, if he has Ambition enough to aspire to a Brick-chimney. Justice herself is but indifferently Lodged, the Court-House having much the Air of a Common Tobacco-House. I believe this is the only Metropolis in the Chris-

---

[1] " Wattled palings," as they are called, are occasionally found in the extremely rural parts of the State to this day.

tian or Mahometan World, where there is neither Church, Chappel, Mosque, Synagogue, or any other Place of Publick Worship of any Sect or Religion whatsoever.

What little Devotion there may happen to be is much more private than their vices. The People seem easy without a Minister, as long as they are exempted from paying Him. Sometimes the Society for propagating the Gospel has had the Charity to send over Missionaries to this Country; but unfortunately the Priest has been too Lewd for the people, or, which oftener happens, they too lewd for the Priest. For these Reasons these Reverend Gentlemen have always left their Flocks as arrant Heathen as they found them. Thus much however may be said for the Inhabitants of Edenton, that not a Soul has the least taint of Hypocrisy, or Superstition, acting very Frankly and aboveboard in all their Excesses.

Provisions here are extremely cheap, and extremely good, so that People may live plentifully at a triffleing expense. Nothing is dear but Law, Physick, and Strong Drink, which are all bad in their Kind, and the last they get with so much Difficulty, that they are never guilty of the Sin of Suffering it to Sour upon their Hands. Their Vanity generally lies not so much in having a handsome Dining-Room, as a Handsome House of Office: in this Kind of Structure they are really extravagant.

They are rarely guilty of Flattering or making any Court to their governors, but treat them with

all the Excesses of Freedom and Familiarity.
They are of Opinion their rulers wou'd be apt to
grow insolent, if they grew Rich, and for that
reason take care to keep them poorer, and more
dependent, if possible, than the Saints in New
England used to do their Governors. They have
very little coin, so they are forced to carry on their
Home-Traffick with Paper-Money. This is the
only Cash that will tarry in the Country, and for
that reason the Discount goes on increasing between that and real Money, and will do so to the
End of the Chapter.

28. Our Time passt heavily in our Quarters, where
we were quite cloy'd with the Carolina Felicity of
having nothing to do. It was really more insupportable than the greatest Fatigue, and made us
even envy the Drudgery of our Friends in the
Dismal. Besides, tho' the Men we had with us
were kept in Exact Discipline, and behav'd without Reproach, yet our Landlord began to be tired
of them, fearing they would breed a Famine in his
Family.

Indeed, so many keen Stomachs made great
Havock amongst the Beef and Bacon, which he
had laid in for his Summer Provision, nor cou'd he
easily purchase More at that time of the Year,
with the Money we paid him, because the People
having no certain Market seldom provide any more
of these Commodities than will barely supply their
own Occasions. Besides the Weather was now
grown too warm to lay in a fresh Stock so late in
the Spring. These Considerations abated some-

what of that chearfulness with which he bidd us
Welcome in the Beginning, and made him think
the time quite as long as we did till the Surveyors
return'd.

While we were thus all hands uneasy, we were
comforted with the News that this Afternoon the
Line was finisht through the Dismal. The Messenger told us it had been the hard work of three
days to measure the Length of only 5 Miles, and
mark the Trees as they past along, and by the
most exact Survey they found the Breadth of the
Dismal in this Place to be completely 15 Miles.

How wide it may be in other Parts, we can give
no Account, but believe it grows narrower towards
the North; possibly towards Albemarle Sound it
may be something broader, where so many Rivers
issue out of it. All we know for certain is, that
from the Place where the Line enter'd the Dismal,
to where it came out, we found the Road round
that Portion of it which belongs to Virginia to be
about 65 Miles. How great the Distance may be
from Each of those Points, round that Part that
falls within the Bounds of Carolina, we had no
certain Information: tho' tis conjectur'd it cannot
be so little as 30 Miles. At which rate the whole
Circuit must be about an Hundred. What a Mass
of Mud and Dirt is treasur'd up within this filthy
circumference, and what a Quantity of Water must
perpetually drain into it from the riseing ground
that Surrounds it on every Side?

Without taking the Exact level of the Dismal,
we may be sure that it declines towards the Places

where the Several Rivers take their Rise, in order to carrying off the constant Supplies of Water. Were it not for such Discharges, the whole Swamp would long Since have been converted into a Lake. On the other Side this Declension must be very gentle, else it would be laid perfectly dry by so many continual drains; Whereas, on the contrary, the Ground seems every where to be thoroughly drencht even in the dryest Season of the Year.

The Surveyors concluded this day's Work with running 25 chains up into the Firm Land, where they waited further Orders from the Commissioners.

29. This day the Surveyors proceeded with the Line no more than 1 Mile and 15 Chains, being Interrupted by a Mill Swamp, thro' which they made no difficulty of wading, in order to make their work more exact.

Thus, like Norway-Mice, these worthy Gentlemen went right forward, without Suffering themselves to be turned out of the way by any Obstacle whatever.

We are told by some Travellers, that those Mice march in mighty Armies, destroying all the fruits of the Earth as they go along. But Something Peculiar to those obstinate little Animals is, that nothing stops them in their career, and if a House happen to stand in their way, disdaining to go an Inch about, they crawl up one side of it, and down the other: or if they meet with any River, or other Body of Water, they are so determin'd, that they swim directly over it, without varying one Point from their course for the Sake of any Safety or Convenience.

The Surveyors were also hinder'd some Time by Setting up Posts in the great Road, to shew the Bounds between the two Colonies.

Our Chaplain return'd to us in the Evening from Edenton, in Company with the Carolina Commissioners. He had preacht there in the Court-House, for want of a consecrated Place, and made no less than 19 of Father Hennepin's Christians.

By the permission of the Carolina Commissioners, Mr. Swan was allow'd to go home, as soon as the Survey of the Dismal was finisht; He met with this Indulgence for a Reason that might very well have excust his coming at all; Namely, that he was lately marry'd.

What remain'd of the Drudgery for this Season was left to Mr. Moseley, who had hitherto acted only in the capacity of a Commissioner. They offer'd to employ Mr. Joseph Mayo as their Surveyor in Mr. Swan's stead, but He thought it not proper to accept of it, because he had hitherto Acted as a Volunteer in behalf of Virginia, and did not care to change Sides, tho' it might have been to his Advantage.

30. The line was advanc'd this day 6 Miles and 35 chains, the Woods being pretty clear, and interrupted with no Swamp, or other wet Ground. The Land hereabout had all the Marks of Poverty, being for the most Part Sandy and full of Pines. This kind of Ground, tho' unfit for Ordinary Tillage, will however bring Cotton and Potatoes in Plenty, and Consequently Food and Raiment

to such as are easily contented, and, like the Wild Irish, find more Pleasure in Laziness than Luxury.

It also makes a Shift to produce Indian-corn, rather by the Felicity of the climate than by the Fertility of the Soil. They who are more Industrious than their Neighbours may make what Quantity of tar they please, tho' indeed they are not always sure of a Market for it.

The Method of burning Tar in Sweden and Muscovy Succeeds not well in this Warmer Part of the World. It seems they kill the Pine-Trees, by barking them quite round at a certain Height, which in those cold countreys brings down the Turpentine into the Stump in a Year's time. But experience has taught us that in warm Climates the Turpentine will not so easily descend, but is either fixt in the upper parts of the Tree, or fryed out by the intense Heat of the Sun.

Care was taken to Erect a Post in Every Road that our Line ran thro', with Virginia carv'd on the North-Side of it, and Carolina on the South, that the Bounds might every where appear. In the Evening the Surveyors took up their Quarters at the House of one Mr. Parker, who, by the Advantage of a better Spot of Land than Ordinary, and a more industrious Wife, lives comfortably, and has a very neat plantation.

31. It rain'd a little this Morning, but this, happening again upon a Sunday, did not interrupt our Business. However the Surveyors made no Scruple of protracting and platting off their work upon

that good day, because it was rather an Amusement than a Drudgery.

Here the Men feasted on the fat of the Land, and believing the dirtiest part of their work was over, had a more than Ordinary Gaiety of Heart. We christen'd two of our Landlord's children, which might have remained Infidels all their lives, had not we carry'd Christianity home to his own Door.

The Truth of it is, our Neighbours of North Carolina are not so zealous as to go much out of their way to procure this benefit for their children: Otherwise, being so near Virginia, they might, without exceeding much Trouble, make a Journey to the next Clergyman, upon so good an Errand.

And indeed should the Neighbouring Ministers, once in two or three years, vouchsafe to take a turn among these Gentiles, to baptize them and their children, twould look a little Apostolical, and they might hope to be requited for it hereafter, if that be not thought too long to tarry for their Reward.

April 1. The Surveyors getting now upon better Ground, quite disengag'd from Underwoods, pusht on the Line almost 12 Miles. They left Sommerton Chappel near two Miles to the Northward, so that there was now no Place of Publick Worship left in the whole Province of North Carolina.

The high Land of North Carolina was barren, and cover'd with a deep Sand; and the Low Grounds were wet and boggy, insomuch that several of our Horses were mir'd, and gave us frequent Opportunitys to shew our Horsemanship.

The Line cut William Spight's Plantation in
two, leaving little more than his dwelling House
and Orchard in Virginia. Sundry other Plantations were Split in the same unlucky Manner,
which made the Owners accountable to both Governments. Wherever we passed we constantly
found the Borderers laid it to Heart if their Land
was taken into Virginia: They chose much rather
to belong to Carolina, where they pay no Tribute,
either to God or to Caesar.

Another reason was, that the Government there
is so Loose, and the Laws so feebly executed, that,
like those in the Neighbourhood of Sydon formerly, every one does just what seems good in his
own Eyes. If the Governor's hands have been
weak in that Province, under the Authority of the
Lord Proprietors, much weaker then were the hands
of the Magistrate, who, tho' he might have had
Virtue enough to endeavour to punish Offendors,
which very rarely happen'd, yet that vertue had
been quite Impotent, for want of Ability to put it
in execution.

Besides, their might have been some Danger, perhaps, in venturing to be so rigorous, for fear of
undergoing the Fate of an honest Justice in Corotuck Precinct. This bold Magistrate, it seems,
taking upon him to order a fellow to the Stocks,
for being disorderly in his Drink, was, for his in-
temperate Zeal, carry'd thither himself, and narrowly escap'd being whippt by the Rabble into the
Bargain.

This easy day's work carried the Line to the

Banks of Somerton-Creek, that runs out of Chowan River, a little below the Mouth of Nottoway.

2. In less than a Mile from Somerton creek the Line was carry'd to Black-water, which is the Name of the upper Part of Chowan, running some Miles above the Mouth of Nottoway. It must be observ'd that Chowan, after taking a compass round the most beautiful part of North Carolina, empties itself into Albermarle Sound, a few Miles above Edenton. The Tide flows 7 or 8 miles higher than where the River changes its Name, and is Navigable thus high for any small vessel. Our Line intersected it exactly half a Mile to the northward of the mouth of Nottoway. However, in Obedience to his Majesty's Command, we directed the Surveyors to come down the River as far as the Mouth of Nottoway, in order to continue our true West Line from thence.

Thus we found the Mouth of Nottoway to lye no more than half a Minute farther to the Northward than Mr. Lawson had formerly done.[1] That Gentleman's Observation, it seems, placed it in 36° 30', and our Working made it out to be 36° 30½'—a very inconsiderable Variance.

The Surveyors crost the River over against the Middle of the Mouth of Nottoway, where it was about 80 yards wide. From thence they ran the Line about half a Mile through a dirty Pocoson, as far as an Indian Field. Here we took up our Lodging in a moist Situation, having the Pocoson

---

[1] John Lawson was one of the surveyors on the part of North Carolina in the futile attempt to run the line in 1710.—EDITOR.

above mention'd on one Side of us, and a Swamp on the other.

In this Camp 3 of the Meherin Indians made us a Visit. They told us that the Small Remains of their Nation had deserted their Ancient Town, situated near the Mouth of Meherin River, for fear of the Cataubas, who had kill'd 14 of their People the Year before; and the few that Survived that Calamity, had taken refuge amongst the English, on the East side of Chowan. Tho', if the complaint of these Indians were true, they are hardly used by our Carolina Friends. But they are the less to be pitied, because they have ever been reputed the most false and treacherous to the English of all the Indians in the Neighbourhood.

Not far from the Place where we lay, I observ'd a large Oak which had been blown up by the Roots, the Body of which was Shiver'd into perfect Strings, and was, in truth, the most Violent Effects of Lightning I ever saw.

But the most curious Instance of that dreadful meteor happen'd at York, where a man was kill'd near a Pine Tree in which the Lightening made a Hole before it Struck the Man, and left an exact Figure of the Tree upon his Breast, with all its Branches, to the wonder of all that beheld it, in which I shall be more particular hereafter.

We made another tryal of the Variation in this place, and found it some Minutes less than we had done at Coratuck-Inlet; but so small a Difference might easily happen thro' some defect in one or

other of the Observations, and, therefore, we
alter'd not our compass for the Matter.

3. By the advantage of clear woods, the Line was
extended 12 miles and three Quarters, as far as the
Banks of Meherin. Tho' the Mouth of this River
lye 15 miles below the Mouth of Nottaway, yet it
winds so much to the Northward, that we came
upon it, after running this Small Distance. During the first 7 Miles, we observed the Soil to be
poor and Sandy; but as we approacht Meherin it
grew better, tho' there it was cut to pieces by
Sundry Miry Branches, which discharge themselves into that River, Several of our Horses
plunged up to the Saddle-Skirts, and were not
disengaged without Difficulty.

The latter Part of our Day's work was pretty
laborious, because of the unevenness of the way,
and becauss the low Ground of the River was full
of Cypress-Snags, as Sharp and Dangerous to our
Horses as so many chevaux-de-frize. We found
the whole distance from the Mouth of Nottaway
to Meherin River, where our Line intersected it,
thirteen Miles and a Quarter.

It was hardly possible to find a level large
enough on the Banks of the River whereupon to
pitch our Tent. But tho' the Situation was, on
that Account, not very convenient for us, yet it
was for our poor Horses, by reason of the Plenty
of Small Reeds on which they fed voraciously.

These Reeds are green here all the Year round,
and will keep cattle in tolerable good Plight during the Winter. But whenever the Hogs come

where they are, they destroy them in a Short time, by ploughing up their Roots, of which, unluckily, they are very fond.

The River was in this place about as wide as the River Jordan, that is, 40 Yards, and wou'd be Navigable very high for flat Bottom-Boats and Canoes, if it were not so choakt up with large Trees, brought down by every Fresh. Tho' the Banks were full 20 feet high from the Surface of the Water, yet we saw certain Marks of their having been Overflow'd.

These Narrow Rivers that run high up into the Country are Subject to frequent Inundations, when the Waters are roll'd down with such Violence as to carry all before them. The Logs that are then floated, are very fatal to the bridges built over these rivers, Which can hardly be contriv'd Strong enough to stand against so much Weight and Violence join'd together.

The Isle of Wight County begins about 3 Miles to the East of Meherin River, being divided from that of Nansimond only by a Line of Markt trees.

4. The River was here hardly fordable, tho' the Season had been very dry. The Banks too were so Steep that our Horses were forced to climb like Mules to get up them. Nevertheless we had the Luck to recover the Opposite Shore without Damage.

We halted for half an hour at Charles Anderson's, who lives on the Western Banks of the River, in order to christen one of his children. In the mean time, the Surveyors extended the Line

2 Miles and 39 chains, in which small Distance Meherin River was so serpentine, that they crost it 3 times.

Then we went on to Mr. Kinchin's, a Man of Figure and Authority in N Carolina, who lives about a Mile to the Southward of the Place where the Surveyors left off. By the Benefit of a little pains, and good Management, this worthy Magistrate lives in much Affluence.

Amongst other Instances of his Industry, he had planted a good Orchard, which is not common in that Indolent climate; nor is it at all Strange, that such improvident People, who take no thought for the Morrow, shou'd save themselves the Trouble to make Improvements that will not pay them for several Years to come. Tho' if they cou'd trust futurity for any thing, they certainly wou'd for Cyder, which they are so fond of, that they generally drink it before it is done working, lest the Fermentation might unluckily turn it Sowr.

It is an Observation, which rarely fails of being true, both in Virginia and Carolina, that those who take care to plant good Orchards are, in their General characters, Industrious People. This held good in our LANDLORD, who had many Houses built on this Plantation, and every One kept in decent Repair. His Wife, too, was tidy, his Furniture clean, his Pewter bright, and nothing seem'd to be wanting to make his Home comfortable.

Mr. Kinchin made us the Compliment of his

House, but because we were willing to be as little
troublesome as possible, we order'd the Tent to be
pitch'd in his Orchard, where the Blossoms of the
Apple Trees contributed not a little to the sweetness of our Lodging.

Because the Spring was now pretty forward,
and the Rattle-Snakes began to crawl out of their
Winter-Quarters, and might grow dangerous, both
to the Men and their Horses, it was determin'd
to proceed no farther with the Line till the Fall.
Besides, the Uncommon Fatigue the People had
undergone for near 6 Weeks together, and the
Inclination they all had to visit their Respective
Familys, made a Recess highly reasonable.

The Surveyors were employ'd great part of the
Day, in forming a Correct and Elegant Map of
the Line, from Corotuck-Inlet to the Place where
they left off.   On casting up the account in the
most accurate manner, they found the whole distance we had run to amount to 73 Miles and 13
chains.   Of the Map they made two fair copies,
which agreeing exactly, were subscrib'd by the
Commissioners of both colonies, and one of them
was delivered to those on the Part of Virginia,
and the other to those on the Part of North Carolina.

6. Thus we finish'd our Spring Campaign, and
having taken leave of our Carolina-Friends, and
agreed to meet them again the Tenth of September following, at the same Mr. Kinchin's, in order
to continue the Line, we crosst Meherin River near
a Quarter of a Mile from the House.   About ten

Miles from that we halted at Mr. Kindred's Plantation, where we Christen'd two Children.

It happen'd that some of Isle of Wight militia
Were exercising in the Adjoining Pasture, and
there were Females enough attending that Martial
Appearance to form a more invincible corps.

Ten miles farther we passed Nottoway River
at Bolton's Ferry, and took up our Lodgings
about three Miles from thence, at the House of
Richard Parker, an honest Planter, whose Labours
were rewarded with Plenty, which, in this country
is the Constant Portion of the Industrious.

7. The Next day being Sunday, we order'd Notice to be sent to all the Neighbourhood that there
wou'd be a Sermon at this Place, and an Opportunity of Christening their Children. But the
Likelihood of Rain got the better of their Devotion, and what perhaps, Might Still be a Stronger
motive of their Curiosity. In the Morning we
despacht a runner to the Nottoway Town, to let
the Indians know we intended them a Visit that
Evening, and our honest Landlord was so kind as
to be our Pilot thither, being about 4 Miles from
his House.

Accordingly in the Afternoon we marcht in
good Order to the Town, where the Female Scouts,
station'd on an Eminence for that purpose, had
no sooner spy'd us, but they gave Notice of our
Approach to their Fellow-Citizens by continual
Whoops and Cries, which cou'd not possibly have
been more dismal at the Sight of their most implacable Enemys.

This Signal Assembled all their Great Men, who receiv'd us in a Body, and conducted us into the Fort. This Fort was a Square Piece of Ground, inclos'd with Substantial Puncheons, or Strong Palisades, about ten feet high, and leaning a little outwards, to make a Scalade more difficult.

Each side of the Square might be about 100 Yards long, with Loop-holes at proper Distances, through which they may fire upon the Enemy.

Within this Inclosure we found Bark Cabanes Sufficient to lodge all their people, in Case they should be obliged to retire thither. These Cabanes are no other but Close Arbours made of Saplings, arched at the top, and cover'd so well with Bark as to be proof against all Weather. The fire is made in the Middle, according to the Hibernian Fashion, the Smoak whereof finds no other Vent but at the Door, and so keeps the whole family Warm, at the Expense both of their Eyes and Complexion.

The Indians have no standing Furniture in their Cabanes but Hurdles to repose their Persons upon, which they cover with Mats or Deer-skins. We were conducted to the best Appartments in the Fort, which just before had been made ready for our Reception, and adorn'd with new Mats, that were sweet and clean.

The Young Men had Painted themselves in a Hideous Manner, not so much for Ornament as Terror. In that frightful Equipage they entertain'd us with Sundry War-Dances, wherein they endeavour'd to look as formidable as possible.

The Instrument they danct to was an Indian-drum, that is, a large Gourd with a Skin bract tort over the Mouth of it. The Dancers all Sang to this Musick, keeping exact Time with their feet, while their Heads and Arms were screw'd into a thousand Menacing Postures.

Upon this occasion the Ladies had array'd them-selves in all their finery. They were Wrapt in their Red and Blue Match-Coats, thrown so Neg-ligently about them, that their Mehogony Skins appear'd in Several Parts, like the Lacedaemonian Damsels of Old. Their Hair was breeded with white and Blue Peak, and hung gracefully in a large Roll upon their Shoulders.

This peak Consists of Small Cylinders cut out of a Conque-Shell, drill'd through and Strung like Beads. It serves them both for Money and Jewels, the Blue being of much greater Value than the White, for the same reason that Ethio-pian Mistresses in France are dearer than French, because they are more Scarce. The Women wear Necklaces and Bracelets of these precious Mate-rials, when they have a mind to appear lovely. Tho' their complexions be a little Sad-Colour'd, yet their Shapes are very Strait and well propor-tion'd. Their Faces are Seldom handsome, yet they have an Air of Innocence and Bashfulness, that with a little less dirt wou'd not fail to make them desirable. Such Charms might have had their full Effect upon Men who had been so long deprived of female conversation, but that the whole Winter's Soil was so crusted on the Skins

of those dark Angels, that it requir'd a very strong
Appetite to approach them.   The Bear's oyl, with
which they anoint their Persons all over, makes
their Skins Soft, and at the Same time protects
them from every Species of Vermin that use to be
troublesome to other uncleanly People.

We were unluckily so many, that they cou'd not
well make us the Complement of Bed-fellows, according to the Indian Rules of Hospitality, tho' a
grave Matron whisper'd one of the Commissioners
very civily in the Ear, that if her Daughter had
been but one year Older, she should have been at
his Devotion.

It is by no means a loss of Reputation among
the Indians, for Damsels that are Single to have
Intrigues with the Men; on the contrary, they
count it an Argument of Superior Merit to be
liked by a great Number of Gallants.   However,
like the Ladys that Game they are a little Mer-
cenary in their Amours, and seldom bestow their
Favours out of Stark Love and Kindness.   But
after these Women have once appropriated their
Charms by Marriage, they are from thenceforth
faithful to their Vows, and will hardly ever be
tempted by an Agreeable Gallant, or be provokt
by a Brutal or even by a fumbling Husband to go
astray.

The little Work that is done among the Indians
is done by the poor Women, while the men are
quite idle, or at most employ'd only in the Gentle-
manly Diversions of Hunting and Fishing.

In this, as well as in their Wars, they now use

nothing but Fire-Arms, which they purchase of
the English for Skins. Bows and Arrows are
grown into disuse, except only amongst their Boys.
Nor is it ill Policy, but on the contrary very prudent, thus to furnish the Indians with Fire-Arms,
because it makes them depend entirely upon the
English, not only for their Trade, but even for
their subsistence. Besides, they were really able to
do more mischief, while they made use of Arrows,
of which they wou'd let Silently fly Several in a
Minute with Wonderful Dexterity, whereas now
they hardly ever discharge their Fire-locks more
than once, which they insidiously do from behind a Tree, and then retire as nimbly as the
Dutch Horse us'd to do now and then formerly in
Flanders.

We put the Indians to no expense, but only of
a little Corn for our Horses, for which in Gratitude we cheer'd their hearts with what Rum we
had left, which they love better than they do their
Wives and Children.

Tho' these Indians dwell among the English,
and see in what Plenty a little Industry enables
them to live, yet they chuse to continue in their
Stupid Idleness, and to Suffer all the Inconveniences of Dirt, Cold, and Want, rather than to disturb their heads With care, or defile their Hands
with labour.

The whole Number of People belonging to the
Notoway Town, if you include Women and Chil-
dren, amount to about 200. These are the only
Indians of any consequence now remaining within

the Limits of Virginia. The rest are either removed, or dwindled to a very inconsiderable Number, either by destroying one another, or else by the Small-Pox and other Diseases. Tho' nothing has been so fatal to them as their ungovernable Passion for Rum, with which, I am sorry to say it, they have been but too liberally supply'd by the English that live near them.

And here I must lament the bad Success Mr. Boyle's Charity[1] has hitherto had towards converting any of these poor Heathens to Christianity. Many children of our Neighbouring Indians have been brought up in the College of William and Mary. They have been taught to read and write, and have been carefully Instructed in the Principles of the Christian Religion, till they came to be men. Yet after they return'd home, instead of civilizeing and converting the rest, they have immediately Relapt into Infidelity and Barbarism themselves.

And some of them too have made the worst use of the Knowledge they acquir'd among the English, by employing it against their Benefactors. Besides, as they unhappily forget all the good they learn, and remember the Ill, they are apt to

[1] Robert Boyle, an influential English chemist, left a sum of money to be invested by his trustees for some worthy charity. Dr. James Blair, who was about the same time in England soliciting funds for the foundation of William and Mary College, induced the trustees to appropriate most of this fund to the education of Indian youths in the new college. The fund was invested in England in an estate called Brafferton, and the building erected at Williamsburg for the use of the Indian students was called Brafferton Hall. It is still standing.—EDITOR.

be more vicious and disorderly than the rest of
their Countrymen.

I ought not to quit this Subject without doing
Justice to the great Prudence of Colo Spotswood
in this Affair.   That Gentleman was lieut Governor of Virginia when Carolina was engaged in
a Bloody War with the Indians.   At that critical
Time it was thought expedient to keep a Watchful
Eye upon our Tributary Savages, who we knew
had nothing to keep them to their Duty but their
Fears.

Then it was that he demanded of each Nation a
Competent Number of their their great Men's
Children to be sent to the College, where they
serv'd as so many Hostages for the good Behaviour of the Rest, and at the same time were
themselves principled in the Christian Religion.
He also Plac'd a School-Master among the Saponi
Indians, at the salary of Fifty Pounds P Annum,
to instruct their Children.   The Person that
undertook that Charitable work was Mr. Charles
Griffin, a Man of good Family, who by the Innocence of his Life, and the Sweetness of his
Temper, was perfectly well qualify'd for that
pious undertaking.   Besides, he had so much the
Secret of mixing Pleasure with instruction, that
he had not a Scholar, who did not love him affec-
tionately.

Such Talents must needs have been blest with a
Proportionable Success, had he not been unluckily
remov'd to the College, by which he left the good
work he had begun unfinisht.   In short, all the

Pains he had undertaken among the Infidels had no other Effect but to make them something cleanlier than other Indians are.

The Care Colo Spotswood took to tincture the Indian Children with Christianity produc'd the following Epigram, which was not publisht during his Administration, for fear it might then have lookt like flattery.

> Long has the Furious Priest assay'd in Vain,
> With Sword and Faggot, Infidels to gain,
> But now the Milder Soldier wisely tryes
> By Gentler Methods to unveil their Eyes.
> Wonders apart, he knew 'twere vain t'engage
> The fix'd Preventions of Misguided Age.
> With fairer Hopes he forms the Indian Youth
> To early Manners, Probity and Truth.
> The Lyon's whelp thus on the Lybian Shore ⎞
> Is tam'd and Gentled by the Artful Moor, ⎬
> Not the Grim Sire, inured to Blood before. ⎠

I am sorry I can't give a Better Account of the State of the Poor Indians with respect to Christianity, altho' a great deal of Pains has been and still continues to be taken with them. For my Part, I must be of Opinion, as I hinted before, that there is but one way of Converting these poor Infidels, and reclaiming them from Barbarity, and that is, Charitably to intermarry with them, according to the Modern Policy of the most Christian King in Canada and Louisiana.

Had the English done this at the first Settlement of the Colony, the Infidelity of the Indians had been worn out at this Day, with their Dark Complexions, and the Country had swarm'd with People more than it does with Insects.

It was certainly an unreasonable Nicety, that prevented their entering into so good-Natur'd an Alliance. All Nations of men have the same Natural Dignity, and we all know that very bright Talents may be lodg'd under a very dark Skin. The principal Difference between one People and another proceeds only from the Different Opportunities of Improvement.

The Indians by no means want understanding, and are in their Figure tall and well-proportion'd. Even their Copper-colour'd Complexion wou'd admit of Blanching, if not in the first, at the farthest in the Second Generation.

I may safely venture to say, the Indian Women would have made altogether as Honest Wives for the first Planters, as the Damsels they us'd to purchase from aboard the Ships. It is Strange, therefore, that any good Christian Shou'd have refused a wholesome, Straight Bed-fellow, when he might have had so fair a Portion with her, as the Merit of saving her Soul.

8. We rested on our clean Mats very comfortably, tho' alone, and the next Morning went to the Toilet of some of the Indian Ladys, where, what with the Charms of their Persons and the Smoak of their Apartments, we were almost blinded. They offer'd to give us Silk-Grass Baskets of their own making, which we Modestly refused, knowing that an Indian present, like that of a

Nun, is a Liberality put out to Interest, and a Bribe plac'd to the greatest Advantage.

Our Chaplain observ'd with concern, that the Ruffles of Some of our Fellow Travellers were a little discolour'd with pochoon, wherewith the good Man had been told those Ladies us'd to improve their invisible charms.

About 10 a Clock we marched out of Town in good order, & the War Captains saluted us with a Volley of Small-Arms. From thence we proceeded over Black-water Bridge to colo' Henry Harrisons, where we congratulated each other upon our Return into Christendom.

Thus ended our Progress for this Season, which we may justly say was attended with all the Success that could be expected. Besides the Punctual Performance of what was Committed to us, we had the Pleasure to bring back every one of our Company in perfect Health. And this we must acknowledge to be a Singular Blessing, considering the Difficulties and Dangers to which they had been expos'd.

We had reason to fear the many Waters and Sunken Grounds, thro' which We were oblig'd to wade, might have thrown the men into Sundry Acute distempers; especially the Dismal, where the Soil was so full of Water, and the Air so full of Damps, that nothing but a Dutchman cou'd live in them.

Indeed the Foundation of all our Success was the Exceeding dry Season. It rain'd during the whole Journey but rarely, and then, as when Herod built his Temple, only in the Night or upon the Sabbath, when it was no hindrance at all to our progress.

THE tenth of September being thought a little too soon for the Commissioners to meet, in order to proceed on the Line, on account of Snakes, 'twas agreed to put it off to the twentieth of the same Month, of which due Notice was sent to the Carolina-Commissioners.

19. We, on the part of Virginia, that we might be sure to be punctual, arriv'd at Mr. Kinchin's, the place appointed, on the 19th, after a Journey of three days, in which nothing Remarkable happen'd.

We found three of the Carolina-Commissioners had taken Possession of the House, having come thither by water from Edenton. By the Great Quantity of Provisions these Gentlemen brought, and the few men they had to eat them, we were afraid they intended to carry the Line to the South sea.

They had 500℔s of bacon and dry'd Beef, and 500℔s of Bisket, and not above three or four men. The misfortune was, they forgot to provide Horses to carry their good things, or else trusted to the Incertainty of hireing them here, which, considering the Place, was leaving too much to that Jilt, Hazard.

On our part we had taken better Care, being completely furnisht with everything necessary for transporting our Baggage and Provisions. Indeed we brought no other Provisions out with us but 1000℔s of Bread, and had Faith enough to depend on Providence for our Meat, being desirous to husband the publick Money as much as possible.

We had no less than 20 men, besides the Chaplain, the Surveyors and all the Servants, to be Subsisted upon this Bread. However, that it might hold out the better, our men had been Order'd to provide themselves at Home with Provision for Ten days, in which time we judg'd we should get beyond the Inhabitants, where Forest-Game of all sorts was like to be plenty at that time of the Year.

20. This being the day appointed for our Rendezvous, great part of it was Spent in the careful fixing our Baggage and Assembling our Men, who were order'd to meet us here. We took care to examine their Arms, and made proof of the Powder provided for the Expedition.

Our Provision-Horses had been hinder'd by the rain from coming up exactly at the Day; but this Delay was the less Disappointment, by reason of the ten days' Subsistence the men had been directed to provide for themselves.

Mr. Moseley did not join us till the afternoon, nor Mr. Swan till Several Days after.

Mr. Kinchin had unadvisedly sold the Men a little Brandy of his own making, which produced much disorder, causing some to be too cholerick, and others too loving; Insomuch that a Damsel, who assisted in the Kitchen, had certainly Suffer'd what the Nuns call Martyrdom, had she not capitulated a little too soon.

This outrage would have call'd for some severe Discipline, had she not bashfully withdrawn herself early in the Morning, & so carry'd off the Evidence.

21. We despatcht away the Surveyors without Loss of Time, who, with all their diligence, could carry the Line no farther than 3 Miles and 176 Poles, by reason the Low-Ground was one entire Thicket. In that distance they crost Meherin River the 4th time. In the mean while the Virginia-Commissioners thought proper to conduct their Baggage a farther way about, for the Convenience of a clearer Road.

The Carolina-Gentlemen did at length, more by Fortune than forecast, hire a clumsy Vehicle, something like a cart, to transport their Effects as far as Roanoak. This wretched Machine, at first Setting out, met with a very rude choque, that broke a Case-Bottle of Cherry Brandy in so unlucky a Manner that not one precious Drop was saved. This Melancholy Beginning forboded an unprosperous Journey, and too quick a Return, to the Persons most immediately concern'd.

In our way we crosst Fountain's Creek, which runs into Meherin River, so call'd from the disaster of an unfortunate Indian Trader who had formerly been drowned in it, and, like Icarus, left his Name to that fatal stream. We took up our Quarters on the Plantation of John Hill, where we pitcht our Tent, with design to tarry till such time as the Surveyors cou'd work their way to us.

22. This being Sunday, we had an Opportunity

of resting from our Labours.   The expectation of such a Novelty as a Sermon in these Parts brought together a Numerous Congregation.   When the Sermon was over, our Chaplain did his part towards making Eleven of them Christians.

Several of our men had Intermitting feavers, but were soon restor'd to their Health again by proper Remedies.   Our chief Medicine was Dogwood Bark, which we used, instead of that of Peru, with good Success.   Indeed, it was given in larger Quantity, but then, to make the Patients amends, they swallowed much fewer Doses.

In the afternoon our Provision-Horses arrived Safe in the Camp.   They had met with very heavy Rains, but, thank God, not a Single Bisket receiv'd the least Damage thereby.

We were furnisht by the Neighbours with very lean Cheese and very fat Mutton, upon which occasion twill not be improper to draw one conclusion, from the Evidence of North Carolina, that Sheep would thrive much better in the Woods than in Pasture Land, provided a careful Shepherd were employed to keep them from Straying, and, by the help of Dogs, to protect them also from the wolves.

23. The Surveyors came to us at Night, tho' they had not brought the Line so far as our Camp, for which reason we thought it needless to go forward till they came up with us.   They cou'd run no more than 4 Miles and 5 Poles, because the Ground was every where grown up with thick Bushes.

The Soil here appear'd to be very good, tho'

much broken betwixt Fountain creek and Roanoak River. The Line crost Meherin the 5th and last time, nor were our People sorry to part with a Stream the Meanders of which had given them so much Trouble.

Our Hunters brought us four wild Turkeys, which at that Season began to be fat and very delicious, especially the Hens.

These Birds seem to be of the Bustard kind, and fly heavily. Some of them are exceedingly large, and weigh upwards of 40 Pounds; Nay, some bold Historians venture to say, upwards of 50. They run very fast, stretching forth their Wings all the time, like the Ostrich, by way of Sails to quicken their Speed.

They roost commonly upon very high Trees, Standing near some River or Creek, and are so stupify'd at the Sight of Fire, that if you make a Blaze in the Night near the Place where they roost, you may fire upon them Several times successively, before they will dare to fly away.

Their Spurs are so Sharp and Strong that the Indians used formerly to point their Arrows with them, tho' now they point them with a Sharp white Stone. In the Spring the Turkey-Cocks begin to gobble, which is the Language wherein they make Love.

It rain'd very hard in the Night, with a violent Storm of Thunder and Lightening, which oblig'd us to trench in our Tent all round, to carry off the Water that fell upon it.

24. So soon as the men could dry their Blan-

kets, we sent out the Surveyors, who now meeting with more favourable Grounds, advanc'd the line 7 Miles and 82 Poles. However, the Commissioners did not think proper to decamp that day, believing they might easily overtake the Surveyors the next. In the mean time they sent out some of their most expert Gunners, who brought in four more wild Turkeys.

This part of the Country being very proper for raising Cattle and Hogs, we observ'd the Inhabitants lived in great plenty without killing themselves with Labour.

I found near our Camp some Plants of that kind of Rattle-Snake Root, called Star-grass. The Leaves shoot out circularly, and grow Horizontally and near the Ground. The Root is in Shape not unlike the Rattle of that Serpent, and is a Strong Antidote against the bite of it. It is very bitter, and where it meets with any Poison, works by Violent Sweats, but where it meets with none, has no Sensible Operation but that of putting the Spirits into a great Hurry, and so of promoting Perspiration.

The Rattle-snake has an utter Antipathy to this Plant, insomuch that if you Smear your hands with the Juice of it, you may handle the Viper Safely. Thus much I can say on my own Experience, that once in July, when these Snakes are in their greatest Vigour, I besmear'd a Dog's Nose with the Powder of this Root, and made him trample on a large Snake Several times, which, however, was so far from biting him, that it perfectly Sicken'd at the Dog's Approach, and turn'd its Head from him with the Utmost Aversion.

Our Chaplain, to shew his Zeal, made an Excursion of 6 Miles to christen 2 children, but without the least regard to the good Chear at these Solemnities.

25. The Surveyors taking the Advantage of clear Woods, pusht on the Line 7 Miles and 40 Poles. In the mean time the Commissioners marcht with the Baggage about 12 miles, and took up their Quarters near the Banks of the Beaver Pond, (which is one Branch of Fountain's creek,) just by the place where the Surveyors were to finish their day's work.

In our march one of the men kill'd a Small Rattle-Snake, which had no more than two Rattles. Those Vipers remain in Vigour generally till towards the End of September, or Sometimes later, if the Weather continue a little warm. On this consideration we had provided three Several Sorts of Rattle-Snake-Root, made up into proper Doses, and ready for immediate use, in case any one of the Men or their Horses had been bitten.

We crosst Fountain's Creek once more in our Journey this day, and found the Grounds very Rich, notwithstanding they were broken and Stony.

Near the place where we encampt the county of Brunswick is divided from *the* Isle of Wight. These Counties run quite on the back of Surry and Prince George, and are laid out in very irregular Figures.

As a Proof the Land mended hereabouts, we found the Plantations began to grow thicker by much than we had found them lower down.

26. We hurry'd away the Surveyors without Loss of time, who extended the Line 10 Miles and 160 Poles, the Grounds proving dry and free from Under-woods. By the way the chain-carriers kill'd two more Rattle-Snakes, which I own was a little ungrateful, because two or three of the Men had Strided over them without receiving any Hurt; tho' one of these Vipers had made bold to Strike at one of the Baggage Horses, as he went along, but by good Luck his Teeth only grazed on the hoof, without doing him any Damage. However, these Accidents were, I think, so many Arguments that we had very good Reason to defer our coming out till the 20th of September.

We observ'd Abundance of St. Andrew's Cross in all the Woods we passed thro', which is the common Remedy used by the Indian traders to cure their horses when they are bitten by Rattle-Snakes.

It grows on a Strait Stem, about 18 Inches high, and bears a Yellow Flower on the Top, that has an Eye of Black in the Middle, with Several Pairs of Narrow Leaves Shooting out at right Angles from the Stalk over against one another.

This Antidote grows Providentially all over the Woods, and upon all Sorts of Soil, that it may be every where at hand in Case a Disaster should Happen, and may be had all the hot Months while the Snakes are dangerous.

About four a'clock in the Afternoon we took up
our Quarters upon Caban Branch, which also discharges itself into Fountain Creek.   On our way
we observed Several Meadows cloth'd with very
rank-Grass, and Branches full of tall Reeds, in
which Cattle keep themselves fat good part of the
Winter.   But Hogs are as injurious to both as
Goats are said to be to Vines, and for that Reason
it was not lawful to Sacrifice them to Bacchus.
We halted by the way to Christen two Children
at a Spring, where their Mothers waylaid us for
that good Purpose.

27. It was ten of the clock before the Surveyors
got to work, because some of the Horses had
straggled to a great Distance from the Camp.
Nevertheless, meeting with Practicable Woods,
they advanct the Line 9 Miles and 104 Poles.
We crosst over Pea-Creek about four Miles from
our Quarters, and three Miles farther, Lizzard-
Creek, both which empty their Waters into Roanoak River.

Between these two Creeks a poor Man waited
for us with five Children to be baptiz'd, and we
halted till the Ceremony was ended.   The Land
seem'd to be very good, by the largeness of the
Trees, tho' very Stony.   We proceeded as far as
Pidgeon-Roost-Creek, which also runs into Roanoak, and there Quarter'd.

We had not the pleasure of the Company of any
of the Carolina-Commissioners in this day's March,
except Mr. Moseley's, the rest tarrying behind to
wait the coming up of their Baggage-Cart, which

they had now not seen nor heard (though the
Wheels made a Dismal Noise) for several days
past.

Indeed it was a very difficult Undertaking to
conduct a Cart thro' such pathless and perplext
Woods, and no wonder if its Motion was a little
Planetary. We would have payd them the Complement of waiting for them, cou'd we have done
it at any other Expense but that of the Publick.

In the Stony Grounds we rode over we found
great Quantity of the true Ipocoacanna, which in
this part of the World is call'd Indian-Physick.
This has Several Stalks growing up from the Same
Root about a Foot high, bearing a Leaf resembling
that of a Straw-Berry. It is not so strong as that
from Brazil, but has the same happy Effects, If
taken in Somewhat a larger Dose. It is an Excellent Vomit, and generally cures intermitting Fevers
and Bloody Fluxes at once or twice taking. There
is abundance of it in the upper part of the Country,
where it delights most in a Stony Soil intermixt
with black Mold.

28. Our Surveyors got early to work, yet cou'd
forward the Line but 6 miles and 121 Poles, because of the uneven Grounds in the Neighbourhood of Roanoak, which they crosst in this Day's
work.

In that Place the River is 49 Poles wide, and
rolls down a crystal Stream of very Sweet water,
Insomuch that when there comes to be a great
Monarch in this Part of the World, he will cause
all the Water for his own Table to be brought

from Roanoak, as the great Kings of Persia did theirs from the Nile and Choaspis, because the Waters of those Rivers were light, and not apt to corrupt.[1]

The great Falls of Roanoak lie about 20 Miles lower, to which a Sloop of Moderate Burthen may come up.   There are, besides these, many Smaller Falls above, tho' none that entirely intercept the Passage of the River, as the great Ones do, by a Chain of Rocks for 8 Miles together.

The River forks about 36 Miles higher, and both Branches are pretty equal in Breadth where they divide, tho' the Southern, now call'd the Dan, runs up the farthest.   That to the North runs away near North-west, and is call'd the Staunton, and heads not far from the Source of Appamatuck River, while the Dan stretches away pretty near West & runs clear thro' the great Mountains.

We did not follow the Surveyors till towards Noon, being detain'd in our camp to Christen Several more Children.   We were conducted a nearer way, by a famous Woodsman, call'd Epaph-roditus Bainton.   This Forester Spends all his time in ranging the Woods, and is said to make great Havock among the Deer, and other Inhabi-tants of the Forest, not much wilder than Himself.

We proceeded to the Canoe-Landing on Roa-noak, where we passt the River with the Baggage.

[1] The same Humour prevails at this day in the Kings of Den-mark, who order all the East India Ships of that nation to call at the Cape of Good Hope, and take in a But of Water from a Spring on the Table Hill, and bring it to Coppenhagen, for their Majesty's own Drink-ing. (Original note.)

But the Horses were directed to a Ford about a Mile higher, call'd by the Indians Moni-seep, which signifies, in their Jargon, Shallow Water. This is the Ford where the Indian-Traders used to cross with their Horses, in their way to the Catauba Nation.

There are many Rocks in the River thereabouts, on which grows a kind of Water Grass, which the wild Geese are fond of, and resort to it in great Numbers.

We landed on the South Side of Roanoak at a Plantation of Colo. Mumford's, where, by that Gentleman's Special Directions, we met with Sundry Refreshments. Here we picht our Tent, for the benefit of the Prospect, upon an Eminence that overlookt a broad Piece of Low Ground, very rich, tho' liable to be overflow'd.

By the way, one of our Men kill'd another Rattle-Snake, with 11 Rattles, having a large Gray Squirrel in his Maw, the head of which was already digested, while the Body remain'd Stil entire.

The way these Snakes catch their Prey is thus: They Ogle the poor little animal, till by force of the Charm he falls down Stupify'd and Senseless on the Ground. In that condition the Snake approaches, and moistens first one Ear and then the Other with his Spawl, and after that the other Parts of the Head, to make all Slippery. When that is done, he draws this Member into his Mouth, and after it, by Slow Degrees, all the rest of the Body.

29. This being Sunday, we had Divine Service and a Sermon, at which Several of the Borderers as-

sisted, and we concluded the Duties of the Day in
the Christening five Children.   Our Devotion being perform'd in the Open Field, like that of Mr.
Whitfield's Flocks, an unfortunate Shower of Rain
had almost disperst our Congregation.   About four
in the Afternoon the Carolina-Commissioners made
a Shift to come up with us, whom we had left at
Pidgeon-Roost Creek the Fryday before, waiting
for their Provisions.   When their Cart came up
they prudently discharg'd it, and rather chose to
hire two Men to carry some part of their Baggage.
The Rest they had been Obliged to leave behind,
in the Crotch of an Old Tree, for want of proper
Conveniences to transport it any farther.

We found in the low Ground Several Plants
of the Fern Root, which is said to be much the
Strongest Antidote yet discover'd against the
Poison of the Rattle-Snake.   The Leaves of it
resemble those of Fern, from whence it obtain'd
its Name.   Several Stalks shoot from the same
Root, about 6 Inches long, that ly mostly on the
Ground.   It grows in a very Rich Soil, under the
Protection of Some tall Tree, that Shades it from
the Meridian Beams of the Sun.   The Root has a
faint Spicy tast, and is preferr'd by the Southern
Indians to all other Counter-poisons in this Country.

But there is another sort preferr'd by the
Northern Indians, that they call Seneca Rattle-
Snake-Root, to which wonderful Vertues are as-
crib'd in the Cure of Pleurisys, Feavers, Rhuma-
tisms, and Dropsys; besides it being a powerful
Antidote against the Venom of the Rattle-Snake.

In the Evening the Messenger we had sent to Christanna return'd with five Saponi Indians. We cou'd not entirely rely on the Dexterity of our own Men, which induced us to send for some of the Indians. We agreed with two of the most expert of them, upon reasonable Terms, to hunt for us the remaining Part of our Expedition. But one of them falling Sick soon after, we were content to take only the other, whose Hunting Name was Bear-skin.

This Indian, either by his Skill or good Luck, Supply'd us plentifully all the way with Meat, Seldom discharging his piece in vain.

By his Assistance, therefore, we were able to keep our men to their Business, without Suffering them to Straggle about the Woods, on pretence of furnishing us with Necessary Food.

30. It had rain'd all night, and made every thing so wet, that our Surveyors cou'd not get to their Work before Noon. They cou'd therefore measure no more than four Miles and 220 Poles, which, according to the best information we cou'd get, was near as high as the uppermost Inhabitant at that time.

We crost the Indian Trading path above-mention'd about a Mile from our Camp, and a Mile beyond that forded Haw-Tree-Creek. The Woods we passed thro' had all the Tokens of Sterility, except a small Poison'd Field, on which grew no Tree bigger than a Slender Sapling. The larger Trees had been destroyed, either by Fire or Caterpillars, which is often the Case in the upland Woods, and the places where such Desolation happens are call'd Poison'd Fields.

We took up our Quarters upon a Branch of Great Creek, where there was tolerable good Grass for the poor Horses. These poor Animals having now got beyond the Latitude of Corn, were obliged to Shift as well as they cou'd for themselves.

On our way the men rous'd a Bear, which being the first we had seen since we came out, the poor Beast had many pursuers. Several Persons contended for the Credit of killing him: tho' he was so poor he was not worth the Powder. This was some Disappointment to our Woodsmen, who commonly prefer the Flesh of Bears to every kind of Venison. There is Something indeed peculiar to this Animal, namely, that its fat is very firm, and may be eaten plentifully without rising in the Stomach. The Paw (which, when stript of the hair, looks like a Human Foot,) is accounted a delicious Morsel by all who are not Shockt at the ungracious Resemblance it bears to a Human Foot.

Oct. 1. There was a white Frost this morning on the Ground, occasion'd by a North-West Wind, which stood our Friend in dispersing all Aguish Damps, and making the Air wholesome at the Same time that it made it cold. Encourag'd therefore by the Weather, Our Surveyors got to work early, and by the Benefit of Clear Woods, and Level Ground, drove the Line 12 Miles and 12 Poles.

At a Small Distance from our Camp we crost Great Creek, and about 7 Miles farther Nut-bush

Creek, so call'd from the many Hazle-Trees growing upon it. By good Luck Many Branches of
these Creeks were full of Reeds, to the great comfort of our Horses. Near five Miles from thence
we encampt on a Branch that runs into Nut-Bush
Creek, where those Reeds flourisht more than
Ordinary. The Land we marcht over was for the
most part broken and Stony, and in some places
cover'd over with Thickets almost impenetrable.

At Night the Surveyors, taking Advantage of a
very clear Sky, made a third Tryal of the Variation, and found it Still something less than 3
Degrees, so that it did not diminish by advancing
towards the West, or by approaching the Mountains, nor yet by encreasing our distance from the
Sea; but remain'd much the Same we had found
it at Corotuck-Inlet.

One of our Indians kill'd a large Fawn, which
was very welcome, tho', like Hudibras's Horse, it
had hardly Flesh enough to cover its Bones.

In the low Grounds the Carolina Gentlemen
shew'd us another Plant, which they said was
used in their country to cure the Bite of the Rattle-Snake. It put forth Several Leaves in figure
like a Heart, and was clouded so like the common
Assarabacca, that I conceived it to be of that
Family.

2. So soon as the Horses cou'd be found, we
hurry'd away the Surveyors, who advanct the Line
9 Miles and 254 Poles. About 3 Miles from the
Camp they crosst a large Creek, which the Indians
call'd Massamoni, Signifying, in their Language,

Paint-Creek, because of the great Quantity of Red ochre found in its banks. This in every Fresh tinges the Water just as the same Mineral did formerly, and to this day continues to tinge, the famous River Adonis, in Phoenicia, by which there hangs a celebrated Fable.

Three Miles beyond that we past another Water with difficulty, call'd Yaypatsco, or Bever Creek. Those industrious Animals had damm'd up the water so high, that we had much ado to get over. Tis hardly credible how much work of this kind they will do in the Space of one Night. They bite young Saplings into proper Lengths with their Fore-teeth, which are exceeding Strong and Sharp, and afterwards drag them to the Place where they intend to Stop the Water.

Then they know how to join Timber and Earth together with so much Skill, that their Work is able to resist the most violent Flood that can happen. In this they are qualify'd to instruct their Betters, it being certain their damms will stand firm when the Strongest that are made by men will be carry'd down the Stream.

We observed very broad low Grounds upon this Creek, with a growth of large Trees, and all the other Signs of Fertility, but seem'd subject to be every where overflow'd in a fresh.

The certain way to catch these Sagacious Animals is thus: Squeeze all the Juice out of the large Pride of the Beaver, and 6 drops out of the small Pride. Powder the inward Bark of Sassafras, and mix it with this Juice, then bait therewith a Steel

Trap, and they will eagerly come to it, and be taken.

About three Miles and a half farther we came to the Banks of another creek, call'd, in the Saponi Language, Ohimpa-moni, Signifying Jumping Creek, from the frequent Jumping of Fish during the Spring Season.

Here we encampt, and by the time the Horses were hobbled, our Hunters brought us no less than a Brace and a half of Deer, which made great Plenty, and consequently great content in our Quarters.

Some of our People had Shot a great Wild Cat, which was that fatal moment making a comfortable Meal upon a Fox-Squirrel, and an Ambitious Sportsman of our Company claim'd the merit of killing this monster after it was dead.

The Wild-cat is as big again as any Household-Cat, and much the fiercest Inhabitant of the Woods. Whenever 'tis disabled, it will tear its own Flesh for madness. Altho' a Panther will run away from a Man, a Wild-cat will only make a Surly Retreat, now and then facing about, if he be too closely pursued; and will even pursue in his turn, if he observe the least Sign of Fear or even of caution in those that pretend to follow Him.

The Flesh of this Beast, as well as of the Panther, is as white as veal, and altogether as sweet and delicious.

3. We got to work early this Morning, and carry'd the line 8 Miles and a 160 Poles. We forded Several Runs of Excellent Water, and afterwards

traverst a large levil of high land full of lofty
Walnut, Poplar, and White Oak Trees, which
are certain Proofs of a fruitful Soil. This levil
was near two Miles in length, and of an unknown
breadth, quite out of Danger of being overflow'd,
which is a misfortune most of the Low Grounds
are liable to in those Parts. As we marcht along
we saw many Buffalo-Tracks, and abundance of
their Dung very Fresh, but could not have the
pleasure of seeing them. They either Smelt us
out, having that sense very Quick, or else were
alarm'd at the Noise that so many People must
necessarily make in marching along. At the
Sight of a Man they will Snort and Grunt, cock
up their ridiculous Short Tails, and tear up the
Ground with a Sort of Timorous Fury.

These wild Cattle hardly ever range alone, but
herd together like those that are tame. They are
Seldom seen so far North as 40° of latitude, delighting much in canes and Reeds, which grow
generally more Southerly.

We quarter'd on the Banks of a Creek that the
Inhabitants call Tewahominy, or Tuskarooda
creek, because one of that Nation had been kill'd
thereabouts, and his Body thrown into the Creek.

Our People had the Fortune to kill a Brace of
does, one of which we presented to the Carolina-
Gentlemen, who were glad to partake of the
Bounty of Providence, at the same time that they
sneer'd at us for depending upon it.

4. We hurry'd away the Surveyors about 9 this
Morning, who extended the Line 7 Miles and 160

Poles, notwithstanding the Ground was exceedingly uneaven. At the Distance of five Miles we forded a stream to which we gave the Name of Blewing creek, because of the great Number of those Fowls that then frequented it.

About 2½ Miles beyond that, we came upon Sugar-Tree-Creek, so call'd from the many Trees of that kind that grow upon it. By tapping this Tree, in the first Warm weather in February, one may get from 20 to 40 Gallons of Liquor, very sweet to the tast and agreeable to the Stomach. This may be boil'd into molosses first, and afterwards into very good Sugar, allowing about 10 Gallons of the Liquor to make a Pound. There's no doubt, too, that a very fine Spirit may be distill'd from the molosses, at least as good as Rum. The Sugar Tree delights only in Rich Ground, where it grows very tall, and by the Softness and Spunginess of the Wood shou'd be a quick Grower.

Near this Creek we discovered likewise Several Spice-Trees, the Leaves of which are fragrant, and the Berries they bear are black when dry, and of a hot tast, not much unlike Pepper.

The low Grounds upon the creek are very wide, sometimes on one Side, Sometimes on the Other; tho' most commonly upon the Opposite Shore the high-land advances close to the Bank, only on the North-Side of the Line it spreads itself into a great Breadth of rich low Ground on both sides the Creek for four Miles together, as far as this Stream runs into Hico-River, whereof I shall presently make mention.

One of our Men Spy'd three Buffaloes, but his Piece being loaded only with Goose-shot, he was able to make no effectual Impression on their thick hides; however, this Disappointment was made up by a Brace of Bucks, and as many Wild Turkeys, kill'd by the rest of the company.

Thus Providence was very Bountiful to our Endeavours, never disappointing those that faithfully rely upon it, and pray heartily for their Daily Bread.

5. This day we met with such uneven Grounds, and thick Underwoods, that with all our Industry we were able to advance the Line but 4 Miles and 312 Poles. In this small Distance it intersected a large stream four times, which our Indian at first mistook for the South Branch of Roanoke River; but, discovering his Error soon after, he assur'd us 'twas a River called Hicootomony,[1] or Turkey-Buzzard River, from the great Number of those unsavoury Birds that roost on the tall Trees growing near its banks.

Early in the Afternoon, to our very great surprize, the Commissioners of Carolina acquainted us with their Resolution to return Home. This Declaration of theirs seem'd the more abrupt, because they had not been so kind as to prepare us, by the least Hint, of their Intention to desert us.

We therefore let them understand they Appear'd to us to abandon the Business they came about with too much Precipitation, this being but the 15th day since we came out the last time. But,

---

[1] Shortened to Hico.

altho' we were to be so unhappy as to lose the
Assistance of their great Abilities, yet we, who
were concern'd for Virginia, determin'd by the
Grace of God, not to do our Work by Halves, but,
all deserted as we were like to be, shou'd think it
our duty to push the Line quite to the Mountains;
and if their Government should refuse to be bound
by so much of the Line as was run without their
Commissioners, yet at least it would bind Virginia,
and Stand as a Direction how far his Majesty's
Lands extend to the Southward.

In short, these Gentlemen were positive, and the
most we could agree upon was to Subscribe plats
of our work as far as we had Acted together; tho'
at the same time we insisted these Plats should be
got ready by Monday Noon at farthest, when we
on the Part of Virginia intended, if we were alive,
to move forward without farther loss of Time, the
Season being then too far advanct to admit of any
unnecessary or complaisant delays.

6. We lay still this day, being Sunday, on the
Bank of Hico River, and had only Prayers, our
Chaplain not having Spirits enough to preach.
The Gentlemen of Carolina assisted not at our
Publick Devotions, because they were taken up
all the Morning in making a formidable Protest
against our Proceeding on the Line without them.

When the Divine Service was over, the Surveyors sat about making the Plats of so much of
the Line as we had run this last Campaign. Our
pious Friends of Carolina assisted in this work
with some Seeming Scruple, pretending it was a

Violation of the Sabbath, which we were the more
Surpriz'd at, because it happen'd to be the first
Qualm of Conscience they had ever been troubled
with dureing the whole journey. They had made
no Bones of Staying from prayers to hammer out
an unnecessary Protest, tho' Divine Service was
no Sooner over, but an unusual Fit of Godliness
made them fancy that finishing the Plats, which
was now matter of necessity, was a prophanation
of the Day. However, the Expediency of losing
no time, for us who thought it our duty to finish
what we had undertaken, made such a Labour
pardonnable.

In the Afternoon, Mr. Fitz William, one of the
Commissioners for Virginia, acquainted his Collegues it was his Opinion, that by his Majesty's
Order they could not proceed farther on the Line,
but in Conjunction with the Commissioners of
Carolina; for which reason he intended to retire,
the Next Morning, with those Gentlemen.

This lookt a little odd in our Brother Commissioner; tho', in Justice to Him, as well as to our
Carolina Friends, they stuck by us as long as our
good Liquor lasted, and were so kind to us as to
drink our good Journey to the Mountains in the
last Bottle we had left.

7. The Duplicates of the plats cou'd not be
drawn fair this day before Noon, when they were
countersign'd by the Commissioners of Each
Government. Then those of Carolina deliver'd
their Protest, which was by this time lickt into
form, and sign'd by them all. And we have been

so just to them as to set it down at full length in
the Appendix, that their Reasons for leaving us
may appear in their full Strength.

After having thus adjusted all our Affairs with
the Carolina Commissioners, and kindly supply'd
them with Bread to carry them back, which they
hardly deserv'd at our hands, we took leave both
of them and our colleague, Mr. Fitzwilliam.

This Gentleman had stil a Stronger Reason for
hurrying him back to Williamsburg, which was,
that neither the General Court might lose an able
Judge, nor himself a double Salary, not despairing
in the least but he shou'd have the whole pay of
Commissioner into the Bargain, tho' he did not
half the Work. This, to be sure, was relying more
on the Interest of his Friends than on the Justice
of his cause; in which, however, he had the misfortune to miscarry, when it came to be fairly
considered.

It was two a clock in the Afternoon before these
arduous Affairs could be despatcht, and then, all
forsaken as we were, we held on our course towards the West. But it was our misfortune to
meet with so many Thickets in this Afternoon's
Work, that we cou'd advance no further than 2
Miles and 260 Poles.

In this small Distance we crosst the Hico the
fifth time, and Quarter'd near Buffalo-Creek, so
nam'd from the frequent Tokens we discover'd of
that American Behemoth.

Here the Bushes were so intolerably thick, that
we were oblig'd to cover the Bread Baggs with

our Deer Skins, otherwise the Joke of one of the Indians must have happen'd to us in good Earnest, that in a few days We must cut up our House to make Bags for the Bread, and so be forct to expose our Backs in compliment to our Bellys.

We computed we had then Bisquet enough left to last us, with good Management, Seven Weeks longer; And this being our chief Dependence, it imported us to be very careful both in the Carriage and the Distribution of it.

We had no other Drink but what Adam drank in Paradise, tho' to our comfort we found the Water excellent, by the Help of which we perceiv'd our Appetites to mend, our Slumbers to Sweeten, the Stream of Life to run cool and peaceably in our Veins, and if ever we dreamt of Women, they were kind.

Our men kill'd a very fat Buck and Several Turkeys. These two kinds of Meat boil'd together, with the addition of a little Rice or French Barley, made excellent Soupe, and, what happens rarely in Other good things, it never cloy'd, no more than an Engaging Wife wou'd do, by being a Constant Dish.

Our Indian was very Superstitious in this Matter, and told us, with a face full of concern, that if we continued to boil Venison and Turkey together, we Shou'd for the future kill nothing, because the Spirit that presided over the Woods would drive all the Game out of our Sight. But we had the Happiness to find this an Idle Superstition, and tho' his Argument could not convince us, yet our repeated Experience at last, with much ado, convinc'd Him.

We observ'd abundance of Colt's foot and Maiden-hair in many Places, and nowhere a larger Quantity than here. They are both Excellent Pectoral Plants, and seem to have greater Vertues much in this part of the World than in more Northern climates; and I believe it may pass for a Rule in Botanicks, that where any Vegetable is planted by the hand of Nature, it has more Vertue than in Places whereto it is transplanted by the Curiosity of Man.

8. Notwithstanding we hurry'd away the Surveyors very early, yet the Underwoods embarrass'd them so much that they cou'd with Difficulty advance the Line 4 Miles and 20 Poles.

Our Cloaths Suffer'd extreamely by the Bushes, and it was really as much as both our hands could do to preserve our Eyes in our Heads. Our poor Horses, too, could hardly drag their Loads thro' the Saplings, which stood so close together that it was necessary for them to draw and carry at the same time.

We quarter'd near a Spring of very fine Water, Soft as oyl and as cold as Ice, to make us amends for the want of Wine. And our Indian knockt down a very fat Doe, just time enough to hinder us from going Supperless to Bed.

The heavy Baggage cou'd not come up with us, because of the Excessive badness of the Ways. This gave us no Small uneasiness, but it went worse with the poor men that guarded it. They had nothing in the World with them but dry Bread, nor durst they eat any of that, for fear of inflaming their Thirst, in a Place where they could find no Water to quench it.

This was, however, the better to be endured, because it was the first Fast any one had kept dureing the whole Journey, and then, Thanks to the gracious Guardian of the Woods! there was no more than a Single Meal lost to a few of the Company.

We were entertain'd this Night with the Yell of a whole Family of Wolves, in which we cou'd distinguish the Treble, Tenor and Bass, very clearly. These Beasts of Prey kept pretty much upon our Track, being tempted by the Garbage of the Creatures we kill'd every day; for which we were Serenaded with their Shrill Pipes almost every Night. This Beast is not so untamable as the Panther, but the Indians know how to gentle their Whelps, and use them about their cabans instead of Dogs.

9. The Thickets were hereabouts so impenetrable, that we were obliged, at first setting off this Morning, to order four Pioneers to clear the way before the Surveyors. But after about 2 Miles of these rough-woods, we had the Pleasure to meet with Open Grounds and not very uneven, by the help of which we were enabled to push the Line about 6 Miles.

The Baggage that lay Short of our camp last Night came up about Noon, and the Men made heavy Complaints, that they had been half Starv'd, like Tantalus, in the midst of plenty, for the Reason above mention'd.

The Soil we past over this Day was generally very good, being cloath'd with large Trees, of Poplar, Hiccory, and Oak. But another certain Token of its Fertility was, that wild Angelica grew plentifully upon it.

The Root of this Plant being very warm and Aromatick, is coveted by Woodsmen extremely as a dry Dram, that is, when Rum, that cordial for all Distresses, is wanting.

Several Deer came into our View as we marcht along, but none into the Pot, which made it necessary for us to sup on the Fragments we had been so provident as to carry along with us. This being but a temperate Repast, made some of our hungry Fellows call the Place we lodg'd at that Night, Bread and Water Camp.

A great Flock of Cranes flew over our Quarters, that were exceeding Clamorous in their Flight. They seem to steer their Course towards the South (being Birds of Passage) in Quest of Warmer Weather. They only took this Country in their way, being as rarely met with, in this part of the World, as a Highwayman or a Beggar.

These Birds travel generally in Flocks, and when they roost they place Sentinels upon some of the highest Trees, which constantly stand upon one leg to keep themselves waking.[1]

[1] Nor are these Birds the only Animals that appoint Scouts to keep the main Body from being surpriz'd. For the Baboons, whenever they go upon any mischievous Expedition, such as robbing an Orchard, they place centinels to look out

Our Indian kill'd nothing all day but a Mountain Patridge, which a little resembled the common Partridge in the Plumage, but was near as large as a Dunghill Hen. These are very frequent towards the Mountains, tho' we had the fortune to meet with very few. They are apt to be Shy, and consequently the Noise of so great a Number of People might easily Scare them away from our Sight.

We found what we conceiv'd to be Good Limestone in several Places, and a great Quantity of Blue Slate.

10. The day began very fortunately by killing a Fat Doe, and Two Brace of wild Turkeys; so the Plenty of the Morning made amends for the Short Commons over Night. One of the new men we brought out with us the last time was unfortunately heard to wish himself at Home, and for that Shew of Impatience was publickly reprimanded at the Head of the men, who were all drawn up to witness his Disgrace.

He was askt how he came so soon to be tired of the Company of so many brave Fellows, and whe-

towards every Point of the Compass, and give notice of any danger. Then ranking themselves in one File, that reaches from the mountains where they harbour, to the Orchard they intend to rob, some of them toss the Fruits from the Trees to those that stand nearest, these throw them to the next, and so from one to tother, til the fruit is all secured in a few Minutes out of Harm's way. In the mean time, if any of the Scouts should be careless at their Posts & Suffer any Surprize, they are torn to pieces without Mercy. In case of danger these centinels Set up a fearful cry, upon which the rest take the alarm, and Scour away to the Mountains as fast as they can. (Original note.)

ther it was the Danger or Fatigue of the Journey
that dishearten'd Him? This publick Reproof
from thenceforward put an effectual Stop to all
complaints, and not a man amongst us after that
pretended so much as to wish himself in Paradise.

A Small Distance from our Camp we crosst a
pleasant Stream of Water call'd Cocquade Creek,
and something more than a Mile from thence our
Line intersected the South Branch of Roanoak
River the first time, which we call'd the Dan. It
was about 200 Yards wide where we forded it, and
when we came over to the West Side, we found
the Banks lin'd with a Forest of Tall canes, that
grew more than a furlong in depth. So that it
cost us abundance of time and Labour to cut a
Passage thro' them wide enough for our Baggage.

In the mean time we had leizure to take a full
view of this charming River. The Stream, which
was perfectly clear, ran down about two Knots, or
two Miles, an Hour, when the water was at the
lowest. The Bottom was cover'd with a coarse
Gravel, Spangled very thick with a Shining Substance, that almost dazzled the eye, and the Sand
upon either Shore Sparkled with the same Splendid
Particles.

At first Sight, the Sun-Beams giving a Yellow
cast to these Spangles made us fancy them to be
Gold-Dust, and consequently that all our Fortunes
were made. Such Hopes as these were the less
extravagant, because several Rivers lying much
about the Same Latitude with this have formerly
abounded with Fragments of that tempting Metal.

Witness the Tagus in Portugal, the Heber in
Thrace, and the Pactolus in Lesser Asia; Not to
mention the Rivers on the Gold Coast in Africa,
which ly in a more Southern Climate.

But we soon found our Selves mistaken, and our
Gold Dust dwindled into small Flakes of ising-
glass.   However, tho' this did not make the River
so rich as we cou'd wish, yet it made it exceedingly Beautiful.

We marcht about two Miles and a half beyond
this River, as far as Cane Creek, so call'd from a
Prodigious Quantity of tall canes that fring'd the
Banks of it.

On the West side of this Creek we markt out
our Quarters, and were glad to find our Horses
fond of the canes, tho' they Scowred them smartly
at first, and discolor'd their Dung.   This beautiful
Vegetable grows commonly from 12 to 16 feet
High, and some of them as thick as a Man's wrist.

Tho' these appear'd large to us, yet they are no
more than Spires of Grass, if compar'd to those
which some curious Travellers tell us grow in the
East Indies, one Joint of which will make a Brace
of Canoes, if saw'd in two in the Middle.   Ours
continue green thro' all the Seasons during the
Space of Six Years, and the Seventh shed their
Seed, wither away and Die.   The Spring following
they begin to Shoot again, and reach their former
Stature the Second or third Year after.

They grow so thick, and their Roots lace together so firmly, that they are the best Guard that
can be of the River-Bank, which wou'd otherwise

be washt away by the frequent Inundations that happen in this part of the World.

They would also serve excellently well to plant on the Borders of Fish-Ponds and Canals, to secure their sides from falling in; tho' I fear they would not grow kindly in a cold Country, being seldom seen here so Northerly as 38 Degrees of Latitude.

11. At the Distance of 4 Miles and 60 Poles from the Place where we encampt, we came upon the River Dan a Second time; tho' It was not so wide in this Place as where we crosst it first, being not above a 150 yards over.

The West Shore continued to be cover'd with the Canes above mention'd, but not to so great a Breadth as before, and 'tis Remarkable that these canes are much more frequent on the West Side of the River than on the East, where they grow generally very scattering.

It was Still a beautiful Stream, rolling down its limpid and murmuring waters among the Rocks, which lay scatter'd here and there, to make up the variety of the Prospect.

It was about two Miles from this River to the End of our Day's Work, which led us mostly over Broken Grounds and troublesome Underwoods. Hereabout, from one of the Highest hills, we made the first Discovery of the Mountains, on the Northwest of our course. They seem'd to lye off at a vast Distance, and lookt like Ranges of Blue clouds rising one above another.

We encampt about two Miles beyond the River, where we made good chear upon a very fat Buck,

that luckily fell in our way. The Indian likewise
Shot a Wild Turkey, but confest he wou'd not
bring it us, lest we shou'd continue to provoke the
Guardian of the Forrest, by cooking the Beasts of
the Field and the Birds of the Air together in one
vessel.

This Instance of Indian Superstition, I confess,
is countenanced in some measure by the Levitical
Law, which forbad the mixing of things of a Dif-
ferent Nature together in the Same field, or in the
Same Garment, and why not then in the same
Kettle?

But, after all, if the Jumbleing of two Sorts of
Flesh together be a Sin, how intolerable an Of-
fence must it be to make a Spanish Ole, that is, a
Hotchpotch of every kind of thing that is eatable?
And the good People of England wou'd have a
great deal to answer for, for beating up so many
different Ingredients into a Pudding.

12. We were so cruelly intangled with Bushes
and Grape-Vines all day, that we could advance
the Line no farther than 5 Miles and 28 Poles.

The Vines grow very thick in these Woods,
twineing lovingly round the Trees almost every
where, especially to the Saplings. This makes it
evident how Natural both the Soil and Climate of
this Country are to Vines, tho' I believe most to
our own Vines.

The Grapes we commonly met with were black,
tho' there be two or three kinds of White Grapes
that grow wild. The Black are very Sweet, but
Small, because the Strength of the Vine spends

itself in Wood; tho' without Question a proper Culture would make the same Grapes both larger and Sweeter. But, with all these Disadvantages, I have Drunk tolerably good Wine prest from them, tho' made without Skill. There is then good Reason to believe it might Admit of great Improvement, if rightly managed.

Our Indian kill'd a Bear, of two years old, that was feasting on these Grapes. He was very fat, as they generally are in that season of the year. In the fall, the Flesh of this Animal has a high Relish, different from that of other Creatures, tho' inclining nearest to that of Pork, or rather of Wild Boar.

A true Woodsman prefers this Sort of meat to that of the fattest Venison, not only for the *Haut-gout* but also because the Fat of it is well tasted, and never rises in the stomach. Another proof of the goodness of this meat is, that it is less apt to corrupt than any other we are acquainted with. As agreeable as such rich Diet was to the men, yet we who were not accustom'd to it, tasted it at first with some sort of Squeamishness, that Animal being of the Dog-kind ; tho' a little Use soon reconcil'd us to this American Venison. And that its being of the Dog kind might give us the less disgust, we had the Example of that Ancient and polite People, the Chinese, who reckon Dog's Flesh too good for any under the Quality of a mandarin.

This Beast is in truth a very clean Feeder, living, while the Season lasts, upon Acorns, Chesnuts and Chinkapins, Wild-Hony and Wild-Grapes.

They are naturally not carniverous, unless Hunger constrains them to it, after the Mast is all gone, and the Products of the Woods quite exhausted.

They are not provident enough to lay up any Hoard, like the Squirrels, nor can they, after all, live very long upon licking their Paws, as Sr John Mandevil and some Travellers tell us, but are forct in the Winter Months to quit the Mountains, and visit the Inhabitants.

Their Errand is then to Surprise a poor Hog at a Pinch to keep them from Starving. And to shew that they are not Flesh-Eaters by Trade, they devour their Prey very awkwardly.

They don't kill it right out, and feast upon its Blood and Entrails, like other ravenous Beasts, but having, after a fair pursuit, seiz'd it with their Paws, they begin first upon the Rump, and so devour one collop after another, till they come to the Vitals, the poor Animal crying all the while, for several Minutes together. However, in so doing, Bruin acts a little imprudently, because the dismal outcry of the Hog alarms the Neighbourhood, and 'tis odds but he pays the forfeit with his Life, before he can Secure his Retreat.

But Bears soon grow weary of this unnatural Diet, and about January, when there is nothing to be got in the Woods, they retire into some cave or hollow Tree, where they Sleep away two or three Months very comfortably. But then they quit their Holes in March, when the Fish begin to run up the Rivers, on which they are forct to keep Lent, till some Fruit or Berry comes in Season.

But Bears are fondest of chesnuts, which grow plentifully towards the Mountains, upon very large Trees, where the Soil happens to be rich. We were curious to know how it happen'd that many of the outward Branches of those Trees came to be brok off in that Solitary Place, and were inform'd that the Bears are so discreet as not to trust their unwieldy Bodies on the Smaller Limbs of the Tree, that would not bear their weight; but after venturing as far as is safe, which they can judge to an Inch, they bite off the End of the Branch, which falling down, they are content to finish their Repast upon the Ground. In the same Cautious Manner they secure the Acorns that grow on the weaker Limbs of the Oak. And it must be allow'd that, in these Instances, a Bear carries Instinct a great way, and Acts more reasonably than many of his Betters, who indiscreetly Venture upon frail Projects that wont bear them.

13. This being Sunday, we rested from our Fatigue, and had leisure to reflect on the signal Mercies of Providence.

The great Plenty of Meat wherewith Bearskin furnisht us in these lonely Woods made us once more Shorten the men's allowance of Bread, from 5 to 4 Pounds of bisket a week. This was the more necessary, because we knew not yet how long our Business might require us to be out.

In the Afternoon our Hunters went forth, and return'd triumphantly with three brace of wild Turkeys. They told us they cou'd see the Moun-

tains distinctly from every Eminence, tho' the Atmosphere was so thick with Smoak that they
appear'd at a greater Distance than they really
were.

In the Evening we examin'd our Friend Bearskin, concerning the Religion of his Country, and
he explain'd it to us, without any of that Reserve
to which his Nation is Subject.

He told us he believ'd there was one Supreme
God, who had Several Subaltern Deities under
Him.   And that this Master-God made the World
a long time ago.   That he told the Sun, the Moon,
and Stars, their Business in the Beginning, which
they, with good looking after, have faithfully perform'd ever Since.

That the same Power that made all things at
first has taken care to keep them in the same
Method and Motion ever since.

He believ'd God had form'd many Worlds before he form'd this, but that those Worlds either
grew old and ruinous, or were destroyed for the
Dishonesty of the Inhabitants.

That God is very just and very good — ever
well pleas'd with those men who possess those
God-like Qualities.   That he takes good People
into his safe Protection, makes them very rich, fills
their Bellies plentifully, preserves them from sickness, and from being surpriz'd or Overcome by
their Enemies.

But all such as tell Lies, and Cheat those they
have Dealings with, he never fails to punish with
Sickness, Poverty and Hunger, and, after all that,

Suffers them to be knockt on the Head and scalpt by those that fight against them.

He believ'd that after Death both good and bad People are conducted by a strong Guard into a great Road, in which departed Souls travel together for some time, till at a certain Distance this Road forks into two Paths, the one extremely Levil, and the other Stony and Mountainous.

Here the good are parted from the Bad by a flash of Lightening, the first being hurry'd away to the Right, the other to the Left. The Right hand Road leads to a charming warm Country, where the Spring is everlasting, and every Month is May; and as the year is always in its Youth, so are the People, and particularly the Women are bright as Stars, and never Scold.

That in this happy Climate there are Deer, Turkeys, Elks, and Buffaloes innumerable, perpetually fat and gentle, while the Trees are loaded with delicious Fruit quite throughout the four Seasons.

That the Soil brings forth Corn Spontaneously, without the Curse of Labour, and so very wholesome, that None who have the happiness to eat of it are ever Sick, grow old, or dy.

Near the Entrance into this Blessed Land Sits a Venerable Old Man on a Mat richly woven, who examins Strictly all that are brought before Him, and if they have behav'd well, the Guards are order'd to open the Crystal Gate, and let them enter into the Land of Delights.

The left Hand Path is very rugged and uneaven, leading to a dark and barren Country, where it is always Winter. The Ground is the whole year round cover'd with Snow, and nothing is to be seen upon the Trees but Icicles.

All the People are hungry, yet have not a Morsel of any thing to eat, except a bitter kind of Potato, that gives them the Dry-Gripes, and fills their whole Body with loathsome Ulcers, that Stink, and are insupportably painfull.

Here all the Women are old and ugly, having Claws like a Panther, with which they fly upon the Men that Slight their Passion. For it seems these haggard old Furies are intolerably fond, and expect a vast deal of Cherishing. They talk much and exceedingly Shrill, giving exquisite Pain to the Drum of the Ear, which in that Place of the Torment is so tender, that every Sharp Note wounds it to the Quick.

At the End of this Path sits a dreadful old Woman on a monstrous Toad-Stool, whose head is cover'd with Rattle-Snakes instead of Tresses, with glaring white Eyes, that strike a Terror unspeakable into all that behold her.

This Hag pronounces Sentence of Woe upon all the miserable Wretches that hold up their hands at her Tribunal. After this they are deliver'd over to huge Turkey-Buzzards, like harpys, that fly away with them to the Place above mentioned.

Here, after they have been tormented a certain Number of years, according to their several Degrees of Guilt, they are again driven back into this World, to try if they will mend their Manners,

and merit a place the next time in the Regions of
Bliss.

This was the Substance of Bearskin's Religion,
and was as much to the purpose as cou'd be expected from a meer State of Nature, without one
Glimpse of Revelation or Philosophy.

It contain'd, however, the three Great Articles
of Natural Religion: The Belief of a God; The
Moral Distinction betwixt Good and Evil; and the
Expectation of Rewards and Punishments in Another World.

Indeed, the Indian Notion of a Future Happiness is a little Gross and Sensual, like Mahomet's
Paradise.   But how can it be otherwise, in a People that are contented with Nature as they find
Her, and have no other Lights but what they receive from purblind Tradition?

14. There having been great Signs of Rain yesterday Evening, we had taken our Precautions in
Securing the Bread, and trenching in our Tent.

The men had also Stretcht their Blankets upon
Poles, Penthouse fashion, against the Weather, so
that nobody was taken unprepar'd.

It began to fall heavily about three a'clock in
the Morning, and held not up till near Noon.
Everything was so thoroughly Soakt, that we laid
aside all thoughts of decamping that Day.

This gave leizure to the most expert of our Gunners to go and try their Fortunes, and they succeeded so well, that they return'd about Noon with
three fat Deer, and 4 wild Turkeys.   Thus Providence took care of us, and however short the Men

might be in their Bread, 'tis certain they had Meat at full Allowance.

The Cookery went on Merrily all Night long, to keep the Damps from entering our Pores; and in truth the Impressions of the Air are much more powerfull upon empty Stomachs.

In such a Glut of Provisions, a true Woodsman, when he has nothing else to do, like our honest countrymen the Indians, keeps eating on, to avoid the imputation of Idleness; Though, in a Scarcity, the Indian will fast with a much better Grace than they. They can Subsist Several days upon a little Rockahominy, which is parcht Indian Corn reduc'd to powder. This they moisten in the hollow of their Hands with a little water, and 'tis hardly credible how small a Quantity of it will Support them. Tis true they grow a little lank upon it, but to make themselves feel full, they gird up their Loins very tight with a Belt, taking up a Hole every day. With this Slender Subsistence they are able to travel very long Journeys; but then, to make themselves Amends, when they do meet with better Chear, they eat without ceasing, till they have raven'd themselves into another Famine.

This was the first time we had ever been detain'd a whole day in our camp by the Rain, and therefore had Reason to bear it with the more patience.

As I sat in the Tent I overheard a learn'd conversation between one of our men and the Indian. He ask't the Englishman what it was that made that rumbling noise when it thunder'd?

The man told him merrily, that the God of the English was firing his great Guns upon the God of the Indians, which made all the roaring in the clouds, and that the Lightening was only the Flash of those Guns.

The Indian carrying on the Humour reply'd very gravely, He believed that might be the case indeed, and that the Rain which follow'd upon the Thunder must be occasion'd by the Indian God's being so scar'd he could not hold his Water.

The few good Husbands amongst us took some thought of their Backs as well as their Bellies, and made use of this Opportunity to put their Habiliments in repair, which had Suffer'd wofully by the Bushes.

The Horses got some rest by reason of the bad weather, but very little Food, the chief of their Forage being a little wild Rosemary, which resembles the Garden Rosemary pretty much in Figure, but not at all in taste or smell. This Plant grows in small Tufts here and there on the Barren Land in these upper Parts, and the Horses liked it well, but the misfortune was, they cou'd not get enough of it to fill their Bellies.

15. After the Clouds brake away in the Morning, the People dryed their Blankets with all diligence. Nevertheless, it was Noon before we were in condition to move forward, and then were so puzzled with passing the river twice in a Small Distance, that we could advance the Line in all no farther than One Single Mile and 300 Poles.

The first time we past the Dan this day was 240

Poles from the Place where we lay, and the Second
time was one Mile and Seven Poles beyond that.
This was now the fourth time we forded that fine
River, which still tended westerly, with many Short
and returning Reaches.

The Surveyors had much Difficulty in getting
over the River, finding it deeper than formerly.
The Breadth of it here did not exceed fifty Yards.
The Banks were about 20 feet high from the Water, and beautifully beset with canes.

Our Baggage Horses crost not the River here
at all, but, fetching a compass, went round the
Bent of it.   On our Way we forded Sable-Creek,
so call'd from the Dark Colour of the Water, which
happen'd, I suppose, by its being Shaded on both
Sides with canes.

In the Evening we quarter'd in a Charming
Situation near the angle of the River, from whence
our Eyes were carried down both Reaches, which
kept a Straight Course for a great way together.

This Prospect was so beautiful, that we were
perpetually climbing up to a Neighbouring eminence, that we might enjoy it in more Perfection.

Now the Weather grew cool, the Wild Geese
began to direct their Flight this way from Hudson's Bay, and the Lakes that lay North-west
of us.

They are very lean at their first coming, but fat-
ten soon upon a Sort of Grass that grows on the
Shores and Rocks of this River.

The Indians call this Fowl Cohunks, from the
hoarse Note it has, and begin the year from the

Coming of the Cohunks, which happens in the Beginning of October.

These Wild Geese are guarded from cold by a Down, that is exquisitely soft and fine, which makes them much more valuable for their Feathers than for their Flesh, which is dark and coarse.

The Men chast a Bear into the River that got safe over, notwithstanding the continual fire from the Shore upon Him. He Seem'd to Swim but heavily, considering it was for his Life.

Where the Water is Shallow, 'tis no Uncommon thing to see a Bear sitting, in the Summer time, on a heap of Gravel in the Middle of the River, not only to cool himself, but likewise for the Advantage of Fishing, particularly for a small Shellfish, that is brought down with the Stream.

In the upper part of James River I have observed this Several times, and wonder'd very much, at first, how so many heaps of small Stones came to be piled up in the Water, till at last we spy'd a Bear Sitting upon one of them, looking with great attention on the Stream, and rakeing up Something with his Paw, which I take to be the Shell-fish above mention'd.

16. It was Ten a'clock this Morning before the Horses cou'd be found, having hidden themselves among the canes, whereof there was great plenty just at hand. Not far from our camp we went over a Brook, whose Banks were edg'd on both Sides with these canes. But three Miles further we forded a larger Stream, which we call'd Low Land

Creek, by reason of the great Breadth of Low Grounds inclos'd between that and the River.

The high Land we travell'd over was very good, and the low Grounds promis'd the greatest Fertility of any I had ever seen.

At the End of 4 Miles and 311 Poles from where we lay, the Line intersected the Dan the fifth time. We had day enough to carry it farther, but the Surveyors cou'd find no Safe ford over the River.

This obliged us to ride two Miles up the River in quest of a Ford, and by the way we traverst Several Small Indian Fields, where we conjectur'd the SAWRO'S had been used to plant Corn, the Town where they had liv'd lying Seven or Eight Miles more Southerly, upon the Eastern Side of the River.

These Indian Fields produc'd a Sweet kind of Grass, Almost knee-high, which was excellent Forage for the Horses.

It must be observ'd, by the way, that Indian Towns, like Religious Houses, are remarkabler for a fruitful Situation; for being by Nature not very Industrious, they choose such a Situation as will Subsist them with the least Labour.

The Trees grew Surprisingly large in this low-Ground, and amongst the rest we observ'd a tall kind of hiccory, peculiar to the Upper Parts of the Country. It is cover'd with a very rough Bark, and produces a Nut with a thick Shell that is easily broken. The Kernel is not so rank as that of the Common Hiccory, but altogether as oily.

And now I am upon the Subject of these Nuts,

it may not be improper to remark, that a very great benefit might be made of Nut-Oyl in this Colony. The Walnuts, the Hiccory-Nuts, and Pig-nuts, contain a vast deal of Oyl, that might be press'd out in great abundance with proper Machines.

The Trees grow very kindly, and may be easily propagated. They bear plenty of Nuts every year, that are now of no other use in the World but to feed Hogs. 'Tis certain there is a large Consumption of this Oyl in Several of our Manufactures, and in some parts of France, as well as in other Countries, it is eaten instead of Oyl-Olive, being tolerably Sweet and wholesome.

The Indian kill'd a fat Buck, and the men brought in four Bears and a Brace of wild Turkeys, so that this was truly a Land of Plenty, both for man and Beast.

17. We detacht a Party this morning early in Search of a Ford, who after all cou'd find None that was safe; tho' dangerous as it was, we determin'd to make use of it, to avoid all further delay. Accordingly we rode over a Narrow Ledge of Rocks, Some of which lay below the Surface of the Water, and some above it.

Those that lay under the Water were as Slippery as Ice; and the Current glided over them so swiftly, that tho' it was only Water, it made us perfectly drunk. Yet we were all so fortunate as to get safe over to the West Shore, with no other Damage than the Sopping some of our Bread by the flounceíng of the Horses.

The tedious time Spent in finding out this Ford, and in getting all the Horses over it, prevented our carrying the Line more than 2 Miles and 250 Poles.

This was the last time we crost the Dan with our Line, which now began to run away more Southerly, with a very flush and plentiful Stream, the Description whereof must be left to future Discoveries, tho' we are well assured by the Indians that it runs thro' the Mountains.

We conducted the Baggage a round about way for the Benefit of evener Grounds, and this carry'd us over a broad Levil of exceeding rich Land, full of large Trees, with Vines marry'd to them, if I may be allow'd to speak so Poetically.

We untreed a young Cub in our March, that made a brave Stand against one of the best of our Dogs. This and a Fawn were all the Game that came in our way.

In this day's Journey, as in many others before, we saw beautiful Marble of Several Colours, and particularly that of the Purple kind with white Streaks, and in some places we came across large pieces of pure Alabaster.

We markt out our Quarters on the Banks of a purling Stream, which we call'd Casquade Creek, by reason of the Multitude of Water-Falls that are in it. But, different from all other Falls that ever I met with, the Rocks over which the water roll'd were Soft, and would Split easily into broad Flakes, very proper for Pavement; and some Fragments of it seem'd soft enough for Hones, and the Grain fine enough.

Near our Camp we found a prickly Shrub, riseing about a foot from the Ground, something like
that which bears the Barberry, tho' much Smaller.
The Leaves had a fresh, agreeable Smell, and I
am perswaded the Ladies would be apt to fancy
a Tea made of them, provided they were told how
far it came, and at the Same time were obliged to
buy it very dear.

About a Mile to the South-West of our Camp
rose a regular Mount, that commanded a full Prospect of the Mountains, and an Extensive View of
the Flat Country.   But being, with respect to the
high Mountains, no more than a Pimple, we call'd
it by that Name.

Presently after Sunset we discovered a great
Light towards the West, too bright for a fire, and
more resembling the Aurora Borealis.   This, all
our Woodsmen told us, was a Common Appearance in the High Lands, and generally foreboded
bad Weather.   Their Explanation happen'd to be
exactly true, for in the Night we had a Violent
Gale of Wind, accompany'd with Smart Hail, that
rattled frightfully amongst the Trees, tho' it was
not large enough to do us any Harm.

[18]. We crost Casquade Creek over a Ledge of
Smooth Rocks, and then Scuffled thro' a mighty
Thicket, at least three Miles long.   The whole
was one continued Tract of rich high Land, the
woods whereof had been burnt not long before.
It was then overgrown with Saplings of Oak,
Hiccory and Locust, interlac'd with Grape Vines.
In this fine Land, however, we met with no Water,

till at the End of three Miles we luckily came upon
a Chrystal Stream, which, like some Lovers of
Conversation, discover'd every thing committed to
its faithless Bosom.

Then we came upon a piece of Rich Low
Ground, covered with large Trees, of the extent
of half a Mile, which made us fancy ourselves not
far from the River; tho' after that we ascended
gently to higher Land, with no other Trees growing upon it except Butter-wood, which is one
Species of White Maple.

This being a dead Levil, without the least De-
clivity to carry off the Water, was moist in many
Places, and produc'd abundance of Grass.   All
our Woodsmen call these flat Grounds High-Land-
Ponds, and in their Trading Journeys are glad to
halt at such Places for Several days together, to
recruit their Jaded Horses, especially in the Winter Months, when there is little or no Grass to be
found in other Places.

This High-Land-Pond extended above two
Miles, our Palfrey's Snatching greedily at the
Tufts of Grass, as they went along.   After we
got over this Level, we descended some Stony
Hills for about half a Mile, and then came upon a
large Branch of the River, which we christen'd the
Irvin, in honour of our learned Professor.   This
River we forded with much Difficulty and some
Danger, by reason of the Hollow-Spaces betwixt
the Rocks, into which our Horses plunged almost
every Step.

The Irvin runs into the Dan about four Miles to

the Southward of the Line, and seem'd to roll down its Waters from the N. N. W. in a very full and Limpid stream, and the Murmur it made, in tumbling over the Rocks, caus'd the Situation to appear very Romantick, and had almost made some of the Company Poetical, tho' they drank nothing but Water.

We encampt on a pleasant Hill, overlooking the River, which seem'd to be deep every where except just where we forded. In the mean time, neither the Chain of Rocks, nor any other that we cou'd observe in this Stream, was so uninterrupted, but that there were Several Breaks where a Canoe, or even a Moderate Flat-bottom'd Boat, might Shear clear. Nor have we reason to believe there are any other Falls (except the great ones, thirty Miles below Moniseep-Ford) that reach quite across, so as to interrupt the Navigation for Small Craft. And I have been inform'd that, even at those Great Falls, the Blowing up a few Rocks wou'd open a Passage at least for canoes, which certainly wou'd be an unspeakable Convenience to the Inhabitants of all that beautiful Part of the Country.

The Indian kill'd a very fat Doe, and came across a Bear, which had been put to Death and was half devour'd by a Panther. The last of these Brutes reigns absolute Monarch of the Woods, and in the keenness of his hunger will venture to attack a Bear; tho' then 'tis ever by surprize, as all Beasts of the cat kind use to come upon their Prey.

Their Play is to take the poor Bears napping, they being very drowsy Animals, and tho' they be exceedingly Strong, yet their Strength is heavy, while the Panthers are too Nimble and cunning to trust themselves within their Hugg.

As formidable as this Beast is to his Fellow Brutes, he never has the confidence to venture upon a Man, but retires from him with great respect, if there be a way open for his Escape. However, it must be confesst, his Voice is a little contemptible for a Monarch of the Forrest, being not a great deal louder nor more awful than the Mewing of a Household Cat.[1]

In South Carolina they call this Beast a Tyger, tho' improperly, and so they do in some parts of the Spanish West Indies.   Some of their Authors, a little more properly, complement it with the Name of a Leopard.   But none of these are the Growth of America, that we know of.

The whole Distance the Surveyors advanc'd the Line this day amounted to 6 Miles and 30 Poles, which was no small Journey, considering the Grounds we had traverst were exceedingly rough and uneven, and in many Places intolerably entangled with Bushes.   All the Hills we ascended

[1] Some Authors, who have given an Account of the Southern Continent of America, wou'd make the World believe there are Lyons; but in all likelihood they were mistaken, imagining these Panthers to be Lyons. What makes this probable is, that the Northern and Southern Parts of America being join'd by the Isthmus of Darien, if there were Lyons in either they would find their way into the other, the Latitudes of each being equally proper for that generous animal. (Original note.)

were encumber'd with Stones, many of which
seem'd to contain a Metallick Substance, and the
Vallies we crost were interrupted with Miry
Branches. From the Top of every Hill we cou'd
discern distinctly, at a great Distance to the
Northward, three or four Ledges of Mountains,
rising one above another; and on the highest of
all rose a Single Mountain, very much resembling
a Woman's Breast.

19. About four Miles beyond the River Irvin, we
forded Matrimony Creek, call'd so by an unfortunate marry'd man, because it was exceedingly
noisy and impetuous. However, tho' the Stream
was Clamorous, yet, like those Women who make
themselves plainest heard, it was likewise perfectly
clear and unsully'd.

Still half a Mile further we saw a Small Mountain, about five Miles to the North-west of us, which
we call'd the Wart, because it appeared no bigger
than a Wart, in Comparison of the great Mountains which hid their haughty Heads in the Clouds.

We were not able to extend the Line farther
than 5 Miles and 135 Poles, notwithstanding we
began our March Early in the Morning, and did
not encamp till it was almost dark.

We made it the later by endeavouring to Quarter in some convenient Situation, either for Grass
or Canes. But Night Surprising us, we were
oblig'd to Lodge at last upon High and uneven
Ground, which was so overgrown with Shrubs
and Saplings, that we cou'd hardly see ten yards
around us.

The most melancholy part of the Story was, that
our Horses had Short Commons.   The poor Creatures were now grown so weak that they Stagger'd
when we mounted them.   Nor wou'd our own Fare
have been at all more plentiful, had we not been so
provident as to carry a Load of Meat along with
us.   Indeed, the Woods were too thick to shew us
any sort of Game but one Wild Turkey, which
help'd to enrich our Soup.

To make us amends, we found abundance of very
Sweet Grapes, which, with the help of Bread,
might have furnish'd out a good Italian Repast, in
the Absence of more Savoury Food.

The men's Mouths water'd at the Sight of a Prodigious Flight of Wild Pigeons, which flew high
over our Heads to the Southward.

The Flocks of these Birds of Passage are so
amazingly great, Sometimes, that they darken the
Sky; nor is it uncommon for them to light in such
Numbers on the Larger Limbs of Mulberry-Trees
and Oaks as to break them down.

In their Travels they make vast Havock among
the Acorns and Berries of all Sorts, that they wast
whole Forrests in a short time, and leave a Famine
behind them for most other Creatures; and under
Some Trees where they light, it is no Strange thing
to find the ground cover'd three Inches thick with
their Dung.   These Wild Pigeons commonly breed
in the uninhabitated parts of Canada, and as the
Cold approaches assemble their Armies and bend
their Course Southerly, Shifting their Quarters, like
many of the Winged kind, according to the Sea-

son.   But the most remarkable thing in their
Flight, as we are told, is that they never have
been observ'd to return to the Northern Countries
the same way they came from thence, but take
quite another Rout, I suppose for their better
Subsistence.

In these long Flights they are very lean, and
their Flesh is far from being white or tender, tho'
good enough upon a March, when Hunger is the
sauce, and makes it go down better than Truffles
and Morels wou'd do.

20. It was now Sunday, which we had like to
have spent in Fasting as well as Prayer; for our
Men, taking no Care for the Morrow, like good
Christians, but bad Travellers, had improvidently
Devour'd all their Meat for Supper.

They were order'd in the Morning to drive up
their Horses, lest they shou'd stray too far from
the Camp and be lost, in case they were let alone
all day.   At their Return they had the very great
Comfort to behold a monstrous fat Bear, which
the Indian had kill'd very Seasonably for their
Breakfast.

We thought it still necessary to make another
Reduction of our Bread, from four to three Pounds
a Week to every man, computing that we had still
enough in that Proportion to last us Three weeks
longer.

The Atmosphere was so smoaky all round us,
that the Mountains were again growing invisible.
This happen'd not from the Hazyness of the Sky,
but from the fireing of the Woods by the Indians,

for we were now near the Route the Northern
Savages take when they go out to War against the
Cataubas and other Southern Nations.

On their way the Fires they make in their
camps are left burning, which, catching the dry
Leaves that ly near, soon put the adjacent Woods
into a flame.

Some of our men in Search of their Horses
discovered one of those Indian camps, where not
long before they had been Furring and dressing
their Skins.

And now I mention the Northern Indians, it
may not be improper to take Notice of their implacable Hatred to those of the South.   Their
Wars are everlasting, without any Peace, Enmity
being the only Inheritance among them that descends from Father to Son, and either Party will
march a thousand Miles to take their Revenge upon
such Hereditary Enemies.

These long Expeditions are Commonly carry'd
on in the following Manner; Some Indian, remarkable for his Prowess, that has rais'd himself to the
Reputation of a War-Captain, declares his Intention of paying a Visit to some southern Nation;
Hereupon as many of the Young Fellows as have
either a Strong Thirst of Blood or Glory, list themselves under his command.

With these Volunteers he goes from One Con-
federate Town to another, listing all the Rabble
he can, til he has gather'd together a competent
Number for Mischief.

Their Arms are a Gun and Tomahawk, and all

the Provisions they carry from Home is a Pouch of Rockahominy.   Thus provided and accoutr'd, they march towards their Enemy's Country, not in a Body, or by a certain Path, but Straggling in Small Numbers, for the greater convenience of Hunting and passing along undiscover'd.

So soon as they approach the Grounds on which the Enemy is used to hunt, they never kindle any Fire themselves, for fear of being found out by the smoak, nor will they Shoot at any kind of Game, tho' they shou'd be half Famisht, lest they might alarm their Foes, and put them upon their Guard.

Sometimes indeed, while they are still at some distance, they roast either Venison or Bear, till it is very dry, and then having Strung it on their Belts, wear it round their Middle, eating very Sparingly of it, because they know not when they shall meet with a fresh Supply.   But coming nearer, they begin to look all round the Hemisphere, to watch if any smoke ascends, and listen continually for the Report of Guns, in order to make some happy Discovery for their own advantage.

It is amazing to see their Sagacity in discerning the Track of a Human Foot, even amongst dry leaves, which to our Shorter Sight is quite undiscoverable.

If by one or more of those Signs they be able to find out the Camp of any Southern Indians, they Squat down in some Thicket, and keep themselves hush and Snug till it is dark; Then creeping up

Softly, they approach near enough to observe all the Motions of the Enemy. And about two a Clock in the Morning, when they conceive them to be in a Profound Sleep, for they never keep Watch and Ward, pour in a Volley upon them, each Singling out his Man. The Moment they have discharg'd their Pieces, they rush in with their Tomahawks, and make sure work of all that are disabled.

Sometimes, when they find the Enemy Asleep around their little Fire, they first Pelt them with little Stones to wake them, and when they get up, fire in upon them, being in that posture a better Mark than when prostrate on the Ground.

Those that are kill'd of the Enemy, or disabled, they Scalp, that is, they cut the Skin all round the Head just below the hair, and then clapping their Feet to the poor Mortal's Shoulders, pull the Scalp off clean, and carry it home in Triumph, being as proud of those Trophies, as the Jews used to be of the Foreskins of the Philistines.

This way of Scalping was practised by the Ancient Scythians, who us'd these hairy Scalps as Towels at Home, and Trappings for their Horses when they went abroad.

They also made Cups of their Enemies' Skulls, in which they drank Prosperity to their country, and Confusion to all their Foes.

The Prisoners they happen to take alive in these expeditions generally pass their time very Scurvily. They put them to all the Tortures that ingenious Malice and cruelty can invent. And (what shews

the baseness of the Indian Temper in Perfection)
they never fail to treat those with the greatest Inhumanity that have distinguish'd themselves most
by their Bravery; and, if he be a War-Captain,
they do him the Honour to roast him alive, and
distribute a Collop to all that had a Share in steal-
ing the Victory.[1]

They are very cunning in finding out new ways
to torment their unhappy Captives, tho', like those
of Hell, their usual Method is by Fire.　Sometimes
they Barbecue them over live-Coals, taking them
off every now and then, to prolong their Misery;
at other times they will Stick Sharp Pieces of
Lightwood all over their Body's, and setting them
afire, let them burn down into the Flesh to the
very Bone.　And when they take a Stout Fellow,
that they believe able to endure a great deal, they
will tear all the Flesh off his Bones with red hot
Pincers.

While these and such like Barbarities are prac-
tising, the Victors are so far from being touch'd
with Tenderness and Compassion, that they dance
and Sing round these wretched Mortals, shewing
all the Marks of Pleasure and Jollity.　And if

---

[1] Tho' who can reproach the poor Indians for this, when Homer makes his celebrated Hero, Achilles, drag the Body of Hector at the Tail of his chariot, for having fought gallantly in defence of his Country. Nor was Alexander the Great, with all his Fam'd Generosity, less inhuman to the brave Tyrians, 2000 of whom he ordered to be crucified in cold Blood, For no other fault but for having defended their City most corageously against Him, dureing a Siege of Seven Months. And what was still more brutal, he dragg'd alive —— at the Tail of his Chariot, thro' all the Streets, for defending the Town with so much Vigour. (Original note.)

such cruelties happen to be executed in their Towns, they employ their Children in tormenting the Prisoners, in order to extinguish in them betimes all Sentiments of Humanity.

In the mean time, while these poor Wretches are under the Anguish of all this inhuman Treatment, they disdain so much as to groan, Sigh, or shew the least Sign of Dismay or concern, so much as in their Looks; on the Contrary, they make it a Point of Honour all the time to Soften their Features, and look as pleas'd as if they were in the Actual Enjoyment of Some Delight; and if they never sang before in their Lives, they will be sure to be Melodious on this sad and Dismal Occasion.

So prodigious a Degree of Passive Valour in the Indians is the more to be wonder'd at, because in all Articles of Danger they are apt to behave like Cowards. And what is still more Surprizeing, the very Women discover, on such Occasions, as great Fortitude and Contempt, both of Pain and Death, as the Gallantest of their Men can do.

21. The Apprehension we had of losing the Horses in these Copse Woods were too well founded, nor were the Precautions we us'd Yesterday of driveing them up Sufficient to prevent their Straying away afterwards, notwithstanding they were securely hobbled.

We therefore Order'd the men out early this Morning to look diligently for them, but it was late before any cou'd be found. It seems they had straggled in quest of Forrage, and, besides all that, the Bushes grew thick enough to conceal them from being Seen at the Smallest Distance. One of the People was so bewilder'd in search of his Horse, that he lost Himself, being no great Forester.

However, because we were willing to save time, we left two of our most expert Woodsmen behind to beat all the Adjacent Woods in Quest of Him.

In the mean while the Surveyors proceeded vigourously on their Business, but were so perplext with Thickets at their first setting off, that their Progress was much retarded.

They were no sooner over that Difficulty, but they were oblig'd to encounter another. The rest of the day's-Work lay over very Sharp Hills, where the dry leaves were so Slippery that there was hardly any hold for their Feet. Such Rubbs as these prevented them from Measuring more than 4 Miles and 270 Poles.

Upon the Sides of these Hills the Soil was rich, tho' full of Stones, and the Trees reasonably large.

The Smoak continued still to Veil the Mountains from our Sight, which made us long for Rain, or a brisk Gale of Wind, to disperse it. Nor was the loss of this wild Prospect all our concern, but we were apprehensive lest the Woods shou'd be burnt in the Course of our Line before us, or happen to take fire behind us, either of which wou'd effectually have Starv'd the Horses, and made us all Foot Soldiers. But we were so happy, thank God! as to escape this Misfortune in every Part of our Progress.

We were exceedingly uneasy about our lost

man, knowing he had taken no Provision of any kind, nor was it much Advantage towards his Support, that he had taken his Gun along with him, because he had rarely been guilty of putting any thing to Death.

He had unluckily wander'd from the Camp Several Miles, and after Steering Sundry unsuccessful Courses, in order to return, either to us or to the Line, was at length so tired he could go no Farther. In this Distress he sat himself down under a Tree, to recruit his jaded Spirits, and at the same time indulge a few Melancholy Reflections.

Famine was the first Phantom that appear'd to him, and was the more frightfull, because he fancy'd himself not quite Bear enough to Subsist long upon licking his Paws.

In the mean time the two Persons we had sent after him hunted diligently great part of the day without coming upon his Track. They fir'd their Pieces towards every Point of the Compass, but cou'd perceive no fireing in return. However, advancing a little farther, at last they made a lucky Shot, that our Straggler had the good Fortune to hear, and he returning the Salute, they soon found each other with no Small Satisfaction. But tho' they lighted of the man, they cou'd by no means light of his Horse, and therefore he was oblig'd to be a Foot Soldier all the rest of the Journey.

Our Indian shot a Bear so prodigiously fat, that there was no way to kill Him but by fireing in at his Ear.

The fore part of the Skull of that Animal being guarded by a double Bone, is hardly penetrable, and when it is very fat, a Bullet aim'd at his Body is apt to lose its force, before it reaches the Vitals. This Animal is of the Dog kind, and our Indians, as well as Woodsmen, are as fond of its Flesh as the Chinese can be of that of the Common Hound.

22. Early in the Morning we sent back two men to make further Search for the horse that was Stray'd away. We were unwilling the Poor man shou'd Sustain such a Damage as wou'd eat out a large Part of his Pay, or that the Publick shou'd be at the Expense of reembursing Him for it.

These foresters hunted all over the Neighbouring Woods, and took as much pains as if the Horse had been their own Property, but all their Diligence was to no purpose.

The Surveyors, in the mean time, being fearful of leaving these men too far behind, advanc'd the Line no farther than One Mile and 230 Poles.

As we rode along we found no less than three Bears and a fat Doe, that our Indian, who went out before us, had thrown in our Course, and we were very glad to pick them up.

About a Mile from the Camp we crost Miry Creek, So call'd because Several of the Horses were mired in its Branches. About 230 Poles beyond that, the Line intersected another River, that seem'd to be a Branch of the Irvin, to which we gave the Name of the Mayo, in complement to the other of our Surveyors. It was about 50 Yards wide where we forded it, being just below a Ledge of Rocks, which reacht across the River, and made a natural casquade.

Our Horses cou'd hardly keep their feet over these Slippery Rocks, which gave Some of their Riders no small Palpitation.

This River forks about a Quarter of a Mile below the Ford, and has Some Scattering Canes growing near the Mouth of it.

We picht our Tent on the Western Banks of the Mayo, for the Pleasure of being lull'd to Sleep by the Casquade. Here our Hunters had leisure to go out and try their Fortunes, and return'd loaden with Spoil. They brought in no less than Six Bears, exceedingly fat, so that the frying pan had no rest all Night. We had now the Opportunity of trying the speed of these lumpish Animals by a fair Course it had with the Nimblest of our Surveyors.

A Cubb of a year Old will run very fast, because, being upon his growth, he is never encumber'd with too much fat; but the Old ones are more Sluggish and unwieldy, especially when Mast is Plenty. Then their Nimblest Gait is only a heavy Gallop, and their Motion is still Slower down hill, where they are oblig'd to Sidle very awkwardly, to keep their Lights from riseing up into their Throat.

These Beasts always endeavour to avoid a man, except when they are wounded, or happen to be engaged in the Protection of their Cubbs.

By the force of these Instincts and that of Self-Preservation, they will now and then throw off all

Reverence for their Maker's Image. For that Reason, excess of hunger will provoke them to the same Desperate Attack, for the support of their Being.

A Memorable Instance of the last Case is said to have happen'd not long ago in New England, where a Bear assaulted a Man just by his own Door, and rearing himself upon his Haunches, offer'd to take him lovingly into his Hug. But the Man's Wife observing the Danger her Husband was in, had the courage to run behind the Bear, and thrust her two Thumbs into his Eyes. This made Bruin quit the Man, and turn short upon the Woman to take his Revenge, but She had the Presence of mind to spring back with more than Female Agility, and so both their Lives were preserv'd.

23. At the Distance of 62 Poles from where we lay, we crost the South Branch of what we took for the Irvin, nor was it without Difficulty we got over, tho' it happen'd to be without Damage.

Great part of the way after that was Mountainous, so that we were no sooner got down one Hill, but we were oblig'd to climb up another. Only for the last Mile of our Stage, we encounter'd a Locust Thicket that was level, but interlac'd terribly with Bryars and Grape Vines.

We forded a large creek, no less than five times, the Banks of which were so steep that we were forc'd to cut them down with a Hough.

We gave it the Name of Crooked creek, because of its frequent Meanders. The Sides of it were

planted with Shrub-Canes, extremely inviting to
the Horses, which were now quite jaded with clam-
bering up so many Precipices, and tugging thro'
so many dismal Thickets, notwithstanding which
we pusht the Line this day Four Miles and 69
Poles.   The men were so unthrifty this Morning
as to bring but a Small Portion of their Abundance
along with them.   This was the more unlucky, because we cou'd discover no Sort of Game the whole
livelong Day.   Woodsmen are certainly good
Christians in one respect, at least, that they always
leave the Morrow to care for itself; tho' for that
very reason they ought to pray more fervently for
their Dayly Bread than most of them remember
to do.

The Mountains were still conceal'd from our
Eyes by a cloud of Smoak.   As we went along we
were alarmed at the Sight of a great Fire, which
shewed itself to the Northward.   This made our
small Corps march in closer Order than we us'd to
do, lest perchance we might be waylaid by Indians.
It made us look out Sharp to see if we cou'd discover any Track or other Token of these insidious
Forresters, but found none.   In the mean time we
came often upon the Track of Bears, which can't
without some Skill be distinguisht from that of
Human Creatures, made with Naked Feet.   And
Indeed a Young Woodsman wou'd be puzzled to
find out the Difference, which consists principally
in a Bear's Paws being something Smaller than a
Man's foot, and in its leaving sometimes the Mark of
its Claws in the Impression made upon the Ground.

The Soil where the Locust Thicket grew, was exceedingly rich, as it constantly is, where that kind of Tree is Naturally and largely produc'd.

But the Desolation made there lately, either by Fire or Caterpillars, had been so general, that we could not see a Tree of any Bigness standing within our Prospect. And the Reason why a Fire makes such a Havock in these lonely Parts is this.

The Woods are not there burnt every year, as they generally are amongst the Inhabitants. But the dead Leaves and Trash of many years are heapt up together, which being at length kindled by the Indians that happen to pass that way, furnish fewel for a conflagration that carries all before it.

There is a beautiful Range of Hills, as levil as a Terrass-Walk, that overlooks the Valley through which Crooked Creek conveys its Spiral Stream.

This Terrass runs pretty near East and West, about two Miles South of the Line, and is almost Parallel with it.

The Horses had been too much harass'd to permit us to ride at all out of our way, for the pleasure of any Prospect, or the gratification of any Curiosity. This confin'd us to the Narrow Sphere of our Business, and is at the same time a just Excuse for not animating our Story with greater Variety.

24. The Surveyors went out the sooner this Morning, by reason the men lost very little time in cooking their Breakfast. They had made but a

Spare Meal over Night, leaving nothing but the
Hide of a Bear for the Morrow. Some of the
keenest of them got up at Midnight to Cook that
nice Morsel after the Indian Manner.

They first Singed the Hair clean off, that none
of it might Stick in their Throats; then they boil'd
the Pelt into Soup, which had a Stratum of Grease
Swimming on it full half an Inch Thick. However,
they commended this Dish extremely; tho' I believe the Praises they gave it were more owing to
their good Stomach than to their good Tast.

The Line was extended 6 Miles and 300 Poles,
and in that Distance crosst Crooked Creek at least
eight times more.

We were forct to scuffle through a Thicket about
two Miles in breadth, planted with Locusts and
hiccory Sapplings, as close as they cou'd stand
together. Amongst these there was hardly a Tree
of Tolerable Growth within View. It was a dead
Plane of Several Miles Extent, and very fertile
Soil. Beyond that the Woods were open for about
three Miles, but Mountainous. All the rest of our
Day's Journey was pester'd with Bushes and
Grape Vines, in the thickest of which we were
obliged to take up our Quarters, near one of the
Branches of Crooked creek.

This Night it was the Men's good fortune to
fare very sumptuously, The Indian had kill'd
two large Bears, the fatest of which he had taken
napping. One of the People too Shot a Raccoon,
which is also of the Dog-kind, and as big as a
small Fox, tho' its Legs are Shorter, and when fat

has much a higher relish than either Mutton or Kid. 'Tis naturally not Carniverous, but very fond of Indian corn and Parsimons.

The fat of this Animal is reckon'd very good to asswage Swellings and Inflammations. Some old Maids are at the Trouble of breeding them up tame, for the pleasure of seeing them play over as many Humorous Tricks as a Munkey. It climbs up small Trees, like a Bear, by embraceing the Bodies of them.

Till this Night we had accustom'd ourselves to go to Bed in our Night-Gowns, believing we should thereby be better secur'd from the cold: but upon tryal found we lay much warmer by Stripping to our Shirts, and Spreading our Gowns over us.

A True Woodsman, if he have no more than a Single Blanket, constantly pulls all off, and, lying on one part of it, draws the other over him, believing it much more refreshing to ly so, than in his cloaths; and if he find himself not warm enough, Shifts his Lodging to Leeward of the Fire, in which Situation the smoak will drive over him, and effectually correct the cold Dews that wou'd otherwise descend upon his Person, perhaps to his great damage.

25. The Air clearing up this Morning, we were again agreeably surprized with a full Prospect of the Mountains. They discover'd themselves both to the North and South of us, on either side, not distant above ten Miles, according to our best Computation.

We cou'd now see those to the North rise in four distinct Ledges, one above another, but those to the South form'd only a Single Ledge, and that broken and interrupted in many Places; or rather they were only single Mountains detacht from each other.

One of the Southern Mountains was so vastly high, it seem'd to hide its head in the Clouds, and the West End of it terminated in a horrible Precipice, that we call'd the Despairing Lover's Leap. The Next to it, towards the East, was lower, except at one End, where it heav'd itself up in the form of a vast Stack of Chimnys.[1]

The Course of the Northern Mountains seem'd to tend West-South-West, and those to the Southward very near West. We cou'd descry other Mountains ahead of us, exactly in the Course of the Line, tho' at a much greater distance. In this Point of View, the Ledges on the right and Left both seem'd to close, and form a Natural Amphi-Theater.

Thus, 'twas our Fortune to be wedg'd in betwixt these two Ranges of Mountains, insomuch that if our Line had run ten Miles on either Side, it had butted before this day either upon one or the other, both of them now Stretching away plainly to the Eastward of us.

It had rain'd a little in the Night, which disperst the smoak and open'd this Romantick Scene to us all at once, tho' it was again hid from our Eyes as we mov'd forwards, by the rough Woods we had the

1 Probably Pilot Mountain.

Misfortune to be engag'd with. The Bushes were
so thick for near four Miles together, that they tore
the Deer-Skins to Pieces that guarded the Bread-
Bags. Tho', as rough as the Woods were, the Soil
was extremely good all the way, being washt down
from the Neighbouring Hills into the Plane Country. Notwithstanding all these Difficulties, the
Surveyors drove on the line 4 Miles and 205 Poles.

In the mean time we were so unlucky as to meet
with no Sort of Game the whole day, so that the
men were oblig'd to make a frugal distribution of
what little they left in the Morning.

We encampt upon a small Rill, where the Horses
came off as temperately as their Masters. They
were by this time grown so thin, by hard Travel
and Spare Feeding, that henceforth, in pure Compassion, we chose to perform the greater Part of
the Journey on foot. And as our Baggage was
by this time grown much lighter, we divided it,
after the best Manner, that every Horse's Load
might be proportion'd to the Strength he had left.
Tho', after all the prudent Measures we cou'd take,
we perceiv'd the Hills began to rise upon us so
fast in our Front, that it wou'd be impossible for
us to proceed much farther.

We saw very few Squirrels in the upper parts,
because the Wild Cats devour them unmercifully.
Of these there are four kinds: The Fox Squirrel,
the Gray, the Flying, and the Ground-Squirrel.

These last resemble a Rat in every thing but
the Tail, and the black and Russet Streaks that
run down the Length of their little Bodies.

26. We found our way grow still more Mountainous, after extending the Line 300 Poles farther. We came then to a Rivulet that ran with a Swift Current towards the South. This we fancy'd to be another Branch of the Irvin, tho' some of these men, who had been Indian Traders, judg'd it rather to be the head of Deep River, that discharges its Stream into that of Pee Dee; but this seem'd a wild Conjecture.

The Hills beyond that River were exceedingly lofty, and not to be attempted by our Jaded Palfreys, which could now hardly drag their Legs after them upon level Ground. Besides, the Bread began to grow Scanty, and the Winter Season to advance apace upon us.

We had likewise reason to apprehend the Consequences of being intercepted by deep Snows, and the Swelling of the many Waters between us and Home. The first of these Misfortunes would starve all our Horses, and the Other ourselves, by cutting off our Retreat, and obliging us to Winter in those Desolate Woods. These considerations determin'd us to Stop short here, and push our Adventures no farther. The last Tree we markt was a Red Oak, growing on the Bank of the River; and to make the Place more remarkable, we blaz'd all the Trees around it.

We found the whole Distance from Corotuck Inlet to the Rivulet Where we left off, to be, in a Strait Line, Two Hundred and Forty-one Miles and Two Hundred and Thirty Poles. And from the Place where the Carolina Commissioners de-

serted us, 72 Miles and 302 Poles.　This last part
of the Journey was generally very hilly, or else
grown up with troublesome Thickets and underwoods, all which our Carolina Friends had the
Discretion to avoid.

We encampt in a dirty Valley near the Rivulet
above-mention'd, for the advantage of the Canes,
and so sacrificed our own Convenience for that of
our Horses.

There was a Small Mountain half a Mile to the
Northward of us, which we had the Curiosity to
Climb up in the Afternoon, in Order to enlarge
our Prospect.　From thence we were able to discover where the two Ledges of Mountains clos'd,
as near as we cou'd guess, about 30 Miles to the
West of us, and lamented that our present circumstances wou'd not permit us to advance the Line
to that Place, which the Hand of Nature had
made so very remarkable.

Not far from our Quarters one of the men pickt
up a pair of Elk's Horns, not very large, and discover'd the Track of the Elk that had Shed them.
It was rare to find any Tokens of those Animals
so far to the South, because they keep commonly
to the Northward of 37 degrees, as the Buffaloes,
for the most part, confine themselves to the Southward of that Latitude.

The Elk is full as big as a Horse, and of the
Deer kind.　The Stags only have Horns, and
those exceedingly large and Spreading.　Their
Colour is Something lighter than that of the Red
Deer, and their Flesh tougher.　Their swiftest

Speed is a large trot, and in that Motion they turn
their Horns back upon their Necks, and Cock their
Noses aloft in the Air.   Nature has taught them
this Attitude to save their Antlers from being
entangled in the Thickets, which they always
retire to.   They are very shy, and have the Sense
of Smelling so exquisite that they wind a man at
a great distance.   For this reason they are Seldom
Seen but when the Air is moist, in which Case
their smell is not so Nice.

They commonly herd together, and the Indians
say, if one of the Drove happen by some Wound
to be disabled from making his Escape, the rest
will forsake their fears to defend their Friend,
which they will do with great obstinacy, till they
are kill'd upon the Spot.   Tho' otherwise, they
are so alarm'd at the Sight of a man, that to avoid
him they will Sometimes throw themselves down
very high Precipices into the River.

A misadventure happen'd here, which gave us
no Small perplexity.   One of the Commissioners
was so unlucky as to bruise his Foot against a
Stump, which brought on a formal Fit of the
Gout.

It must be own'd there cou'd not be a more un-
seasonable time, nor a more improper Situation,
for any one to be attackt by that cruel Distemper.
The Joint was so inflam'd that he cou'd neither
draw Shoe nor Boot upon it; and to ride without
either wou'd have expos'd him to so many rude
knocks and Bruises, in those rough Woods, as to
be intolerable even to a Stoick.

It was happy, indeed, that we were to rest here the next day, being Sunday, that there might be leisure for trying some Speedy Remedy. Accordingly he was persuaded to bathe his Foot in Cold Water, in Order to repel the Humour and asswage the Inflamation. This made it less painful, and gave us hopes, too, of reducing the Swelling in a Short time.

Our men had the fortune to kill a Brace of Bears, a fat Buck, and a Wild Turkey, all which paid them with Interest for Yesterday's Abstinence. This constant and Seasonable Supply of all our daily Wants made us reflect thankfully on the Bounty of Providence.

And that we might not be unmindful of being all along fed by Heaven in this great and Solitary Wilderness, we agreed to Wear in our Hats the Maosti, which is, in Indian, the Beard of the Wild Turkey-Cock, and on our Breasts the Figure of that Fowl with its Wings extended, and holding in its Claws a scrowl with this Motto, "VICE COTURNICUM," meaning that we had been Supported by them in the Wilderness in the room of Quails.

27. This being Sunday we were not wanting in our Thanks to Heaven for the Constant Support and Protection we had been favour'd with. Nor did our Chaplain fail to put us in mind of Our Duty by a Sermon proper for the Occasion.

We order'd a Strict Inquiry to be made into the Quantity of Bread we had left, and found no more than wou'd Subsist us a Fortnight at Short Allowance. We made a fair Distribution of our whole Stock, and at the Same time recommended to the Men to manage this, their last Stake, to the best advantage, not knowing how long they would be oblig'd to live upon it.

We likewise directed them to keep a Watchfull eye upon their Horses, that none of them might be missing the next Morning, to hinder our Return.

There fell some Rain before Noon, which made our Camp more a Bogg than it was before. This moist Situation began to infect some of the men with Fevers, and some with Fluxes, which however we soon remov'd with Peruvian Bark and Ipocoacanah.

In the Afternoon we marcht up again to the top of the Hill to entertain our Eyes a Second time with the View of the Mountains, but a perverse Fog arose that hid them from our Sight.

In the Evening we deliberated which way it might be most proper to return. We had at first intended to cross over at the foot of the Mountains to the head of James River, that we might be able to describe that Natural Boundary so far. But, on Second Thoughts, we found many good Reasons against that laudable Design, Such as the Weakness of our Horses, the Scantiness of our Bread, and the near approach of Winter. We had Cause to believe the way might be full of Hills, and the farther we went towards the North, the more danger there wou'd be of Snow. Such considerations as these determin'd us at last to make the best of our way back upon the Line, which was the Strait-

est, and Consequently the shortest way to the Inhabitants. We knew the worst of that Course,
and were sure of a beaten Path all the way, while
we were totally ignorant what Difficulties and
Dangers the other Course might be attended with.
So Prudence got the better for once of Curiosity,
and the Itch for new Discoveries gave Place to
Self-preservation.

Our Inclination was the Stronger to cross over
according to the Course of the Mountains, that we
might find out whether James River and Appamat-
tock River head there, or run quite thro' them.
'Tis Certain that Potomec passes in a large Stream
thro' the Main Ledge, and then divides itself into
two considerable Rivers. That which Stretches
away to the Northward is call'd the Cohungaroota,[1]
and that which flows to the South-west, hath the
Name of Sharantow.[2]

The Course of this last Stream is near parallel
to the Blue Ridge of Mountains, at the distance
only of about three or four Miles. Tho' how far it
may continue that Course has not yet been sufficiently discover'd, but some Woodsmen pretend to
say it runs as far as the source of Roanoak; Nay,
they are so very particular as to tell us that Roanoak, Sharantow, and another Wide Branch of the
Missassippi, all head in one and the Same Mountain.

What dependence there may be upon this Con-

[1] Which by a Late Survey has
been found to extend above 200
Miles before it reaches its
Source, in a Mountain, from
whence Allegany, one of the
Branches of Missassippi, takes
its Rise, and runs South-West,
as this River dos South-East.
(Original note.)

[2] Shenandoah.—EDITOR.

jectural Geography, I wont pretend to say, tho'
'tis certain that Sharantow keeps close to the
Mountains, as far as we are acquainted with its
Tendency.   We are likewise assur'd that the South
Branch of James River, within less than 20 Miles
East of the Main Ledge, makes an Elbow, and runs
due South-west, which is parallel with the Mountains on this side.   But how far it Stretches that
way, before it returns, is not yet certainly known,
no more than where it takes its Rise.

In the mean time it is Strange that our Woodsmen
have not had Curiosity enough to inform themselves
more exactly of these particulars, and it is Stranger
Still that the Government has never thought it
worth the Expense of making an accurate Survey
of the Mountains, that we might be Masters of that
Natural Fortification before the French, who in some
Places have Settlements not very distant from it.

It therefore concerns his Majesty's Service very
nearly, and the Safety of His Subjects in this part
of the World, to take Possession of so important a
Barrier in time, lest our good Friends, the French,
and the Indians, thro' their Means, prove a perpetual Annoyance to these Colonies.

Another Reason to invite us to Secure this great
Ledge of Mountains is, the Probability that very
Valuable Mines may be discover'd there.   Nor
wou'd it be at all extravagant to hope for Silver
Mines, among the rest, because Part of these
Mountains ly exactly in the same Parallel, as well
as upon the Same Continent with New Mexico, and
the Mines of St. Barb.

28. We had given Orders for the Horses to be brought up early, but the likelyhood of more Rain prevented our being over-hasty in decamping. Nor were we out in our conjectures, for about ten a'clock it began to fall very plentifully.

Our Commissioner's Pain began now to abate, as the Swelling encreas'd. He made an excellent Figure for a Mountaineer, with one boot of Leather and the other of Flannel. Thus accowtur'd, he intended to mount, if the Rain had not happen'd opportunely to prevent him.

Tho', in Truth, it was hardly possible for Him to ride with so Slender a Defense, without exposing his Foot to be bruis'd and tormented by the Saplings, that stood thick on either side of the Path. It was therefore a most Seasonable Rain for Him, as it gave more time for his Distemper to abate.

Tho' it may be very difficult to find a certain Cure for the Gout, yet it is not improbable but some things may ease the Pain, and Shorten the Fits of it. And those Medicines are most likely to do this, that Supple the Parts, and clear the Passage Through the Narrow Vessels, that are the Seat of this cruel Disease. Nothing will do this more Suddenly than Rattle-snake's Oyl, which will even penetrate the Pores of Glass when warm'd in the sun.

It was unfortunate, therefore, that we had not taken out the Fat of those Snakes we had kill'd some time before, for the Benefit of so useful an Experiment, as well as for the Relief of our Fellow-Traveller.

But lately the Seneca Rattle-Snake-Root has been discover'd in this Country, which being infus'd in Wine, and drank Morning and Evening, has in Several Instances had a very happy Effect upon the Gout, and enabled Cripples to throw away their Crutches and walk several Miles, and, what is Stranger Still, it takes away the Pain in half an hour.

Nor was the Gout the only Disease among us that was hard to cure. We had a man in our Company who had too Voracious a Stomach for a Woodsman. He ate as much as any other two, but all he Swallow'd stuck by him till it was carry'd off by a Strong Purge. Without this Assistance, often repeated, his Belly and Bowels wou'd swell to so enormous a Bulk that he cou'd hardly breathe, especially when he lay down, just as if he had had an Asthma; tho', notwithstanding this oddness of constitution, he was a very Strong, lively Fellow, and us'd abundance of Violent Exercise, by which 'twas wonderfull the Peristaltick Motion was not more Vigorously promoted.

We gave this poor Man Several Purges, which only eas'd Him for the present, and the next day he wou'd grow as burly as ever. At last we gave Him a Moderate Dose of ippocoacanah, in Broth made very Salt, which turn'd all its Operations downwards. This had so happy an Effect that, from that day forward to the End of our Journey, all his Complaint ceas'd, and the passages continued unobstructed.

The Rain continued most of the Day and Some

Westover Gate (North).

part of the Night, which incommoded us much in
our Dirty Camp, and made the men think of
Nothing but Eating, even at the time when nobody cou'd Stir out to make provision for it.

29. Tho' we were flattered in the morning with
the usual Tokens of a fair Day, yet they all blew
over, and it rain'd hard before we cou'd make
ready for our Departure.

This was still in favour of our Podagrous Friend,
whose Lameness was now grown better, and the
Inflamation fallen. Nor did it seem to need above
one day more to reduce it to its Natural Proportion, and make it fit for the Boot; And effectually
The Rain procur'd this Benefit for him, and gave him
particular Reason to believe his Stars propitious.

Notwithstanding the falling Weather, our Hunt-
ers sally'd out in the afternoon, and drove the
Woods in a Ring, which was thus performed.
From the circumference of a large Circle they all
march't inwards, and drove the Game towards the
center. By this means they shot a Brace of fat
Bears, which came very seasonably, because we
had made clean Work in the Morning and were in
Danger of dining with St. Anthony, or his Grace
Duke Humphry.

But in this Expedition the unhappy man who
had lost himself once before, Straggled again so
far in Pursuit of a Deer, that he was hurry'd a
second time quite out of his knowledge. And
Night coming on before he cou'd recover the
Camp, he was obliged to lie down, without any of
the Comforts of Fire, Food or covering; Nor

would his Fears suffer him to Sleep very Sound, because, to his great disturbance, the Wolves howl'd all that Night, and the Panthers scream'd most frightfully.

In the Evening a brisk North-Wester swept all the Clouds from the Sky, and expos'd the mountains as well as the Stars to our Prospect.

That which was the most lofty to the Southward, and which we call'd the Lover's Leap, some of our Indian Traders fondly fancy'd was the Kiawan mountain, which they had formerly seen from the country of the Cherokees.

They were the more positive by reason of the prodigious Precipice that remarkably distinguished the West End of it.

We seem'd however not to be far enough South for that, tho' 'tis not improbable but a few miles farther the Course of our Line might carry us to the most Northerly Towns of the Cherokees.

What makes this the more credible, is the North West Course, that our Traders take from the Catawbas for some hundred miles together, when they carry Goods that round-about way to the Cherokees.

It was a great Pity that the want of Bread, and the Weakness of our Horses, hinder'd us from making the Discovery. Tho' the great Service of such an Excursion might have been to the Country wou'd certainly have made the attempt not only pardonable, but much to be commended.

Our Traders are now at the vast Charge and Fatigue of travelling above five hundred miles for

the Benefit of that traffique which hardly quits cost.
Wou'd it not then be worth the Assembly's while
to be at some charge to find a Shorter cut to carry
on so profitable a Trade, with more advantage,
and less hazard and Trouble, than they do at present? For I am persuaded it will not then be half
the Distance that our Traders make it now, nor
half so far as Georgia lies from the Northern
Clans of that Nation.

Such a Discovery would certainly prove an unspeakable Advantage to this Colony, by facilitating
a Trade with so considerable a nation of Indians,
which have 62 Towns, and more than 4000 Fighting Men. Our Traders at that rate would be able
to undersell those sent from the other Colonies so
much, that the Indians must have reason to deal
with them preferable to all others.

Of late the new Colony of Georgia has made
an act obliging us to go 400 miles to take out a
License to traffick with these Cherokees, tho' many
of their Towns ly out of their Bounds, and we had
carry'd on this Trade 80 years before that Colony
was thought of.

30. In the Morning early the man who had gone
astray the day before found his way to the Camp,
by the Sound of the Bells that were upon the
Horses' Necks.

At nine a'clock we began our March back toward
the rising Sun; for tho' we had finisht the Line,
yet we had not yet near finisht our Fatigue. We
had after all 200 good miles at least to our several
Habitations, and the Horses were brought so low,

that we were oblig'd to travel on foot great part of the way, and that in our Boots, too, to save our Legs from being torn to pieces by the Bushes and Briars. Had we not done this, we must have left all our Horses behind, which cou'd now hardly drag their Legs after them, and with all the favour we cou'd show the poor Animals, we were forc'd to set Seven of them free, not far from the foot of the Mountains.

Four men were despatcht early to clear the Road, that our Lame Commissioner's leg might be in less danger of being bruis'd, and that the Baggage Horses might travel with less difficulty and more expedition.

As we past along, by favour of a Serene Sky, we had still, from every Eminence, a perfect view of the Mountains, as well to the North as to the South. We could not forbear now and then facing about to survey them, as if unwilling to part with a Prospect, which at the same time, like some Rake's, was very wild and very Agreeable.

We encourag'd the Horses to exert the little Strength they had, and being light, they made a shift to jog on about Eleven Miles. We Encampt on Crooked Creek, near a Thicket of Canes. In the front of our Camp rose a very beautiful Hill, that bounded our View at about a Mile's Distance, and all the Intermediate space was cover'd with green canes. Tho', to our Sorrow, Fire-wood was Scarce, which was now the harder upon us, because a north-wester blew very cold from the Mountains.

The Indian kill'd a stately, fat Buck, & we pickt

his Bones as clean as a score of Turky-Buzzards cou'd have done.

By the advantage of a clear night, we made tryal once more of the Variation, and found it much the same as formerly.

This being his Majesty's Birth-Day, we drank all the Loyal Healths in excellent Water, not for the sake of the drink, (like many of our fellow subjects,) but purely for the Sake of the Toast. And because all Public Mirth shou'd be a little noisy, we fir'd several volleys of Canes, instead of Guns, which gave a loud report.

We threw them into the Fire, where the Air enclosed betwixt the Joints of the Canes, being expanded by the violent Heat, burst its narrow Bounds with a considerable explosion!

In the Evening one of the men knockt down an Opossum, which is a harmless little Beast, that will seldom go out of your way, and if you take hold of it, it will only grin, and hardly ever bite. The Flesh was well tasted and Tender, approaching nearest to Pig, which it also resembles in Bigness. The colour of its Fur was a Goose Gray, with a Swine's Snout, and a Tail like a Rat, but at least a foot long. By twisting this Tail about the arm of a Tree, it will hang with all its weight, and swing to any thing it wants to take hold of.

It has five Claws on the fore Feet of equal length, but the hinder feet have only Four claws, and a sort of Thumb standing off at a proper Distance.

Their Feet being thus form'd, qualify them for

climbing up Trees to catch little Birds, which they are very fond of.

But the greatest Particularity of this creature, and which distinguishes it from most others that we are acquainted with, is the FALSE BELLY of the FEMALE, into which her Young retreat in time of Danger. She can draw the Slit, which is the Inlet into this Pouch, so close, that you must look narrowly to find it, especially if she happen to be a Virgin.

Within the False Belly may be seen seven or eight Teats, on which the young Ones grow from their first Formation till they are big enough to fall off, like ripe Fruit from a Tree. This is so odd a method of Generation, that I should not have believed it without the Testimony of mine own Eyes. Besides a knowing and credible Person has assur'd me he has more than once observ'd the Embryo Possums growing to the Teat before they were compleatly Shaped, and afterwards wacht their daily growth till they were big enough for Birth. And all this he could the more easily pry into, because the Damm was so perfectly gentle and harmless, that he could handle her just as he pleas'd.

I cou'd hardly persuade myself to publish a thing so contrary to the Course that Nature takes in the Production of other Animals, unless it were a Matter Commonly believ'd in all Countries where that Creature is produc'd, and has been often observed by Persons of undoubted credit and understanding.

They say that the Leather-winged Bats produce their Young in the same uncommon Manner. And that young Sharks at Sea, and the Young Vipers ashoar, run down the Throats of their Damms when they are closely pursued.

The frequent crossing of Crooked Creek, and mounting the Steep Banks of it, gave the finishing stroke to the foundering of our Horses: and no less than two of them made a full stop here, and would not advance a foot farther, either by fair means or foul.

We had a Dreamer of Dreams amongst us, who warned me in the Morning to take care of myself, or I shou'd infallibly fall into the Creek; I thank'd him kindly, and used what Caution I cou'd, but was not able it seems to avoid my Destiny, for my Horse made a false step and laid me down at my full Length in the water.

This was enough to bring dreaming into credit, and I think it much for the Honour of our expedition, that it was grac'd not only with PRIEST but also with a PROPHET.

We were so perplext with this Serpentine Creek, as well as in Passing the Branches of the Irvin, (which were swell'd since we saw them before,) that we could reach but 5 miles this whole day. In the Evening We pitched our Tent near Miry creek, (tho' an uncomfortable place to lodge in) purely for the advantage of the Canes.

Our Hunters killed a large Doe and two Bears, which made all other misfortunes easy. Certainly no Tartar ever lov'd Horse-flesh, or Hottentot Guts and Garbage, better than Woodsmen do Bear. The truth of it is, it may be proper food perhaps for such as Work or Ride it off, but, with our Chaplain's Leave, who lov'd it much, I think it not a very proper dyet for saints, because 'tis apt to make them a little too rampant.

And now, for the good of mankind, and for the better Peopling an Infant colony, which has no want but that of Inhabitants, I will venture to publish a Secret of Importance, which our Indian disclos'd to me. I askt him the reason why few or none of his Countrywomen were barren? To which curious Question he answered, with a Broad grin upon his Face, they had an infallible SECRET for that. Upon my being importunate to know what the secret might be, he informed me that, if any Indian woman did not prove with child at a decent time after Marriage, the Husband, to save his Reputation with the women, forthwith entered into a Bear-dyet for Six Weeks, which in that time makes him so vigorous that he grows exceedingly impertinent to his poor wife and 'tis great odds but he makes her a Mother in Nine Months.

And thus I am able to say, besides, for the Reputation of the Bear Dyet, that all the Marryed men of our Company were joyful Fathers within forty weeks after they got Home, and most of the Single men had children sworn to them within the same time, our chaplain always excepted, who, with much ado, made a shift to cast out that importunate kind of Devil, by Dint of Fasting and Prayer.

Nov. 1. By the negligence of one o the Men in not hobbling his Horse, he straggled so far that he could not be found. This stopt us all the Morning long; Yet, because our Time should not be entirely lost, we endeavoured to observe the Latitude at twelve a clock. Though our observation was not perfect, by reason the Wind blew a little too fresh, however, by Such a One as we cou'd make, we found ourselves in 36° 20' only.

Notwithstanding our being thus delay'd, and the unevenness of the Ground, over which we were oblig'd to walk, (for most of us serv'd now in the Infantry,) we travell'd no less than 6 miles, Tho' as merciful as we were to our poor Beasts, another of 'em tired by the way, & was left behind for the Wolves & Panthers to feast upon.

As we marcht along, we had the fortune to kill a Brace of Bucks, as many Bears, and one wild Turkey. But this was carrying Sport to wantonness, because we butchered more than we were able to transport. We ordered the Deer to be quarter'd and divided amongst the Horses for the lighter Carriage, and recommended the Bears to our dayly attendants, the Turkey-Buzzards.

We always chose to carry Venison along with us rather than Bear, not only because it was less cumbersome, but likewise because the People cou'd eat it without Bread, which was now almost spent. Whereas the other, being richer food, lay too heavy upon the stomach, unless it were lightened by something farinaceous. This is what I thought proper to remarque, for the service of all those

whose Business or Diversion shall oblige them to
live any time in the Woods.

And because I am persuaded that very usefull
Matters may be found out by Searching this great
Wilderness, especially the upper parts of it about
the Mountains, I conceive it will help to engage
able men in that good work, if I recommend a
wholesome kind of Food, of very small Weight
and very great Nourishment, that will secure them
from Starving, in case they shou'd be so unlucky
as to meet with no Game. The Chief discourage-
ment at present from penetrating far into the Woods
is the trouble of carrying a Load of Provisions. I
must own Famine is a frightful Monster, and for
that reason to be guarded against as well as we
can. But the common precautions against it, are
so burthensome, that People can't tarry long out,
and go far enough from home, to make any effectual
Discovery.

The Portable Provisions I would furnish our
Foresters withal are Glue-Broth and rockahomini:
one contains the Essence of Bread, the other of
Meat.

The best way of making Glue-Broth is after the
following method: Take a Leg of Beef, Veal,
Venison, or any other Young Meat, because Old
Meat will not so easily Jelly. Pare off all the fat,
in which there is no Nutriment, and of the Lean
make a very strong Broth, after the usual Manner,
by boiling the meat to Rags till all the Goodness
be out. After Skimming off what fat remains,
pour the Broth into a wide Stew-Pan, well tinn'd,

& let it simmer over a gentle, even Fire, till it come to a thick Jelly. Then take it off and set it over Boiling Water, which is an Evener Heat, and not so apt to burn the Broth to the Vessel. Over that let it evaporate, stirring it very often till it be reduc'd, when cold, into a Solid Substance like Glue. Then cut it into small Pieces, laying them Single in the Cold, that they may dry the Sooner. When the Pieces are perfectly dry, put them into a Cannister, and they will be good, if kept Dry, a whole East India Voyage.

This Glue is so Strong, that two or three Drams, dissolv'd in boiling Water with a little Salt, will make half a pint of good Broth, & if you shou'd be faint with fasting or Fatigue, let a small piece of this Glue melt in your Mouth, and you will find yourself surprisingly refreshed.

One Pound of this cookery wou'd keep a man in good heart above a Month, and is not only Nour-ishing, but likewise very wholesome. Particularly it is good against Fluxes, which Woodsmen are very liable to, by lying too near the moist ground, and guzzling too much cold Water. But as it will be only us'd now and then, in times of Scarcity, when Game is wanting, two Pounds of it will be enough for a Journey of Six Months.

But this Broth will be still more heartening, if you thicken every mess with half a Spoonful of Rockahominy, which is nothing but Indian Corn parched without burning, and reduced to Powder. The Fire drives out all the Watery Parts of the Corn, leaving the Strength of it behind, and this being very dry, becomes much lighter for carriage and less liable to be Spoilt by the Moist Air.

Thus half a Dozen Pounds of this Sprightful Bread will sustain a Man for as many Months, provided he husband it well, and always Spare it when he meets with Venison, which, as I said before, may be very Safely eaten without any Bread at all.

By what I have said, a Man needs not encumber himself with more than 8 or 10 Pounds of Provisions, tho' he continue half a year in the Woods.

These and his Gun will support him very well during that time, without the least danger of keeping one Single Fast. And tho' some of his days may be what the French call *Jours maigres*, yet there will happen no more of those than will be necessary for his health, and to carry off the Excesses of the Days of Plenty, when our Travellers will be apt to indulge their Lawless Appetites too much.

2. The Heavens frowned this Morning, and threaten'd abundance of Rain, but our Zeal for returning made us defy the Weather, and decamp a little before Noon. Yet we had not advanct two Miles, before a Soaking Shower made us glad to pitch our Tent as fast as we could. We chose for that purpose a rising Ground, half a mile to the East of MATRIMONY CREEK. This was the first and only time we were caught in the Rain, during the whole Expedition. It us'd before to be so civil as to fall in the night, after we were safe in our Quarters, and had trencht ourselves in; or else it

came upon us on Sundays, when it was no Interruption to our Progress, nor any Inconvenience to our Persons.

We had, however, been so lucky in this Particular before, that we had abundant Reason to take our present soaking patiently, and the Misfortune was the less, because we had taken the Precaution to keep all our Baggage and Bedding perfectly dry.

This Rain was enliven'd with very loud Thunder, which was echo'd back by the Hills in the Neighbourhood in a frightful Manner. There is something in the Woods that makes the Sound of this Meteor more awfull, and the Violence of the Lightening more Visible. The Trees are frequently Shiver'd quite down to the Root, and sometimes perfectly twisted. But of all the Effects of Lightening that ever I heard of, the most amazing happen'd in this country, in the Year 1736.

In the Summer of that year a Surgeon of a Ship, whose Name was Davis, came ashoar at York to visit a Patient. He was no sooner got into the House, but it began to rain with many terrible Claps of Thunder. When it was almost dark there came a dreadful Flash of Lightning, which Struck the Surgeon dead as he was walking about the Room, but hurt no other Person, tho' several were near him. At the same time it made a large Hole in the Trunk of a Pine Tree, which grew about Ten Feet from the Window. But what was most surprising in this Disaster was, that on the Breast of the unfortunate man that was kill'd was the

Figure of a Pine Tree, as exactly delineated as any Limner in the World could draw it, nay, the Resemblance went so far as to represent the colour of the Pine, as well as the Figure. The Lightning must probably have passed thro' the Tree first before it struck the Man, and by that means have printed the Icon of it on his breast.

But whatever may have been the cause, the Effect was certain, and can be attested by a Cloud of Witnesses who had the curiosity to go and see this Wonderful Phenomenon.

The worst of it was, we were forced to Encamp in a barren place, where there was hardly a blade of Grass to be seen, Even the wild Rosemary failed us here, which gave us but too just apprehensions that we should not only be oblig'd to trudge all the way home on foot, but also to lug our Baggage at our Backs into the Bargain.

Thus we learnt by our own Experience, that Horses are very improper animals to use in a long Ramble into the Woods, and the better they have been used to be fed, they are still the worse. Such will fall away a great deal faster, and fail much sooner, than those which are wont to be at their own keeping. Besides, Horses that have been accustom'd to a Plane and Champaign Country will founder presently, when they come to clamber up Hills, and batter their Hoofs against continal Rocks.

We need Welsh Runts, and Highland Galloways to climb our Mountains withal; they are us'd to Precipices, and will bite as close as Banstead

Down Sheep. But I should much rather recommend Mules, if we had them, for these long and
painful Expeditions; tho' till they can be bred, certainly Asses are the fittest Beasts of Burthen
for the Mountains. They are sure-footed, patient
under the heaviest Fatigue, and will subsist upon
Moss, or Browsing on Shrubs all the Winter. One
of them will carry the Necessary Luggage of four
Men, without any Difficulty, and upon a Pinch will
take a Quarter of Bear or Venison upon their
Backs into the Bargain.

Thus, when the Men are light and disengaged
from every thing but their Guns, they may go the
whole Journey on foot with pleasure. And tho'
my Dear Countrymen have so great a Passion for
riding, that they will often walk two miles to catch
a Horse, in Order to ride One, yet, if they'll please
to take my Word for't, when they go into the
Woods upon Discovery, I would advise them by
all Means to march a-foot, for they will then be
deliver'd from the great Care and Concern for
their Horses, which takes up too large a portion of
their time.

Over Night we are now at the trouble of hobbling them out, and often of leading them a mile
or two to a convenient place for Forrage, and then
in the morning we are some Hours in finding them
again, because they are apt to stray a great way
from the place where they were turn'd out. Now
and then, too, they are lost for a whole day together, and are frequently so weak and jaded, that
the Company must ly still Several days, near some

Meadow, or High-land Pond, to recruit them. All these delays retard their Progress intolerably; whereas, if they had only a few Asses, they wou'd abide close to the Camp, and find Sufficient food everywhere, and in all Seasons of the Year. Men wou'd then be able to travel Safely over Hills and Dales, nor wou'd the Steepest Mountains obstruct their Progress.

They might also search more narrowly for Mines and other Productions of Nature, without being confin'd to level grounds, in Compliment to the jades they ride on. And one may foretell, without the Spirit of Divination, that so long as Woodsmen continue to range on Horse-back, we shall be Strangers to our own Country, and a few or no valuable Discoveries will ever be made.

The FRENCH COURIERS *de Bois*, who have run from one End of the Continent to the other, have performed it all on foot, or else in all probability must have continued as ignorant as we are.

Our Country has now been inhabited more than 130 years by the English, and still we hardly know any thing of the Appallachian Mountains, that are no where above 250 miles from the sea. Whereas the French, who are later comers, have rang'd from Quebec Southward as far as the Mouth of Mississippi, in the bay of Mexico, and to the West almost as far as California, which is either way above 2000 miles.

3. A North-west Wind having clear'd the Sky, we were now tempted to travel on a Sunday, for the first time, for want of more plentiful Forage,

though some of the more Scrupulous amongst us we[re] unwilling to do Evil, that good might come of it, and make our Cattle work a Good part of the Day in order to fill their Bellies at Night. However, the Chaplain put on his casuistical Face, and offer'd to take the sin upon Himself. We therefore consented to move a Sabbath Day's Journey of 3 or 4 Miles, it appearing to be a Matter of some necessity.

On the way our unmerciful Indian kill'd no less than two Brace of Deer and a large Bear. We only prim'd the Deer, being unwilling to be encumbered with their whole Carcasses. The rest we consign'd to the Wolves, which in Return seranaded us great part of the Night. They are very clamerous in their Banquets, which we know is the way some other Brutes have, in the extravagance of their Jollity and Sprightliness, of expressing their thanks to Providence.

We came to our Old camp, in Sight of the River Irvin, whose Stream was Swell'd now near four feet with the Rain that fell the Day before. This made it impracticable for us to ford it, nor could we guess when the water wou'd fall enough to let us go over.

This put our Mathematical Professor, who shou'd have set a better Example, into the Vapours, fearing he shou'd be oblig'd to take up his Winter Quarters in that doleful Wilderness. But the rest were not affected with his want of Faith, but preserv'd a Firmness of Mind Superior to such little Adverse Accidents. They trusted that the same good

Providence which had most remarkably prosper'd them hitherto, would continue his goodness and conduct them safe to the End of their Journey.

However, we found plainly that travelling on the Sunday, contrary to our constant Rule, had not thriven with us in the least. We were not gainers of any distance by it, because the River made us pay two days for Violating one.

Nevertheless, by making this Reflection, I would not be thought so rigid an observer of the Sabbath as to allow of no Work at all to be done, or Journeys to be taken upon it. I should not care to ly still and be knockt on the head, as the Jews were heretofore by Antiochus, because I believ'd it unlawful to stand upon my Defense on this good day. Nor would I care, like a certain New England Magistrate, to order a Man to the Whipping Post, for daring to ride for a Midwife on the Lord's Day.

On the contrary, I am for doing all acts of Necessity, Charity, and Self-Preservation, upon a Sunday as well as other days of the Week. But, as I think our present March cou'd not Strictly be justify'd by any of these Rules, it was but just we should suffer a little for it.

I never could learn that the Indians set apart any day of the Week or the Year for the Service of God. They pray, as Philosophers eat, only when they have a stomach, without having any set time for it. Indeed these Idle People have very little occasion for a sabbath to refresh themselves after hard Labour, because very few of them ever Labour at all. Like the wild Irish, they would

rather want than Work, and are all men of Pleasure, to whom every day is a day of rest.

Indeed, in their Hunting, they will take a little
Pains; but this being only a Diversion, their spirits
are rather rais'd than depress'd by it, and therefore
need at most but a Night's Sleep to recruit them.

4. By some Stakes we had driven into the River
yesterday, we perceiv'd the Water began to fall,
but fell so Slowly that we found we must have patience a day or two longer.   And because we were
unwilling to ly altogether Idle, we sent back some
of the men to bring up the two Horses that tir'd
the Saturday before. They were found near the
place where we had left them, but seemed too
sensible of their Liberty to come to us.   They
were found Standing indeed, but as Motionless as
the Equestrian statue at CHARING-CROSS.

We had great reason to apprehend more Rain
by the clouds that drove over our Heads. The
boldest amongst us were not without some Pangs
of uneasiness at so very Sullen a Prospect.   However, God be prais'd! it all blew over in a few
Hours.

If much Rain had fallen, we resolv'd to make a
Raft and bind it together with Grape Vines, to
Ferry ourselves and Baggage over the River.
Tho', in that Case, we expected the Swiftness of
the Stream wou'd have carry'd down our Raft a
long way before we cou'd have tugg'd it to the
opposite shoar.

One of the Young Fellows we had sent to bring
up the tired Horses entertained us in the Evening

with a remarkable adventure he had met with that day.

He had straggled, it seems, from his Company in a mist, and made a cub of a year old betake itself to a Tree. While he was new-priming his piece, with intent to fetch it down, the Old Gentlewoman appeared, and perceiving her Heir apparent in Distress, advanc'd open-mouth'd to his relief.

The man was so intent upon his Game, that she had approacht very near him before he perceived her. But finding his Danger, he faced about upon the Enemy, which immediately rear'd upon her posteriors, & put herself in Battle Array.

The Man, admiring at the Bear's assurance, endeavour'd to fire upon Her, but by the Dampness of the Priming, his Gun did not go off. He cockt it a second time, and had the same misfortune. After missing Fire twice, he had the folly to punch the Beast with the muzzle of his Piece; but mother Bruin, being upon her Guard, seized the Weapon with her Paws, and by main strength wrenched it out of the Fellow's Hands.

The Man being thus fairly disarm'd, thought himself no longer a Match for the Enemy, and therefore retreated as fast as his Legs could carry him.

The brute naturally grew bolder upon the flight of her Adversary, and pursued him with all her heavy speed. For some time it was doubtful whether fear made one run faster, or Fury the other. But after an even course of about 50 yards, the Man had the Mishap to Stumble over a Stump,

and fell down his full Length. He now wou'd
have sold his Life a Penny-worth; but the Bear,
apprehending there might be some Trick in the
Fall, instantly halted, and lookt with much attention on her Prostrate Foe.

In the mean while, the Man had with great presence of Mind resolved to make the Bear believe he
was dead, by lying Breathless on the Ground, in
Hopes that the Beast would be too generous to
kill him over again. To carry on the Farce, he
acted the Corpse for some time without dareing to
raise his head, to see how near the Monster was to
him. But in about two Minutes, to his unspeakable Comfort, he was rais'd from the Dead by the
Barking of a Dog, belonging to one of his companions, who came Seasonably to his Rescue, and
drove the Bear from pursuing the Man to take
care of her Cub, which she fear'd might now fall
into a second Distress.

5. We Judg'd the Waters were assuag'd this
morning to make the River fordable. Therefore
about Ten we try'd the Experiment, and every
Body got over Safe, except one man, whose Horse
Slipt from a Rock as he forded over, and threw
him into the River. But being able to swim, he
was not Carry'd down the Stream very far before
he recover'd the North Shore.

At the Distance of about 6 miles we passt Cas-
cade Creek, and 3 Miles farther we came upon
the Banks of the Dan, which we crost with much
Difficulty, by reason the Water was risen much
higher than when we forded it before.

Here the same unlucky Person happen'd to be
duckt a Second time, and was a Second time
Sav'd by Swimming.   My own Horse too plunged
in such a Manner that his Head was more than
once under Water, but with much more ado recover'd his Feet, tho' he made so low an obeisance,
that the water ran fairly over my Saddle.

We continued our march as far as LOWLAND
CREEK, where we took up our Lodging, for the
benefit of the Canes and Winter Grass that grew
upon the rich Grounds thereabouts.   On our way
thither we had the Misfortune to drop another
Horse, though he carry'd nothing the whole day
but his Saddle.   We showed the same favour to
most of our Horses, for fear, if we did not do it,
we should in a little time be turned into Beasts of
Burthen ourselves.

Custom had now made travelling on foot so familiar, that we were able to walk ten Miles with
Pleasure.   This we cou'd do in our Boots, notwithstanding our way lay over rough Woods and
uneven Grounds.

Our learning to walk in heavy Boots was the
same advantage to us that learning to Dance High
Dances in Wooden Shoes is to the French, it made
us most exceedingly Nimble without them.

The Indians, who have no way of travelling but
on the Hoof, make nothing of going 25 miles a
day, and carrying their little Necessaries at their
backs, and Sometimes a Stout Pack of Skins into
the Bargain.   And very often they laugh at the
English, who can't Stir to Next Neighbour with-

out a Horse, and say that 2 Legs are too much for such lazy people, who cannot visit their next neighbour without six.

For their Parts, they were utter Strangers to all our Beasts of Burthen or Carriage, before the Slothful Europeans came amongst them. They had on no part of the American Continent, or in any of the Islands, either Horses or Asses, Camels, Dromedaries or Elephants, to ease the Legs of the Original Inhabitants, or to lighten their Labour.

Indeed, in South America, and particularly in Chili, they have a useful animal call'd "paco." This creature resembles a Sheep pretty much; only in the Length of the Neck, and figure of the Head, it is more like a Camel. It is very near as high as the ass, and the Indians there make use of it for carrying moderate Burthens.

The Fleece that grows upon it is very Valuable for the fineness, length and Glossiness of the Wool. It has one remarkable Singularity, that the Hoofs of its fore-feet have three Clefts, and those behind no more than one. The Flesh of this Animal is something drier than our Mutton, but altogether as well tasted.

When it is Angry, it has no way of resenting its wrongs, but by spitting in the Face of those that provoke it: and if the Spawl happen to light on the bare Skin of any Person, it first creates an Itching, and afterwards a Scab, if no Remedy be applied. The way to manage these pacos, and make them tractable, is, to bore a hole in their ears, through which they put a Rope, and then guide them just as they please.

In Chili, they wear a beautiful kind of Stuff, with thread made of this Creature's Wool, which has a Gloss Superior to any Camlet, and is sold very dear in that country.

6. The Difficulty of finding the Horses among the tall Canes made it late before we decampt. We traversed very hilly Grounds, but to make amends it was pretty clear of Underwood.

We avoided crossing the Dan twice by taking a Compass round the bent of it. There was no passing by the angle of the River without halting a moment to entertain our Eyes again with that Charming Prospect. When that pleasure was over we proceeded to Sable Creek, and encamped a little to the East of it.

The River thereabouts had a charming effect, its Banks being adorn'd with green canes, sixteen feet high, which make a Spring all the year, as well as plenty of Forage all the Winter.

One of the Men wounded an Old Buck, that was gray with years, and seem'd by the Reverend Marks he bore upon him, to confirm the current Opinion of that animal's Longevity. The Smart of his Wounds made him not only turn upon the Dogs, but likewise pursue them to some Distance with great Fury.

However he got away at last, though by the blood that issued from his Wound he could not run far before he fell, and without doubt made a comfortable repast for the wolves. However the Indian had better Fortune, and supply'd us with a fat Doe, and a young Bear two years old. At that Age they are in their Prime, and, if they be fat withal, they are a Morsel for a Cardinal.

All the Land we Travell'd over this day, and the day before, that is to say from the river Irvin to Sable Creek, is exceedingly rich, both on the Virginia Side of the Line, and that of Carolina.[1] Besides whole Forests of Canes, that adorn the Banks of the River and Creeks thereabouts, the fertility of the Soil throws out such a Quantity of Winter Grass, that Horses and Cattle might keep themselves in Heart all the cold Season without the help of any Fodder. Nor have the low Grounds only this advantage, but likewise the Higher Land, and particularly that which we call the Highland Pond, which is two miles broad, and of a length unknown.

I question not but there are 30,000 Acres at least, lying Altogether, as fertile as the Lands were said to be about Babylon, which yielded, if Herodotus tells us right, an Increase of no less that 2 or 300 for one. But this hath the Advantage of being a higher, and consequently a much healthier, Situation than that. So that a Colony of 1000 families might, with the help of Moderate Industry, pass their time very happily there.

[1] It was this tract of land which Byrd bought from the North Carolina commissioners, to whom it was granted in payment for their services. Byrd called it "The Land of Eden"; but when he surveyed his tract he found a good deal of it was highland and by no means very attractive.—EDITOR.

Besides grazing and Tillage, which would abundantly compensate their Labour, they might plant Vineyards upon the Hills, in which Situation the richest Wines are always produc'd.

They might also propagate white Mulberry Trees, which thrive exceedingly in this climate, in order to the feeding of silk-worms, and making of Raw Silk.

They might too produce Hemp, Flax and Cotton, in what quantity they pleas'd, not only for their own use, but likewise for Sale. Then they might raise very plentiful Orchards, of both Peaches and Apples, which contribute as much as any Fruit to the Luxury of Life. There is no Soil or Climate will yield better Rice than this, which is a Grain of prodigious Increase, and of very wholesome Nourishment. In short every thing will grow plentifully here to supply either the Wants or Wantonness of Man.

Nor can I so much as wish that the more tender Vegetables might grow here, such as Orange, Lemon, and Olive Trees, because then we shou'd lose the much greater benefit of the brisk North-West Winds, which purge the Air, and sweep away all the Malignant Fevers, which hover over countries that are always warm.

The Soil wou'd also want the advantages of Frost, and Snow, which by their Nitrous Particles contribute not a little to its Fertility. Besides the Inhabitants wou'd be depriv'd of the Variety and Sweet Vicissitude of the Season, which is much more delightful than one dull and Constant Succession of Warm Weather, diversify'd only by Rain and Sun Shine.

There is also another convenience, that happens to this country by cold weather — it destroys a great Number of Snakes, and other Venomous Reptiles, and troublesome Insects, or at least lays them to Sleep for Several Months, which otherwise would annoy us the whole year round, & multiply beyond all Enduring.

Though Oranges and Lemons are desirable Fruits, and Usefull enough in many Cases, yet, when the Want of them is Supply'd by others more useful, we have no cause to complain.

There is no climate that produces every thing, since the Deluge Wrencht the Poles of the World out of their Place, nor is it fit it shou'd be so, because it is the Mutual Supply one country receives from another, which creates a mutual Traffic and Intercourse amongst men. And in Truth, were it not for the correspondence, in order to make up for each other's Wants, the Wars betwixt Bordering Nations, like those of the Indians and other barbarous People, wou'd be perpetual and irreconcileable.

As to Olive Trees, I know by Experience they will never stand the Sharpness of our Winters, but their Place may be Supply'd by the Plant call'd Sessamun, which yields an infinite quantity of large Seed, from whence a Sweet Oyl is prest, that is very wholesome and in use amongst the People of Lesser Asia. Likewise it is us'd in Egypt, preferably to oyl olive, being not so apt to make those

that eat it Constantly break out into Scabs, as they
do in many parts of Italy.   This would grow very
kindly here, and has already been planted with
good Success in North Carolina, by way of Experiment.

  7. After crossing the Dan, we made a march of
8 miles, over Hills and Dales as far as the next
Ford of that River.   And now we were by Practice become such very able Footmen, that we easily
outwalkt our Horses, and cou'd have marcht much
farther, had it not been in pity to their Weakness.
Besides here was plenty of Canes, which was
reason enough to make us Shorten our Journey.
Our Gunners did great Execution as they went
along, killing no less than two Brace of Deer, and
as many Wild Turkeys.

  Though Practice will soon make a man of tolerable Vigour an able Footman, yet, as a Help to
bear Fatigue I us'd to chew a Root of Ginseng as
I Walk't along.   This kept up my Spirits, and
made me trip away as nimbly in my half Jack-
Boots as younger men cou'd in their Shoes.   This
Plant is in high Esteem in China, where it sells
for its Weight in Silver.   Indeed it does not grow
there, but in the Mountains of Tartary, to which
Place the emperor of China Sends 10,000 Men
every Year on purpose to gather it.   But it grows
so scattering there, that even so many hands can
bring home no great Quantity.   Indeed it is a
Vegetable of so many vertues, that Providence
has planted it very thin in every Country that has

the happiness to produce it. Nor indeed is Mankind worthy of so great a Blessing, since Health and long Life are commonly Abus'd to ill Purposes. This noble Plant grows likewise at the Cape of Good Hope, where it is Call'd kanna, and is in wonderful Esteem among the Hottentots. It grows also on the northern continent of America, near the Mountains, but as Sparingly as Truth & Public Spirit. It answers exactly both to the Figure and vertues of that which grows in Tartary, so that there can be no doubt of its being the Same.

Its vertues are, that it gives an uncommon Warmth and Vigour to the Blood, and frisks the Spirits, beyond any other Cordial. It chears the Heart even of a Man that has a bad Wife, and makes him look down with great Composure on the crosses of the World. It promotes insensible Perspiration, dissolves all Phlegmatick and Viscous Humours, that are apt to obstruct the Narrow channels of the Nerves. It helps the Memory, and would quicken even Helvetian dullness. 'Tis friendly to the Lungs, much more than Scolding itself. It comforts the Stomach, and Strengthens the Bowels, preventing all Colicks and Fluxes. In one Word, it will make a Man live a great while, and very well while he does live. And what is more, it will even make Old Age amiable, by rendering it lively, chearful, and good-humour'd. However 'tis of little use in the Feats of Love, as a great prince once found, who hearing of its invigorating Quality, sent as far as China for some of it, though his ladys could not boast of any Advantage thereby.[1]

We gave the Indian the Skins of all the Deer that he Shot himself, and the Men the Skins of what they Kill'd. And every Evening after the Fires were made, they stretcht them very tight upon Sticks, and dry'd them. This, by a Nocturnal Fire, appear'd at first a very odd Spectacle, every thing being dark and gloomy round about. After they are Dry'd in this manner they may be folded up without Damage, till they come to be dress'd according to Art.

The Indians dress them with Deer's Brains, and so do the English here by their example. For Expedition's Sake they often Stretch their Skins over Smoak in order to dry them, which makes them smell so disagreeably that a Rat must have a good Stomach to gnaw them in that condition; nay, 'tis said, while that Perfume continues in a Pair of Leather Breeches, the Person who wears them will be in no Danger of that Villainous little insect the French call Morpion. And now I am upon the subject of Insects, it may not be improper to mention some few Remedies against those that are most Vexatious in this Climate. There are two Sorts without Doors, that are great Nuisances, the Tikes, and the Horse Flies. The Tikes are either Deer-tikes, or those that annoy the Cattle. The first kind are long, and take a very Strong Gripe, being most in remote Woods, above the Inhabitants.

---

[1] Ginseng is still found in Virginia and constitutes a considerable article of trade in some of the interior counties.—EDITOR.

The other are round, and more generally insinu-
ate themselves into the Flesh, being in all places
where Cattle are frequent. Both these Sorts are
apt to be troublesome during the Warm Season,
but have such an aversion to Penny Royal, that
they will attack no Part that is rubb'd with the
Juice of that fragrant Vegetable. And a Strong
Decoction of this is likewise the most effectual
Remedy against Seed-tikes, which bury themselves
in your Legs, when they are so small you can
hardly discern them without a MICROSCOPE.

The Horse Flies are not only a great Grievance
to Horses, but likewise to those that ride them.
These little Vixons confine themselves chiefly to
the Woods, and are most in moist Places. Tho'
this Insect be no bigger than an Ordinary Fly, it
bites very Smartly, darting its little Proboscis into
the Skin the instant it lights upon it. These are
offensive only in the hot months, and in the Day
time, when they are a great Nuisance to Travellers; insomuch that it is no Wonder they were formerly employed for one of the Plagues of Egypt.
But Dittany, which is to be had in the Woods all
the while those Insects remain in Vigor, is a Sure
Defense against them. For this purpose, if you
stick a Bunch of it on the Head-Stall of your
Bridle, they will be sure to keep a respectful
Distance.

Thus, in what part of the Woods soever any
thing mischievous or troublesome is found, kind
Providence is sure to provide a Remedy. And
'tis probably one great Reason why God was

pleas'd to create these, and many other Vexatious Animals, that Men sho'd exercise their Wits and Industry, to guard themselves against them.

Bears' Oyl is used by the Indians as a General Defence, against every Species of Vermin. Among the rest, they say it keeps both Bugs and Musquetas from assaulting their Persons, which wou'd otherwise devour Such uncleanly People. Yet Bears' Grease has no strong Smell, as that Plant had which the Egyptians formerly us'd against musquetas, resembling our palma Christi, the Juice of which smelled so disagreeably, that the Remedy was worse than the Disease.

Against musquetas, in Egypt, the Richer Sort us'd to build lofty Towers, with Bed-chambers in the Tops of them, that they might rest undisturbed. 'Tis certain that these Insects are no High Fliers, because their Wings are weak and their Bodies so light, that if they mount never so little, the wind blows them quite away from their Course, and they become an easy prey to the Martins, East India Bats, and other Birds that fly about in continual Quest of them.

8. As we had twice more to cross the Dan over two fords, that lay no more than 7 miles from each other, we judg'd the Distance wou'd not be much greater to go round the Bent of it. Accordingly we sent the Indian and two white Men that way, who came up with us in the Evening, after fetching a compass of about 12 Miles.

They told us that, about a mile from our last Camp, they passed a creek fortify'd with Steep

Cliffs, which therefore gain'd the name of Cliff
Creek.　Near 3 miles beyond that they forded a
Second Creek, on the Margin of which grew abundance of Tall canes and this was call'd Hix's creek,
from one of the Discoverers.　Between these two
creeks lies a level of exceeding rich Land, full of
large Trees, and cover'd with black Mould, as
fruitful, if we believe them, as that which is yearly
overflow'd by the Nile.

We who marched the nearest way upon the Line
found the Ground rising and falling between the
two Fords of the Dan, which almost broke our
own Wind, and the Hearts of our Jaded Palfreys.
When we had passed the last Ford, it was a Sensible Joy to find ourselves Safe over all the Waters
that might cut off our Retreat.　And we had the
greater Reason to be Thankfull, because so late in
the Year it was very unusual to find the rivers so
fordable.

We catcht a large Tarapin in the River, which
is one kind of Turtle.　The flesh of it is wholesome, and good for Consumptive People.　It lays
a great Number of Eggs, not larger but rounder
than those of Pigeons.　These are Soft, but
withal so tough that 'tis difficult to break them, yet
are very Sweet and invigorating, so that some
Wives recommend them earnestly to their Husbands.

One of the Men, by an Overstrain, had unhappily got a Running of the Reins, for which I gave
him every Morning a little Sweet Gumm dissolv'd
in Water, with good success.　This gumm distils

from a large Tree, call'd the Sweet-Gum Tree, very Common in Virginia, and is as healing in its Virtue as Balm of Gilead, or the Balsams of Tolu and of Peru. It is likewise a most Agreeable parfume, very little inferior to Ambergris.

And now I have mention'd Ambergris, I hope it will not be thought an unprofitable digression, to give a faithful Account how it is produced, in Order to reconcile the various Opinions concerning it. It is now certainly found to be the Dung of the Sper Maceti Whale, which is at first very black and unsavoury. But after having been washt for some Months in the Sea, and blanch'd in the Sun, it comes at length to be of a Gray colour, and from a most offensive Smell, contracts the finest fragrancy in the World.

Besides the Fragrancy of this Animal Substance, 'tis a very rich and innocent Cordial, which raises the spirits without Stupifying them afterwards, like Opium, or intoxicating them like Wine. The Animal Spirits are amazingly refreshed by this Cordial, without the Danger of any ill consequence, and if Husbands were now and then to dissolve a little of it in their Broth, their Consorts might be the better for it, as well as themselves. In the Bahama Islands (where a great Quantity is found, by reason the Sperma Ceti Whales resort thither continually,) it is us'd as an Antidote against the Venomous Fish which abound thereabouts, wherewith the People are apt to Poison themselves.

We are not only oblig'd to that Whale for this rich parfume, but also for the Sper Maceti itself,

which is the Fat of that Fish's Head boil'd and
purg'd from all its impuritys. What remains is of
a balsamick and detersive Quality, very friendly
to the Lungs, and usefull in many other Cases.

The Indian had kill'd a fat Doe in the compass
he took round the Elbow of the River, but was
content to Prime it only, by reason it was too
far off to lug the whole Carcass upon his Back.
This, and a Brace of Wild Turkeys which our
Men had Shot, made up all our Bill of Fare this
Evening, but could only afford a Philosophical
Meal to so many craving Stomachs.

The Horses were now so lean that any thing
would gall those that carry'd the least Burthen;
no Wonder then if Several of them had sore
Backs, especially now the Pads of the Saddles
and Packs were press'd flat with long and constant Use. This would have been another Misfortune, had we not been provided with an easy
Remedy for it.

One of the Commissioners, believing that Such
Accidents might happen in a far Journey, had furnisht himself with Plasters of Strong Glue spread
pretty thick. We laid on these, after making
them running hot, which, Sticking fast, never fell
off till the Sore was perfectly heal'd. In the
mean time it defended the part so well, that the
Saddle might bear upon it without Danger of
further Injury.

9. We reckon'd ourselves now pretty well out
of the Latitude of Bears, to the great Grief of
most of the company. There was Still Mast

enough left in the Woods to keep the Bears from drawing so near to the Inhabitants. They like not the neighbourhood of Merciless Man, till Famine compels them to it. They are all Black in this part of the World, and so is their Dung, but it will make Linnen white, being tolerably good Soap, without any Preparation but only drying.

These Bears are of a Moderate Size, whereas within the Polar Circles they are white, and much larger. Those of the Southern Parts of Muscovy are of a Russet Colour, but among the SAMOEIDS, as well as in GREENLAND and NOVA ZEMBLA, they are as white as the snow they converse with, and by some Accounts are as large as a Moderate Ox.

The Excessive Cold of that Climate sets their Appetites so Sharp, that they will Attack a Man without Ceremony, and even climb up a Ship's Side to come at him. They range about and are very Mischievous all the time the Sun is above the Horizon, which is something more than Five Months; but after the Sun is Set for the rest of the Year, they retire into Holes, or bury themselves under the Snow, and Sleep away the Dark Season without any Sustenance at all. 'Tis pitty our Beggars and Pickpockets Cou'd not do the Same.

Our Journey this day was above 12 Miles, and more than half the way terribly hamper'd with Bushes. We tir'd another Horse, which we were oblig'd to leave two miles short of where we Encampt, and indeed Several others were upon the

Careen almost every Step. Now we wanted one
of those celebrated Musicians of Antiquity, who,
they tell us, among many other Wonders of their
Art, cou'd play an air which, by its Animateing
Briskness wou'd make a Jaded Horse caper and
curvet much better than any Whip, Spur, or even
than Swearing. Tho' I fear our poor Beasts were
so harast that it wou'd have been beyond the Skill
of Orpheus himself so much as to make them
prick up their ears.

For Proof of the Marvellous Power of Music
among the Ancients, some Historians say, that one
of those Skilful Masters took upon him to make
the great Alexander start up from his Seat, and
handle his Javelin, whether he would or not, by
the force of a sprightly Tune, which he knew how
to play to Him. The King ordered the man to
bring his Instrument, and then fixing himself
firmly in his chair, and determining not to Stir, he
bade him to Strike up as soon as he pleas'd. The
Musician obey'd, and presently rous'd the Hero's
Spirits with such Warlike Notes, that he was con-
strain'd, in Spite of all his Resolution, to spring up
and fly to his Javelin with great martial Fury.

We can the easier credit these Prophane Stories
by what we find recorded in the Oracles of Truth,
where we are told the Wonders David performed
by Sweetly touching his Harp. He made nothing
of driving the Evil Spirit out of Saul, tho' a certain rabbi assures us he could not do so much by
his Wife, MICHAL, when she happen'd to be in
her Ayrs.

The greatest Instance we have of the Power of Modern Music is that which cures those who in Italy are bitten by the little Spider called the Tarantula. The whole method of which is perform'd in the following manner.

In Apulia it is a common Misfortune for People to be bitten by the Tarantula, and most about Taranto and Gallipoli. This is a gray spider, not very large, with a narrow Streak of white along the Back. It is no wonder there are many of these Villanous Insects, because, by a Ridiculous Superstition 'tis accounted great Inhumanity to kill them. They believe, it seems, that if the Spider come to a Violent Death, all those who had been bitten by it will certainly have a Return of their Frenzy every Year as long as they live. But if it dye a Natural Death, the Patient will have a chance to recover in two or three Years.

The Bite of the tarantula gives no more pain than the Bite of a musqueta, and makes little or no inflamation on the Part, especially when the Disaster happens in April or May; but, its Venom encreasing with the Heat of the Season, has more fatal Consequences in July and August. The Persons who are so unhappy as to be bitten in those Warm Months, fall down on the Place in a few Minutes, and lye senseless for a considerable time, and when they come to themselves feel horrible Pains, are very Sick at their Stomachs, and in a Short time break out into foul Sores; but those who are bitten in the Milder Months have much gentler Symptoms. They are longer before the

Distemper Shows itself, and then they have a small
Disorder in their Senses, are a little sick, and perhaps have some Moderate Breakings-out.

However, in both cases, the Patient keeps upon
the Bed, not caring to stir, till he is rous'd by a
Tune, proper for his particular case. Therefore,
as soon as the Symptoms discover themselves, a
Tarantula Doctor is sent for, who, after viewing
carefully the condition of the Person, first tries
one Tune and then another, until he is so fortunate
as to hit the Phrenetic turn of the Patient. No
sooner does this happen but he begins to Wag a
finger, then a Hand, and afterwards a Foot, till at
last he springs up and dances Round the Room,
with a Surprising Agility, rolling his Eyes and
looking wild the whole time. This dancing-Fit
lasts commonly about 25 minutes, by which time
he will be all in a Lather. Then he sits down, falls
a laughing, and returns to his Senses. So Plentiful a Perspiration discharges so much of the Venom
as will keep off the Return of the Distemper for a
whole Year. Then it will Visit Him again, and
must be remov'd in the Same Merry Manner. But
three dancing Bouts will do the Business, unless,
peradventure, the Spider, according to the Vulgar
Notion, has been put to a Violent Death.

The Tunes Play'd to expel this Whimsical
Disorder, are of the Jigg-kind, and exceed not
15 in number. The Apulians are frequently
dancing off the Effects of this Poison, and no
Remedy is more commonly apply'd to any other
Distemper elsewhere, than those Sprightly Tunes

are to the Bite of the Tarantula in that part of
Italy.

It is remarkable that these Spiders have a greater
Spight to the Natives of the Place than they have
to Strangers, and Women are oftener bitten than
Men. Tho' there may be a Reason for the last,
because Women are more confin'd to the House,
where these Spyders keep, and their coats make
them liable to Attacks unseen, whereas the Men
can more easily discover, and brush them off their
Legs. Nevertheless, both Sexes are cur'd the
Same way, and thereby Show the Wonderful
Effects of Music.

Considering how far we had walkt, and consequently how hungry we were, we found but Short
commons when we came to our Quarters. One
Brace of Turkeys was all the Game we cou'd meet
with, which almost needed a Miracle to enable
them to Suffice so many Voracious Appetites.
However, they just made a Shift to keep Famine,
and consequently Mutiny, out of the Camp. At
Night we lodg'd upon the Banks of Buffalo Creek,
where none of us cou'd complain of loss of Rest,
for having eaten too heavy and Luxurious a
Supper.

10. In a Dearth of Provisions our Chaplain pro-
nounc'd it lawful to make bold with the Sabbath,
and send a Party out a-Hunting. They fired the
Dry Leaves in a Ring of five Miles' circumference,
which, burning inwards, drove all the Game to the
Centre, where they were easily killed.

It is really a pitiful Sight to see the extreme

Distress the poor deer are in, when they find themselves Surrounded with this Circle of Fire; they weep and Groan like a Human Creature, yet can't move the compassion of those hard-hearted People, who are about to murder them. This unmerciful Sport is called Fire Hunting, and is much practic'd by the Indians and Frontier Inhabitants, who sometimes, in the Eagerness of their Diversion, are Punish't for their cruelty, and are hurt by one another when they Shoot across at the Deer which are in the Middle.

What the Indians do now by a Circle of Fire, the ancient Persians performed formerly by a circle of Men: and the same is practis'd at this day in Germany upon extraordinary Occasions, when any of the Princes of the Empire have a Mind to make a General Hunt, as they call it. At such times they order a vast Number of People to Surround a whole Territory. Then Marching inwards in close Order, they at last force all the Wild Beasts into a Narrow Compass, that the Prince and his Company may have the Diversion of Slaughtering as many as they please with their own hands.

Our Hunters massacred two Brace of Deer after this unfair way, of which they brought us one Brace whole, and only the Primings of the rest. So many were absent on this Occasion, that we who remained excusd the Chaplain from the Trouble of spending his Spirits by Preaching to so thin a Congregation. One of the men, who had been an old Indian Trader, brought me a Stem of Silk Grass, which was about as big as my little

Finger. But, being so late in the Year that the Leaf was fallen off, I am not able to describe the Plant.

The Indians use it in all their little Manufactures, twisting a Thread of it that is prodigiously Strong. Of this they make their Baskets and the Aprons which their Women wear about their Middles, for Decency's Sake. These are long enough to wrap quite round them and reach down to their Knees, with a Fringe on the under part by way of Ornament.

They put on this modest covering with so much art, that the most impertinent curiosity can't in the Negligentest of their Motions or Postures make the least discovery. As this species of Silk Grass is much Stronger than Hemp, I make no doubt but Sail Cloth and Cordage might be made of it with considerable Improvement.

11. We had all been so refresht by our day of rest, that we decamp'd earlier than Ordinary, and passed the Several Fords of Hico River. The Woods were thick great Part of this Day's Journey, so that we were forced to scuffle hard to advance 7 miles, being equal in fatigue to double that distance of Clear and Open Grounds.

We took up our Quarters upon Sugar-tree Creek, in the same camp we had lain in when we came up, and happen'd to be entertained at Supper with a Rarity we had never had the fortune to meet with before, during the whole Expedition.

A little wide of this creek, one of the men had the Luck to meet with a Young Buffalo of two

Years Old. It was a Bull, which, notwithstanding he was no older, was as big as an ordinary Ox. His Legs are very thick and very Short, and his Hoofs exceeding broad. His Back rose into a kind of Bunch a little above the Shoulders, which I believe contributes not a little to that creature's enormous Strength. His Body is vastly deep from the shoulders to the Brisket, sometimes 6 feet in those that are full grown. The portly figure of this Animal is disgrac'd by a Shabby little Tail, not above 12 Inches long. This he cocks up on end whenever he's in a Passion, and, instead of lowing or bellowing, grunts with no better grace than a Hog.

The Hair growing on his Head and Neck is long and Shagged, and so Soft that it will Spin into Thread not unlike Mohair, which might be wove into a Sort of Camlet. Some People have Stockings knit of it, that would have serv'd an Israelite during his forty Years' march thro' the Wilderness.

Its horns are short and Strong, of which the Indians make large Spoons, which they say will Split and fall to Pieces whenever Poison is put into them. Its Colour is a dirty Brown, and its hide so thick that it is Scarce penetrable. However, it makes very Spongy Sole Leather by the ordinary method of Tanning, tho' this fault might by good Contrivance be mended.

As thick as this poor Beast's Hide was, a Bullet made Shift to enter it and fetch him down. It was found all alone, tho' Buffaloes Seldom are. They usually range about in Herds, like other cattle, and, tho' they differ something in figure, are certainly of the Same Species.   There are two Reasons for this Opinion: the Flesh of both has exactly the same taste, and the mixed Breed betwixt both, they say, will generate.   All the Difference I could perceive between the Flesh of Buffalo and Common Beef was, that the Flesh of the first was much Yellower than that of the other, and the Lean something tougher.

The Men were so delighted with this new dyet, that the Gridiron and Frying-Pan had no more rest all night, than a poor Husband Subject to Curtain Lectures.   Buffaloes may be easily tamed when they are taken Young.   The best way to catch them is to carry a Milch Mare into the Woods, and when you find a Cow and a Calf, to kill the Cow, and then having catch'd the Calf to Suckle it upon the Mare.   After once or twice Sucking Her, it will follow her Home, and become as gentle as another calf.

If we cou'd get into a breed of them, they might be made very usefull, not only for the Dairy, by giving an Ocean of Milk, but also for drawing vast and cumbersome Weights by their prodigious Strength.   These, with the other Advantages I mention'd before, wou'd make this sort of Cattle more profitable to the owner, than any other we are acquainted with, though they would need a world of Provender.

Before we marcht this Morning, every man took care to pack up some Buffalo Steaks in his Wallet,

besides what he crammed into his Belly. When
Provisions were Plenty, we always found it Difficult to get out early, being too much Embarrast
with a long-winded Breakfast.

However, by the Strength of our Beef, we made
a shift to walk about 12 Miles, crossing Blewing
and Tewaw-homini Creeks. And because this last
Stream receiv'd its Appelation from the Disaster
of a Tuscarora Indian, it will not be Straggling
much out of the way to say something of that Particular Nation.

These Indians were heretofore very numerous
and powerful, making, within time of Memory, at
least a Thousand Fighting Men. Their Habitation, before the War with Carolina, was on the
North Branch of Neuse River, commonly call'd
Connecta Creek, in a pleasant and fruitful Country. But now the few that are left of that Nation
live on the North Side of MORATUCK, which is
all that Part of Roanok below the great Falls,
towards ALBEMARLE Sound.

Formerly there were Seven Towns of these Savages, lying not far from each other, but now their
Number is greatly reduc'd.

The Trade they have had the Misfortune to
drive with the English has furnisht them constantly
with Rum, which they have used so immoderately,
that, what with the Distempers, and what with the
Quarrels it begat amongst them, it has proved a
double Destruction.

But the greatest Consumption of these savages
happen'd by the war about Twenty-Five years

ago, on Account of some Injustice the Inhabitants of that Province had done them about their Lands.

It was on that Provocation they resented their wrongs a little too severely upon Mr. Lawson, who, under Colour of being Surveyor gen'l, had encroacht too much upon their Territories, at which they were so enrag'd, that they waylaid him, and cut his Throat from Ear to Ear, but at the same time releas'd the Baron de Graffenried, whom they had Seized for Company, because it appear'd plainly he had done them no Wrong.[1]

This Blow was followed by some other Bloody Actions on the Part of the Indians, which brought on the War, wherein many of them were but [sic] off, and many were oblig'd to flee for Refuge to the Senecas, so that now there remain so few, that they are in danger of bing [sic] quite exterminated by the Catawbas, their mortal Enemies.

These Indians have a very odd Tradition amongst them, that many years ago, their Nation was grown so dishonest, that no man cou'd keep any Goods, or so much as his loving Wife to himself. That, however, their God, being unwilling to root them out for their crimes, did them the honour to send a Messenger from Heaven to instruct them, and set Them a perfect Example of Integrity and kind Behavior towards one another.

But this holy Person, with all his Eloquence and Sanctity of Life, was able to make very little

---

[1] For an account of this massacre see De Graffenreid's narrative in the Colonial Records of North Carolina, I. 905.

Reformation amongst them. Some few Old Men did listen a little to his Wholesome Advice, but all the Young fellows were quite incorrigible. They not only Neglected his Precepts, but derided and Evil Entreated his Person. At last, taking upon Him to reprove some Young Rakes of the Conechta Clan very sharply for their impiety, they were so provok'd at the Freedom of his Rebukes, that they tied him to a Tree, and shot him with Arrows through the Heart. But their God took instant Vengeance on all who had a hand in that Monstrous Act, by Lightning from Heaven, & has ever since visited their Nation with a continued Train of Calamities, nor will he ever leave off punishing, and wasting their People, till he shall have blotted every living Soul of them out of the World.

Our Hunters shot nothing this whole day but a straggling Bear, which happen'd to fall by the Hand of the very Person who had been lately dis-arm'd and put to flight, for which he declar'd War against the whole Species.

13. We pursued our Journey with all Diligence, and forded Ohimpamony Creek about Noon, and from thence proceeded to Yatapsco, which we cou'd not cross without difficulty. The Beavers had dammed up the Water much higher than we found it at our going up, so that we were oblig'd to lay a Bridge over a part that was shallower than the rest, to facilitate our passage.

Beavers have more of Instinct, that Half-Brother of Reason, than any other Animal, especially in matters of Self-Preservation. In their Houses they always contrive a Sally-Port, both towards the Land and towards the Water, that so they may escape by One, if their Retreat shou'd happen to be cut off at the other.

They perform all their Works in the Dead of Night, to avoid Discovery, and are kept diligently to it by the Master Beaver, which by his age or strength has gain'd to himself an Authority over the rest. If any of the Gang happen to be lazy, or will not exert himself to the utmost in felling of Trees, or dragging them [to] the place where they are made use of, this Superintendent will not fail to chastise him with the Flat of the Tail, where-with he is able to give unmerciful strokes.

They lie Snug in their Houses all day, unless some unneighbourly Miller chance to disturb their repose, by demolishing their Dams for supplying his Mill with Water.

It is rare to see one of them, and the Indians for that Reason have hardly any way to take them, but by laying Snares near the place where they dam up the Water. But the English Hunters have found out a more effectual Method, by using the following receipt. Take the large Pride of the Beaver, Squeeze all the Juice out of it, then take the small Pride, and Squeeze out about 5 or 6 Drops. Take the inside of Sassafras Bark, Pow-der it, and mix it with the Liquor, and place this Bait conveniently for your Steel Trap.

The Story of their biting off their Testicles to compound for their Lives, when they are pur-sued, is a story taken upon trust by Pliny, like

many others.   Nor is it the Beaver's Testicles that
carry the Perfume, but they have a Pair of Glands
just within the Fundament, as Sweet as Musk, that
perfume their Dung, and communicate a strong
scent to their Testicles, by being plac'd near them.

It is true Several creatures have Strange instincts
for their Preservation, as the Egyptian Frog, we
are told by Elian, will carry a whole Joint of a
Reed across its Mouth, that it may not be swallow'd
by the ibis.

And this Long-neckt fowl will give itself a
clyster with its Beak, whenever it finds itself too
costive or feverish.   The Dogs of that Country
lap the Water of the Nile in a full Trot, that they
may not be Snapped by the Crocodiles.   Both
Beavers and Wolves, we know, when one of their
Legs is caught in a Steel Trap, will bite it off, that
they may escape with the rest.   The Flesh of the
Beavers is tough and dry, all but the Tail, which,
like the Parrot's Tongue, was one of the far-
fetched Rarities with which Heliogabalus used to
furnish his Luxurious Table.

The Fur of these creatures is very valuable,
especially in the more Northern Countries, where
it is longer and finer.   This the Dutch have lately
contriv'd to mix with their Wool, and Weave into
a Sort of Drugget, that is not only warm, but won-
derfully light and Soft.   They also make Gloves
and Stockings of it, that keep out the Cold almost
as well as the Fur itself, and do not look quite so
Savage.

There is a deal of Rich low Ground on Yapatsco

Creek, but I believe liable to be overflow'd in a fresh. However, it might be proper enough for Rice, which receives but little Injury from Water.

We encamp on the Banks of Massamony Creek, after a Journey of more than 11 Miles. By the way we Shot a fat Doe and a wild Turkey, which fed us all plentifully. And we have reason to say, by our own happy Experience, that no man need to despair of his daily Bread in the Woods, whose faith is but half so large as his Stomach.

14. Being at length happily arriv'd within 20 Miles of the uppermost Inhabitants, we despacht two Men who had the ablest Horses, to go before, and get a Beef kill'd and some Bread bak'd to refresh their Fellow Travellers, upon their arrival. They had likewise Orders to hire an express to carry a Letter to the Governor, giving an Account that we were all returned in Safety. This was the more necessary, because we had been so long absent that many now began to fear we were, by this time, Scalpt and barbecu'd by the Indians.

We decampt with the rest of the People about ten a clock, and marched near 12 Miles. In our way we Crost Nutbush Creek, and 4 Miles farther we came upon a beautiful Branch of Great Creek, where we took up our Quarters. The Tent was pitched upon an Eminence, which overlookt a wide Piece of low Grounds, cover'd with Reeds and watered by a Crystal Stream, gliding thro' the Middle of it. On the Other Side of this delightful Valley, which was about half a Mile wide, rose a Hill that terminated the View, and in the figure of a Semicircle closed in upon the opposite Side of the Valley. This had a most agreeable Effect upon the Eye, and wanted nothing but Cattle grazing in the Meadow, and Sheep and Goats feeding on the Hill, to make it a Compleat Rural LANDSCAPE.

The Indian kill'd a Fawn, which, being upon its growth, was not fat, but made some amends by being tender. He also Shot an Otter, but our People were now better fed than to eat such Coarse Food. The truth of it is, the Flesh of this Creature has a rank Fishy taste, and for that reason might be a proper Regale for the Samoeids, who drink the CZAR of MUSCOVY's health and toast their Mistresses in a Bumper of Train Oil.

The Carthusians, to save their Vow of eating no Flesh, pronounce this Amphibious Animal to be a Fish, and feed upon it as such, without Wounding their Consciences.

The Skin of the Otter is very Soft, and the Swedes make Caps and Socks of it, not only for Warmth, but also because they fancy it Strengthens the Nerves, and is good against all Distempers of the Brain.

The otter is a great Devourer of Fish, which are its Natural Food, and whenever it betakes itself to a Vegetable Dyet, it is as some high-Spirited Wives obey their Husbands, by pure Necessity. They dive after their Prey, tho' they can't continue long under Water, but thrust their Noses up to the Surface now and then for Breath. They are great Enemies to Weirs Set up in the Rivers to catch Fish, devouring or biting to pieces all they find there. Nor is it either easy to fright them from this kind of Robbery, or to destroy them. The best way I cou'd ever find was to float an Old Wheel just by the Weir, and so soon as the Otter has taken a large Fish, he will get upon the Wheel to eat it more at his ease, which may give you an Opportunity of firing upon him from the Shoar.

One of our People Shot a large Gray Squirrel with a very Bushy Tail, a singular use of which our merry Indian discover'd to us. He said whenever this little Animal has occasion to cross a run of Water, he launches a Chip or Piece of Bark into the Water, on which he embarks, and, holding up his Tail to the wind, he Sails over very Safely. If This be true, it is probable men learnt at first the use of Sails from these ingenious little Animals, as the Hottentots learnt the Physical use of most of their Plants from the Baboons.

15. About three Miles from our Camp we passed GREAT CREEK, and then, after traversing very barren grounds for 5 Miles together, we crost the Tradeing Path, and soon after had the pleasure of reaching the uppermost Inhabitant. This was a Plantation belonging to colonel Mumford, where our Men almost burst themselves with Potatoes and Milk. Yet as great a Curiosity as a House was to us Foresters, still we chose to lie in the Tent, as being much the cleaner and sweeter Lodging.

The Tradeing Path above-mention'd receives its

Name from being the Route the Traders take with their Caravans, when they go to traffick with the Catawbas and other Southern Indians. The Catawbas live about 250 Miles beyond Roanoke River, and yet our Traders find their Account in transporting Goods from Virginia to trade with them at their own Towne.

The Common Method of carrying on this Indian Commerce is as follows: Gentlemen send for Goods proper for such a Trade from England, and then either Venture them out at their own Risk to the Indian Towns, or else credit some Traders with them of Substance and Reputation, to be paid in Skins at a certain Price agreed betwixt them.

The Goods for the Indian Trade consist chiefly in Guns, Powder, Shot, Hatchets, (which the Indians call Tomahawks,) Kettles, red & blue Planes, Duffields, Stroudwater blankets, and some Cutlary Wares, Brass Rings and other Trinkets.

These Wares are made up into Packs and Carry'd upon Horses, each Load being from 150 to 200 Pounds, with which they are able to travel about 20 Miles a day, if Forage happen to be plentiful.

Formerly a Hundred Horses have been employ'd in one of these Indian Caravans, under the Conduct of 15 or 16 Persons only, but now the Trade is much impair'd, insomuch that they seldom go with half that Number.

The Course from Roanoke to the Catawbas is laid down nearest South-west, and lies thro' a fine Country, that is Water'd by Several beautiful Rivers.

Those of the greatest Note are, first, Tar river, which is the upper Part of Pamptico, Flat river, Little river and Eno river, all three Branches of Neuse.

Between Eno and Saxapahaw rivers are the Haw old fields, which have the Reputation of containing the most fertile high land in this part of the World, lying in a Body of about 50,000 acres.

This Saxapahaw is the upper Part of Cape Fair River, the falls of which lye many Miles below the Trading Path.

Some Mountains overlook this Rich Spot of Land, from whence all the Soil washes down into the Plane, and is the cause of its exceeding Fertility.   Not far from thence the Path crosses ARAMANCHY River, a branch of Saxapahaw, and about 40 Miles beyond that, Deep River, which is the N Branch of Pedee.   Then 40 miles beyond that, the Path intersects the Yadkin, which is there half a Mile over, and is supposed to be the South Branch of the same Pedee.

The Soil is exceedingly rich on both sides the Yadkin, abounding in rank Grass and prodigiously large Trees; and for plenty of Fish, Fowl and Venison, is inferior to No Part of the Northern Continent.   There the Traders commonly lie Still for some days, to recruit their Horses' Flesh as well as to recover their own Spirits.   Six Miles further is Crane Creek, so nam'd from its being the Rendezvous of great Armies of Cranes, which wage a more cruel War at this day, with the Frogs and

the Fish, than they us'd to do with the Pigmies in
the Days of Homer.

About three-score Miles more bring you to the
first Town of the Catawbas, call'd Nauvasa, situ-
ated on the banks of Santee river.   Besides this
Town there are five Others belonging to the same
Nation, lying all on the same Stream, within the
Distance of 20 Miles.

These Indians were all call'd formerly by the
general Name of the Usherees, and were a very
Numerous and Powerful People. But the frequent
Slaughters made upon them by the Northern Indians, and, what has been still more destructive by
far, the Intemperance and Foul Distempers intro-
duc'd amongst them by the Carolina Traders, have
now reduc'd their Numbers to little More than 400
Fighting Men, besides Women & Children.   It is
a charming Place where they live, the Air very
Wholesome, the Soil fertile, and the Winters ever
mild and Serene.

In Santee river, as in Several others of Carolina,
a Small kind of allegator is frequently seen, which
perfumes the Water with a Musky Smell.   They
Seldom exceed Eight Feet in Length in these
parts, whereas, near the Equinoctial, they come up
to twelve or Fourteen.   And the heat of the Climate don't only make them bigger, but more Fierce
and Voracious.   They watch the Cattle there when
they come to drink and Cool themselves in the
River; and because they are not able to drag them
into the Deep Water, they make up by Strategem
what they want in Force.   They Swallow great

Stones, the Weight of which being added to their Strength, enables them to tug a Moderate Cow under Water, and as soon as they have drown'd her, they discharge the Stones out of their Maw and then feast upon the Carcass. However, as Fierce and Strong as these Monsters are, the Indians will surprise them Napping as they float upon the Surface, get astride upon their Necks, then whip a short piece of wood like a Truncheon into their Jaws, & holding the Ends with their two hands, hinder them from diving by keeping their mouths open, and when they are almost Spent, they will make to the shoar, where their Riders knock them on the Head and Eat them. This Amphibious Animal is a Smaller kind of Crocodile, having the Same Shape exactly, only the Crocodile of the Nile is twice as long, being when full grown from 20 to Thirty Feet. This Enormous Length is the more to be wonder'd at, because the Crocodile is hatcht from an Egg very little larger than that of a Goose. It has a long Head, which it can open very wide, with very Sharp & Strong teeth. Their Eyes are Small, their Legs Short, with Claws upon their Feet. Their Tail makes half the Length of their Body, and the whole is guarded with hard impenetrable Scales, except the Belly, which is much Softer and Smoother. They keep much upon the Land in the day time, but towards the Evening retire into the Water to avoid the Cold Dews of the Night. They run pretty fast right forward, but are very awkward and Slow in turning, by reason of their unwieldy Length. It is an

Error that they have no Tongue, without which they cou'd hardly Swallow their Food; but in eating they move the upper Jaw only, Contrary to all other Animals. The way of catching them in Egypt is, with a Strong Hook fixt to the End of a chain, and baited with a joynt of Pork, which they are very fond of. But a live Hog is generally tyed near, the Cry of which allures them to the Hook. This Account of the Crocodile will agree in most particulars with the Alligator, only the Bigness of the last cannot entitle it to the Name of "Leviathan," which Job gave formerly to the crocodile, and not to the Whale, as some Interpreters wou'd make us believe.

So Soon as the Catawba Indians are inform'd of the Approach of the Virginia Caravans, they send a Detachment of their Warriors to bid them Welcome, and escort them Safe to their Town, where they are receiv'd with great Marks of Distinction. And their Courtesys to the VIRGINIA Traders, I dare say, are very Sincere, because they sell them better Goods and better Pennyworths than the Traders of Carolina. They commonly reside among the Indians till they have barter'd their Goods away for Skins, with which they load their Horses and come back by the Same Path they went.

There are generally some Carolina Traders that constantly live among the Catawbas, and pretend to Exercise a dictatorial Authority over them. These petty Rulers don't only teach the honester Savages all sorts of Debauchery, but are unfair in their dealings, and use them with all kinds of Oppression. Nor has their Behaviour been at all better to the rest of the Indian Nations, among whom they reside, by abusing their Women and Evil-entreating their Men; and, by the way, this was the true Reason of the fatal War which the Nations roundabout made upon Carolina in the year 1713.

Then it was all that the Neighbouring Indians, grown weary of the Tyranny and Injustice with which they had been abus'd for many Years, resolv'd to endure their bondage no longer, but enter'd into General Confederacy against their Oppressors of Carolina.

The Indians open'd the War by knocking most of those little Tyrants on the Head that dwelt amongst them, under pretence of regulating their Commerce, and from thence Carry'd their Resentment so far as to endanger both NORTH and SOUTH CAROLINA.

16. We gave Orders that the Horses shou'd pass Roanoak River at Monisep Ford, while most of the Baggage was transported in a Canoe.

We landed at the Plantation of cornelius Keith, where I beheld the wretchedest Scene of Poverty I had ever met with in this happy Part of the World. The Man, his Wife and Six Small Children, liv'd in a Penn, like so many Cattle, without any Roof over their Heads but that of Heaven. And this was their airy Residence in the Day time, but then there was a Fodder Stack not far from this Inclosure, in which the whole Family shelter'd themselves a night's and in bad weather.

However, 'twas almost worth while to be as poor as this Man was, to be as perfectly contented. All his Wants proceeded from Indolence, and not from Misfortune. He had good Land, as well as good Health and good Limbs to work it, and, besides, had a Trade very useful to all the Inhabitants round about. He cou'd make and set up Quern Stones very well, and had proper Materials for that purpose just at Hand, if he cou'd have taken the pains to fetch them.

There is no other kind of Mills[1] in those remote parts, and, therefore, if the Man wou'd have Workt at his Trade, he might have liv'd very comfortably. The poor woman had a little more Industry, and Spun Cotton enough to make a thin covering for her own and her children's Nakedness.

I am sorry to say it, but Idleness is the general character of the men in the Southern Parts of this Colony as well as in North Carolina. The Air is so mild, and the Soil so fruitful, that very little Labour is requir'd to fill their Bellies, especially where the Woods afford such Plenty of Game. These Advantages discharge the Men from the Necessity of killing themselves with Work, and then for the other Article of Raiment, a very little of that will suffice in so temperate a Climate. But so much as is absolutely Necessary falls to the good women's Share to provide. They all Spin, weave and knit, whereby they make a good Shift

---

[1] The Editor has seen old quern-mills, or hand-mills, in some of the remote sections of North Carolina, which tradition said were in use well into the nineteenth century.

to cloath the whole Family; and to their credit be it recorded, many of them do it very completely, and thereby reproach their Husbands' Laziness in the most inoffensive way, that is to say, by discovering a better Spirit of Industry in themselves.

From thence we mov'd forward to Colo Mumford's other Plantation, under the Care of Miles Riley, where, by that Gentleman's Directions, we were again Supply'd with many good things. Here it was we discharg'd our Worthy Friend and Fellow Travellaur, Mr. Bearskin, who had so plentifully Supplyed us with Provisions during our long Expedition. We rewarded Him to his Heart's content, so that he return'd to his Town loaden, both with Riches and the Reputation of haveing been a great Discoverer.

17. This being Sunday, we were Seasonably put in mind how much we were oblig'd to be thankfull for our happy return to the Inhabitants. Indeed, we had great reason to reflect with Gratitude on the Signal Mercies we had receiv'd. First, that we had, day by day, been fed by the Bountifull hand of Providence in the desolate Wilderness, Insomuch that if any of our People wanted one Single Meal during the whole Expedition, it was intirely owing to their own imprudent Management.

Secondly, that not one Man of our whole Company, had any Violent Distemper or bad Accident Befall him, from One End of the Line to the other. The very worst that happen'd was, that One of them gave himself a Smart cut on the Pan of his knee with a Tomahawk, which we had the good

Fortune to cure in a Short time, without the help of a Surgeon.

As for the Misadventures of Sticking in the Mire and falling into Rivers and Creeks, they were rather Subjects of Mirth than complaint, and serv'd only to diversify our Travels with a little farcicall Variety. And, lastly, that many uncommon Incidents have concurr'd to prosper our Undertaking. We had not only a dry Spring before we went out, but the preceding Winter, and even a Year or two before, had been much dryer than Ordinary. This made not only the Dismal, but likewise most of the Sunken Grounds near the Sea-Side, just hard enough to bear us, which otherwise had been quite unpassible.

And the whole time we were upon the Business, which was in all about Sixteen Weeks, we were never catch't in the Rain except once, Nor was our Progress Interrupted by bad Weather above 3 or 4 days at most. Besides all this, we were Surpriz'd by no Indian Enemy, but all of us brought our Scalps back Safe upon our Heads.

This cruel Method of Scalping of Enemies is practis'd by all the Savages in America, and perhaps is not the least proof of their Original from the Northern Inhabitants of Asia. Among the Ancient Scythians it was constantly us'd, who carry'd about these hairy Scalps as Trophies of Victory. They serv'd them too as Towels at home, and Trappings for their Horses abroad. But these were not content with the Skin of their Enemies' Heads, but also made use of their Sculls

for cups to drink out of upon high Festival
days, & made greater Ostentation of them than
if they had been made of Gold or the purest
crystal.

Besides the Duties of the Day, we christen'd
one of our Men who had been bred a Quaker. The
Man desir'd this of his own mere Motion, without
being tamper'd with by the Parson, who was willing every one shou'd go to Heaven his own way.
But whether he did it by the Conviction of his
Own Reason, or to get rid of some Troublesome Forms and Restraints, to which the Saints
of that Perswasion are Subject, I can't Positively
say.

18. We proceeded over a Levil Road 12 Miles,
as far as George Hixe's Plantation, on the South
Side Meherrin River, Our Course being for the
most part North-East. By the way we hired a
Cart to transport our Baggage, that we might the
better befriend our Jaded Horses.

Within 2 Miles of our Journey's End this day,
we met the Express We had sent the Saturday
before to give Notice of our Arrival. He had
been almost as Expeditious as a carrier Pigeon,
rideing in 2 Days no less than 200 Miles.

All the Grandees of the Sappony Nation did us
the Honour to repair hither to meet us, and our
worthy Friend and Fellow Traveller, Bearskin,
appear'd among the gravest of them in his Robes
of ceremony. Four Young Ladies of the first
Quality came with them, who had more the Air
of cleanliness than any copper-Colour'd Beauties I

had ever seen; Yet we resisted all their Charms,
notwithstanding the long Fast we had kept from
the Sex, and the Bear Dyet we had been so long
engag'd in.   Nor can I say the Price they sat upon
their Charms was at all Exorbitant.   A Princess
for a Pair of Red Stockings can't, surely, be thought
buying Repentance much too dear.

The Men had something great and Venerable in
their countenances, beyond the common Mien of
Savages; and indeed they ever had the Reputation
of being the Honestest, as well as the bravest Indians we have ever been acquainted with.

This People is now made up of the Remnant of
Several other Nations, of which the most considerable are the Sapponys, the Occaneches, and Steu-
kenhocks, who not finding themselves Seperately
Numerous enough for their Defence, have agreed
to unite into one Body, and all of them now go
under the Name of the Sapponys.

Each of these was formerly a distinct Nation,
or rather a Several clan or Canton of the Same
Nation, Speaking the Same Language, and using
the same Customs.   But their perpetual Wars
against all other Indians, in time, reduc'd them so
low as to make it Necessary to join their Forces
together.

They dwelt formerly not far below the Mountains, upon Yadkin River, about 200 Miles West
and by South from the Falls of Roanoak.   But
about 25 Years ago they took Refuge in Virginia,
being no longer in condition to make Head not
only against the Northern Indians, who are their

Implacable enemies, but also against most of those to the South. All the Nations round about, bearing in mind the Havock these Indians us'd formerly to make among their Ancestors in the Insolence of their Power, did at length avenge it Home upon them, and made them glad to apply to this Government for protection.

Colo Spotswood, our then lieut. governor, having a good Opinion of their Fidelity & Courage, Settled them at Christanna, ten Miles north of Roanoak, upon the belief that they wou'd be a good Barrier on that Side of the Country, against the Incursion of all Foreign Indians. And in Earnest they wou'd have Serv'd well enough for that Purpose, if the White People in the Neighbourhood had not debauch't their Morals, and ruin'd their Health with Rum, which was the Cause of many disorders, and ended at last in a barbarous Murder committed by one of these Indians when he was drunk, for which the poor Wretch was executed when he was sober.

It was a matter of great Concern to them, however, that one of their Grandees should be put to so ignominious a Death. All Indians have as great an Aversion to hanging as the Muscovites, tho' perhaps not for the same cleanly reason: These last believing that the Soul of one that dies in this manner, being forc'd to Sally out of the Body at the Postern, must needs be defiled. The Sapponys took this Execution so much to Heart, that they soon after quitted their Settlement and remov'd in a Body to the Cataubas.

The Daughter of the TETERO KING went away with the Sapponys, but being the last of her Nation, and fearing she Shou'd not be treated according to her Rank, poison'd herself, like an Old Roman, with the Root of the Trumpet-Plant. Her Father dy'd 2 Years before, who was the most intrepid Indian we have been acquainted with. He had made himself terrible to all other Indians by His Exploits, and had escaped so many Dangers that he was esteem'd invulnerable. But at last he dy'd of a Pleurisy, the last Man of his Race and Nation, leaving only that unhappy Daughter behind him, who would not long survive Him.

The most uncommon Circumstance in this Indian visit Was, that they all came on Horse-back, which was certainly intended for a Piece of State, because the Distance was but 3 Miles, and 'tis likely they had walk't a foot twice as far to catch their Horses. The Men rode more awkwardly than any Dutch Sailor, and the Ladies bestrode their Palfreys a la mode de France, but were so bashful about it, that there was no persuading them to Mount till they were quite out of our Sight.

The French Women use to ride a-straddle, not so much to make them sit firmer in the Saddle, as from the hopes the same thing might peradventure befall them that once happen'd to the Nun of ORLEANS, who escaping out of a Nunnery, took Post en CAVALIER, and in ten Miles' hard rideing had the good Fortune to have all the Tokens of a Man break out upon her.

This Piece of History ought to be the more

credible, because it leans upon much the same
Degree of Proof as the Tale of Bishop Bur-
net's Two Italian Nuns, who, according to his
Lordship's Account, underwent the Same happy
Metamorphosis, probably by some other Violent
Exercise.

19. From hence we despatch't the Cart with our
Baggage under a Guard, and crosst Meherrin
River, which was not 30 Yards wide in that Place.
By the help of Fresh Horses that had been sent us,
we now began to mend our Pace, which was also
quicken'd by the Strong Inclinations we had to get
Home.

In the Distance of 5 Miles we forded Meherrin creek, which was very near as broad as the
River.   About 8 Miles farther we came to Stur-
geon-Creek, so call'd from the Dexterity an
Occaanechy Indian shewed there in Catching
one of those Royal Fish, which was perform'd
after the following Manner.

In the Summer time 'tis no unusual thing for
Sturgeons to Sleep on the Surface of the Water,
and one of them having wander'd up into this
Creek in the Spring, was floating in that drowsy
condition.

The Indian, above mention'd, ran up to the Neck
into the Creek a little below the Place where he
discover'd the Fish, expecting the Stream wou'd
soon bring his Game down to Him.   He judg'd
the Matter right, and as Soon as it came within
his Reach, he whip't a running Noose over his
Jole.   This waked the Sturgeon, which being

Strong in its own Element darted immediately under Water and dragg'd the Indian after Him. The Man made it a Point of Honour to keep his Hold, which he did to the Apparent Danger of being drown'd. Sometimes both the Indian and the Fish disappear'd for a Quarter of a Minute, & then rose at some Distance from where they dived. At this rate they continued flouncing about, Sometimes above, and sometimes under Water, for a considerable time, till at last the Hero Suffocated his Adversary, and haled his Body ashoar in Triumph.

About Six Miles beyond that, we passed over Wicco-quoi creek, Named so from the Multitude of Rocks over which the Water tumbles in a Fresh, with a bellowing Noise. Not far from where we went over, is a Rock much higher than the rest, that Strikes the Eye with agreeable Horror, and near it a very Talkative Eccho, that, like a fluent Helpmeet, will return her good Man Seven Words for one, & after all, be Sure to have the Last. It speaks not only the Language of Men, but also of Birds & Beasts, and often a Single Wild Goose is cheated into the Belief that Some of his Company are not far off, by hearing his own cry multiply'd; & 'tis pleasant to see in what a flutter the Poor Bird is, when he finds himself disappointed.

On the Banks of this creek are very broad low-Grounds in many Places, and abundance of good high-Land, tho' a little Subject to Floods.

We had but two Miles more to Capt. Em-

BRY'S, where we found the Housekeeping much
better than the House. Our Bountifull Landlady
had set her Oven and all her Spits, Pots, Grid-
irons and Saucepans to work, to diversify our
Entertainment, tho' after all it prov'd but a Ma-
hommetan Feast, there being Nothing to drink but
Water. The worst of it was, we had unluckily
outrid the Baggage, and for that Reason were
oblig'd to Lodge very Sociably in the Same Apartment with the Family, where, reckoning Women
and Children, we muster'd in all no less than Nine
Persons, who all pigg'd loveingly together.

20. In the Morning colo Bolling, who had been
Surveying in the Neighbourhood, and Mr. Walker,
who dwelt not far off, came to visit us; And the
last of these Worthy Gentlemen, fearing that our
drinking so much Water might incline us to Pleurisys, brought us a kind Supply both of Wine and
cyder.

It was Noon before we cou'd disengage Ourselves from the Courtesies of this Place, and then
the two Gentlemen above-mention'd were so good
as to accompany us that day's Journey, tho' they
cou'd by no means approve of our LITHUANIAN
Fashion of Dismounting now and then, in order to
walk part of the way on foot.

We cros't Nottoway River not far from our
Landlord's House, where it seem'd to be about 25
Yards over. This River divides the County of
Prince George from that of BRUNSWICK. We
had not gone 8 Miles farther before our Eyes were
bless'd with the Sight of Sapponi chappel, which

was the first House of Prayer we had seen for
more than two calendar Months.

About 3 Miles beyond that, we passed over
Stony Creek, where One of those that Guarded
the Baggage kill'd a Polcat, upon which he made
a comfortable Repast. Those of his company were
so SQUEAMISH they cou'd not be persuaded at
first to tast, as they said, of so unsavoury an Animal; but seeing the Man Smack his Lips with more
pleasure than usual, they ventur'd at last to be
of his Mess, and instead of finding the Flesh rank
and high-tasted, they owned it to be the Sweetest
Morsel they had ever eat in their Lives.

The ill Savour of this little Beast lys altogether
in its Urine, Which Nature has made so detestably
ill-scented on purpose to furnish a helpless Creature with Something to defend itself. For as
some Brutes have Horns and Hoofs, and others
are arm'd with Claws, Teeth and Tushes for their
Defence; and as Some Spit a Sort of Poison at
their Adversaries, like the Paco; and others dart
Quills at their Pursuers, like the Porcupine; and
as some have no Weapons to help themselves but
their Tongue, and others none but their Tails; so
the poor Polcat's safety lies altogether in the irre-
sistible Stench of its Water; insomuch that when
it finds itself in Danger from an Enemy, it Moistens its bushy Tail plentifully with this Liquid
Amunition, and, then with great fury, Sprinkles it
like a Shower of Rain full into the Eyes of its
Assailant, by which it gains time to make its
Escape.

Nor is the Polcat the only Animal that defends itself by a Stink. At the CAPE OF GOOD HOPE is a little Beast, call'd a Stinker, as big as a Fox, and Shap't like a Ferret, which being pursued has no way to save himself but by farting and Squittering. And then such a Stench ensues that None of its Pursuers can Possibly stand it.

At the End of 30 good Miles, we arriv'd in the Evening at colo Bolling's, where first, from a Primitive Course of Life, we began to relapse into Luxury. This Gentleman lives within Hearing of the Falls of Appamatuck River, which are very Noisy whenever a Flood happens to roll a greater stream than ordinary over the Rocks.

The River is Navigable for Small Craft as high as the Falls, and at Some distance from thence fetches a compass, and runs nearly parallel with James River almost as high as the Mountains.

While the Commissioners tared Sumptuously here, the poor Chaplain and two Surveyors, stoppt Ten Miles Short at a poor Planter's House, in Pity to their Horses, made a Saint ANTHONY's Meal, that is, they Supp't upon the Pickings of what Stuck in their Teeth ever since Breakfast. But to make them amends, the good Man laid them in his own Bed, where they all three nestled together in one cotton Sheet and one of Brown Oznabrugs, made Still Something Browner by two Months' Copious Perspiration.

21. But those worthy Gentlemen were so alert in the Morning after their light Supper, that they

came up with us before Breakfast, & honestly paid their Stomachs all they ow'd them.

We made no more than a Sabbath day's Journey from this to the next Hospitable House, namely, that of our great Benefactor, Colo Mumford. We had already been much befriended by this Gentleman, who, besides sending Orders to his Overseers at ROANOAK to let us want for nothing, had, in the Beginning of our Business, been so kind as to recommend most of the Men to us who were the faithfull Partners of our Fatigue.

Altho' in most other ATCHIEVEMENTS those who command are apt to take all the HONOUR to themselves of what perhaps was more owing to the Vigour of those who were under them, Yet I must be more just, and allow these brave Fellows their full Share of credit for the Service we perform'd, & must declare, that it was in a great Measure owing to their Spirit and indefatigable Industry that we overcame many Obstacles in the Course of our Line, which till then had been esteem'd unsurmountable.

Nor must I at the Same time omit to do Justice to the Surveyors, and particularly to Mr. Mayo, who besides an eminent degree of Skill, encounter'd the same Hardships and underwent the Same Fatigue that the forwardest of the Men did, and that with as much Chearfulness as if Pain had been his Pleasure, and Difficulty his real Diversion.

Here we discharg'd the few Men we had left, who were all as Ragged as the GIBEONITE AM-

BASSADORS, tho', at the Same time, their Rags were very honourable, by the Service they had so Vigorously performed in making them so.

22. A little before Noon we all took leave and dispers't to our Several Habitations, where we were so happy as to find all our Familys well. This crown'd all our other Blessings, and made our Journey as prosperous as it had been painfull.

Thus ended our Second Expedition, in which we extended the Line within the Shadow of the Chariky Mountains, where we were oblig'd to Set up our Pillars, like Hercules, and return Home.

We had now, upon the whole, been out Sixteen Weeks, including going and returning, and had travell'd at least Six Hundred Miles, and no Small part of that Distance on foot. Below, towards the Sea Side, our Course lay through MARSHES, SWAMPS, and great Waters; and above, over Steep HILLS, Craggy ROCKS, and Thickets, hardly penetrable. Notwithstanding this variety of Hardships, we may say, without Vanity, that we faithfully obey'd the King's Orders, and perform'd the Business effectually, in which we had the Honour to be employ'd.

Nor can we by any Means reproach Ourselves of having put the Crown to any exorbitant Expense in this difficult affair, the whole Charge, from Beginning to End, amounting to no more than One Thousand Pounds. But let no one concern'd in this painful Expedition complain of the Scantiness of his Pay, so long as His Majesty has been Graciously pleas'd to add to our Reward the HONOUR

of his ROYAL approbation, and to declare, not-
withstanding the Desertion of the CAROLINA COM-
MISSIONERS, that the Line by us run shall hereafter
Stand as the true Boundary betwixt the GOVERN-
MENTS OF VIRGINIA AND NORTH CAROLINA.

APPENDIX

APPENDIX

To the Foregoing Journal, containing the second Charter to the Proprietors of CAROLINA, confirming and enlarging the first, and also several other acts to which it refers. These are plac'd by themselves at the End of the Book, that they may not interrupt the Thread of the Story, and the Reader will be more at liberty whether he will please to read them or not, being something dry and unpleasant.

The Second Charter granted by KING CHARLES 2D to the Proprietors of CAROLINA.

[Here follows the full text of the Charter. Only the beginning, the part which concerns boundaries, is here given. The complete document is easily accessible to the general reader. It may be found in the Colonial Records of North Carolina, Vol. I., p. 102.—EDITOR.]

CHARLES, by the GRACE of GOD, &c. : WHEREAS, by our LETTERS PATENT, bearing date the four and twentieth day of march, in the fifteenth year of our Reign, we were graciously pleas'd to grant unto our right trusty and right well beloved cousin and councellor, Edward, Earl of Clarendon, our high Chancellor of England, Our right trusty and right intirely beloved Cousin and Counsellor, George, Duke of Albemarle, Master of our Horse, our right trusty and well beloved William, now Earl of Craven, our Right trusty and well beloved Counsellor, Anthony, Lord Ashley, Chancellor of our Exchequer, our right trusty and well beloved Counsellor, Sir George Carterett, Knight and Baronet, vice Chamberlain of our household, our right trusty and well beloved, Sir John Colleton, Knight and Baronet, and Sir William Berkley,[1] Knight, all that Province, Territory,

[1] The name of John Berkeley is omitted.—EDITOR.

or Tract of Ground, called Carolina, situate, lying and being within our Dominions of America, extending from the North End of the Island called Luke Island, which lys in the Southern Virginia Seas, and within Six and thirty Degrees of the Northern Latitude; and to the West as far as the South Seas; & so respectively as far as the River of Mathias, which bordereth upon the Coast of Florida, & within one and thirty Degrees of the Northern Latitude, and so west in a direct Line as far as the South Seas aforesaid. Now know ye, that, at the humblest request of the said Grantees in the aforesaid Letters Patent named, and as a further mark of our especial favour towards them, we are graciously pleas'd to enlarge our said Grant unto them according to the Bounds & limits hereafter Specify'd & in favour to the pious and noble purpose of the said Edward, Earl of Clarendon, George, Duke of Albemarle, William, Earl of Craven, John, Lord Berkley, Anthony, Lord Ashley, Sir George Carterett, Sir John Colleton, and Sir William Berkley, we do give and grant to them, their Heirs and Assigns, all that Province, Territory, or tract of Ground, Situate, lying and being within our Dominions of America aforesaid, extending North and Eastward as far as the North end of Carahtuke River or Inlet, upon a Streight westerly line to Wyonoake Creek, which lys within or about the Degrees of thirty-six and thirty Minutes Northern Latitude, and so West in a Direct line as far as the South Seas; & south and westward as far as the Degrees of twenty-nine inclusive Northern Latitude, & so west in a direct line as far as the South seas; together with all and Singular ports, harbours, Bays, rivers & inlets belonging unto the Province or Territory aforesaid, etc.

———

*At the Court of St James's the 1st day of March, 1710.—
Present, The Queen's most Excellent Majesty in Council.*

Upon reading this day at the Board a Representation from the Rt Honble the Lords Commissioners for trade &

Plantations, in the Words following : In pursuance of your Majesty's Pleasure, Commissioners have been appointed on the Part of your Majesty's Colony of Virginia, as likewise on the Part of the Province of Carolina, for the settling the Bounds between those Governments ; And they have met several times for that purpose, but have not agreed upon any one Point thereof, by reason of the trifleing delays of the Carolina Commissioners, & of the many difficulties by them rais'd in relation to the proper Observations & survey they were to make. However, the Commissioners for Virginia have deliver'd to your Majesty's Lieut Governor of that Colony an Account of their proceedings, which Account has been under the Consideration of your Majesty's Council of Virginia, &c they have made a Report thereon to the said Lieut Governor, who haveing lately transmitted unto us a Copy of that Report, we take leave humbly to lay the Substance thereof before your Majesty, which is as follows :

That the Commissioners of Carolina are both of them Persons engag'd in Interest to obstruct the Settling the Boundarys between that Province and the Colony of Virginia ; for one of them has for several Years been Surveyor General of Carolina, has acquired to himself great Profit by surveying Lands within the controverted Bounds, & has taken up several Tracts of Land in his own Name, & sold the same to others, for which he stands still oblig'd obtain Patents from the Government of Carolina. The other of them is at this time Surveyor General, & hath the same Prospect of advantage by making future surveys within the said Bounds. That the Behavior of the Carolina Commissioners has tended visibly to no other End than to protract and defeat the Settling this Affair : and particularly Mr. Moseley has us'd so many Shifts & Excuses to disappoint all Conferences with the Commissioners of Virginia, as plainly shew his Aversion to proceed in a Business that tends so manifestly to his disadvantage. His prevaricating on this occasion has been so undiscreet and so unguarded, as to be discover'd in the presence of the Lieut Governor

of Virginia. He started so many objections to the Powers
granted to the Commissioners of that Colony, with design to
render their conferences ineffectual, that his Joint Commissioner cou'd hardly find an excuse for him. And when the
Lieut Governor had with much adoe prevail'd with the said
Mr. Moseley to appoint a time for meeting the Commissioners of Virginia, & for bringing the necessary Instruments to
take the Latitude of the Bounds in dispute, which Instruments he owned were ready in Carolina, he not only fail'd
to comply with his own appointment, but after the Commissioners of Virginia had made a Journey to his House,
and had attended him to the Places proper for observing
the Latitude, he wou'd not take the trouble of carrying his
own Instrument, but contented himself to find fault with
the Quadrant produc'd by the virginia Commissioners, tho
that Instrument had been approv'd by the best Mathemati-
cians, and is of universal Use. From all which it is evident
how little hopes there are of Settling the Boundarys above-
mention'd, in concert with the present Commissioners for
Carolina. That tho the Bounds of the Carolina Charter
are in express words limited to Weyanoak Creek, lying in
or about 36° 30′ of Northern Latitude, yet the Commissioners for Carolina have not by any of their Evidences
pretended to prove any such Place as Weyanoak Creek, the
amount of their Evidence reaching no further than to prove
which is Weyanoak River, & even that is contradicted by
affidavit taken on the part of Virginia; by which affidavits
it appears that, before the Date of the Carolina Charter to
this day, the place they pretend to be Weyanoak River
was, & is still, called Nottoway River. But supposing the
same had been called Weyanoak River, it can be nothing to
their purpose, there being a great difference between a
River & a Creek. Besides, in that Country there are divers
Rivers & Creeks of the same Name, as Potomeck River &
Potomeck Creek, Rappahannock River, & Rappahannock
Creek, & several others, tho there are many Miles' distance
between the mouths of these Rivers and the mouths of these
Creeks. It is also observable, that the Witnesses on the

APPENDIX 263

Part of Carolina are all very Ignorant persons, & most of them of ill fame & Reputation, on which Account they had been forced to remove from Virginia to Carolina. Further, there appeared to be many contradictions in their Testimonys, whereas, on the other hand, the witnesses to prove that the Right to those Lands is in the Government of Virginia are Persons of good Credit, their knowledge of the Lands in question is more ancient than any of the witnesses for Carolina, & their Evidence fully corroborated by the concurrent Testimony of the Tributary Indians. And that right is farther confirm'd by the Observations lately taken of the Latitude in those parts, by which tis plain, that the Creek proved to be Weyanoak Creek by the Virginia Evidences, & sometimes call'd Wicocon, answers best to the Latitude described in the Carolina Charter, for it lys in 36° 40', which is ten Minutes to the Northward of the Limits described in the Carolina grant, Whereas Nottoway River, lys exactly in the Latitude of 37°,[1] and can by no construction be suppos'd to be the Boundary described in their Charter; So that upon the whole Matter, if the Commissioners of Carolina had no other view than to clear the just right of the Proprietors, such undeniable Demonstrations wou'd be Sufficient to convince them; but the said Commissioners gave too much Cause to suspect that they mix their own private Interest with the Claim of the Proprietors, & for that reason endeavor to gain time in order to obtain Grants for the Land already taken up, and also to secure the rest on this occasion, we take notice, that they proceed to survey the Land in dispute, notwithstanding the assurance given by the Government of Carolina to the Contrary by their letter of the 17th of June, 1707, to the Government of Virginia, by which letter they promised that no lands shou'd be taken up within the controverted bounds till the same were settled.[2]

[1] The commissioners in 1728 found that it was really in 36° 30½'. See above, p. 88.
[2] There is not space enough here to give the North Carolina side of this controversy. Byrd's own statement goes far toward justifying that colony. (See in-

Whereupon we humbly propose, that the Lords Proprietors be acquainted with the foregoing Complaint of the trifleing delays of their Commissioners, which delays tis reasonable to believe have proceeded from the self-Interest of those Commissioners, and that therefore your Majesty's pleasure be signify'd to the said Lords Proprietors, that by the first Opportunity they send Orders to their Governour or Commander in Chief of Carolina for the time being, to issue forth a new Commission, to the purport of that lately issued, therby constituting two other Persons, not having any personal Interest in, or claim to, any of the Land lying within the Boundary's in the room of Edward Moseley & John Lawson.   The Carolina Commissioners to be appointed being strictly required to finish their Survey, & to make a return thereof in conjunction with the Virginia Commissioners, within six months, to be computed from the time, that due notice shall be given by your Majesty's Lieut Governor of Virginia to the Governor or Commander in Chief of Carolina, of the time & place, which your Majesty's said Lieut Governor shall appoint for the first meeting of the Commissioners on one part & the other.   In order whereunto we humbly offer, that directions be sent to the said Lieut Governor, to give such Notice accordingly ; & if after Notice so given, the Carolina Commissioners shall refuse or neglect to Join with those on the part of Virginia, in making such survey, as likewise a Return thereof within the time before mention'd ; that then and in such Case, the Commissioners on the part of Virginia be directed to draw up an Account of the proper observations and Survey which

fra, pp. 24, 88.) In 1699 North Carolina had sent commissioners to Virginia to make arrangements for running the line ; but the latter colony refused to move in the matter, because Harvey, the deputy governor of North Carolina, had not been confirmed by the king. After this the southern colony, satisfied that the disputed territory belonged to it, seems to have been rather indifferent to the matter, till Virginia urged its final settlement. The whole matter may well be taken up in a separate treatment.

they shall have made for ascertaining the Bounds between Virginia & Carolina, and to deliver the same in Writing under their Hands and Seals to the Lieut Governor and Council of Virginia, to the end the same may be laid before your Majesty, for your Majesty's final Determination therein, within, with regard to the Settling of those Boundarys; the Lords Proprietors haveing, by an Instrument under their Hands, submitted the same to Your Majesty's royal determination, which instrument, dated in March, 1708, is lying in this Office.

And lastly, we humbly propose, that your Majesty's further pleasure be signifyd to the said Lords Proprietors, and in like manner to the Lieut Governor of Virginia, that no Grants be pass'd by either of those Governments of any of the Lands lying within the controverted Bounds, until such Bounds shall be ascertain'd and settled as aforesaid, whereby it may appear whether those Lands do of Right belong to your Majesty, or to the Lords Proprietors of Carolina.

Her Majesty in Council, approveing of the said Representation, is pleas'd to order, as it is hereby ordered, that the Rt Honble the Lords Commissioners for Trade & Plantations Do signifye her Majesty's pleasure herein to her Majesty's Lieut Governor or Commander in Chief of Virginia for the time being, and to all Persons to whom it may belong, as is propos'd by their Lordships in the said Representation, and the Rt Honble the Lords Proprietors of Carolina are to do what on their part does appertain.

EDW SOUTHWELL.

PROPOSALS for determining the Controversy relating to the Bounds between the Governments of Virginia and North Carolina, most humbly offered for his Majesty's Royal Approbation, and for the Consent of the Rt Honble the Lords Proprietors of Carolina.

Forasmuch as the dispute between the said two Governments about their true Limits continues still, notwithstanding the several meetings of the Commissioners, and all the proceedings of many Years past, in order to adjust that affair, & seeing no speedy Determination is likely to ensue, unless some Medium be found out, in which both Partys may incline to acquiesce, wherefore both the underwritten Governors having met, and consider'd the prejudice both to the King & the Lords Proprietors' Interests, by the continuance of this contest, and truly endeavouring a Decision, which they Judge comes nearest the Intention of Royal Charter granted to the Lords Proprietors, do, with the advice & consent of their respective Councils, propose as follows.

That from the mouth of Corotuck River or Inlet, & setting the Compass on the North Shoar, thereof a due West Line be run & fairly mark'd, & if it happen to cut Chowan River, between the mouths of Nottoway River and Wicocon Creek, then shall the same direct Course be continued towards the Mountains, and be ever deem'd the Sole divideing line between Virginia & Carolina.

That if the said West Line cuts Chowan River to the Southward of Wicocon Creek, then from point of Intersection the Bounds shall be allow'd to continue up the middle of the said Chowan River to the middle of the Entrance into the said Wicocon Creek, and from thence a due West Line shall divide the said two Governments.

That if a due West Line shall be found to pass through Islands or to cut out small Slips of Land, which might much more conveniently be included in one Province or the other by Natural Water Bounds, In such Cases the Persons appointed for runing the Line shall have power to settle Natural Bounds, provided the Commissioners of both Sides agree thereto, and that all such Variations from the West Line, be particularly Noted in the Maps or Plats, which they shall return, to be put upon the Records of both Governments, all which is Humbly submitted by

CHALES EDEN.
A. SPOTSWOOD.

*Order of the King and Council upon the foregoing Proposals,
At the Court of St. James's the 28th day of March, 1729.*[1]
Present, the King's most Excellent Majesty in Council.

WHEREAS it has been represented to his Majesty at the
Board, that for adjusting the disputes, which have Subsisted
for many Years past, between the Colonys of Virginia and
North Carolina, concerning their true Boundarys, the late
Governors of the said colonys did some time since agree
upon certain Proposals for regulating the said Boundarys
for the future, to which Proposals the Lords Proprietors of
Carolina have given their assent; And whereas the said
Proposals were this day presented to his Majesty as proper
for his Royal Approbation,

His Majesty is thereupon pleas'd, with the Advice of his
Privy Council, to approve of the said Proposals, a copy
whereof is hereunto annex't, and to order, as it is hereby
order'd, that the Governor or Commander in Chief of the
Colony of Virginia, do settle the said Boundarys, in conjunction with the Governor of North Carolina, agreeable to
the said Proposals.

EDWARD SOUTHWELL.

---

*The Lieut Governor of Virginia's Commission
in obedience to His Majesty's Order.*

George the second, by the Grace of God, of great Britain,
France and Ireland King, Defender of the Faith, to our
trusty and well beloved William Byrd, Richard Fitz-William, and William Dandridge, Esqrs., members of our
council of the Colony and Dominion of Virginia, Greeting :
Whereas our late Royal Father of Blessed memory was
graciously pleas'd, by Order in his Privy Council, bearing
date the 28 day of March 1727, to approve of certain Proposals agreed upon by Alexander Spotswood, Esqr. late Lieut

[1] It should be 1727.—EDITOR.

Governor of Virginia, on the one part, and Charles Eden
Esqr. late Governoor of the Province of North Carolina, for
determining the Controversy relating to the Bounds between
the said two Governments, and was farther pleased to direct
and Order, that the said Boundarys shoud be laid out &
settled agreeable to the said Proposals. Know ye, therefore, that reposing special trust and confidence in your
Ability & Provident circumspection, have assign'd, constituted & appointed, & by these presents do assign, constitute
& appoint you & every of you jointly & severally, our Commissioners for & on behalf of our Colony & Dominion of
Virginia, to meet the Commissioners appointed or to be
appointed on the part of the Province of North Carolina,
and in conjunction with them to cause a Line or Lines of
Division to be run and markt, to divide the said two Governments according to the proposals above-mention'd, &
the order of our late Royal Father, Copies of both which
you will herewith receive. and we do further give and
grant unto you, and in case of the Death or absence of any
of you, such of you as shall be present, full power and
Authority to treat & agree with the said Commissioners of
the Province of North Carolina on such rules and Methods
as you shall Judge most expedient for the adjusting and
finally determining all disputes or controversies which
may arise, touching any Islands or other small Slips of Land
which may happen to be intersected or cut off by the dividing Line aforesaid, and which may with more conveniency
be included in the One Province or the other by natural
water bounds, agreeable to the proposals aforemention'd,
and generally to do and perform all matters and things
requisite for the final determination and Settlement of the
said Boundarys, according to the said Proposals. And to
the end our Service herein may not be disappointed through
the refusal or delay of the Commissioners for the Province
of North Carolina, to act in Conjunction with you in settling
the Boundarys aforesaid, we do hereby give & grant unto
you, or such of you as shall be present at the time and place

appointed for running the dividing Line aforesaid, full power and Authority to cause the said Line to be run and mark'd out, conformable to the said proposals, having due regard to the doing equal Justice to Us, and to the Lords Proprietors of Carolina, any refusal, disagreement, or opposition of the said Commissioners of North Carolina notwithstanding. And in that case we hereby require you to make a true report of your proceedings to our Lieut Governor, or Commander in Chief of Virginia, in order to be laid before us for our approbation, and final determination herein. And in case any Person or Persons whatsoever shall presume to disturb, Molest or resist you, or any of the Officers or Persons by your direction, in running the said Line, and executing the Powers herein given you, we do by these presents Give and Grant unto you, or such of you as shall be attending the service aforesaid, full power & Authority by Warrant under your or any of your hands and Seals, to order and command all and every the Militia Officers in our counties of Princess Anne, Norfolk, Nansemond, & Isle of Wight, or other the adjacent Counties, together with the Sheriff of each of the said Counties, or either of them, to raise the Militia & posse of the said Several Counties, for the removing all force and opposition, which shall or may be made to you in the due Execution of this our Commission, & we do hereby will and require, as well the Officers of the said militia, as all other our Officers & loving Subjects within the said Counties, & all others whom it may concern, to be obedient, aiding & assisting unto you in all & Singular the Premises. And we do in like manner command & require you, to cause fair Maps & descriptions of the said Dividing Line, and the remarkable places through which it shall pass, to be made and return'd to our Lieut Governor or Commander in Chief of our said Colony for the time being, in order to be entered on Record in the proper Offices within our said Colony. Provided that you do not, by colour of this our Commission, take upon you or determine any Private man's property, in or to the Lands which shall by the said dividing Line be included within the Limits of Virginia, nor of any other matter or thing that doth not relate immediately to the adjusting, settling & final Determination of the Boundary aforesaid, conformable to the Proposals hereinbefore mention'd, and not otherwise.   In Witness whereof we have caused these presents to be made.   Witness our trusty and well beloved William Gooch, Esqr. our Lieut Governor & Commander in Chief of our Colony & Dominion of Virginia, under the seal of our said Colony, at Williamsburgh the 14th day of December, 1727. in the first Year of our Reign.

WILLIAM GOOCH.

The Governour of N. Carolina's Commission in Obedience to His Majesty's Order.

Sir Richard Everard, Baronet, Governor, Captain General, Admiral, and Commander in Chief of the said Province : To Christopher Gale, Esqr. Chief Justice, John Lovick Esqr., Secretary, Edward Moseley, Esqr., Surveyor General & William Little Esqr., Attorney General, Greeting : Whereas many disputes & differences have formerly been between the Inhabitants of this province and those of his Majesty's Colony of Virginia, concerning the Boundarys and Limits between the said two Governments, which having been duly considered by Charles Eden, Esqr., late Governor of this Province, and Alexander Spotswood, Esqr., late Governor of Virginia, they agreed to certain proposals for determining the said controversy, & humbly offer'd the same for his Majesty's Royal Approbation, and the consent of the true & absolute Lords Proprietors of Carolina.   and his Majesty having been pleas'd to signify his Royal approbation of those proposals (consent'd unto by the true and absolute Lords Proprietors of Carolina) and given directions for adjusting & settling the Boundarys as near as may be to the said Proposals :

I, therefore, reposing especial trust and confidence in you the said Christopher Gale, John Lovick, Edward Moseley and William Little, to be Commissioners, on the part of the true and absolute Lords Proprietors, and that you in conjunction with such Commissioners as shall be nominated for Virginia, use your utmost Endeavours, and take all necessary care in adjusting and settling the said boundarys, by drawing such a distinct Line or Lines of Division between the said two Provinces, as near as reasonable you can to the Proposals made by the two former Governours, and the Instructions herewith given you. Given at the Council Chamber in Edenton, under my hand, and the Seal of the Colony, the 21st day of February, anno Dom 1727,[1] and in the first year of the Reign of our sovereign Lord, King George the Second.

RICHARD EVERARD.

The Protest of the Carolina Commissioners, against our Proceeding on the Line without them.

We the underwritten Commissioners for the Government of N. Carolina, in conjunction with the Commissioners on the part of Virginia, having run the Line for the division of the two Colonys from Corotuck Inlet, to the South Branch of Roanoak River; being in the whole about 170 Miles, and near 50 Miles without the Inhabitants, being of Opinion we had run the Line as far as would be requisite for a long time, Judged the carrying it farther would be a needless charge and trouble. And the Grand Debate which had so long Subsisted between the two Governments, about Wyanoke River or Creek, being settled at our former meeting in the Spring, when we were ready on our parts to have gone with the Line to the utmost Inhabitants, which if it had been done, the Line at any time after might have been continued at an easy expense by a Surveyor on each

[1] February 21, 1728, by New Style.—EDITOR.

side ; and if at any time hereafter there shou'd be occasion
to carry the Line on further than we have now run it, which
we think will not be in an Age or two, it may be done in
the same easy manner, without the great Expense that now
attends it.   And on the Conference of all the Commissioners,
we have communicated our sentiments thereon, and declar'd
our Opinion, that we had gone as far as the Service required, and thought proper to proceed no farther ; to which
it was answered by the Commissioners for Virginia, that
they Should not regard what we did, but if we desisted,
they wou'd proceed without us.   But we, conceiving by
his Majesty's Order in Council they were directed to Act
in conjunction with the Commissioners appointed for Carolina, & having accordingly run the Line jointly so far, and
Exchanged Plans, thought they cou'd not carry on the
Bounds singly ; but that their proceedings without us wou'd
be irregular & invalid, and that it wou'd be no Boundary,
and thought proper to enter our Dissent thereto.   Wherefore, for the reasons aforesaid, in the name of his Excellency
the Lord Palatine, and the rest of the true and absolute
Lords proprietors of Carolina, we do hereby dissent and
Disallow of any farther proceedings with the Bounds without our Concurrence, and pursuant to our Instructions do
give this our DISSENT in Writing.

EDWARD MOSELEY.
WILL LITTLE.
C. GALE.
J. LOVICK.

October 7th, 1728.

———

The Answer of the Virginia Commissioners
to the foregoing protest.

WHEREAS, on the 7th of October last, a paper was deliver'd to us by the Commissioners of N. Carolina, in the
Stile of a Protest, against our carrying any farther, without
them, the dividing Line between the 2 Governments, we,

the underwritten Commissioners on the part of Virginia, having maturely considered the reasons offer'd in the said PROTEST, why those Gentlemen retir'd so soon from that Service, beg leave to return the following answer:

They are pleas'd in the first place to alledge, by way of Reason, that having run the Line near 50 Miles beyond the Inhabitants, it was Sufficient for a long time, in their Opinion for an Age or two. To this we answer that, by breaking off so soon, they did but imperfectly obey his Majesty's Order, assented to by the Lords Proprietors. The plain meaning of that Order was, to ascertain the Bounds betwixt the two Governments as far towards the Mountains as we cou'd, that neither the King's Grants may hereafter encroach on the Lords Proprietors', nor theirs on the Right of his Majesty. And tho the distance towards the great Mountains be not precisely determin'd, yet surely the West line shou'd be carry'd as near them as may be, that both the King's Lands and those of their Lordships, may be taken up the faster, and that his Majesty's Subjects may as soon as possible extend themselves to that Natural Barrier. This they will certainly do in a few Years, when they know distinctly in which Government they may enter for the Land, as they have already done in the more northern parts of Virginia. So that 'tis Strange the Carolina Commissioners should affirm, that the distance only of 50 Miles above the Inhabitants wou'd be sufficient to carry the Line for an Age or two, especially considering that, two or three days before the date of their Protest, Mr. Mayo had enter'd with them for 2000 Acres of Land, within 5 Miles of the Place where they left off. Besides, if we reflect on the richness of the Soil in those parts, & the convenience for Stock, we may foretell, without the Spirit of Divination, that there will be many Settlements higher than those Gentlemen went, in less than ten Years, and Perhaps in half that time.

Another reason mention'd in the Protest for their retiring so soon from the Service is, that their going farther wou'd be a needless charge and Trouble. And they alledge that the rest may be done by one Surveyor on a side, in an easy manner, whenever it shall be thought necessary.

To this we answer, that Frugality for the Public is a rare virtue, but when the public Service must Suffer by it, it degenerates into a Vice. And this will ever be the Case when Gentlemen Execute the orders of their Superiors by halves. but had the Carolina Commissioners been sincerely frugal for their Government, why did they carry out Provisions Sufficient to support them and their Men for ten Weeks, when they intended not to tarry half that time? This they must own to be true, since they brought 1000 lbs. of Provisions along with them. Now, after so great an Expence in their preparations, it had been no mighty Addition to their Charge, had they endured the Fatigue 5 or 6 Weeks longer. It wou'd at most have been no more than they must be at, whenever they finish their Work, even tho they shou'd fancy it proper to trust a matter of that consequence to the Management of one Surveyor. Such a one must have a Number of Men along with him, both for his assistance and Defense, and those Men must have Provisions to Support them.

These are all the reasons these Gentlemen think fit to mention in their protest, tho they had in truth a more Powerful argument for retiring so abruptly, which, because they forgot, it will be neighbourly to help them out. The provisions they intended to bring along with them, for want of Horses to carry them, were partly droppt by the way, & what they cou'd bring was husbanded so ill, that after 18 days, (which was the whole time we had them in our Company,) they had no more left, by their own confession, than two Pounds of Biscuit for each Man, to carry them home. However, tho this was an unanswerable Reason for Gentlemen for leaving the Business unfinisht, it was none at all for us, who had at that time Bread Sufficient for 7 Weeks longer. Therefore, lest their want of Management might put a stop to his Majesty's Service, & frustrate his Royal intentions, we judg'd it our Duty to proceed without them, and have extended the Dividing Line so far West as to leave the great Mountains on each hand to the Eastward of us. And this we have done with the same fidelity & exactness as if the Gentlemen had continued with us. Our surveyors (whose Integrity I am perswaded they will not call in Question) continued to Act under the same Oath, which they had done from the beginning. Yet, notwithstanding all this, if the Government of N. Carolina shou'd not hold itself bound by that part of the Line which we made without the assistance of the Commissioners, yet we shall have this benefit in it at least, that his Majesty will know how far his Lands reach towards the South, & consequently where his Subjects may take it up, & how far they may be granted without Injustice to the Lords Proprietors. To this we may also add, that having the Authority of our Commission, to act without the Commissioners of Carolina, in Case of their disagreement or refusal, we thought ourselves bound upon their Retreat to finish the Line without them, lest his Majesty's Service might Suffer by any honour or neglect on their part.

WILLIAM DANDRIDGE.
W. BYRD.

The Names of the Commissioners to direct the running of the Line between Virginia and North Carolina.

WILLIAM BYRD,
RICH'D FITZ-WILLIAM,
WILLIAM DANDRIDGE,
          Esqrs. } Commissioners for Virginia.

CHRISTOPHER GALE,
JOHN LOVEWICK,
EDWARD MOSELEY,
W'M LITTLE,
          Esqrs, } Commissioners for Carolina.

ALEX'R IRVIN,
WILLIAM MAYO, } Surveyors for Virginia.

EDW'D MOSELEY,
SAM'LL SWAN,   } Surveyors for N. Carolina.

THE REV'D PETER FOUNTAIN, Chaplain.

Names of the Men employ'd on the part of Virginia to run the Line between that Colony and N. Carolina.

On the first expedition.	On the 2d expedition.
1. Peter Jones,	Peter Jones,
2. Thomas Jones,	Thomas Jones,
3. Thomas Short,	Thomas Short,
4. Robert Hix,	Robert Hix,
5. John Evans,	John Evans,
6. Stephen Evans,	Stephen Evans,
7. John Ellis,	John Ellis,
8. John Ellis, Jr.	John Ellis, Jr.
9. Thomas Wilson,	Thomas Wilson,
10. George Tilman,	George Tilman,
11. Charles Kimbal,	Charles Kimbal,
12. George Hamilton,	George Hamilton,
13. Robert Allen,	Thomas Jones, Junr.
14. Thomas Jones, Junr.	James Petillo,
15. James Petillo,	Rich'd Smith,
16. Richard Smith,	Abraham Jones,
17. John Rice.	Edward Powell,
	William Pool,
	William Calvert,
	James Whitlock,
	Thomas Page.

Account of the Expence of running the Line between Virginia and N. Carolina.

To the Men's Wages in Currant Money . . .	227	10	0 [1]
To Sundry Disbursements for Provisions, &c. .	174	01	6
To Paid the Men for 7 Horses lost	44	0	0
	£495	11	6

[1] There is an error, either in transcribing these amounts or in finding their sum.—EDITOR.

The Sum of £495 11 6 Current Money reduc't
at 15 p cent. Sterling amounts to 430   8 10
To paid to colo Byrd 142   5   7
To paid to colo Dandridge 142   5   7
To paid to Mr. Fitz-William 94   0   0
To paid to the Chaplain, Mr. Fountain . . . 20   0   0
To paid to Mr. William Mayo 75   0   0
To paid to Mr. Alex Irvin 75   0   0
To paid for a Tent and Marquis 20   0   0
                                         ─────────────
                                         £1000   0   0

This Summ was discharg'd by a Warrant out of His Majesty's Quitrents from the Lands in Virginia.

A JOURNEY TO
THE LAND OF EDEN

A JOURNEY TO
THE LAND OF EDEN:

Anno 1733.

EPT. 11.   Having recommended my Family to the Protection of the Almighty, I crost the river with 2 Servants and 4 Horses, and rode to Colo. Mumford's.   There I met my Friend, Mr Banister, who was to be the kind Companion of my Travels.   I stayed dinner with the Good Colonel, while Mr. Banister made the best of his way home, to get his Equipage ready, in order to join me the next day.   After dining plentifully, and wishing all that was good to the household, I proceeded to Major Mumford's, who had also appointed to go along with me.   I was the more obliged to Him, because he made me the Complement to leave the Arms of a pretty Wife, to lye on the Cold Ground for my Sake. She seemed to chide me with her Eyes, for coming to take her Bed-fellow from her, now the Cold

weather came on, and to make my peace, I was forced to promise to take abundance of Care of Him, in Order to restore him Safe and Sound to her Embraces.

12. After the Major had cleared his Pipes, in calling with much Authority about him, he made a Shift to truss up his Baggage about Nine a'Clock. Near the Same Hour my Old Friend and Fellow Travellor, Peter Jones, came to us compleatly accoutred. Then we fortifi'd ourselves with a Beef-Steake, kis't our Landlady for good Luck, and mounted about ten. The Major took one Robin Bolling with him, as Squire to his Body, as well as Conductor of his Baggage. Tom Short had promised to attend me, but had marry'd a Wife and could not come. We cros't Hatcher's Run, Gravelly Run, Stony Creek, and in the distance of about 20 Miles reach't Sappony chappel, where Mr. Banister join'd us. Thus agreeably reinforc't we proceeded ten Miles further, to Major Embry's, on the South Side of Nottoway River. The Major was ill of a purging and vomiting, attended with a Feaver which had brought him low; but I prescribed him a Gallon or two of Chicken Broth, which wash't him as clean as a Gun, and quench't his feaver. Here Major Mayo met us, well equip't for a March into the Woods, bringing a Surveyor's Tent, that would Shelter a Small Troop. Young Tom Jones also repaired hither to make his Excuse; but Old Tom Jones, by the priviledge of his Age, neither came nor sent, so that we were not so strong as we intended, being disappointed of 3 of our Ablest

Foresters. The Entertainment we met with was
the less Sumptuous by Reason of our Landlord's
Indisposition. On this Occasion we were as little
Troublesome as possible, by sending part of our
Company to Richard Birch's, who lives just by the
Bridge over the River. We sent for an Old Indian called Shacco-Will, living about 7 Miles off,
who reckon'd himself 78 years Old. This fellow
pretended he could conduct us to a Silver Mine,
that lyes either upon Eno River, or a Creek of it,
not far from where the Tuscaruros once lived.
But by some Circumstances in his Story, it seems
to be rather a Lead than a Silver Mine. However, such as it is, he promised to go and Shew it
to me whenever I pleased. To comfort his Heart,
I gave him a Bottle of Rum, with which he made
himself very happy, and all the Familey very miserable by the horrible Noise he made all Night.

13. Our Landlord had great relief from my
Remedy, and found himself easy this Morning.
On this Account we took our departure with more
Satisfaction, about Nine, and having pick't up our
Friends at Mr. Birch's, pursued our Journey over
Quoique Creek, and Sturgeon Run, as far as
Brunswick Court house, about 12 Miles beyond
Notoway. By the way, I sent a Runner half a
Mile out of the Road to Colo. Drury Stith's, who
was so good as to come to us. We cheer'd Our
hearts with Three Bottles of pretty good Madeira,
which made Drury talk very hopefully of his cop-
per Mine. We easily prevailed with him to let us
have his Company, upon condition we would take

the Mine in our way.   From thence we proceeded
to Meherin River, which lys 8 Miles beyond the
Court house, and in our way forded Great Creek.
For fear of being belated, we called not at my
Quarter, where Dom Pedro is Overseer, and lives in
good Repute amongst his Neighbours.   In Complement to the little Major we went out of our
way, to ly at a Settlement of his upon Cock's
Creek, 4 Miles Short of Roanoak.   Our Fare here
was pretty Coarse, but Mr. Banister and I took
possession of the Bed, while the rest of the Company lay in Bulk upon the Floor.   This Night the
little Major made the first discovery of an impatient and peevish Temper, equally unfit both for a
Traveller and a Husband.

14. In the Morning my friend Tom Wilson made
me a Visit, and gave me his Parole that he would
meet us at Blue Stone Castle.   We took Horse
about Nine, and in the distance of Ten Miles
reach't a Quarter of Colo. Stith's, under the
Management of John Tomasin.   This Plantation
lies on the West Side of Stith's Creek, which was
so full of Water, by reason of a Fresh in the
River, that we cou'd not ford it, but we and our
Baggage were paddled over in a canoe, and our
Horses swam by our Sides.   After Staying here
an Hour, with some of Diana's Maids of Honour,
we cross't Miles' Creek a Small Distance off, and
at the End of Eight Miles were met by a tall, mea-
gre Figure, which I took at first for an Apparition,
but it proved to be Colo. Stith's Miner.   I concluded that the unwholesome Vapours arising from

the Copper Mine had made this Operator such a
Skeleton, but upon Enquiry understood that it
was Shear Famine had brought him so low. He
told us his Stomach had not been bles't with one
Morsel of Meat for more than three Weeks, and
that too he had been obliged to Short Allowance
of Bread, by reason Corn was Scarce and to be
fetch't from Tomasin's, which was ten long Miles
from the Mine where he liv'd. However, in Spite
of this Spare dyet, the man was chearfull, and ut-
tered no Complaint. Being conducted by him, we
reach't the Mines about five a'clock, and pitch't
our Tents, for the first time, there being yet no
building erected but a Log-house, to Shelter the
Miner and his two Negroes. We examined the
Mine and found it dip't from East to West, and
shew'd but a Slender Vein, embody'd in a hard
rock of White Spar. The Shaft they had opened
was about 12 feet deep, and 6 Over. I saw no
more than one Peck of good Ore above Ground,
and that promis'd to be very Rich. The Engineer
seem'd very sanguine, and had not the least doubt
but his Employer's Fortune was made. He made
us the Complement of 3 Blasts, and We filled his
Belly with good Beef in return, which in his
hungry Circumstances was the most agreeable
Present we cou'd make him.

15. It rain'd in the Morning, which made us decamp later than we intended, but the Clouds clearing away about ten, We wish't good luck to the
Mine and departed. We left Colo. Stith there to
keep fast with his Miner, and directed our Course

thro' the Woods to Boucher's Creek, which hath
its Name from an honest Fellow that lives upon it.
This place is about 6 Miles from Colo. Stith's
works, and can also boast of a very fair Shew of
Copper Oar.   It is dug out of the side of a Hill,
that rises gradually from the Creek to the House.
The good Man was from Home himself; but his
Wife, who was as old as one of the Sybills, refresh't us with an Ocean of Milk.   By the Strength
of that Entertainment, we proceeded to Mr. Mumford's Quarter, about 5 Miles off, where Joseph
Colson is Overseer.   Here our thirsty Companions
rais'd their drooping Spirits with a chearfull Dram,
and having wet both Eyes, we rode on 7 Miles
farther to Blue Stone Castle, 5 whereof were thro'
my own Land, that is to say, all above Sandy
Creek.   My Land there in all extends 10 Miles
upon the River; and 3 charming Islands, namely,
Sapponi, Occaneeche, and Totero, run along the
whole length of it.   The lowest of these Islands is
three Miles long, the next 4, and the uppermost 3,
divided from each other by only a Narrow Strait.
The Soil is rich in all of them, the Timber large,
and a kind of Pea, very gratefull to Cattle and
Horses, holds green all the Winter.   Roanoke
River is divided by these Islands; that part which
runs on the North Side is about 80 Yards, and that
on the South more than 100.   A large Fresh will
overflow the lower part of these Islands, but never
covers all, so that the Cattle may alwcys recover a
Place of Security.   The Middlemost Island, called
Occaneeche Island, has several fields in it where

Occaneeche Indians formerly lived, and there are still some remains of the Peach Trees they planted. Here grow likewise excellent wild Hops without any Cultivation. My Overseer, Harry Morris, did his utmost to entertain me and my Company; the worst of it was, we were obliged all to be litter'd down in one Room, in Company with my Landlady and four children, one of which was very Sick, and consequently very fretfull.

16. This being Sunday, and the place where we were quite out of Christendom, very little Devotion went forward. I thought it no harm to take a Sabbath day's Journey, & rode with my Overseer to a new Entry I had made upon Blue Stone Creek, about 3 Miles from the Castle, and found the Land very fertile & convenient. It consists of Low Grounds and Meadows on both Sides the Creek. After taking a View of this, we rode 2 Miles farther to a Stony Place, where there were some Tokens of a Copper Mine, but not hopefull enough to lay me under any Temptation. Then we return'd to the Company, and found Tom Wilson was come according to his promise, in order to proceed into the Woods along with Us. Jo. Colson likewise entered into pay, having cautiously made his Bargain for a Pistole. There were 3 Tuskeruda Indians, (which I understood had been kept on my Plantation to hunt for Harry Morris,) that with much ado were also persuaded to be of the party. My Landlady cou'd not forbear discovering some broad Signs of the fury, by breaking out into insolent & passionate Expressions against the poor

Negroes. And if my Presence cou'd not awe Her,
I concluded she could be very outrageous when I
was an hundred Miles off. This inference I came
afterwards to understand was but too true, for,
between the Husband and the Wife, the Negroes
had a hard time of it.

17. We set off about nine from Blue Stone
Castle, and rode up the River 6 Miles, (one half
of which distance was on my own Land,) as far as
Major Mumford's Quarter, where Master Hogen
was Tenant upon Halves. Here were no great
Marks of Industry, the Weeds being near as high
as the Corn. My Islands run up within a little
way of this Place, which will expose them to the
Inrode of the Major's Creatures. That call'd
Totero Island, lyes too convenient not to receive
Damage that way; but we must guard against it
as well as we can. After the Major had convinct
Himself of the Idleness of his Tenant, he return'd
back to Blue Stone, and Harry Morris and I went
in quest of a fine Copper Mine, which he had
Secured for me in the Fork. For which purpose,
about a Quarter of a Mile, higher than Hogen's,
we crost a Narrow Branch of the River into a
small Island, not yet taken up, and after traversing
that, forded a much wider Branch into the Fork of
the Roanoke River. Where we landed was near 3
Miles higher up than the Point of the Fork. We
first directed our Course Easterly towards that
Point, which was very Sharp, and each Branch of
the River Where it divided first seem'd not to
exceed 80 Yards in Breadth. The Land was

broken and barren off from the River, till we came
within half a Mile of the Point where the Low-
grounds began. The Same Sort of Low Ground
run up each Branch of the River. That on the
Staunton (being the Northern Branch) was but
Narrow, but that on the South, which is called the
Dan, seem'd to carry a wedth of at least half a
Mile. After discovering this Place, for which I
intended to enter, we rode up the Mid-land 5 Miles
to view the Mine, which in my Opinion hardly
answered the Trouble of riding so far out of our
way. We returned downwards again about 4
Miles, and a Mile from the Point found a good
Ford over the North Branch, into the upper end of
Totero Island. We crost the River there, and
near the Head of the Island saw a large Quantity
of Wild Hops growing, that smelt fragrantly, and
seem'd to be in great perfection. At our first
Landing we were so hampered with Brambles, Vines
and Poke Bushes, that our Horses could hardly
force their way thro' them. However, this Diffi-
culty held only about 25 Yards at each end of the
Island, all the rest being very level and free from
Underwood. We met with Old Fields where the
Indians had formerly liv'd, and the Grass grew as
high as a Horse and his Rider. In one of these
Fields were large Duck Ponds, very firm at the
Bottom, to which Wild fowl resort in the Winter.
In the Woody part of the Island grows a Vetch,
that is green all the Winter, and a great Support
for Horses & Cattle, tho' it is to be fear'd the
Hogs will root it all up. There is a Cave in this

Island, in which the last Totero King, with only 2
of his Men, defended himself against a great Host
of Northern Indians, & at last oblig'd them to
retire. We forded the Streight out of this into
Occaneechy Island, which was full of large Trees,
and rich Land, and the South part of it is too high
for any flood less than Noah's to drown it, we rode
about 2 Miles down this Island, (being half the
length of it,) where finding ourselves opposite to
Blue Stone Castle, we pass't the River in a canoe,
which had been ordered thither for that purpose, &
join'd our Friends, very much tired, not so much
with the length of the Journey, as with the heat of
the Weather.

18. We lay by till the return of the Messenger
that we sent for the Amunition, and other things
left at the Court house. Nor had the Indians yet
join'd us according to their Promise, which made
us begin to doubt of their Veracity. I took a Solitary Walk to the first Ford of Blue Stone Creek,
about a Quarter of a Mile from the House. This
Creek had its Name from the Colour of the Stones,
which pav'd the Bottom of it, and are so smooth
that tis probable they will burn into Lime. I took
care to return to my Company by Dinner time that
I might not trespas upon their Stomachs. In the
Afternoon I was paddled by the Overseer and one
of my Servants up the Creek, but cou'd proceed
little farther than a Mile because of the Shoal
Water. All the way we perceiv'd the Bottom of
the Creek full of the Blue Stones above mention'd,
Sufficient in quantity to build a large Castle. At

our return we went into the Middle of the River, and stood upon a large Blue Rock to Angle, but without any Success. We broke off a Fragment of the Rock, and found it as heavy as so much Lead. Discouraged by our ill Luck, we repair'd to the Company, who had procured some Pieces of Copper Oar from Cargil's Mine, which seem'd full of Metal. This Mine lies about 2 Miles higher than Major Mumford's Plantation, and has a better Shew than any yet discover'd. There are so many appearances of Copper in these Parts, that the Inhabitants seem to be all Mine-mad, and neglect making of Corn for their present necessitys, in hopes of growing very Rich hereafter.

19. The Heavens lowr'd a little upon us in the Morning, but, like a Damsel ruffled by too bold an Address, it soon clear'd up again. Because I detested Idleness, I caus'd my Overseer to paddle me up the River as far as the Streight that divides Occaneechy from Totero Island, which is about 20 Yards wide. There runs a Swift Stream continually out of the South part of the River into the North, and is in some places very deep. We crost the South part of the opposite Shoar, to view another entry I had made, beginning at Buffalo Creek and running up the River to guard my Islands, and keep off bad Neighbours on that Side. The Land seems good enough for Corn along the River, but a Quarter of a Mile back tis broken, and full of Stones. After satisfying my Curiosity, I return'd the way that I came, and shot the same Streight back again, and paddled down the River

to the Company.   When we got home, we laid the
foundation of two large Citys.   One at Shacco's,
to be called Richmond, and the other at the Point
of Appamattuck River, to be nam'd Petersburgh.[1]
These Major Mayo offered to lay out into Lots
without Fee or Reward.   The Truth of it is, these
two places being the uppermost Landing of James
and Appamattux Rivers, are naturally intended for
Marts, where the Traffick of the Outer Inhabitants
must Center.   Thus we did not build Castles only,
but also Citys in the Air.   In the Evening our
Ammunition arrived safe, and the Indians came to
us, resolving to make part of our Company, upon
Condition of their being Supply'd with Powder and
Shot, and having the Skins of all the Deer they
kill'd to their own proper use.

20. Every thing being ready for a March, we
left Blue Stone Castle about ten.   My Company
consisted of 4 Gentlemen (Namely, Maj Mayo,
Maj Mumford, Mr. Banister and Mr. Jones,) and
5 Woodsmen, Thomas Wilson, Henry Morris, Joseph Colson, Robert Bolling and Thomas Hooper,
4 Negroes and 3 Tuscaruda Indians.   With this
small Troop we proceeded up the River as far as
Hogen's, above which, about a quarter of a Mile,
we forded into the little Island, and from thence
into the Fork of the River.   The Water was risen
so high, that it ran into the Top of my Boots,

---

[1] Richmond took its name
from a fancied resemblance to
the site of the town by the same
name near London. Its lots
were advertised for sale in the
Virginia Gazette, April, 1737.
(See Campbell's Hist. of Va.,
p. 421.)   Petersburg took its
name from a local inhabitant.

but without giving me any Cold, altho I rid in my wet Stockings. We Landed 3 Miles above the point of the Fork, and, after marching three Miles farther, reacht the Tenement of Peter Mitchell, the highest Inhabitant on Roanoke River. Two Miles above that we forded a Water, which we named Birche's Creek, not far from the Mouth, where it discharges itself into the Dan. From thence we rode thro charming Low-Grounds, for 6 Miles together, to a larger Stream, which we agreed to call Banister River. We were puzzled to find a Ford by reason the Water was very high, but at last got safe over, about 1½ Mile from the Banks of the Dan. In our way we kill'd 2 very large Rattle-Snakes, One of 15 and the other of 12 Rattles. They were both fat, but nobody would be persuaded to carry them to our Quarters, altho they would have added much to the Luxury of our Supper. We pitcht our Tents upon Banister River, where we feasted on a Young Buck which had the ill luck to cross our way. It rain'd great part of the Night, with very loud Thunder, which rumbled frightfully amongst the tall Trees that Surrounded us in that low Ground, but, thank God! without any Damage. Our Indians kill'd 3 deer, but were so lazy they brought them not to the Camp, pretending for their Excuse that they were too lean.

21. The necessity of drying our Baggage prevented us from marching till 11 a'clock. Then we proceeded thro low-Grounds which were tolerably wide for 3 Miles together, as far as a Small Creek,

named by us Morris's Creek.   This Tract of Land
I persuaded Mr. Banister to enter for, that he
might not be a loser by the Expedition.   The Low
Grounds held good a Mile beyond the Creek, and
then the Highland came quite to the River, and
made our travelling more difficult.   All the way
we went we perceiv'd there had been tall Canes
lately growing on the Bank of the River, but were
universally kill'd; And inquiring into the reason
of this destruction, we were told that the Nature
of those Canes was, to shed their Seed but once in
Seven Years, and the Succeeding Winter to dye,
and make Room for Young ones to grow up in
their Places.   Thus much was certain, that 4 Years
before we saw Canes grow and flourish in Several
Places, where they now lay dead and dry upon the
Ground.   The whole distance we travell'd in this
day by Computation was 15 Miles, and then the
Appearance of a black Cloud, which threaten'd a
Gust, oblig'd us to take up our Quarters.   We had
no sooner got our Tents over our Heads, but it
began to rain and thunder furiously, and one Clap
succeeded the Lightening the same Instant, and
made all tremble before it.   But, blessed be God!
it spent its fury upon a tall Oak just by our Camp.
Our Indians were so fearfull of falling into the
hands of the Cataubas, that they durst not lose
Sight of us all day; so they kill'd nothing, and we
were forc'd to make a temperate Supper upon
Bread and Cheese.   It was Strange we met with
no Wild Turkeys, this being the Season in which
great Numbers of them used to be seen towards

the Mountains. They commonly perch on the high
Trees near the Rivers and Creeks. But this Voyage, to our great Misfortune, there were none to be
found. So that we cou'd not commit that Abomination, in the Sight of all Indians, of mixing the
Flesh of Deer & Turkey in our Broth.

22. We were again oblig'd to dry our Baggage, which had thoroughly soakt with the heavy
Rain that fell in the Night. While we staid for that,
our Hunters knockt down a Brace of Bucks, wherewith we made ourselves amends for our Scanty
Supper the aforegoing Night. All these Matters
being duly perform'd made it near Noon before
we Sounded to Horse. We marcht about 2 Miles
over fine low-Grounds to a most pleasant Stream,
which we nam'd the Medway, and by the way discover'd a rich Neck of Highland that lay on the
South Side of the Dan, and lookt very tempting.
Two Miles beyond the Medway, we forded another
Creek, which we called Maosty Creek. The whole
distance between these 2 Streams lay exceeding
rich Land, & the same continued 2 Miles higher.
This body of Low-Ground tempted me to enter for
it, to serve as a Stage between my Land at the
Fork, and the Land of Eden. The Heavens lookt
so menacing that we resolved to take up our Quarters 2 Miles above Maosty Creek, where we in-
trencht ourselves on a rising Ground. We had no
sooner taken these Precautions, but it began to
rain unmercifully, and to put out our Fire as fast
as we cou'd kindle it; nor was it only a hasty
Shower, but continued with great impetuosity most

part of the Night.   We preferred a dry Fast to a
Wet Feast, being unwilling to expose the People
to the Weather, to gratify an unreasonable Appetite.   However it was some comfort, in the Midst
of our Abstinence, to dream of the delicious Breakfast we intended to make next Morning, upon a
fat Doe and two-year-Old Bear our Hunters had
kill'd the Evening before.   Notwithstanding all
the Care we cou'd take, several of the Men were
dripping wet, and among the rest, Harry Morris
dabbled so long in the Rain, that he was seized
with a Violent Fit of an Ague that Shook him
almost out of all his Patience.

23. It was no loss of time to rest in our Camp
according to the Duty of the day, because our
Baggage was so wet it needed a whole day to dry
it.   For this purpose we kindled 4 Several Fires,
in the absence of the Sun, which vouchsaft us not
one kind look the whole day.   My Servant had
dropt his Great-Coat Yesterday, and 2 of the men
were so good-Natured as to ride back and look for
it to-day, and were so lucky as to find it.   Our Indians having no Notion of the Sabbath, went out
to hunt for Something for dinner, and brought a
Young Doe back along with them.   They laught
at the English for losing one day in Seven; tho
the Joke may be turned upon them for losing the
whole Seaven, if Idleness and doing nothing to the
purpose may be called loss of time.   I lookt out
narrowly for Ginseng, this being the Season when
it wears its Scarlet Fruit, but neither now nor
any other time during the whole Journey cou'd I

find one Single Plant of it. This made me conclude that it delighted not in quite so Southerly a
Climate; And in truth I never heard of its growing
on this Side of 38 Degrees of Latitude. But to
make amends we saw abundance of Sugar Trees in
all these Low-Grounds, which the whole Summer
long the Woodpeckers tap, for the sweet Juice that
flows out of them. Towards the Evening, a Strong
Norwester was so kind as to sweep all the Clouds
away, that had blacken'd our Sky, and moisten'd
our Skins, for some time past.

24. The rest the Sabbath had given us made
every Body alert this Morning, so that we mounted
before Nine a'clock. This Diligence happened to
be the more necessary, by reason the Woods we
encountered this day were exceedingly Bushy and
uneven. At the distance of 4 Miles we forded
both Branches of Forked Creek, which lay within
1000 Paces from each other. My Horse fell twice
under me, but, thank God! without any Damage
either to Himself or his Rider; and Maj'r Mayo's
Baggage Horse roll'd down a Steep Hill, and
Ground all his Biscuit to Rocahominy. My greatest disaster was that, in mounting one of the Precipices, my Steed made a Short turn and gave my
Knee an unmerciful Bang against a Tree, & I
felt the Effects of it Several Days after. However, this was no Interruption of our Journey, but
we went merrily on, and 2 Miles farther crost
Peter's Creek, and 2 Miles after that Jones' Creek.
Between these Creeks was a Good breadth of
Low-Grounds, with which Mr. Jones was tempted,

tho he shook his head at the distance. A little above Jones' Creek, we met with a pleasant Situation, where the Herbage appear'd more inviting than usual. The Horses were so fond of it that we determin'd to Camp there, altho' the Sun had not near finisht his Course. This gave some of our Company leisure to go out and search for the Place where our Line first crost the Dan, and by good luck they found it within half a Mile of the Camp. But the Place was so altered by the desolation which had happen'd to the Canes, (which had formerly fringed the Banks of the River a full Furlong deep,) that we hardly knew it again. Pleas'd with this discovery, I forgot the Pain in my knee, and the whole Company ate their Venison without any other Sauce than keen Appetite.

25. The Weather now befriending us, we despatcht our little Affairs in good time, and marcht in a Body to the Line. It was already grown very dimm, by reason many of the markt Trees were burnt or blown down. However, we made Shift, after riding little more than half a Mile, to find it, and having once found it, stuck as close to it as we could. After a March of 2 Miles, we got upon Cane Creek, where we saw the same Havock amongst the Old Canes that we had observ'd in other places, & a whole Forest of Young Ones Springing up in their Stead. We pursued our Journey over Hills and Dales till we arriv'd at the Second Ford of the Dan, which we past with no other Damage than Sopping a little of our Bread, and Shipping some Water at the Tops of our Boots.

The late Rains having been a little immoderate,
had rais'd the Water and made a currant in the
River.   We drove on 4 Miles farther to a plentifull
Run of very clear Water, and quarter'd on a rising
Ground a Bow-Shot from it.   We had no sooner
pitcht the Tents, but one of our Woodsmen alarm'd
us with the News that he had follow'd the Track
of a great Body of Indians to the place where they
had lately encampt.   That there he had found no
less than Ten Huts, the Poles whereof had Green
Leaves still fresh upon them.   That each of these
Huts had Shelter'd at least Ten Indians, who, by
some infallible Marks, must have been Northern
Indians.   That they must needs have taken their
departure from thence no longer ago than the day
before, having erected those Huts to protect themselves from the late Heavy Rains.   These Tidings
I could perceive were a little Shocking to some of
the Company, and particularly the little Major,
whose Tongue had never lain still, was taken
Speechless for 16 Hours.   I put as good a Countenance upon the Matter as I cou'd, assuring my
Fellow Travellers, that the Northern Indians were
at Peace with us, and altho one or two of them may
now and then commit a Robbery or a Murder, (as
other Rogues do,) yet nationally and avowedly
they would not venture to hurt us.   And in Case
they were Cataubas, the Danger would be as little
from them, because they are too fond of our Trade
to loose it for the pleasure of Shedding a little
English Blood.   But Supposing the worst, that
they might break thro all the Rules of Self-Inter-

est, and attack us, yet we ought to stand bravely
on our defence, and sell our lives as dear as we
could.   That we should have no more fear on this
Occasion, than just to make us more watchfull and
better provided to receive the Enemy, if they had
the Spirit to venture upon us.   This reasoning of
mine, tho it could not remove the Panick, yet it
abated something of the Palpitation, and made us
double our Guard.   However, I found it took off
the Edge of most of our Appetites, for every thing
but the Rum Bottle, which was more in favour than
ever, because of its Cordial Quality.   I Hurt my
other Knee this afternoon, but not enough to spoil
either my dancing or my Stomach.

26. We liked the place so little that we were
glad to leave it this Morning as soon as we could.
For that reason we were all on Horseback before
Nine, and after riding 4 Miles arriv'd at the Mouth
of Sable Creek.   On the Eastern Bank of that
Creek, 6 Paces from the Mouth, and just at the
Brink of the River Dan, stands a Sugar Tree,
which is the beginning of my fine Tract of land in
Carolina, call'd the Land of Eden.   I caus'd the
Initial Letters of my name to be cut on a large
Poplar and Beech near my Corner, for the more
easy finding it another time.   We then made a
beginning of my Survey, directing our Course due
South from the Sugar Tree above-mention'd.   In
a little way we perceived the Creek forkt, and the
Western Branch was wide enough to merit the
name of a River.   That to the East was much less,
which we intersected with this Course.   We ran

Southerly a Mile, and found the Land good all the
way, only towards the End of it we saw the Trees
destroy'd in such a Manner that there were hardly
any left to mark my Bounds.   Haveing finisht this
Course, we encampt in a charming Peninsula,
form'd by the Western Branch of the Creek.   It
contain'd about 40 Acres of very Rich Land, gradually descending to the Creek, and is a delightful
Situation for the Manor House.   My Servant had
fed so intemperately upon Bear, that it gave him a
Scouring, and that was followed by the Piles,
which made riding worse to him than Purgatory.
But annointing with the Fat of the same Bear, he
soon grew easy again.

27. We were stirring early from this enchanting
place, and ran 8 Miles of my back Line, which
tended South 84½ Westerly. We found the Land
uneaven, but tolerably good, tho very thin of Trees,
and those that were standing fit for little but fewel
and Fence-Rails. Some Conflagration had effectually open'd the Country, and made room for the
Air to circulate. We crost both the Branches of
Low Land Creek, and Sundry other Rills of fine
Water. From every Eminence we discover'd the
Mountains to the N. West of us, tho' they seem'd
to be a long way off. Here the Air felt very refreshing and agreeable to the Lungs, having no
Swamps or Marshes to taint it. Nor was this the
only good Effect it had, but it likewise made us
very hungry, so that we were forc'd to halt and
pacify our Appetites with a frugal Repast out of
our Pockets, which we washt down with Water

from a Purling Stream just by. My knees pain'd
me very much, tho' I broke not the Laws of Travelling by uttering the least Complaint. Measuring
and marking spent so much of our Time, that we
could advance no further than 8 Miles, and the
Chain Carryer's thought that a great way. In the
Evening we took up our Quarters in the Low-
Grounds of the River, which our Scouts inform'd
us was but 200 Yards ahead of us. This was no
Small surprize, because we had flatter'd ourselves
that this Back Line would not have Intersected the
Dan at all; but we found Ourselves mistaken, and
plainly perceived that it ran more Southerly than
we imagined, and in all likelihood pierces the
Mountains where they form an Amphitheater. The
Venison here was lean; and the misfortune was
we met no Bear in so open a Country, to grease
the way and make it Slip down. In the Night our
Centinel alarm'd us with an Idle Suspicion that he
heard the Indian Whistle, (which amongst them is
a Signal for attacking their Enemies.) This made
every one Stand manfully to his Arms in a Moment,
and I found no Body more undismayed in this Surprize than Mr. Banister; But after we had put
ourselves in Battle Array, we discover'd this
Whistle to be nothing but the Nocturnal Note of
a little harmless Bird, that inhabits those Woods.
We were glad to find the Mistake, and commending
the Centinel for his great Vigilance, compos'd our
Noble Spirits again to rest till the Morning. However, some of the Company dream'd of nothing but
Scalping all the rest of the Night.

28. We snapt up our Breakfast as fast as we
cou'd, that we might have the more leisure to pick
our way over a very bad Ford across the River.
Tho', bad as it was, we all got safe on the other
side. We were no sooner Landed, but we found
ourselves like to encounter a very rough and almost
impassable Thicket. However, we Scuffled thro'
it without any dismay or Complaint. This was a
Copse of young Saplins, consisting of Oak, Hiccory
and Sassafras, which are the growth of a fertile
Soil. We gain'd no more than 2 Miles in 3 Hours
in this perplext Place, and after that had the Pleasure to issue out into opener Woods. The Land
was generally good, tho' pretty bare of Timber,
and particularly we traverst a rich Levil of at least
2 Miles. Our whole day's Journey amounted not
quite to 5 Miles, by reason we had been so hamper'd
at our first setting out. We were glad to take
up our Quarters early in a piece of fine low-
Grounds, lying about a Mile N. of the River.
Thus we perceiv'd the River edged away gently
towards the South, and never likely to come in the
way of our Course again. Nevertheless, the last
time we saw it, it kept much the same Breadth and
depth that it had where it divided its Waters from
the Staunton, and in all likelihood holds its own
quite as high as the Mountains.

29. In Measuring a Mile and a half farther we
reacht the lower Ford of the Irvin, which branches
from the Dan about 2 Miles to the S. S. E. of this
place. This River was very near Three Score
Yards over, and in many places pretty deep. From

thence, in little more than a Mile, we came to the
End of this Course, being in length 15 Miles and
88 Poles.   And so far the Land held reasonably
good; but when we came to run our Northern
Course of 3 Miles, to the place where the Country
line intersects the same Irvin higher up, we past
over nothing but Stony Hills, and barren Grounds,
cloth'd with little Timber, and refresht with less
Water.   All my hopes were in the Riches that
might lye under Ground, there being many goodly
Tokens of Mines.   The Stones which paved the
River, both by their Weight & Colour, promis'd
abundance of Metal; but whether it be Silver,
Lead or Copper, is beyond our Skill to discern.
We also discover'd many shews of Marble, of a
white ground, with Streaks of red and purple.   So
that tis possible the Treasure in the Bowels of the
Earth may make ample amends for the Poverty of
its Surface.   We encampt on the Bank of this
River, a little below the Dividing Line, and near
the lower end of an Island half a Mile long,
which, for the Metallick Appearances, we dignify'd
with the Name of Potosi.   In our way to this place
we treed a Bear, of so mighty a Bulk, that when
we fecht her down she almost made an Earthe-
quake.   But neither the Shot nor the fall disabled
her so much, but she had like to have hugg'd one
of our Dogs to Death in the Violence of her Embrace.   We exercis'd the Discipline of the Woods,
by tossing a very careless Servant in a Blanket,
for lossing one of our Axes.

30. This being Sunday, we were glad to rest

from our Labours; and, to help restore Our Vigour, several of us plung'd into the River, notwithstanding it was a frosty morning. One of our Indians went in along with us, and taught us their way of Swimming. They strike not out both hands together, but alternately one after another, whereby they are able to swimm both farther and faster than we do. Near the Camp grew Several large Chesnut trees very full of Chesnuts. Our men were too lazy to climb the Trees for the sake of the Fruit, but, like the Indians, chose rather to cut them down, regardless of those that were to come after. Nor did they esteem such kind of Work any breach of the Sabbath, so long as it helpt to fill their Bellys. One of the Indians shot a Bear, which he lugg'd about half a Mile for the good of the Company. These Gentiles have no distinction of Days, but make every day a Sabbath, except when they go out to war or a hunting, and then they will undergo incredible Fatigues. Of other work the Men do none, thinking it below the dignity of their Sex, but make the poor Women do all the Drudgery. They have a blind Tradition amongst them, that work was first laid upon Mankind by the fault of a Female, and therefore tis but just that Sex should do the greatest part of it. This they plead in their Excuse; but the true reason is, that the Weakest must always go to the Wall, and Superiority has from the beginning ungenerously impos'd Slavery on those who are not able to resist it.

Oct. 1. I plung'd once more into the River Irvin

this Morning, for a Small Cold I had caught, and
was intirely cured by it.   We ran the 3 Mile Course
from a White Oak standing on my Corner upon
the Western Bank of the River, and intersected the
place, where we ended the Back line exactly, and
fixt that corner at a Hiccory.   We steer'd South
from thence about a Mile, and then came upon the
Dan, which thereabouts makes but narrow Low-
Grounds.   We forded it about a Mile and a half
to the Westward of the place where the Irvin runs
into it.   When we were over, we determin'd to
ride down the River on that Side, and for 3 Miles
found the High-Land come close down to it, pretty
barren and uneaven.   But then on a Sudden the
Scene chang'd, and we were supriz'd with an Opening of large Extent, where the Sauro Indians once
liv'd, who had been a considerable Nation.   But
the frequent Inroads of the Senecas annoy'd them
incessantly, and oblig'd them to remove from this
fine Situation about 30 Years ago.   They then retired more Southerly, as far as Pee Dee River, and
incorporated with the Kewawees, where a Remnant
of them is still surviveing.   It must have been a
great Misfortune to them to be oblig'd to abandon
so beautiful a dwelling, where the Air is wholesome, and the Soil equal in Fertility to any in the
World.   The River is about 80 Yards wide, always
confin'd within its lofty Banks, and rolling down
its Waters, as sweet as Milk, and as clear as Crystal.   There runs a charming Level, of more than a
Mile Square, that will bring forth like the Lands
of Egypt, without being overflow'd once a Year.

There is scarce a Shrub in View to intercept your Prospect, but Grass as high as a Man on Horseback. Towards the Woods there is a gentle Ascent, till your Sight is intercepted by an Eminence, that overlooks the whole Landskape. This sweet Place is bounded to the East by a fine Stream, call'd Sauro Creek, which running out of the Dan, and tending Westerly, makes the whole a Peninsula. I cou'd not quit this Pleasant Situation without Regret, but often faced about to take a Parting look at it as far as I could see, and so indeed did all the rest of the Company. But at last we left it quite out of Sight, and continued our Course down the River, till where it intersects my Back line, which was about 5 Miles below Sauro Town. We took up our Quarters at the same Camp where we had a little before been alarm'd with the Suppos'd Indian Whistle, which we could hardly get out of our heads. However, it did not Spoil our rest; but we dreamt all Night's of the delights of Tempe and the Elysian Fields.

2. We awak'd early from these innocent Dreams, and took Our way along my Back line till we came to the Corner of it. From thence we Slanted to the Country Line, and kept down as far as the next fording place to the River, making in the whole 18 Miles. We breath'd all the way in pure Air, which seem'd Friendly of the Lungs, and circulated the Blood and Spirits very briskly. Happy will be the People destin'd for so wholesome a Situation, where they may live to fulness of days, and which is much better Still, with much Content and Gaiety of

Heart. On every riseing Ground we faced about
to take our leave of the Mountains, which still
shew'd their Towering Heads. The Ground was
uneaven, rising into Hills, and sinking into Valleys
great part of the way, but the Soil was good,
abounding in most places with a greasy black
Mould. We took up our Quarters on the Western Bank of the River, where we had forded it at
our coming up. One of our Men, Joseph Colson
by Name, a timorous, lazy Fellow, had squandered
away his Bread, and grew very uneasy when his
own ravening had reduced him to Short Allowance.
He was one of those Drones who love to do little
and eat much, and are never in humour unless their
Bellies are full. According to this wrong turn of
Constitution, when he found he could no longer
revel in Plenty, he began to break the Rules by
complaining and threatening to desert. This had
like to have brought him to the Blanket, but his
submission repriev'd him. Tho' Bread grew a
little Scanty with us, we had Venison in abundance, which a true Woodsman can eat contentedly without any Bread at all. But Bear's flesh
needs something of the Farinaceous, to make it
pass easily off the Stomach. In the Night we
heard a Dog bark at some distance, as we thought,
when we saw all our own Dogs lying about the
Fire. This was another Alarm; but we soon discover'd it to be a Wolf, which will sometimes
Bark very like a Dog, but something Shriller.

3. The fine Season continuing, we made the most
of it by leaving our Quarters as soon as possible.

We began to measure and mark the Bounds of
Maj'r Mayo's Land on the South of the Country
Line. In order to do this we marcht round the
Bent of the River, but he being oblig'd to make a
traverse, we cou'd reach no farther than 4 Miles.
In the Distance of about a Mile from where we
lay, we crost Cliff Creek, which confin'd its Stream
within such high Banks that it was difficult to find
a Passage over. We kept close to the River, and
2 Miles farther came to Hixe's Creek, where
abundance of Canes lay dry and prostrate on the
Ground, having Suffer'd in the late Septennial
Slaughter of that Vegetable. A Mile after that we
forded another Stream, which we called Hatcher's
Creek, from two Indian Traders of that Name,
who us'd formerly to carry Goods to the Sauro
Indians. Near the Banks of this Creek I found a
Large Beech Tree, with the following Inscription
cut upon the Bark of it, " J. H., H. H., B. B., lay
here the 24th of May, 1673." It was not difficult
to fill up these Initials with the following Names,
Joseph Hatcher, Henry Hatcher and Benjamin
Bullington, 3 Indian Traders, had lodged near that
Place 60 Years before, in their way to the Sauro
Town. But the Strangest part of the Story was
this, that these letters, cut in the Bark, sho'd remain perfectly legible so long. Nay, if no Accident befalls the Tree, which appears to be still in
a flourishing Condition, I doubt not but this piece
of Antiquity may be read many years hence. We
may also learn from it, that the Beech is a very
long-liv'd Tree, of which there are many exceed-

ingly large in these Woods.   The Major took in a
pretty deal of rich low-Ground into his Survey,
but unhappily left a greater Quantity out, which
proves the Weakness of making Entrys by guess.
We found the Dan fordable hereabouts in most
places.   One of the Indians shot a Wild Goose,
that was very lousy, which nevertheless was good
meat, and prov'd those Contemptible Tasters to
be no bad Tasters.   However, for those Stomachs
that were so unhappy as to be Squeamish, there
was plenty of fat Bear, we having kill'd two in this
day's March.

4. I caus'd the Men to use double Diligence to
assist Maj'r Mayo in fixing the Bounds of his Land,
because he had taken a great deal of pains about
Mine.   We therefore mounted our Horses as soon
as we had swallow'd our Breakfast.   Till that is
duly perform'd a Woodsman makes a Conscience
of exposeing himself to any Fatigue.   We proceeded then in his Survey, and made an End before
Night, tho' most of the Company were of Opinion
the Land was hardly worth the Trouble.   It seem'd
most of it before below the Character the Discoverers had given him of it.   We fix'd his Eastern
Corner on Cocquade Creek, and then continued
our March, over the Hills and far away along the
Country Line 2 Miles farther.   Nor had we stopt
there, unless a likelihood of Rain had oblig'd us
to encamp on an Eminence where we were in no
danger of being overflow'd.   Peter Jones had a
smart fit of an Ague, which Shook him severely,
tho' he bore it like a Man; but the small Major had

The Gate at Westover, in front of house, with Byrd Coat of Arms.

a small Fever, and bore it like a Child.   He groan'd
as if he had been in Labour, and thought verily it
wou'd be his Fate to die like a Mutinous Israelite
in the Wilderness, and be bury'd under a heap of
Stones.   The Rain was so kind as to give us Leisure to secure our Selves against it, but came however time enough to interrupt our Cookery, so that
we supt as temperately as so many Philosophers,
and kept ourselves Snug within our Tents.   The
worst part of the Story was, that the Centinels
could hardly keep our Fires from being extinguisht by the heaviness of the Shower.

5. Our Invalids found themselves in travelling
Condition this Morning, and began to conceive
hopes of returning home and dying in their own
Beds.   We pursued our Journey thro' uneven and
perplext Woods, and in the thickest of them had
the Fortune to knock down a Young Buffalo, 2
Years old.   Providence threw this vast Animal in
our way very Seasonably, just as our Provisions
began to fail us.   And it was the more welcome
too, because it was change of dyet, which of all
Varietys, next to that of Bed-fellows, is the most
agreeable.   We had liv'd upon Venison and Bear
til our Stomachs loath'd them almost as much as
the Hebrews of Old did their Quails.   Our Butchers
were so unhandy at their Business that we grew
very lank before we cou'd get our Dinner.   But
when it came, we found it equal in in goodness to the
best Beef.   They made it the longer because they
kept Sucking the Water out of the Guts, in imita-
tion of the Catauba Indians, upon the belief that it

is a great Cordial, and will even make them drunk, or at least very Gay. We encampt upon Hico River, pretty high up, and had much ado to get our house in order, before a heavy Shower descended upon us. I was in pain lest our sick men might suffer by the Rain, but might have spar'd myself the Concern, because it had the Effect of a Cold bath upon them, and drove away their distemper, or rather chang'd it into a Canine Appetite, that devour'd all before it. It rain'd Smartly all Night long, which made our Situation on the Low-Ground more fit for Otters than Men.

6. We had abundance of drying Work this Morning after the Clouds broke away and shew'd the Sun to the happy Earth. It was impossible for us to strike the Tents till the afternoon, and then we took our departure, and made an easy march of 4 Miles to another Branch of Hico River, which we call'd Jesuit's Creek, because it misled us. We lugg'd as many of the dainty Pieces of the Buffalo along with us as our poor Horses cou'd carry, envying the Wolves the pleasure of such Luxurious dyet. Our Quarters were taken upon a delightful Eminence, that Scornfully overlookt the Creek, and afforded us a dry habitation. We made Our Supper on the Tongue and Udder of the Buffalo, which were so good, that a Cardinal Legat might have made a comfortable Meal upon them during the Carnaval. Nor was this all, but we had still a rarer Morsel, the Bunch riseing up between the Shoulders of this Animal, which is very tender and very fat. The Primeings of a Young Doe, which

one of the Men brought to the Camp, were slighted
amidst these Daintys, nor wou'd even our Servants
be fobb'd off with Cates so common. The Low-
Grounds of this creek are wide in many places,
and Rich, but seem to ly within reach of every
Inundation; and this is commonly the Case with
most low-Grounds, that ly either on the Rivers or
on the Creeks that run into them. So great an
Inconvenience lessens their Value very much, and
makes High-Land, that is just tolerable, of greater
Advantage to the Owner. There he will be more
likely to reap the fruits of his Industry every year,
and not run the risque, after all his Toil, to see the
Sweat of his Brow carry'd down the Stream, and
perhaps many of his Cattle drown'd into the Bargain. Perhaps in times to come People may Bank
their Low-Grounds as they do in Europe, to confine
the Water within its natural Bounds to prevent
these Inconveniences.

7. The Scarcity of Bread, join'd to the Impatience of some of our Company, laid us under a
kind of Necessity to hasten our Return home.
For that reason we thought we might be excused
for making a Sabbath day's Journey of about 5
Miles, as far as our Old Camp upon Sugar Tree
Creek. On our way we forded Buffalo Creek,
which also empties its Waters into Hico River.
The Woods we rode thro' were open, and the Soil
very promising, great part thereof being Low-
Grounds, full of tall and large Trees. A She Bear
had the ill luck to cross our way, which was large
enough to afford us several Luxurious Meals. I

paid for Violateing the Sabbath by loseing a pair
of Gold Buttons.   I pitcht my Tent on the very
spot I had done when we ran the Dividing Line
between Virginia and Carolina.   The Beech whose
bark recorded the names of the Carolina Commissioners was still Standing, and we did them the
Justice to add to their Names a Sketch of their
Characters.   We got our House in order time
enough to walk about and make some slight observations.   There were Sugar Trees innumerable
growing in the Low-Grounds of this Creek, from
which it receiv'd its name.   They were many of
them as tall as large Hiccories, with Trunks from
15 to 20 Inches through.   The Woodpeckers, for
the pleasure of the sweet Juice which these Trees
yield, pierce the Bark in many places, and do great
damage, tho' the Trees live a great while under all
these Wounds.   There grows an infinite quantity
.of Maidenhair, which seems to delight most in Rich
grounds.   The Sorrel Tree is frequent there, whose
leaves, brew'd in Beer, are good in Dropsyes,
Green-Sickness, and Cachexys.   We also saw in
this Place abundance of papa Trees, the Wood
whereof the Indians make very dry on purpose to
rub Fire out of it.   Their Method of doing it is
this: They hold one of these dry Sticks in each
hand, and by rubbing them hard and quick together,
rarify the Air in such a Manner as to fetch Fire in
ten Minutes.   Whenever they offer any Sacrifice
to their God, they look upon it as a Profanation to
make use of Fire already kindled, but produce
fresh Virgin Fire for that purpose, by rubbing 2

of these Sticks together that never had been us'd before on any Occasion.

8. After fortifying ourself with a Bear Breakfast, Majr Mayo took what help he thought necessary, and began to Survey the Land, with which the Commissioners of Carolina had presented him upon this Creek. After running the bounds, the Major was a little disappointed in the Goodness of the Land, but as it had cost him nothing it cou'd be no bad pennyworth, as his upper Tract really was. While that business was carrying on, I took my old Friend and Fellow Traveller, Tom Wilson, and went to view the Land I had enter'd for upon this Creek, on the North of the Country Line. We rode down the Stream about 6 Miles, crossing it sundry times, and found very wide Low Grounds on both sides of it, only we observed, wherever the Low-Grounds were Broad on one side the Creek, they were narrow on the Other. The High Lands we were oblig'd to pass over were very good, & in some places descended so gradually to the edge of the Low-grounds, that they form'd very agreeable Prospects and pleasant Situations for building. About 4 Miles from the Line, Sugar Tree Creek empty'd itself into the Hico, which with that Addition swell'd into a fine River. In this Space we saw the most, and most promising good Land we had met with in all our Travels. In our way we shot a Doe, but she not falling immediately, we had lost our Game had not the Ravens, by their Croaking, conducted us to the Thicket where she fell. We plunged the Carcass of the Deer into

the Water, to secure it from these Ominous Birds till we return'd, but an Hour afterwards were surpriz'd with the Sight of a wolf which had been fishing for it, and devour'd one Side. We knockt down an antient She Bear that had no flesh upon her Bones, so we left it to the Free-Booters of the Forrest. In coming back to the Camp we discover'd a Solitary Bull Buffalo, which boldly stood his Ground, contrary to the Custom of that Shy Animal, we spar'd his Life, from a principle of never Slaughtering an Innocent Creature to no purpose. However, we made ourselves some Diversion, by trying if he wou'd face our Dogs. He was so far from retreating at their Approach, that he ran at them with great fierceness, cocking up his ridiculous little Tail, and grunting like a Hog. The Dogs in the mean time only plaid about him, not venturing within reach of his Horns, and by their nimbleness came off with a whole Skin. All these Adventures we related at our return to the Camp, and what was more to the purpose, we carry'd to them the side of Venison which the Wolf had vouchsaft to leave us. After we had compos'd ourselves to rest, Our Horses ran up to Our Camp as fast as their Hobbles would let them. This was to some of us a certain Argument that Indians were near, whose scent the Horses can no more endure than they can their Figures; tho' it was more likely they had been scar'd by a Panther or some other Wild Beast, the glaring of whose Eyes are very terrifying to them in a dark Night.

9. Majr Mayo's Survey being no more than half

done, we were oblig'd to amuse Ourselves another day in this Place. And that the time might not be quite lost, we put our Garments and Baggage into good repair. I for my part never spent a day so well during the whole Voyage. I had an impertinent Tooth in my upper Jaw, that had been loose for some time, and made me chew with great Caution. Particularly I cou'd not grind a Biscuit but with much deliberation and presence of mind. Tooth-Drawers we had none amongst us, nor any of the Instruments they make use of. However, Invention supply'd this want very happily, and I contriv'd to get rid of this troublesome Companion by cutting a Caper. I caused a Twine to be fasten'd round the Root of my Tooth, about a Fathom in Length, and then ty'd the other End to the Snag of a Log that lay upon the Ground, in such a Manner that I cou'd just stand upright. Having adjusted my String in this manner, I bent my Knees enough to enable me to spring vigorously off the Ground, as perpendicularly as I cou'd. The force of the Leap drew out the Tooth with so much ease that I felt nothing of it, nor should have believ'd it was come away, unless I had seen it dangling at the End of the String. An Under tooth may be fecht out by standing off the Ground and fastning your String at due distance above you. And having so fixt your Gear, jump off your Standing, and the weight of your Body, added to the force of the Spring, will poize out your Tooth with less pain than any Operator upon Earth cou'd draw it. This new way of Tooth-drawing, being so silently and

deliberately perform'd, both surprized and delighted all that were present, who cou'd not guess
what I was going about.   I immediately found the
benefit of getting rid of this troublesome Companion, by eating my Supper with more comfort than I
had done during the whole Expedition.

In the Morning we made an End of our Bread,
and all the rest of Our Provision, so that now we
began to travel pretty light.   All the Company
were Witnesses how good the Land was upon
Sugar Tree Creek, because we rode down it 4
Miles, till it fell into Hico River.   Then we directed
our Course over the High Land, thinking to Shorten
our way to Tom Wilson's Quarter.   Nevertheless,
it was our Fortune to fall upon the Hico again, and
then kept within sight of it several Miles together,
till we came near the Mouth.   Its Banks were high
and full of precipices on the East Side, but it afforded some Low-Grounds on the West.   Within
2 Miles of the Mouth are good shews of Copper
Mines, as Harry Morris told me, but we saw nothing of them.   It runs into the Dan just below a
large Fall, but the chain of Rocks dont reach
quite cross the River, to intercept the Navigation.
About a Mile below lives Aaron Pinston, at a
Quarter belonging to Thomas Wilson, upon Tewahominy Creek.   This man is the highest Inhabitant
on the South side of the Dan, and yet reacons himself perfectly safe from danger.   And if the Bears,
Wolves, and Panthers were as harmless as the
Indians, his Stock might be so too.   Tom Wilson offer'd to knock down a Steer for us, but I would by no

means accept of his Generosity. However, we were glad of a few of his Peas and Potatoes, and some Rashers of his Bacon, upon which we made good Chear. This Plantation lys about a Mile from the Mouth of Tewahominy, and about the same distance from the Mouth of Hico River, and contains a good piece of Land. The Edifice was only a Log House, affording a very free passage for the Air thro' every part of it, nor was the cleanliness of it any temptation to lye out of our Tents, so we encampt once more, for the last time, in the open Field.

11. I tippt our Landlady with what I imagined a full Reward for the Trouble we had given her, and then mounted our Horses, which prickt up their Ears after the 2 Meals they had eaten of Corn. In the Distance of about a Mile we reacht the Dan, which we forded with some difficulty into the Fork. The Water was pretty high in the River, and the Currant something Rapid, nevertheless all the Company got over safe, with only a little Water in their boots. After traversing the Fork, which was there at least 2 good Miles across, We forded the Stanton into a little Island, & then the narrow Branch of the same to the main Land. We took Majr Mumford's Tenant in Our way, where we moisten'd Our Throats with a little Milk, and then proceeded in good Order to Blue Stone Castle. My Landlady received us with a grim Sort of a welcome, which I did not expect, since I brought her Husband back in good Health, tho' perhaps that might be the Reason. Tis sure some-

thing or other did teize her, and she was a female
of too strong Passions to know how to dissemble.
However, she was so Civil as to get us a good Dinner, which I was the better pleas'd with because
Colo. Cock and Mr. Mumford came time enough
to partake of it.   The Colo. had been Surveying
Lands in these parts, and particularly that on which
Mr. Stith's Copper Mine lys, as likewise a Tract
on which Cornelius Cargill has fine Appearances.
He had but a poor Opinion of Mr. Stith's Mine,
foretelling it would be all labour in vain, but
thought something better of Mr. Cargill's.   After
Dinner these Gentlemen took their Leaves, and at
the same time I discharg'd 2 of my fellow travel-
lors, Thomas Wilson and Joseph Colson, after
having made their Hearts merry, and giving each
of them a piece of Gold to rub their Eyes with.
We now return'd to that Evil Custom of lying in
a house, and an evil one it is, when ten or a dozen
People are forct to pig together in a Room, as
we did, and were troubled with the Squalling of
peevish, dirty Children into the Bargain.

12. We eat our Fill of Potatoes and Milk, which
seems delicious Fare to those who have made a
Campaign in the Woods.   I then took my first
Minister, Harry Morris, up the Hill, & markt out
the place where Blue stone Castle was to Stand,
and overlook the Adjacent Country.   After that I
put my Friend in mind of many things he had done
amiss, which he promis'd faithfully to reform.   I
was so much an Infidel to his fair Speeches, (having been many times deceiv'd by them,) that I was

forc'd to threaten him with my highest displeasure,
unless he mended his Conduct very much. I also
let him know, that he was not only to Correct his
own Errors, but likewise those of his Wife, since
the power certainly belong'd to him, in Vertue of his
Conjugal Authority. He Scratcht his head at this
last Admonition, from whence I inferred that the
Gray Mare was the better Horse. We gave our
heavy Baggage 2 hours' Start, and about noon follow'd them, and in 12 Miles reacht John Butcher's,
calling by the way for Master Mumford, in order
to take him along with us. Mr. Butcher receiv'd
us kindly, and we had a true Roanoke Entertainment of Pork upon Pork, and Pork again upon
that. He told us he had been one of the first
Seated in that remote part of the Country, and in
the beginning had been forct, like the great Nebu-
chadnezzar, to live a considerable time upon Grass.
This honest man sat a mighty Value on the Mine
he fancyed he had in his Pasture, and shew'd Us
some of the Oar, which he was made to believe was
a Gray Copper, and wou'd certainly make his Fortune. But there is a bad Distemper rages in those
parts, that grows very Epidemical. The People
are all Mine mad, and neglecting to make Corn,
starve their Familys in hopes to live in great Plenty
hereafter. Mr. Stith was the first that was seiz'd
with the Frenzy, and has spread the Contagion far
and near. As you ride along the Woods, you see
all the large Stones knockt to pieces, nor can a
poor Marcasite rest quietly in its Bed for these Curious Inquirers. Our conversation ran altogether

upon this darling Subject, til the hour came for
our lying in bulk together.

13. After breaking our fast with a Sea of Milk
and potatos, we took our leave, and I crosst my
Landlady's hand with a piece of Money. She refus'd the Offer at first, but, like a true Woman,
accepted of it when it was put Home to Her. She
told me the utmost she was able to do for me was
a trifle in Comparison of some favour I had formerly done Her; but what that favour was, neither
I cou'd recollect, nor did she think proper to explain. Tho' it threaten'd Rain, we proceeded on
our Journey, and jogg'd on in the New Road for
20 Miles, that is as far as it was clear'd at that
time, and found it wou'd soon come to be a very
good one after it was well grubb'd. About 9 Miles
from John Butcher's, we crosst Allen's Creek, 4
Miles above Mr. Stith's Mine. Near the Mouth of
this Creek is a good Body of rich Land, whereof
Occaneechy Neck is a part. It was enter'd for
many Years ago by Colo. Harrison and Colo. Allen,
but to this day is held without Patent or Improvement. And they say Mr. Bolling dos the same,
with a Thousand Acres lying below John Butcher's.
After beating the new Road for 20 Miles, we struck
off towards Meherrin, which we reacht in 8 Miles
farther, & then came to the Plantation of Joshua
Nicholson, where Daniel Taylor lives for Halves.
There was a poor dirty house, with hardly any
thing in it but Children, that wallow'd about like
so many Pigs. It is a common Case in this part
of the Country, that People live worst upon good

Land; and the more they are befriended by the
Soil and the clymate, the less they will do for
themselves. This man was an Instance of it, for
tho' his Plantation would make Plentiful returns
for a little Industry, yet he wanting that, wanted
every thing. The Woman did all that was done
in the Family, and the few Garments they had to
cover their dirty Hides were owing to her Industry.
We cou'd have no Supplys from such Neighbours
as these, but depended on our own KnapSacks, in
which we had some Remnants of cold Fowls that
we brought from Bluestone Castle. When my
House was in Order, the whole Family came and
admir'd it, as much as if it had been the Grand
Vizier's Tent in the Turkish·Army.

14. The sabbath was now come round again,
and altho' our Horses wou'd have been glad to
take the benefit of it, yet we determin'd to make a
Sunday's Journey to Brunswick Church, which
lay about 8 Miles off. Tho' our Landlord cou'd
do little for us, nevertheless, we did him all the
good we were able, by bleeding his sick Negro,
and giving him a Dose of Indian Physick. We
got to Church in decent time, and Mr. Betty, the
Parson of the Parish, entertain'd us with a good
honest Sermon, but whether he bought it, or borrow'd it, would have been uncivil in us to inquire.
Be that as it will, he is a decent Man, with a double Chin that fits gracefully over his Band, and his
Parish, especially the Female part of it, like him
well. We were not crowded at Church, tho' it
was a new thing in that remote part of the Coun-

try. What Women happen'd to be there, were very
gim and tydy in the work of their own hands, which
made them look tempting in the Eyes of us Foresters. When Church was done, we refresht our
Teacher with a Glass of Wine, and then receiving
his Blessing, took Horse and directed our Course
to Maj'r Embry's. The Distance thither was reputed 15 Miles, but appear'd less by the Company
of a Nymph of those Woods, whom Innocence,
and wholesome Flesh and Blood made very allur-
ing. In our way we crost Sturgeon Creek and
Queocky Creek, but at our Journey's end were so
unlucky as not to find either Master or Mistress
at home. However, after 2 hours of hungry Expectation, the good Woman luckily found her way
home, and provided very hospitably for us. As
for the Major, he had profited so much by my Pre-
scription, as to make a Journey to Williamsburgh,
which required pretty good health, the distance
being little Short of 100 Miles.

15. After our Bounteous Landlady had cherisht
us with Roast Beef and Chicken-Pye, we thankfully took Leave. At the same time we separated
from our good Friend and Fellow Traveller, Maj'r
Mayo, who steer'd directly home. He is certainly
a very useful, as well as an agreeable Companion
in the Woods, being ever cheerful & good-humour'd, under all the little Crosses, disasters, and
disappointments of that rambling Life. As many
of us as remain'd jogg'd on together to Saponi
Chapel, where I thankt Major Mumford and Peter
Jones for the trouble he had taken in this long

Journey. That Ceremony being duly perform'd, I filed off with my honest Friend, Mr. Banister, to his Habitation on Hatcher's Run, which lay about 14 Miles from the Chapel above-mention'd. His good-humour'd little Wife was glad to see her Runaway Spouse return'd in Safety, and treated us kindly. It was no small pleasure to me, that my worthy Friend found his Family in good Health, and his Affairs in good Order. He came into this Ramble so frankly, that I shou'd have been sorry if he had been a Sufferer by it. In the Gaiety of our hearts we drank our bottle a little too freely, which had an unusual Effect on Persons so long accustom'd to Simple Element. We were both of us rais'd out of our Beds in the same Manner, and near the same time, which was a fair proof that people who breath the same Air, and are engaged in the same Way of living, will be very apt to fall into the same Indispositions. And this may explain why Distempers sometimes go round a Family, without any reason to believe they are infectious, according to the Superstition of the Vulgar.

16. After pouring down a Basin of Chocolate, I wisht Peace to that House, and departed. As long as Mr. Banister had been absent from his Family, He was yet so kind as to conduct me to Major Mumford's, & which was more, his wife very obligingly consented to it. The Major seem'd overjoy'd at his being return'd Safe and Sound from the perils of the Woods, tho' his Satisfaction had some Check from the Change his pretty Wife had suffer'd in her Complexion. The Vermillion of her Cheeks

had given place a little to the Saffron, by means of
a small Tincture of the Yellow Jaundice.   I was
sorry to see so fair a flower thus faded, and Recommended the best Remedy I cou'd think of.
After a refreshment of about an hour, we went on
to Colo. Bolling's, who was so gracious as to send
us an Invitation.   As much in haste as I was to
return to my Family, I spent an hour or two at that
place, but cou'd by no means be persuaded to stay
Dinner, nor could even Madam de Graffenriedt's
Smiles on one Side of her Face shake my Resolution.   From thence we proceeded to Colo. Mumford's, who seem'd to have taken a new Lease,
were any dependence to be upon looks, or any
Indulgence allow'd to the Wishes of his Friends.
An honester Man, a fairer Trader, or a kinder
Friend, this Country never produced: God send
any of his Sons may have the Grace to take after
him.   We took a running Repast with this good
Man, and then bidding Adieu both to him and Mr.
Banister, I mounted once more, and obstinately
pursued my Journey home, tho' the clouds threat-
en'd, and the Heavens lookt very lowring.   I had
not past the Court-house before it began to pour
down like a Spout upon me.   Nevertheless, I
pusht forward with Vigour, and got dripping wet
before I could reach Merchant's hope Point.   My
Boat was there luckily waiting for me, and wafted
me safe over.   And the Joy of meeting my Family
in Health made me in a Moment forget all the
Fatigues of the Journey, as much as if I had been
Husquenawed.   However, the good Providence

that attended me, and my whole Company, will I
hope stick fast in my Memory, and make me ever-
lastingly thankful.

A List of our Company of all Sorts.

Myself,	Thomas Wilson,	Lawson,
Maj'r Mayo,	Joseph Colson,	3 Indians,
Maj'r Mumford,	Harry Morris,	3 negroes,
Mr. Banister,	Robert Bolling,	20 horses,
Mr. Jones,	Thomas Hooper,	4 dogs.

An Account of the Distances of Places.

	MILES.
From Westover to Colo. Mumford's, ...	16
From Colo. Mumford's to maj'r Mumford's, .	6
From thence to Sappony Chappel, ...	20
From thence to major Embry's on Notoway, .	10
From thence to Brunswick Court-house, . .	15
From thence to Meherin River, ...	8
From thence to the Ford on Roanoak, . . .	12
From thence to Colo. Stith's Copper Mine, .	20
From thence to Butcher's Creek, ...	6
From thence to Bluestone Castle, ...	12
From thence to the Ford into the Fork, . .	7
From thence to Birche's Creek, ...	5
From thence to Banister River, ...	6
From thence to Morris Creek, ...	3
From thence to the Medway, ...	14
From thence to Maostie Creek, ...	2
From hence to Fork Creek, ...	6

MILES.

From hence to Peter's Creek, ...	2
From hence to Jones' Creek, ...	2
From hence to the first Ford over the Dan, .	$1\frac{1}{2}$
From hence to Cane Creek, ...	$2\frac{1}{2}$
From hence to the Second Ford of the Dan,	$4\frac{1}{2}$
From hence to the Mouth of Sable creek, .	8
From hence to the S-E Corner of my Land,	1
From thence to the Dan on my Back Line, .	8
From thence to the Irvin on my back Line, .	6
From thence to my S-W Corner, ...	1
From thence to my Corner on the W. of the Irvin, ...	3
From thence to the Dan along my Upper-Line, ...	$4\frac{1}{2}$
Sum	212

From thence to the Mouth of the Irvin, . .	$1\frac{1}{2}$
From thence to Sauro Creek, ...	$2\frac{1}{2}$
From thence to where my Back-line crosses the Dan, ...	5
From thence to my South-East Corner, . .	8
From thence to Cliff Creek, ...	10
From thence to Hixe's Creek, ...	2
From thence to Hatcher's Creek, ...	1
From thence to Cocquade Creek, ...	5
From thence to the upper Ford of Hico River,	7
From thence to Jesuit's Creek, ...	4
From thence to where the Line cuts Sugar Tree Creek, ...	5
From thence to the Mouth of Sugar Tree Creek, ...	4

	MILES.
From thence to the Mouth of Hico River, . .	7
From thence to Wilson's Quarter on Tewahominy Creek, ...	1
From thence to the Dan, ...	1
From thence across the Fork to the Stanton,	2
From thence to Blue Stone Castle, ...	7
From thence to Sandy Creek, ...	5
From thence to Mr. Mumford's Plantation, .	2
From thence to Butcher's Creek, ...	5
From thence to Allen's Creek, ...	9
From thence to Joshua Nicholson's on Meherin, ...	18
From thence to Brunswick Court-house, . .	8
From thence to Notoway Bridge, ...	14
From thence to Sappony Chappel, ...	10
From thence to Mr. Banister's on Hatcher's Run, ...	12
From thence to Colo. Bolling's Plantation, .	9
From thence to Colo. Mumford's Plantation, .	5
From thence to Westover, ...	16

184

A PROGRESS TO THE MINES

A PROGRESS TO THE MINES,

In the Year 1732.

EPT. 18. For the Pleasure of the good Company of Mrs. Byrd, and her little Governour, my Son, I went about half way to the Falls in the Chariot. There we halted, not far from a purling Stream, and upon the Stump of a propagate Oak picket the Bones of a piece of Roast Beef. By the Spirit which that gave me, I was the better able to part with the dear Companions of my Travels, and to perform the rest of my Journey on Horseback by myself. I reacht Shaccoa's before 2 a'clock, and crost the River to the Mills. I had the Grief to find them both stand as still for the want of Water, as a dead Woman's Tongue, for want of Breath. It had rain'd so little for many Weeks above the Falls, that the Naides had hardly Water enough left to wash their Faces. However, as we ought to turn all our Misfortunes to the best Advantage, I directed Mr.

333

Booker, my first Minister there, to make use of the lowness of the Water for blowing up the Rocks at the Mouth of the Canal. For that purpose I order'd Iron Drills to be made about 2 foot long, pointed with Steel, Chizzel fashion, in order to make holes, into which we put our Cartridges of Powder, containing each about 3 Ounces. There wanted Skill among my Engineers to chuse the best parts of the Stone for boring, that we might blow to the most advantage. They made all their Holes quite perpendicular, whereas they should have humour'd the Grain of the Stone for the more effectual Execution. I order'd the points of the Drills to be made Chizzel way, rather than the Diamond, that they might need to be Seldomer repair'd, tho' in Stone the Diamond points would make the most despatch. The Water now flow'd out of the River so slowly, that the Miller was oblig'd to pond it up in the Canal, by setting open the Flood-gates at the Mouth, and shutting those close at the Mill. By this contrivance, he was able at any time to grind two or three Bushels, either for his choice Customers, or for the use of my Plantations. Then I walkt to the place where they broke the Flax, which is wrought with much greater ease than the Hemp, and is much better for Spinning. From thence I paid a Visit to the Weaver, who needed a little of Minerva's Inspiration to make the most of a piece of fine Cloth. Then I lookt in upon my Caledonian Spinster, who was mended more in her looks than in her Humour. However, she promised much, tho' at the same time intended to perform little.

She is too high-Spirited for Mr. Booker, who hates
to have his sweet Temper ruffled, and will rather
suffer matters to go a little wrong sometimes, than
give his righteous Spirit any uneasiness.   He is
very honest, and would make an admirable Overseer where Servants will do as they are bid.   But
Eye-Servants, who want abundance of overlooking,
are not so proper to be committed to his Care.   I
found myself out of order, and for that reason retir'd Early; yet with all this precaution had a gentle
feaver in the Night, but towards morning Nature
sat open all her Gates, and drove it out in a plentiful perspiration.

19. The worst of this feaver was, that it put me
to the Necessity of taking another Ounce of Bark.
I moisten'd every dose with a little Brandy, and
fill'd the Glass up with Water, which is the least
Nauseous way of taking this Popish Medicine, and
besides hinders it from Purging. After I had
swallow'd a few Poacht Eggs, we rode down to
the Mouth of the Canal, and from thence crost
over to the broad Rock Island in a Canoe.   Our
errand was to view some Iron Ore, which we dug
up in two places.   That on the Surface seem'd
very spongy and poor, which gave us no great
Encouragement to search deeper, nor did the
Quantity appear to be very great.   However, for
my greater Satisfaction, I order'd a hand to dig
there for some time this Winter.   We walkt from
one End of the Island to the other, being about
half a Mile in length, and found the Soil very good,
and too high for any Flood, less than that of Deu-

calion, to do the least damage. There is a very wild prospect both upward and downward, the River being full of Rocks, over which the Stream tumbled with a Murmur, loud enough to drown the Notes of a Scolding Wife. This Island would make an agreeable Hermitage for any good Christian, who had a mind to retire from the World. Mr. Booker told me how Dr. Ireton had cured him once of a Looseness, which had been upon him two whole years. He order'd Him a Dose of Rhubarb, with directions to take 25 Drops of Laudanum so Soon as he had had 2 Physical Stools. Then he rested one day, and the next order'd him another Dose of the same Quantity of Laudanum to be taken, also after the 2d Stool. When this was done, he finisht the Cure by giving him 20 drops of Laudanum every night for five Nights running. The Doctor insisted upon the necessity of Stopping the Operation of the Rhubarb before it workt quite off, that what remained behind might strengthen the Bowels. I was punctual in Swallowing my Bark, and that I might use exercise upon it, rode to Prince's Folly, and my Lord's Islands, where I saw very fine Corn. In the mean time Vulcan came in Order to make the Drills for boring the Rocks, And gave me his Parole he wou'd, by the grace of God, attend the works till they were finisht, which he perform'd as lamely as if he had been to labour for a dead Horse, and not for ready Money. I made a North Carolina Dinner upon Fresh pork, tho' we had a plate of Green Peas after it, by way of Desert, for the Safety of our Noses. Then my first Minister and I had some serious Conversation about my Affairs, and I find nothing disturb'd his peaceable Spirit so much as the misbehaviour of the Spinster above-mention'd. I told him I cou'd not pity a Man, who had it always in his Power to do himself and her Justice, and wou'd not. If she were a Drunkard, a Scold, a Thief, or a Slanderer, we had wholesome Laws, that would make her Back Smart for the diversion of her other Members, and twas his Fault he had not put those wholesome Severitys in Execution. I retired in decent time to my own Appartment, and Slept very comfortably upon my Bark, forgetting all the little crosses arising from Overseers and negroes.

20. I continued the Bark, and then tost down my Poacht Eggs, with as much ease as some good Breeders Slip Children into the World. About Nine I left the Prudentest Orders I could think of with my Visier, & then crost the River to Shaccoe's. I made a running Visit to 3 of my Quarters, where, besides finding all the People well, I had the Pleasure to see better Crops than usual both of Corn and Tobacco. I parted there with my Intendant, and pursued my Journey to Mr. Randolph's, at Tuckahoe, without meeting with any Adventure by the way. Here I found Mrs. Fleming, who was packing up her Baggage with design to follow her Husband the next day, who was gone to a new Settlement in Goochland. Both he and She have been about Seaven Years persuading themselves to remove to that retired part of the Country, tho' they had the two strong Arguments of Health and

Interest for so doing. The Widow smiled graciously upon me, and entertain'd me very handsomely. Here I learnt all the tragical Story of
her Daughter's humble Marriage with her Uncle's
Overseer. Besides the meanness of this mortal's
Aspect, the Man has not one visible Qualification,
except Impudence, to recommend him to a Female's
Inclinations. But there is sometimes such a Charm
in that Hibernian Endowment, that frail Woman
cant withstand it, tho' it stand alone without any
other Recommendation. Had she run away with
a Gentleman or a pretty Fellow, there might have
been some Excuse for her, tho' he were of inferior
Fortune: but to stoop to a dirty Plebian, without
any kind of merit, is the lowest Prostitution. I
found the Family justly enraged at it; and tho' I
had more good Nature than to join in her Con-
demnation, yet I cou'd devise no Excuse for so
senceless a Prank as this young Gentlewoman had
play'd. Here good Drink was more Scarce than
good Victuals, the Family being reduc'd to the last
Bottle of Wine, which was therefore husbanded
very carefully. But the Water was excellent.
The Heir of the Family did not come home till late
in the Evening. He is a pretty Young Man, but
had the misfortune to become his own master too
soon. This puts young Fellows upon wrong pursuits, before they have Sence to Judge rightly for
themselves. Tho' at the same time they have a
strange conceit of their own Suffiency, when they
grow near 20 Years old, especially if they happen
to have a small Smattering of Learning. Tis then

they fancy themselves wiser than all their Tutors
and Governors, which makes them headstrong to
all advice, and above all Reproof and Admonition.

21. I was sorry in the morning to find myself
stopt in my Career by bad Weather brought upon
us by a North-East Wind. This drives a World
of Raw unkindly Vapours upon us from Newfound-
land, loaden with Blite, Coughs, and Pleurisys.
However, I complain'd not, lest I might be sus-
pected to be tir'd of the good Company. Tho'
Mrs. Fleming was not so much upon her Guard,
but mutiny'd strongly at the Rain, that hinder'd
her from pursuing her dear Husband. I said what
I cou'd to comfort a Gentlewoman under so sad a
Disappointment. I told her a Husband, that staid
so much at Home as her's did, cou'd be no such
violent Rarity, as for a Woman to venture her
precious Health, to go daggling thro' the Rain
after him, or to be miserable if she happen'd to be
prevented. That it was prudent for marry'd people
to fast Sometimes from one another, that they
might come together again with the better Stomach.
That the best things in this World, if constantly
us'd, are apt to be cloying, which a little absence
and Abstinence wou'd prevent. This was Strange
Doctrine to a fond Female, who fancys People
shou'd love with as little Reason after Marriage as
before. In the Afternoon Monsieur Marij, the
Minister of the Parish, came to make me a Visit.
He had been a Romish Priest, but found Reasons,
either Spiritual or temporal, to quit that gay Religion. The fault of this new Convert is, that he

looks for as much Respect from his Protestant Flock, as is paid to the Popish Clergy, which our ill-bred Hugonots dont understand. Madam Marij, had so much Curiosity as to want to come too; but another Horse was wanting, and she believ'd it would have too Vulgar an Air to ride behind her Husband. This Woman was of the true Exchange Breed, full of Discourse, but void of Discretion, and marry'd a Parson, with the Idle hopes he might some time or other come to be his Grace of Canterbury. The Gray Mare is the better Horse in that Family, and the poor man Submits to her wild Vagarys for Peace' Sake. She has just enough of the fine Lady, to run in debt, and be of no signification in her Household. And the only thing that can prevent her from undoing her loving Husband will be, that nobody will trust them beyond the 16000,[1] which is soon run out in a Goochland store. The way of Dealing there is, for some small Merchant or Pedler to buy a Scots Pennyworth of Goods, and clap 150 p cent. upon that. At this Rate the Parson cant be paid much more for his preaching than tis worth. No sooner was our Visiter retired, but the facetious Widow was so kind as to let me into all this Secret History, but was at the same time exceedingly Sorry that the Woman should be so indiscreet, and the man so tame as to be govern'd by an unprofitable and fantastical Wife.

22. We had another wet day, to try both Mrs.

---

[1] 16,000 pounds of tobacco, which was the legal salary of a minister.

Fleming's Patience and my good Breeding. The
N E Wind commonly sticks by us 3 or 4 days,
filling the Atmosphere with damps, injurious both
to man and Beast. The worst of it was, we had no
good Liquor to warm our Blood, and fortify our
Spirits against so strong a Malignity. However,
I was cheerful under all these Misfortunes, and
exprest no Concern but a decent Fear lest my
long visit might be troublesome. Since I was like
to have thus much Leizure, I endeavour'd to find
out what Subject a dull marry'd man cou'd introduce that might best bring the Widow to the Use
of her Tongue. At length I discover'd she was a
notable Quack, and therefore paid that regard to
her Knowledge, as to put some Questions to her
about the bad distemper that raged then in the
Country. I mean the Bloody Flux, that was
brought us in the Negro-ship consigned to Colo.
Braxton. She told me she made use of very Simple remedys in that Case, with very good Success.
She did the Business either with Hartshorn Drink,
that had Plantain Leaves boil'd in it, or else with
a Strong decoction of St. Andrew's Cross, in New
milk instead of Water. I agreed with her that
those remedys might be very good, but would be
more effectual after a dose or two of Indian Physick. But for fear this Conversation might be too
grave for a Widow, I turn'd the discourse, and
began to talk of Plays, & finding her Taste lay
most towards Comedy, I offer'd my Service to
read one to Her, which she kindly accepted. She
produced the 2d part of the Beggar's Opera, which

had diverted the Town for 40 Nights successively, and gain'd four thousand pounds to the Author. This was not owing altogether to the Wit or Humour that Sparkled in it, but to some Political Reflections, that seem'd to hit the Ministry. But the great Advantage of the Author was, that his Interest was solicited by the Dutchess of Queensbury, which no man could refuse who had but half an Eye in his head, or half a Guinea in his Pocket. Her Grace, like Death, spared nobody, but even took my Lord Selkirk in for 2 Guineas, to repair which Extravagance he liv'd upon Scots Herrings 2 Months afterwards. But the best Story was, she made a very Smart Officer in his Majesty's Guards give her a Guinea, who Swearing at the same time twas all he had in the World, she sent him 50 for it the next day, to reward his Obedience. After having acquainted my Company with the History of the Play, I read 3 Acts of it, and left Mrs. Fleming and Mr. Randolph to finish it, who read as well as most Actors do at a Rehearsal. Thus we kill'd the time, and triumpht over the bad Weather.

23. The Clouds continued to drive from the N-Est, and to menace us with more Rain. But as the Lady resolved to venture thro' it, I thought it a Shame for me to venture to flinch. Therefore, after fortifying myself with 2 capacious Dishes of Coffee, and making my Complements to the Ladyes, I mounted, and Mr. Randolph was so kind as to be my Guide. At the distance of about 3 Miles, in a Path as narrow as that which leads to Heaven,

but much more dirty, we reacht the homely dwelling of the Reverend Mr. Marij. His Land is much more barren than his Wife, and needs all Mr. Bradley's Skill in Agriculture to make it bring Corn. Thence we proceeded five Miles farther, to a Mill of Mr. Randolph's, that is apt to stand still when there falls but little Rain, and to be carry'd away when there falls a great deal. Then we pursued a very blind Path 4 Miles farther, which puzzled my Guide, who I suspect led me out of the way. At length we came into a great Road, where he took leave, after giving me some very confus'd Directions, and so left me to blunder out the rest of the Journey by myself. I lost myself more than once, but soon recover'd the right way again. About 3 Miles after quitting my Guide, I passed the S Branch of Pomunky River, near 50 Yards over, and full of Stones. After this, I had 8 Miles to Mr. Chiswell's, where I arriv'd at about 2 a'Clock, and sav'd my Dinner. I was very handsomely entertain'd, finding every thing very clean, and very Good. I had not seen Mrs Chiswell in 24 Years, which, alas! had made great Havoc with her pretty Face, and plow'd very deep Furrows in her fair Skin. It was impossible to know her again, so much the flower was faded. However, tho' she was grown an Old Woman, yet she was one of those absolute Rarities, a very good old Woman. I found Mr. Chiswell a sensible, well-bred Man, and very frank in communicating his knowledge in the Mystery of making Iron, wherein he has had long Experience. I told him I was come to Spy the Land, and inform myself of the Expence of carrying on an Iron work with Effect. That I sought my Instruction from Him, who understood the whole Mystery, having gain'd full Experience in every part of it; Only I was very sorry he had bought that Experience so dear. He answer'd that he would, with great Sincerity, let me into the little knowledge he had, and so we immediately entered upon the Business. He assured me the first step I was to take was to acquaint myself fully with the Quantity and Quality of my Oar. For that reason I ought to keep a good Pick-ax Man at work a whole Year to search if there be a Sufficient Quantity, without which it would be a very rash undertaking. That I shou'd also have a Skilful person to try the richness of the oar. Nor is it great Advantage to have it exceeding rich, because then it will yield Brittle Iron, which is not valuable. But the way to have it tough is to mix poor Oar and Rich together, which makes the poorer sort extremely necessary for the production of the best Iron. Then he shew'd me a Sample of the Richest Oar they have in England, which yields a full Moiety of Iron. It was of a Pale red Colour, smooth and greasy, and not exceedingly heavy; but it produced so brittle a Metal, that they were oblig'd to melt a poorer Oar along with it. He told me, after I was certain my Oar was good and plentiful enough, my next inquiry ought to be, how far it lyes from a Stream proper to build a furnace upon, and again what distance that Furnace will be from Water Carriage; Because the Charge of

Carting a great way is very heavy, and eats out a great part of the Profit. That this was the Misfortune of the Mines of Fredericksville, where they were oblig'd to Cart the Oar a Mile to the Furnace, and after twas run into Iron, to carry that 24 Miles, over an uneven Road to Rappahannock River, about a Mile below Fredericksburgh, to a Plantation the Company rented of Colo. Page. If I were satisfy'd with the Situation, I was in the next place to consider whether I had Woodland enough near the Furnace to Supply it with Charcoal, whereof it wou'd require a prodigious Quantity. That the properest Wood for that purpose was that of Oyly kind, such as Pine, Walnut, Hiccory, Oak, and in short all that yields Cones, Nuts, or Acorns. That 2 Miles Square of Wood, wou'd supply a Moderate furnace; so that what you fell first may have time to grow up again to a proper bigness (which must be 4 Inches over) by that time the rest is cut down. He told me farther, that 120 Slaves, including Women, were necessary to carry on all the Business of an Iron Work, and the more Virginians amongst them the better; Tho' in that number he comprehended Carters, Colliers, and those that planted the Corn. That if there should be much Carting, it would require 1600 Barrels of Corn Yearly to Support the People, & the Cattle employ'd; nor dos even that Quantity suffice at Fredericksville. That if all these Circumstances shou'd happily concur, and you cou'd procure honest Colliers and Firemen, which will be difficult to do, you may easily run 800 Tuns of Sow Iron a Year.

The whole charge of Freight, Custom, Commission, and other Expences in England, will not exceed 30 Shillings a Tun, and twill commonly sell for £6, and then the clear profit will amount to £4, , 10. So that allowing the ten Shillings for Accidents, you may reasonably expect a clear Profit of £4, which being multiplied by 800, will amount to £3200 a year, to pay you for your Land and Negroes. But then it behooved me to be fully inform'd of the whole Matter myself, to prevent being imposed upon; and if any offer'd to put tricks upon me, to punish them as they deserve. Thus ended our Conversation for this day, and I retir'd to a very clean Lodging in another House, and took my Bark, but was forced to take it in Water, by reason a light finger'd Damsel had ransackt my Baggage, and drunk up my Brandy. This unhappy Girl, it seems, is a Baronet's Daughter; but her Complexion, being red hair'd, inclin'd her so much to Lewdness, that her Father sent her, under the Care of the virtuous Mr. Cheep, to seek her fortune on this Side the Globe.

24. My Friend, Mr. Chiswell, made me reparation for the Robbery of his Servant, by filling my Bottle again with good Brandy. It being Sunday, I made a Motion for going to Church, to see the growth of the Parish, but unluckily the Sermon happen'd to be at the Chappel, which was too far off. I was unwilling to tire my Friend with any farther discourse upon Iron, and therefore turn'd the Conversation to other Subjects. And talking of Management, he let me into 2 Secrets worth re-

membering. He said the quickest way in the world
to stop the Fermentation of any Liquor was to keep
a lighted Match of Brimstone under the Cask for
some time. This is useful in so warm a Country
as this, where cyder is apt to work itself off both
of its Strength and sweetness. The other Secret
was to keep Weevels out of Wheat and other
Grain. You have nothing to do, said he, but to
put a Bag of Pepper into every heap, or Cask,
which those Insects have such an Antipathy to that
they will not approach it. These Receipts he gave
me, not upon Report, but upon his own repeated Experience. He farther told me he had brew'd as good
Ale of Malt made of Indian Corn as ever he tasted;
all the objection was, he cou'd neither by Art, or
Standing, ever bring it to be fine in the Cask. The
Quantity of Corn he employed in brewing a Cask of
40 Gallons was 2 Bushels and a half, which made
it very Strong and pleasant. We had a Hanch of
Venison for Dinner, as fat and well tasted as if it
had come out of Richmond Park. In these upper
parts of the Country the Deer are in better Case
than below, tho' I believe the Buck which gave us
so good a Dinner had eaten out his Value in Peas,
which will make Deer exceeding fat. In the Afternoon, I walkt with my Friend to his Mill, which
is half a Mile from his House. It is built upon a
Rock very firmly, so that tis more apt to suffer by
too little Water, (the Run not being over plentiful,) than too much. On the other side of this
Stream lye several of Colo. Jones' Plantations.
The poor Negroes upon them are a kind of Adam-

ites, very Scantily supply'd with cloaths and other
necessaries; Nevertheless, (which is a little incom-
prehensible,) they continue in perfect health, and
none of them dye, except it be of Age. However,
they are even with their Master, and make him but
indifferent Crops, so that he gets nothing by his
unjustice, but the Scandal of it. And here I must
make One Remarque, which I am a little unwilling
to do for fear of encouraging of Cruelty, that those
Negroes which are kept the barest of cloaths &
Bedding are commonly the freest from Sickness.
And this happens, I suppose, by their being all
Face, and therefore better proof against the sudden
changes of Weather, to which this Climate is
unhappily Subject.

25. After saying some very civil things to
Mrs. Chiswell, for my handsome Entertainment, I
mounted my Horse, and Mr. Chiswell his Phaeton,
in order to go to the Mines at Fredericksville. We
cou'd converse very little by the way, by reason
of our different Voitures. The Road was very
Straight and level the whole Journey, which was
25 Miles, the last ten whereof I rode in the Chair,
and my Friend on my Horse, to ease ourselves by
that Variety of Motion. About a Mile before we
got to Fredericksville, we forded over the North
Branch of Pomunky, about 60 Yards over. Neither this nor the South Branch run up near so high
as the Mountains, but many Miles below them spread
out into a kind of Morass, like Chickahominy.
When we approacht the Mines, there open'd to
our View a large Space of clear'd Ground, whose

Wood had been cut down for coaling. We Arriv'd
here about 2 A'Clock, and Mr. Chiswell had been
so provident as to bring a Cold Venison Pasty,
with which we appeased our Appetites, without
the Impatience of waiting. When our Tongues
were at leizure for discourse, my Friend told me
there was one Mr. Harison, in England, who is
so universal a dealer in all Sorts of Iron, that he
cou'd govern the Market just as he pleas'd. That
it was by his artful Management that our Iron
from the Plantations sold for less than that made
in England, tho' it was generally reckon'd much
better. That Ours wou'd hardly fetch 6£ a Tun,
when their's fetcht 7 or 8, purely to serve that
Man's Interest. Then he explain'd the Several
Charges upon our Sow Iron, after it was put on
Board the Ships. That in the first place it paid
7ƒ6 a Tun for Freight, being just so much clear
gain to the Ships, which carry it as Ballast, or
wedge it in among the Hogsheads. When it gets
Home, it pays 3ƒ9 custome. These Articles together make no more than 11ƒ 3, and yet the Merchants, by their great Skill in Multiplying Charges,
Swell the account up to near 30ƒ a Tun by that
time it gets out of their Hands, and they are continually adding more and more, as they serve us in
our Accounts of Tobacco. He told me a strange
thing about Steel, that the making of the best
remains at this day a profound Secret in the breast
of a very few, and therefore is in danger of being
lost, as the Art of Staining of Glass, and many
others, have been. He cou'd only tell me they

us'd Beech Wood in the making of it in Europe,
& burn it a Considerable time in powder of Charcoal; but the Mystery lies in the Liquor they
quench it in.   After dinner we took a walk to
the Furnace, which is elegantly built of Brick, tho'
the Hearth be of Fire-Stone.   There we saw the
Founder, Mr. Derham, who is paid 4 Shillings for
every Tun of Sow Iron that he runs, which is a
Shilling cheaper than the last Workman had.   This
Operator lookt a little Melancholy, because he had
nothing to do, the Furnace having been Cold ever
since May, for want of Corn to Support the Cattle.
This was however no neglect of Mr. Chiswell, because all the Persons he had contracted with had
basely disappointed him.   But having receiv'd a
small Supply, they intended to blow very soon.
With that view they began to heat the Furnace,
which is 6 Weeks before it comes to that intense
heat required to run the Metal in perfection.   Nevertheless, they commonly begin to blow when the
Fire has been kindled a Week or ten days.   Close
by the Furnace stood a very spacious House full
of Charcoal, holding at least 400 Loads, which will
be burnt out in 3 Months.   The Company has contracted with Mr. Harry Willis to fall the Wood,
and then maul it and cut it into pieces of 4 feet in
length, and bring it to the Pits where it is to be
coal'd.   All this he has undertaken to do for 2
Shillings a Cord, which must be 4 foot broad, 4
foot high, and 8 foot long.   Being thus carry'd to
the Pits, the Collier has contracted to Coal it for 5
Shillings a Load, consisting of 160 Bushels.   The

Fire in the Furnace is blown by 2 Mighty pair of
Bellows, that cost one Hundred pounds each, and
these Bellows are mov'd by a great Wheel of 26
foot diameter. The Wheel again is carry'd round
by a small Stream of Water, conveyed about 350
Yards over Land in a Trough, from a Pond made by
a wooden Dam. But there is great want of Water
in a dry Season, which makes the Furnace often blow
out, to the great prejudice of the Works. Having
thus fill'd my Head with all these Particulars, we
return'd to the House, where, after talking of Colo.
Spotswood, and his Strategems to shake off his Partners, and secure all his Mines to himself, I retired
to a homely Lodging, which, like a homespun Mistress, had been more tolerable, if it had been sweet.

26. Over our Tea, Mr. Chiswell told me the
expence which the Company had been already at
amounted to near Twelve Thousand Pounds: But
then the Land, Negroes, and Cattle were all included in that Charge. However, the Money
began now to come in, they having run 1200 Tuns
of Iron, and all their heavy disbursements were
over. Only they were stil forct to buy great
Quantitys of Corn, because they had not strength
of their own to make it. That they had not more
than 80 Negroes, and few of those Virginia born.
That they need 40 Negroes more to carry on all
the Business with their own Force. They have
15000 Acres of Land, tho' little of it rich except in
Iron, and of that they have a great Quantity. Mr.
FitzWilliams took up the mine tract, and had the
address to draw in the Governor, Capt. Pearse, Dr.

Nicolas and Mr. Chiswell to be jointly concern'd
with him, by which contrivance he first got a good
price for the Land, and then, when he had been
very little out of Pocket, sold his Share to Mr.
Nelson for 500£; and of these Gentlemen the
Company at present consists.   And Mr. Chiswell
is the only person amongst them that knows any
thing of the matter, and has 100£ a year for looking after the Works, and richly deserves it.   After
breaking our Fast we took a walk to the principal
Mine, about a Mile from the Furnace, where they
had sunk in some places about 15 or 20 foot deep.
The Operator, Mr. Gordon, rais'd the Oar, for
which he was to have by contract 1ƒ 6 p Cart-Load
of 26 Hundred Weight.   This man was oblig'd to
hire all the Laborers he wanted for this Work of
the Company, after the rate of 25ƒ a Month, and
for all that was able to clear 40£ a-year for himself.   We saw here several large Heaps of oar of
2 sorts, one of rich, and the other Spongy and poor,
which they melted together to make the Metal
more tough.   The way of raising the oar was by
blowing it up, which Operation I saw here from
beginning to End.   They first drill'd a hole in the
Mine, either upright or Slopeing, as the grain of it
required.   This hole they cleansed with a Rag
fasten'd to the End of an Iron with a Worm at the
end of it.   Then they put in a Cartridge of Powder containing about 3 Ounces, and at the same
time a Reed full of fuse that reacht to the Powder.
Then they ramm'd dry Clay, or soft Stone very
hard into the Hole, and lastly they fired the fuse

with a Paper that had been dipt in a Solution of
Saltpetre and dry'd, which burning Slow and Sure,
gave leizure to the Engineer to retire to a proper
distance before the Explosion.   This in the Miner's
Language is call'd making a Blast, which will
losen several hundred Weight of Oar at once: and
afterwards the Laborers easily separate it with
Pick-axes and carry it away in Baskets up to the
Heap.   At our return we saw near the Furnace
large Heaps of Mine with Charcoal mixet with it,
a Stratum of each alternately, beginning first with
a layer of Charcoal at the Bottom.   To this they
put Fire, which in a little time spreads thro' the
whole Heap, and calcines the Oar, which afterwards easily crumbles into small pieces fit for the
Furnace.   Then was likewise a mighty Quantity
of Limestone, brought from Bristol, by way of
ballast, at 2/6 a Tun, which they are at the
Trouble to Cart hither from Rappahanock River,
but contrive to do it when the Carts return from
carrying of Iron.   They put this into the Furnace
with the Iron Oare, in the proportion of one Tun
of Stone to ten of Oar, with design to absorb the
Sulphur out of the Iron, which wou'd otherwise
make it brittle.   And if that be the use of it, Oyster
Shells wou'd certainly do as well as LimeStone,
being altogether as strong an Alkali, if not
Stronger.   Nor can their being taken out of Salt
water be any Objection, because tis pretty certain
the West India LimeStone, which is thrown up by
the Sea, is even better than that imported from
Bristol.   But the founders who never try'd either

of these will by no means be perswaded to go out
of their way, tho' the Reason of the thing be never
so evident.   I observ'd the richer Sort of Mine,
being of a dark Colour Mixt with rust, was laid in
a heap by itself, and so was the poor, which was of
a Liver or Brick Colour.   The Sow Iron is in the
Figure of a half-round, about two feet and a half-
long, weighing 60 or 70 Pounds, whereof 3000
weight make a Cart-load drawn by 8 Oxen, which
are commonly shod to save their Hoofs in those
Stony ways.   When the Furnace blows, it runs
about 20 Tuns of Iron a Week.   The founders find
it very hot work to tend the Furnace, especially in
Summer, and are oblig'd to spend no small part of
their Earnings in strong Drink, to recruit their
Spirits.   Besides the Founder, the Collier, and
Miner, who are paid in proportion to their Work,
the Company have several other Officers upon
Wages, a Stock-taker, who weighs and measures
every thing, a Clerk, who keeps an Account of all
Receipts and Disbursements, a Smith to Shoe their
Cattle, and keep all their Iron work in repair, a
wheel-Wright, Cartwright, Carpenter, and Several
Carters.   The Wages of all these Persons amount
to one Hundred Pounds a Year; so that including
Mr. Chiswell's Salary, they disburse 200£ p Annum
in standing Wages.   The Provisions too are a heavy
Article, which their Plantations dont yet produce in
a Sufficient Quantity, tho' they are at the Charge
of a general Overseer.   But while Corn is so short
with them, there can be no great Increase of Stock
of any kind.

27. Having now pretty well exhausted the Subject of Sow Iron, I askt my Friend some Questions about Bar-Iron. He told me we had as yet no Forge erected in Virginia, tho' we had 4 Furnaces. But there was a very good one set up at the head of the Bay in Maryland, that made exceeding good Work. He let me know that the duty in England upon Bar Iron was 24ʄ a Tun, and that it sold there from Ten to 16 pounds a Tun. This wou'd pay the Charge of Forging abundantly, but he doubted the Parliament of England would soon forbid us that Improvement, lest after that we shou'd go farther, and manufacture Our Bars into all Sorts of Iron Ware, as they already do in New England & Pennsylvania. Nay, he question'd whether we shou'd be suffer'd to cast any Iron, which they can do themselves at their Furnaces. Thus ended our Conversation, and I thankt my Friend for being so free in communicating everything to me. Then, after tipping a Pistole to the Clerk, to drink prosperity to the Mines with all the Workmen, I accepted the kind offer of going part of my Journey in the Phaeton. I took my Leave about ten, and drove over a Spacious Level Road ten Miles, to a Bridge built over the River Po, which is one of the 4 Branches of the Matopany, about 40 Yards wide. Two Miles beyond that, we passed by a Plantation belonging to the Company, of about 500 Acres, where they keep a great Number of Oxen to relieve those that have dragg'd their loaded Carts thus far. Three Miles farther we came to the Germanna Road,

where I quitted the Chair, and continued my Journey on Horseback. I rode 8 Miles together over a Stony Road, and had on either side continual poisen'd Fields, with nothing but Saplins growing on them. Then I came into the Main County Road, that leads from Fredericksburgh to Germanna, which last place I reacht in Ten Miles more. This famous Town consists of Colo. Spotswood's enchanted Castle on one Side of the Street, and a Baker's Dozen of ruinous Tenements on the other, where so many German Familys had dwelt some Years ago; but are now remov'd ten Miles higher, in the Fork of Rappahannock, to Land of their Own. There had also been a Chappel about a Bow-Shot from the Colonel's house, at the End of an Avenue of Cherry Trees, but some pious people had lately burnt it down, with intent to get another built nearer to their own homes. Here I arriv'd about three a'clock, and found only Mrs. Spotswood at Home, who receiv'd her Old acquaintance with many a gracious Smile. I was carry'd into a Room elegantly set off with Pier Glasses, the largest of which came soon after to an odd Misfortune. Amongst other favourite Animals that cheer'd this Lady's Solitude, a Brace of Tame Deer ran familiarly about the House, and one of them came to stare at me as a Stranger. But unluckily Spying his own Figure in the Glass, he made a spring over the Tea Table that stood under it, and shatter'd the Glass to pieces, and falling back upon the Tea Table, made a terrible Fracas among the China. This Exploit was so sudden,

and accompany'd with such a Noise, that it surpriz'd me, and perfectly frighten'd Mrs. Spotswood.
But twas worth all the Damage to shew the Moderation and good humour with which she bore this
disaster. In the Evening the noble Colo. came
home from his Mines, who saluted me very civily,
and Mrs. Spotswood's Sister, Miss Theky, who had
been to meet him *en Cavalier*, was so kind too as
to bid me welcome. We talkt over a Legend of
old Storys, supp'd about 9, and then prattl'd with
the Ladys, til twas time for a Travellour to retire.
In the mean .time I observ'd my old Friend to be
very Uxorious, and exceedingly fond of his Children. This was so opposite to the Maxims he us'd
to preach up before he was marryed,[1] that I cou'd
not forbear rubbing up the Memory of them. But
he gave a very good-natur'd turn to his Change of
Sentiments, by alleging that whoever brings a poor
Gentlewoman into so solitary a place, from all her
Friends and acquaintance, wou'd be ungrateful not
to use her and all that belongs to her with all
possible Tenderness.

28. We all kept Snug in our several apartments
till Nine, except Miss Theky, who was the Housewife of the Family. At that hour we met over a
Pot of Coffee, which was not quite strong enough
to give us the Palsy. After Breakfast the Colo.
and I left the Ladys to their Domestick Affairs,

---

[1] Spotswood was married in
1724 to Miss Butler Brayne, of
England. This was after his
term of office as governor was
expired. "Miss Theky" was
Dorothy Brayne, sometimes
written Bryan, and she married
Elliott Benger, of Virginia, and
had issue. (See Va. Histl.
Mag., II. 340.)

and took a turn in the Garden, which has nothing
beautiful but 3 Terrace Walks that fall in Slopes
one below another.   I let him understand, that besides the pleasure of paying him a Visit, I came to
be instructed by so great a Master in the Mystery
of Making of Iron, wherein he had led the way, and
was the Tubal Cain of Virginia.   He corrected me
a little there, by assuring me he was not only
the first in this Country, but the first in North
America, who had erected a regular Furnace.
That they ran altogether upon Bloomerys in New
England & Pennsilvania, till his Example had
made them attempt greater Works.   But in this
last Colony, they have so few Ships to carry their
Iron to Great Britain, that they must be content to
make it only for their own use, and must be oblig'd
to manufacture it when they have done.   That he
hoped he had done the Country very great Service
by setting so good an Example.   That the 4 Furnaces now at work in Virginia circulated a great
Sum of Money for Provisions and all other necessarys in the adjacent Countys.   That they took
off a great Number of Hands from Planting Tobacco, and employ'd them in Works that produced
a large Sum of Money in England to the persons
concern'd, whereby the Country is so much the
Richer.   That they are besides a considerable advantage to Great Britain, because it lessens the
Quantity of Bar Iron imported from Spain, Holland, Sweden, Denmark and Muscovy, which used
to be no less than 20,000 Tuns yearly, tho' at the
same time no Sow Iron is imported thither from

any Country but only from the Plantations. /For most of this Bar Iron they do not only pay Silver, but our Friends in the Baltick are so nice, they even expect to be paid all in Crown Pieces. On the contrary, all the Iron they receive from the Plantations, they pay for it in their own Manufactures, and send for it in their own Shipping. Then I inquired after his own Mines, and hoped, as he was the first that engaged in this great undertaking, that he had brought them to the most perfection. He told me he had Iron in several Parts of his great Tract of Land, consisting of 45,000 Acres. But that the Mine he was at work upon was 13 Miles below Germanna. That his Oar (which was very rich) he rais'd a Mile from his Furnace, and was oblig'd to Cart the Iron, when it was made, 15 Miles to Massaponux, a Plantation he had upon Rappahanock River; But that the Road was exceeding good, gently declining all the way, and had no more than one Hill to go up in the whole Journey. For this reason his loaded carts went it in a day without difficulty. He said it was true His works were of the oldest Standing: but that his long absence in England, and the wretched Management of Mr. Greame, whom he had entrusted with his Affairs, had put him back very much. That what with Neglect and Severity, above 80 of his Slaves were lost while he was in England, and most of his Cattle starved. That his Furnace stood still great part of the time, and all his Plantations ran to ruin. That indeed he was rightly serv'd for committing his Affairs to the care of a Mathematician, whose thoughts were always among the Stars. That nevertheless, since his return, he had apply'd himself to rectify his Steward's Mistakes, and bring his Business again into Order. That now he had contriv'd to do every thing with his own People, except raising the Mine and running the Iron, by which he had contracted his Expence very much. Nay, he believ'd that by his directions he cou'd bring sensible Negroes to perform those parts of the Work tolerably well. But at the same time he gave me to understand, that his Furnace had done no great Feats lately, because he had been taken up in building an Air Furnace at Massaponux, which he had now brought to perfection, and shou'd be thereby able to furnish the whole Country with all Sorts of Cast Iron, as cheap and as good as ever came from England. I told him he must do one thing more to have a full Vent for those Commoditys, he must keep a Chaloupe running into all the Rivers, to carry his Wares home to people's own Doors. And if he wou'd do that I wou'd set a good Example, and take of a whole Tun of them. Our Conversation on this Subject continued till Dinner, which was both elegant and plentifull. The afternoon was devoted to the ladys, who shew'd me one of their most beautiful Walks. They conducted me thro' a Shady Lane to the Landing, and by the way made me drink some very fine Water that issued from a Marble Fountain, and ran incessantly. Just behind it was a cover'd Bench, where Miss Theky often sat and bewail'd

her Virginity.   Then we proceeded to the River,
which is the South Branch of Rappahanock, about
50 Yards wide, and so rapid that the Ferry Boat
is drawn over by a Chain, and therefore called the
Rapidan.   At night we drank prosperity to all the
Colonel's Projects in a Bowl of Rack Punch, and
then retired to our Devotions.

29. Having employ'd about 2 hours in Retire-
ment, I Sally'd out at the first Summons to Breakfast, where our conversation with the Ladys, like
Whip Sillabub, was very pretty, but had nothing
in it.   This it seems was Miss Theky's Birth day,
upon which I made her my Compliments, & wish't
she might live twice as long a marry'd Woman as
she had liv'd a Maid.   I did not presume to pry
into the Secret of her Age, nor was she forward to
disclose it, for this humble Reason, lest I shou'd
think her Wisdom fell short of her Years.   She contriv'd to make this day of her Birth a day of Mourn-
ing, for having nothing better at present to set her
Affections upon, she had a Dog that was a great
Favourite.   It happen'd that very Morning the
poor Curr had done something very uncleanly upon
the Colo's Bed, for which he was condemn'd to
dye.   However, upon her entreaty, she got him a
Reprieve; but was so concern'd that so much severity shou'd be intended on her Birth day, that
she was not to be comforted; and lest such another
Accident might Oust the poor Curr of his Clergy,
she protested she would board out her Dog at
a Neighbour's House, where she hoped he wou'd
be more kindly treated.   Then the Colo. and I took

another turn in the Garden, to discourse farther on
the Subject of Iron.   He was very frank in communicating all his dear-bought Experience to me,
and told me very civily he wou'd not only let me
into the whole Secret, but wou'd make a Journey
to James River, and give me his faithful Opinion
of all my Conveniences.   For his part he wisht
there were many more Iron works in the Country,
provided the partys concerned wou'd preserve a
constant Harmony among themselves, and meet
and consult frequently, what might be for their
common Advantage.   By this they might be better
able to manage the Workmen, and reduce their
Wages to what was just and reasonable.   After
this frank Speech, he began to explain the whole
charge of an Iron-work.   He said, there ought at
least to be an Hundred Negroes employ'd in it,
and those upon good Land would make Corn, and
raise Provisions enough to support themselves and
the Cattle, and do every other part of the Business.   That the Furnace might be built for 700£,
and made ready to go to work, if I went the nearest way to do it, especially since coming after so
many, I might correct their Errors and avoid their
Miscarriages.   That if I had Oar and Wood
enough, and a convenient Stream of Water to set
the Furnace upon, having neither too much nor too
little Water, I might undertake the Affair with a
full Assurance of Success.   Provided the distance
of Carting be not too great, which is exceedingly
burdensome.   That there must be abundance of
Wheel Carriages, shod with Iron, and several

Teams of Oxen, provided to transport the Wood
that is to be coal'd, and afterwards the Coal and
Oar to the Furnace, and last of all the Sow Iron to
the nearest Water Carriage, and carry back Limestone & other necessarys from thence to the
Works; and a Sloop also would be useful to carry
the Iron on Board the Ships, the Masters not being
always in the Humour to fetch it. Then he enu-
merated the people that were to be hired, viz.: a
Founder, a Mine-raiser, a Collier, a Stock-taker, a
Clerk, a Smith, a Carpenter, a Wheelwright, and
Several Carters. That these altogether will be a
Standing charge of about £500 a Year. That the
amount of Freight, Custom, Commission and other
Charges in England, comes to 27ƒ a Tun. But
that the Merchants yearly find out means to inflame the Account with New Articles, as they do
in those of Tobacco. That, upon the whole matter, the Expences here and in England may be
computed modestly at 3£ a Tun. And the rest
that the Iron sells for will be clear gain, to pay for
the Land and Negros, which tis to be hoped will
be £3 more for every Tun that is sent over. As
this Account agreed pretty near with that which
Mr. Chiswell had given me, I set it down (notwithstanding it may seem a Repetition of the same
thing) to prove that both these Gentlemen were
sincere in their Representations. We had a Mich-
aelmas Goose for Dinner, of Miss Theky's own
raising, who was now goodnatur'd enough to forget the Jeopardy of her Dog. In the afternoon
we walkt in a Meadow by the River side, which

winds in the form of a Horseshoe about Germanna, making it a Peninsula, containing about 400 Acres. Rappahanock forks about 14 Miles below this place, the Northern Branch being the larger, and consequently must be the River that bounds My Lord Fairfax's Grant of the Northern Neck.

30. The Sun rose clear this Morning, and so did I, and finisht all my little Affairs by Breakfast. It was then resolv'd to wait on the Ladys on Horseback, since the bright Sun, the fine Air, and the wholesome Exercise, all invited us to it. We forded the River a little above the Ferry, and rode 6 Miles up the Neck to a fine Level piece of Rich Land, where we found about 20 Plants of Ginseng, with the Scarlet Berrys growing on the top of the Middle Stalk. The Root of this is of wonderful Vertue in many Cases, particularly to raise the Spirits and promote Perspiration, which makes it a Specifick in Colds and Coughs. The Colo. complemented me with all we found, in return for my telling him the Vertues of it. We were all pleas'd to find so much of this King of Plants so near the Colonel's habitation, and growing too upon his own Land; but were, however, surprized to find it upon level Ground, after we had been told it grew only upon the North Side of Stony Mountains. I carry'd home this Treasure, with as much Joy, as if every Root had been a Graft of the Tree of Life, and washt and dry'd it carefully. This Airing made us as Hungry as so many Hawks, so that between Appetite and a very good Dinner, twas difficult to eat like a Philosopher. In the After-

noon the Ladys walkt me about amongst all their
little Animals, with which they amuse themselves,
and furnish the Table; the worst of it is, they are
so tender-hearted, they Shed a Silent Tear every
time any of them are kill'd.   At Night the Colo.
and I quitted the threadbare Subject of Iron, and
changed the Scene to Politicks.   He told me the
Ministry had receded from their demand upon New
England, to raise a standing Salary for all succeeding Governors, for fear some curious Members
of the House of Commons shou'd enquire How the
Money was dispos'd of, that had been rais'd in the
other American Colonys for the Support of their
Governors.   And particularly what becomes of the
$4\frac{1}{2}$ p cent., paid in the Sugar Colonys for that purpose.   That Duty produces near £20,000 a Year,
but being remitted into the Exchequer, not one of
the West India Governors is paid out of it; but
they, like Falcons, are let loose upon the People,
who are complaisant enough to settle other
Revenues upon them, to the great impoverishing
of these Colonys.   In the mean time, tis certain
the money rais'd by the $4\frac{1}{2}$ p cent. moulders away
between the Minister's Fingers, no body knows
how, like the Quitrents of Virginia.   And tis for
this Reason that the Instructions, forbidding all
Governors to accept of any presents from their
Assemblys, are dispens'd with in the Sugar Islands,
while tis strictly insisted upon every where else,
where the Assemblys were so wise as to keep their
Revenues among themselves.   He said further,
that if the Assembly in New England would stand

Bluff, he did not see how they cou'd be forct to raise Money against their Will, for if they shou'd direct it to be done by Act of Parliament, which they have threaten'd to do, (though it be against the Right of Englishmen to be taxt, but by their Representatives,) yet they wou'd find it no easy matter to put such an Act in Execution.   Then the Colonel read me a Lecture upon Tar, affirming that it cant be made in this warm Clymate, after the manner they make it in Sweden and Muscovy, by barking the Tree 2 Yards from the Ground, whereby the Turpentine descends all into the Stump in a Year's time, which is then split in pieces in order for the Kiln.   But here the Sun fries out the Turpentine in the Branches of the Tree, when the leaves are dry'd, and hinders it from descending. But, on the Contrary, those who burn Tar of Light-wood in the common way, and are careful about it, make as good as that which comes from the East Country, nor will it burn the Cordage more than that dos.   Then we enter'd upon the Subject of Hemp, which the Colonel told me he never cou'd raise here from foreign Seed, but at last sow'd the Seed of Wild Hemp, (which is very common in the upper parts of the Country) and that came up very thick.   That he sent about 500 ℔s. of it to Eng-land, and that the Commissioners of the Navy, after a full tryall of it, reported to the Lords of the Admiralty, that it was equal in goodness to the best that comes from Riga.   I told him if our Hemp were never so good, it would not be worth the making here, even tho' they shou'd continue the Bounty. And my Reason was, because labour is not more than two pence a day in the East Country where they produce Hemp, and here we cant compute it at less than Ten Pence, which being five times as much as their Labour, and considering besides, that our Freight is 3 times as dear as theirs, the Price that will make them rich will ruin us, as I have found by wofull Experience. Besides, if the King, who must have the Refusal, byys our Hemp, the Navy is so long in paying both the price and the Bounty, that we who live from Hand to Mouth cant afford to wait so long for it. And then our good Friends, the Merchants, load it with so many charges, that they run away with great part of the profit themselves. Just like the Bald Eagle, which after the Fishing Hawk has been at great pains to catch a Fish, pounces upon and takes it from him. Our conversation was interrupted by a Summons to Supper, for the Ladys, to shew their power, had by this time brought us tamely to go to Bed with our Bellys full, thou' we both at first declar'd positively against it. So very pliable a thing is frail Man, when Women have the bending of him.

Oct. 1. Our Ladys overslept themselves this Morning, so that we did not break our Fast till Ten. We drank Tea made of the Leaves of Ginseng, which has the Vertues of the Root in a weaker Degree, and is not disagreeable. So Soon as we cou'd force our Inclinations to quit the Ladys, we took a turn on the Terrace walk, and discourst upon quite a New Subject. The Colo. explain'd to me the dif-

ference betwixt the Galleons and the Flota, which
very few People know. The Galleons, it seems,
are the Ships which bring the Treasure and other
Rich Merchandize to Carthagene from Portobel,
to which place it is brought over Land, from Pan-
ama & Peru.   And the Flota is the Squadron that
brings the Treasure, &c., from Mexico and New
Spain, which make up at La Vera Cruz.   Both
these Squadrons rendezvous at the Havanna, from
hence they shoot the Gulph of Florida, in their
return to Old Spain.   That this important Port of
the Havanna is very poorly fortify'd, and worse
garrison'd & provided, for which reason it may be
easily taken.   Besides, both the Galleons and Flota,
being confin'd to Sail thro' the gulph, might be intercepted by our Stationing a Squadron of Men of
War at the most convenient of the Bahama Islands.
And that those Islands are of vast consequence
for that purpose.   He told me also that the assogue
Ships are they that carry QuickSilver to Porto-
bello and La Vera Cruz, to refine the Silver, and
that, in Spanish, assogue signifys Quicksilver.
Then my Friend unriddled to me the great mystery,
why we have endured all the late Insolences of the
Spaniards so tamely.   The Assiento Contract, and
the Liberty of sending a Ship every Year to the
Spanish West Indies, make it very necessary for
the South Sea Company to have Effects of great
Value in that part of the World.   Now these being
always in the Power of the Spaniards, make the
Directors of that Company very fearful of a Breach,
and consequently very generous in their offers to

the Ministry to prevent it. For fear these worthy
Gentlemen shou'd Suffer, the English Squadron,
under Admiral Hofier, lay Idle at the Bastimentos,
till the Ships' Bottoms were eaten out by the
Worm, and the Officers and Men, to the number
of 5000, dyed like Rotten sheep, without being
suffer'd, by the Strictest Orders, to Strike one
Stroke, tho' they might have taken both the Flota
and Galleons, and made themselves Masters of the
Havanna into the Bargain, if they had not been
chain'd up from doing it. All this Moderation,
our peaceable Ministry shew'd even at a time when
the Spaniards were furiously attacquing Gibraltar,
and taking all the English Ships they could, both in
Europe and America, to the great and Everlasting
Reproach of the British Nation. That some of
the Ministry, being tired out with the Clamours of
the Merchants, declared their Opinion for War,
and while they entertain'd those Sentiments they
pitch't upon him, Colo. Spotswood, to be Governor
of Jamaica, that by his Skill and Experience in the
Art Military, they might be the better able to execute their design of taking the Havanna. But the
Courage of these worthy Patriots soon cool'd, and
the Arguments us'd by the South Sea Directors,
perswaded them once again into more pacifick
Measures. When the Scheme was drop't, His Government of Jamaica was drop't at the same time,
and then General Hunter was judg'd fit enough to
rule that Island in time of peace. After this the
Colo. endeavour'd to convince me that he came
fairly by his Place of PostMaster-General, not-

withstanding the Report of some Evil dispos'd persons to the Contrary. The case was this, Mr. Hamilton, of New Jersey, who had formerly had that Post, wrote to Colo. Spotswood, in England, to favour him with his Interest to get it restor'd to him. But the Colo. considering wisely that Charity began at Home, instead of getting the Place for Hamilton, secured it for a better Friend: tho', as he tells the Story, that Gentleman was absolutely refus'd, before he spoke the least good word for himself.

2. This being the day appointed for my departure from hence, I pack't up my Effects in good time; but the lad'ys, whose dear compan'ys we were to have to the Mines, were a little tedious in their Equipment. However, we made a Shift to get into the Coach by ten a'clock; but little Master, who is under no Government, would by all means go on Horseback. Before we set out I gave Mr. Russel the Trouble of distributing a Pistole among the Servants, of which I fancy the Nurse had a pretty good share, being no small Favorite. We drove over a fine Road to the Mines, which lye 13 Measured Miles from the Germanna, each mile being mark't distinctly upon the Trees. The Colo. has a great deal of Land in his Mine tract exceedingly barren, and the growth of Trees upon it is hardly big enough for Coaling. However, the Treasure under Ground makes amends, and renders it worthy to be his Lady's Jointure. We lighted at the Mines, which are a Mile nearer to Germanna than the Furnace. They raise abun-

dance of Oar there, great part of which is very
Rich. We saw his Engineer blow it up after the
following Manner. He drill'd a hole about 18
Inches deep, humouring the Situation of the Mine.
When he had dryed it with a Rag fastened to a
worm, he charged it with a Cartridge containing 4
Ounces of Powder, including the Priming. Then
he ramm'd the Hole up with soft Stone to the very
Mouth; after that he pierced thro' all with an Iron
called a Primer, which is taper and ends in a Sharp
point. Into the hole the Primer makes the Priming
is put, which is fired by a paper moisten'd with a
Solution of SaltPetre. And this burns leizurely
enough, it seems, to give time for the Persons concerned to retreat out of Harm's way. All the
Land hereabouts seems pav'd with Iron Oar; so
that there seems to be enough to feed a Furnace
for many Ages. From hence we proceeded to the
Furnace, which is built of rough Stone, having
been the first of that kind erected in the Country.
It had not blown for Several Moons, the Colo.
having taken off great part of his People to carry
on his Air Furnace at Massaponux. Here the
Wheel that carry'd the Bellows was no more than
20 Feet Diameter; but was an Overshot Wheel
that went with little Water. This was necessary
here, because Water is something Scarce, notwithstanding tis supply'd by 2 Streams, One of which
is conveyed 1900 Feet thro' wooden Pipes, and the
other 60. The Name of the Founder employed at
present is one Godfrey, of the Kingdom of Ireland,
whose Wages are 3∫6 ℔ Tun for all the Iron he

runs, and his provisions.   This Man told me that
the best Wood for Coaling is red Oak.   He Complain'd that the Colo. Starves his Works out of
Whimsicalness and Frugality, endeavouring to do
every thing with his own people, and at the same
time taking them off upon every Vagary that
comes into his Head.   Here the Cole carts discharge their Load at folding Doors, made at the
Bottom, which is sooner done, and Shatters the cole
less.   They carry no more than 110 Bushels.   The
Colo. advised me by all means to have the coal
made on the same side of the River with the Furnace, not only to avoid the Charge of Boating and
Baggs, but likewise to avoid breaking of the coals,
and making them less fit for use.   Having pick't
the Bones of a Surloin of Beef, we took leave of
the Ladys, and rode together about 5 Miles, where
the Roads parted.   The Colo. took that to Massaponux, which is 15 Miles from his Furnace, and
very level, and I that to Fredericksburgh, which
cant be less than 20.   I was a little benighted, and
should not have seen my way, if the Lightening,
which flash't continually in my Face, had not befriended me.   I got about seven a'clock to Colonel
Harry Willis's, a little moisten'd with the Rain;
but a Glass of good Wine kept my Pores open,
and prevented all Rheums and Defluxions for that
time.

    3. I was oblig'd to rise Early here, that I might
not starve my Landlord, whose constitution requires
him to Swallow a BeefSteak before the Sun blesses
the World with its genial Rays.   However, he was

so complaisant as to bear the gnawing of his
Stomach, till 8 a'Clock for my Sake. Colo. Waller,
after a Score of loud Hems to clear his Throat,
broke his fast along with us. When this necessary affair was despatched, Col. Willis walk't
me about his Town of Fredericksburgh. It is
pleasantly situated on the South Shore of Rappahannock River, about a Mile below the Falls.
Sloops may come up and lye close to the Wharf,
within 30 Yards of the Public Warehouses, which
are built in the figure of a Cross. Just by the
Wharf is a Quarry of White Stone that is very
soft in the Ground, and hardens in the Air, appearing to be as fair and fine grain'd as that of Port-
land. Besides that, there are several other Quarrys
in the River Bank, within the Limits of the Town,
sufficient to build a great City. The only Edifice
of Stone yet built is the Prison; the Walls of
which are strong enough to hold Jack Sheppard,
if he had been transported thither. Tho' this be a
commodious and beautiful Situation for a Town,
with the Advantages of a Navigable River, and
wholesome Air, yet the Inhabitants are very few.
Besides Colo. Willis, who is the top man of the
place, there are only one Merchant, a Taylor, a
Smith and an Ordinary keeper; though I must not
forget Mrs. Levistone, who Acts here in the Double
Capacity of a Doctress and Coffee Woman. And
were this a populous City, she is qualify'd to exercise 2 other callings. Tis said the Court-house
and the Church are going to be built here, and
then both Religion and Justice will help to en-

large the Place. 2 Miles from this place is a
Spring strongly impregnated with Alom, and so is
the Earth all about it. This water dos wonders
for those that are afflicted with a Dropsy. And
on the other side the River, in King George
County, 12 Miles from hence, is another Spring of
strong Steel water, as good as that at Tunbridge
Wells. Not far from this last Spring are England's Iron Mines, call'd so from the Chief Manager of them, tho' the Land belongs to Mr.
Washington. These Mines are 2 miles from the
Furnace, and Mr. Washington raises the Oar, and
Carts it thither for 20ƒ the Tun of Iron that it
yields. The Furnace is built on a Run, which discharges its waters into Potomeck. And when the
Iron is cast, they Cart it about 6 Miles to a Landing on that River. Besides Mr. Washington and
Mr. England, there are several other Persons, in
England, concerned in these Works. Matters are
very well managed there, and no Expence is spared
to make them profitable, which is not the case in
the works I have already mention'd. Mr. England
can neither write nor read; but without those
helps, is so well skill'd in Iron works, that he dont
only carry on this Furnace, but has likewise the
Chief Management of the Works at Principia, at
the head of the Bay, where they have also erected
a Forge & make very good Bar Iron. Colo. Willis
had built a Flue to try all sorts of Oar in, which
was contriv'd after the following manner. It was
built of Stone 4 foot Square with an Iron grate
fixed in the Middle of it for the Fire to lye upon.

It was open at the Bottom, to give a free passage
to the Air up to the Grate. Above the Grate was
another Opening that carry'd the Smoke into a
chimney. This makes a Draught upward, and the
fire Rarifying the air below, makes another draught
underneath, which causes the fire to burn very
fiercely, and Melt any Oar in the Crucibles that
are set upon the Fire. This was erected by a
Mason call'd Taylor, who told me he built the
Furnace at Frederickville, and came in for that
purpose at 3ƒ 6 a day, to be paid Him from the
time he left his House in Gloucestershire, to the
time he returned thither again, unless he chose
rather to remain in Virginia after he had done his
Work. It happen'd to be Court day here, but the
Rain hinder'd all but the most quarrelsome People
from coming. The Colo. brought 3 of his Brother
Justices to dine with us, namely, John Taliefero,
Majr Lightfoot, & Captain Green, and in the Evening Parson Kenner edify'd us with his Company,
who left this Parish for a better, without any regard to the poor Souls he had half saved, of the
Flock he abandon'd.

4. The Sun rising very bright, invited me to leave
this Infant City; accordingly, about ten, I took
leave of my Hospitable Landlord, and persuaded
parson Kenner to be my Guide to Massaponux,
lying 5 Miles off, where I had agreed to meet Colo.
Spotswood. We arriv'd there about 12, and found
it a very pleasant and commodious Plantation.
The Colo. receiv'd us with open Arms, and carry'd
us directly to his Air Furnace, which is a very in-

genious and profitable contrivance.   The use of it
is to melt his Sow Iron, in Order to cast it into
sundry Utensils, such as Backs for Chimneys,
Andirons, Fenders, Plates for Hearths, Pots, Mor-
tars, Rollers for Gardeners, Skillets, Boxes for
Cart Wheels; and many other things, which, one
with another, can be afforded at 20ƒ a Tun, and
deliver'd at People's own Homes.   And, being
cast from the Sow Iron, are much better than those
which come from England, which are cast immediately from the Oar for the most part.   Mr
Flowry is the Artist that directed the Building of
this Ingenious Structure, which is contrived after
this Manner.   There is an Opening about a foot
Square for the fresh Air to pass thro' from without.   This leads up to an Iron Grate that holds
about half a Bushel of Sea Coal, and is about 6
fᴖot higher than the opening.   When the Fire is
kindled, it rarifys the Air in such a Manner as
to make a very strong Draught from without.
About too foot above the Grate is a hole that
leads into a kind of Oven, the Floor of which is
laid Shelving towards the Mouth.   In the Middle
of this Oven, on one Side, is another hole that
leads into the Funnel of a Chimney, about 40 foot
high.   The Smoak mounts up this way, drawing
the Flame after it with so much force, that in less
than an hour it melts the Sows of Iron that are
thrust towards the upper end of the Oven.   As the
Mettal melts it runs towards the Mouth into a hollow place, out of which the Potter lades it in Iron
Ladles, in order to pour it into the Several Moulds

just by. The Mouth of the Oven is Stopt close with a
Moveable stone Shutter, which he removes so soon
as he perceives, thro' the peep holes, that the Iron is
melted. The inside of the Oven is lined with soft
Bricks, made of Sturbridge or Windsor Clay, because no other will endure the intense heat of the
Fire. And over the Floor of the Oven they strew
sand taken from the Land, and not from the Water
side. This Sand will melt the 2d Heat here, but
that which they use in England will bear the fire 4
or 5 times. The Potter is also oblig'd to Plaister
over his Ladles with the same Sand moisten'd, to
save them from melting. Here are 2 of these Air
Furnaces in one Room, that so in case one want
repair, the other may work, they being exactly
of the same Structure. The Chimneys and other
outside work of this building are of Free-Stone,
rais'd near a Mile off, on the Colonel's own land.
And were built by his Servant, whose Name is
Kerby, a very compleate Workman. This Man
disdains to do any thing of rough work, even where
neat is not required, lest any one might say hereafter, Kerby did it. The Potter was so complaisant as to shew me the whole Process, for which I
paid him and the other Workmen my respects in
the most agreeable way. There was a great deal
of Ingenuity in the framing of the Moulds, wherein
they cast the Several Utensils, but without breaking them to pieces, I found there was no being let
into that Secret. The Flakes of Iron that fall at
the Mouth of the Oven are call'd Geets, which are
melted over again. The Colo. told me, in my Ear,

that Mr. Robert Cary, in England, was concerned
with him, both in this and his other Iron works,
not only to help support the Charge, but also to
make Friends to the Undertaking at home.   His
Honour has settled his Cousin, Mr. Greame, here
as PostMaster, with a Salary of £60 a Year, to reward him for having ruin'd his Estate while he
was absent.   Just by the Air Furnace stands a
very Substantial Wharf, close to which any Vessel
may ride in Safety.   After satisfying our Eyes
with all these Sights, we Satisfy'd our Stomachs
with a Surloin of Beef, and then the Parson and I
took leave of the Colo., and left our Blessing upon
all his works.   We took our way from thence to
Major Woodford's, 7 Miles off, who lives upon a
high Hill that affords an extended Prospect.   On
which Account tis dignify'd with the Name of
Windsor.   There we found Rachel Cocke, who
stayed with her Sister some time, that she might
not lose the use of her Tongue in this lonely Place.
We were receiv'd graciously, and the Evening was
Spent in talking and toping, and then the Parson
and I were conducted to the same Apartment, the
House being not yet finisht.

5. The Parson slept very peaceably, and gave
me no disturbance, so I rose fresh in the Morning,
and did Credit to the Air by eating a hearty
Breakfast.   Then Major Woodford carry'd me to
the house where he cuts Tobacco.   He Manufactures about 60 Hogsheads yearly, for which he
gets after the Rate of 11 pence a Pound, and pays
himself liberally for his Trouble.   The Tobacco he

cuts is long Green, which, according to its name,
bears a very long leaf, and consequently each
Plant is heavyer than common Sweet-scented or
Townsend Tobacco. The worst of it is the Veins
of the Leaf are very large, so that it loses its
weight a good deal by Stemming. This kind of
Tobacco is much the Fashion in these parts, and
Jonathan Forward (who has great Interest here)
gives a good price for it. This Sort the Major
cuts up, and has a Man that performs it very
handily. The Tobacco is stemm'd clean in the
first place, and then laid straight in a Box, and
press'd down hard by a press that gos with a Nut.
This Box is shov'd forward towards the Knife by
a Screw, receiving its motion from a Treadle, that
the Engineer sets a-going with his Foot. Each
Motion pushes the Box the exact length which the
Tobacco ought to be of, according to the Saffron
or oblong cut, which it seems yields one penny in
a Pound more at London than the Square Cut, tho'
at Bristol they are both of equal price. The Man
strikes down the Knife once at every Motion of
the Screw, so that his hand and foot keep exact
pace with each other. After the Tobacco is cut in
this Manner, tis Sifted first thro' a Sand Riddle,
and then thro' a Dust Riddle, till tis perfectly
clean. Then tis put into a tight Hogshead, and
prest under the Nut, till it weighs about a Thousand Neat. One Man performs all the work after
the Tobacco is stemm'd, so that the Charge bears
no proportion to the Profit. One considerable
Benefit from planting long Green Tobacco is, that

tis much hardyer, and less Subject to fire than other
sweet scented, tho' it smells not altogether so fragrant.   I surpriz'd Mrs. Woodford in her House-
wifery in the meat-house, at which she blush'd as
if it had been a Sin.   We all walkt about a Mile
in the Woods, where I shew'd them several useful
Plants, and explained the Vertues of them.   This
Exercise, and the fine Air we breath'd in, sharpen'd
our appetites so much that we had no mercy on a
Ribb of Beef that came attended with Several other
good things at dinner.   In the afternoon, we
tempted all the Family to go along with us to
Major Ben. Robinson's, who lives on a high Hill,
call'd Moon's Mount, about 5 Miles off.   On the
Road we came to an Eminence, from whence we
had a plain View of the Mountains, which seem'd
to be no more than 30 Miles from us, in a straight
line, tho', to go by the Road, it was near double
that distance.   The Sun had just time to light us
to our Journey's End, and the Major receiv'd us
with his usual good Humour.   He has a very Industrious wife, who has kept him from Sinking by
the Weight of Gaming & Idleness.   But he is now
reform'd from those ruinous Qualities, and by the
help of a Clerk's place, in a Quarrelsome County,
will soon be able to clear his old Scores.   We
drank exceeding good Cyder here, the juice of
the White Apple, which made us talkative till ten
a'clock, and then I was conducted to a Bed-chamber,
where there was neither Chair nor Table; however,
I slept sound, and waked with strong tokens of
Health in the Morning.

6. When I got up about Sunrise, I was surpriz'd to find that a Fog had covered this high Hill; but there is a Marsh on the other side the River that sends its filthy Exhalation up to the Clouds. On the Borders of that Morass lives Mr. Lomax, a Situation fit only for Frogs and Otters. After fortifying myself with Toast and Cyder, and sweetening my Lips with saluteing the Lady, I took Leave, and the 2 Majrs conducted me about 4 Miles on my Way, as far as the Church. After that, Ben Robinson order'd his East Indian to conduct me to Colo. Martin's. In about ten Miles, we reacht Caroline Court-house, where Colo. Armstead and Colo. Will. Beverly, have each of 'em, erected an ordinary, well supply'd with Wine and other Polite Liquors, for the Worshipful Bench. Besides these, there is a Rum Ordinary for Persons of a more Vulgar tast. Such Liberal Supplys of Strong Drink often make Justice nod, and drop the Scales out of her hands. Eight Miles beyond the Ordinary, I arriv'd at Colo. Martin's, who receiv'd me with more Gravity than I expected. But, upon inquiry, his Lady was Sick, which had lengthened his Face and gave him a very mournful Air. I found him in his Night-Cap and Banian, which is his ordinary dress in that retired part of the Country. Poorer Land I never saw than what he lives upon; but the wholesomeness of the Air, and the goodness of the Roads, make some amends. In a clear day the Mountains may be seen from hence, which is, in truth, the only Rarity of the Place. At my first Arrival, the Colo. saluted me

with a Glass of good Canary, and soon after filled
my Belly with good Mutton and Cauliflowers.
Two People were as indifferent Company as a man
and his Wife, without a little Inspiration from the
Bottle; and then we were forced to go as far as
the Kingdom of Ireland, to help out our Conversation. There, it seems, the Colo. had an Elder
Brother, a Physician, who threatens him with an
Estate some time or other; Tho' possibly it might
come to him sooner if the Succession depended on
the death of one of his Patients. By 8 a'Clock at
Night we had no more to say, and I gaped wide as
a Signal for retiring, whereupon I was conducted
to a clean Lodging, where I would have been glad
to exchange one of the Beds for a Chimney.

7. This Morning Mrs. Martin was worse, so that
there was no hopes of seeing how much she was
alter'd. Nor was this all, but the Indisposition of
his Consort made the Colo. intolerably grave and
thoughtful. I prudently eat a Meat Breakfast, to
give me Spirits for a long Journey, and a long
Fast. My Landlord was so good as to send his
Servant along with me, to guide me thro' all the
turnings of a difficult way. In about 4 Miles we
crost Mattaoponi River at Norman's Ford, and then
Slanted down to King William County Road.
We kept along that for about 12 Miles, as far as
the New Brick Church. After that I took a blind
Path, that carry'd me to several of Colo. Jones's
Quarters, which border upon my Own. The Colonel's Overseers were all abroad, which made me
fearful I shou'd find mine as Idle as them. But I

was mistaken, for when I came to Gravel Hall, the first of my Plantations in King William, I found William Snead (that looks after 3 of them) very honestly about his business.   I had the Pleasure to see my People all well, and my Business in good forwardness.   I visited all the 5 Quarters on that Side, which spent so much of my time, that I had no leizure to see any of those on the Other side the River; Tho' I discourst Thomas Tinsley, one of the Overseers, who informed me how matters went. In the Evening Tinsley conducted me to Mrs. Sym's House, where I intended to take up my Quarters.   This Lady, at first Suspecting I was some Lover, put on a Gravity that becomes a Weed; but so soon as she learnt who I was, brighten'd up into an unusual cheerfulness and Serenity.   She was a portly, handsome Dame, of the Family of Esau, and seem'd not to pine too much for the Death of her Husband, who was of the Family of the Saracens.   He left a Son by her, who has all the Strong Features of his Sire, not soften'd in the least by any of hers, so that the most malicious of her Neighbours cant bring his Legitamacy in Question, not even the Parson's Wife, whose unruly Tongue, they say, dont Spare even the Reverend Doctor, her Husband.   This Widow is a Person of a lively & cheerful Conversation, with much less Reserve than most of her Countrywomen.   It becomes her very well, and sets off her other agreeable Qualities to Advantage. We tost off a Bottle of honest Port, which we Relisht with a broil'd Chicken.   At Nine I retir'd

to my Devotions, And then Slept so Sound that
Fancy itself was Stupify'd, else I shou'd have
dreamt of my most obliging Landlady.

8. I moisten'd my Clay with a Quart of Milk and
Tea, which I found altogether as great a help to
discourse as the Juice of the Grape. The courteous Widow invited me to rest myself there that
good day, and go to Church with Her, but I excus'd myself, by telling her she wou'd certainly
spoil my Devotion. Then she civily entreated me
to make her House my Home whenever I visited
my Plantations, which made me bow low, and thank
her very kindly. From thence I crost over to
Shaccoe's, and took Thomas Tinsley for my guide,
finding the Distance about 15 Miles. I found every
Body well at the Falls, blessed be God, tho' the
Bloody Flux raged pretty much in the Neighbourhood. Mr. Booker had receiv'd a Letter the day
before from Mrs. Byrd, giving an Account of great
desolation made in our Neighbourhood, by the
Death of Mr. Lightfoot, Mrs. Soan, Capt. Gerald
and Colo. Henry Harrison. Finding the Flux had
been so fatal, I desired Mr. Booker to make use of
the following Remedy, in case it shou'd come
amongst my People. To let them Blood immediately about 8 Ounces; the next day to give them a
Dose of Indian Physic, and to repeat the Vomit
again the Day following, unless the Symptoms
abated. In the mean time, they shou'd eat nothing
but Chicken Broth, and Poacht Eggs, and drink
nothing but a Quarter of a Pint of Milk boil'd with
a Quart of Water, and Medicated with a little

Mullein Root, or that of the prickly Pear, to restore
the Mucus of the Bowels, and heal the Excoriation.
At the same time, I order'd him to communicate
this Method to all the poor Neighbours, and especially to my Overseers, with Strict Orders to use
it on the first appearance of that Distemper, because in that, and all other Sharp Diseases, Delays
are very dangerous. I also instructed Mr. Booker
in the way I had learnt of Blowing up the Rocks,
which were now Drill'd pretty full of Holes, and
he promised to put it in Execution. After discours-
ing seriously with the Father about my Affairs, I
joked with the Daughter in the evening, and about
8 retired to my Castle, and recollected all the
Follys of the Day, the little I had learnt, and still
less good I had done.

9. My long Absence made me long for the
Domestick Delights of my own Family, for the
Smiles of an Affectionate Wife, and the prattle of
my Innocent Children. As soon as I sally'd out
of my Castle, I understood that Colo. Carter's
Samm was come, by his Master's leave, to shew my
people how to blow up the Rocks in the Canal.
He pretended to great Skill in that matter, but perform'd very little, which however might be the
Effect of Idleness rather than Ignorance. He
came upon one of my Horses, which he ty'd to a
Tree at Shacoe's, where the poor Animal kept a
Fast of a Night and a day. Tho' this Fellow workt
very little at the Rocks, yet my Man, Argalus, stole
his Trade, and perform'd as well as he. For this
good turn, I order'd Mr. Samuel half a Pistole, all

which he laid out with a New England Man for Rum, and made my Weaver and Spinning Woman, who has the happiness to be called his Wife, exceedingly drunk. To punish the Varlet for all these Pranks, I ordered him to be banisht from thence for ever, under the penalty of being whipt home, from Constable to Constable, if he presum'd to come again. I left my Memorandums with Mr. Booker, of every thing I order'd to be done, and mounted my Horse about ten, and in little more reacht Bermuda Hundred, and crost over to Colo. Carter's. He, like an Industrious Person, was gone to oversee his overseers at North Wales, but his Lady was at home, and kept me till Supper time before we went to dinner. As soon as I had done Justice to my Stomach, I made my honours to the good humour'd little Fairy, and made the best of my way home, where I had the great Satisfaction to find all that was dearest to me in good health, nor had any disaster happen'd in the Family since I went away. Some of the neighbours had Worm fevers, with all the Symptoms of the Bloody Flux; but, blessed be God! their Distempers gave way to proper Remedys.

MISCELLANEOUS LETTERS

AND

REPORT OF THE COMMISSIONERS TO LAY OUT THE BOUNDS OF THE NORTHERN NECK

MISCELLANEOUS LETTERS,[1] ETC.

VIRGINIA the 2 of December 1735

SIR

I am sorry your Excellency had so unhappy a Reason
for not honouring us with your Company at our last Genll.
Court. The Seasonings in that moist Climate are probably
more rude and unmercifull to Strangers than they are here,
tho even amongst us, People sometimes meet with an indifferent welcome. I reckon yours are as bad as Zealand
Agues, which almost shake the bones out of joint. Never
the less I make no doubt but the Bark will subdue them, if
it be good, and has not undergone, a gentle Decoction before
it came hither. But then the repeating ounce must be
swallow'd, or the Distemper will as surely return, as speech
to a silent woman.

Your Excellency gives me just pleasure in the hopes of
Kissing your hand here at Westover: the worst of it is
those hopes sicken a little at their being so long deferr'd.
I wish you had changed your air just after your Illness, and
permitted us to nurse you into a perfect recovery. Such a
small Excursion too, might have been some Relief to your
cares, some truce to the Fatigue of making a stubborn
People happy against their Wills. That is a difficult Task,
but Prudence and moderation, a Deaf Ear to violent Councils, & making your officers detest oppression as mortally as
you do yourself, will go a great way towards performing it.

I humbly thank you Sir for your kind disposition to
favour me all you can about my Land. But I hope where

[1] These letters are selected
from a much larger number in
the possession of the Virginia
Historical Society, and are
printed as samples of Byrd's
letters through the courtesy of
Mr. W. G. Stannard, the society's efficient secretary.

there is so much Justice there will be the less need of favour. I purchased my Land for a valuable consideration, of those who had it given them by that Government, for the charge & fatigue they had been at in running the Dividing Line. My Patent was an Authentick Patent, signd by the Governour and Council, without any manner of Fraud, & dated too on the 9th day of December 1728 and the Kings Purchase was not til July 1729. For that reason I wonder who coud misinform your Excellency so grossly, as to tell you it was after the Kings right accrued. Thus I shall never be under any apprehension in an English Government, where Truth & Justice will have a fair Hearing, at least not in the Administration of a Gentleman who is not only a Friend, but a Pattern of these Vertues.

My Intention was to settle a little Colony up that way, which woud not only be a Guard to the Frontiers, but would encourage the takeing up of Lands in those parts. How that good project may be obstructed by any Cavils about my Title I cant tell, but I shall be cautious, til I see what your Court of Equity shall determine, which I wish may decide matters in such a manner as to deserve its Name.

I heartily wish you may bring your good purposes into execution but if I know any thing of that people, I fear you will meet with great difficultys. Confussion is not easily reduced into order, nor will a high hand do it, without you had some Regiment to back it. Your Excellency will pardon my freedom, but turning People out of their possessions, & reducing them to beggary and dispair, is a new way to quiet a Country in the opinion of Sr

Yours etc.

To Govr Johnston.[1]

THE HUMBLE REPRESENTATION OF WILLIAM BYRD ESQ OF VIRGINIA.

On the back of the British Colonies on the Continent of America about 250 Miles from the Ocean, runs a chain of

[1] Of North Carolina.

High Mountains stretching away from the North East to the South, and holding near parellel with the Sea Coaste. Several Rivers which fall Eastward lead in these Mountains, as do some of the Missapippi tending towards the West.

As the French have settlements on these Western Rivers, it will be greatly for their advantage, to be beforehand with the English in gaining possession of the Mountains, and for so doing (besides their encroaching Temper) they will have the following Temptations. First that they may make themselves Masters of all the Mines, with which there is reason to believe these Mountains abound. Amongst the rest, if credit may be given to the Indians, there are several Mines of Silver. And this is the more probable because the Mountains on the back of Virginia and Carolina lye in the same Parellel with the Mines of New Mexico.

In the next place, that they may engross all the Trade with western Indians for Skins and Furrs, which besides being very profitable, will engage those numerous Natives to the French Interests, in order to Side with them against His Majesty's Subjects, as those bordering upon Canada are already engaged to be troublesome to the Adjacent British Colonys.

And lastly that they may build Forts to command the Passes thro the said Mountains, whereby they will be not only in condition to secure their own Traffick and Settlements Westward, but also to invade the British Colonies from thence. Nor are these Views so distant . . . . .nary as some may imagine, because a Scheme for that purpose was some years ago laid before Sieur Croisat, and approved, but not at that time thought ripe for execution, which I hope we shall not Sit Still and expect.

These inducements to the French make it prudent for a British Ministry to be watchfull and prevent their Seizing this important Barrier. In order wherewith it may be proper to employ some fitt Person to reconnoitre these Mountains very diligently, in order to discover what Mines may be found there, as likewise to observe, what nations of

Indians dwell near them, and where lye the most considerable Passes, in order to their being secured by proper
Fortifications. And this will be the more necessary to be
very soon done, not only to be beforehand with the French,
but also to prevent the Negroes takeing Refuge there, as
they do in the mountains of Jamaica, to the great annoyance of the Kings Subjects, and these will be the more
dangerous, because the French will be always ready to
Supply them with Arms, and to make use of them against
us on all occasions. In the mean time it may be necessary
to encourage Foreign Protestants to come over, and Seat
themselves in the Valleys of these Mountains, which are
exceedingly rich, and the air perfectly wholesome. And
the better to tempt them to it, it would be worth while to
pass an Act of Naturalization for all such, and suffer them
to enjoy a certain Portion of Land for each Family free from
Quitrents for ten years, and if these coud be transported
without charge it woud be an effectual Temptation to them,
and no loss to Great Britain by any means.

In the course of these Discoverys enough Ginseng may be
gathered . . . have much better health & meet with fewer
difficul . . . .. zards than their countrymen have done in the
favorite Cou . . . Georgia. They may here exercise their
industry upon every thing Genius leads them to, they may
plant Vinyards, which nature encourages them to, by twisting a Vine round almost every Tree. They may make Silk,
no place being more Kindly for Mulberry Trees. They
may produce as fine Flax as any in the universe, for a
miner Manufacture. They may raise Hemp as good as any
from Riga, for cordage of all kinds. They may also go upon
a Manufacture of Silk-grass, which is stronger much than
Hemp. Nutt Oyl they may also make in what Quantity they
please, of the great Variety of Nuts that the Woods produce. And what may Surprise you most, I can assure you
from Experience many times repeated, that you may make
exceeding good Sugar from a Tree we call a Sugar Tree,

which is very plenty in these parts. This Tree they tap in the spring and a sweet Liquor issues from the wound that may be boild into Sugar, and I question not but a Spirit may be drawn from it equal to Arrack. Many more Improvements may be made in that fine part of the Country, but I shall mention no more but only that of Provisions of every kind, which may be produced with little Labour in the greatest Plenty. It is a fine Place for Cattle and Hoggs, for Sheep and Goats, and particularly there is a large Creature of the Beef Kind, but much larger, called a Buffalo, which may be bred up tame, and is good both for Food and Labour. Then the Ground will produce any Grain you please with a Surprizing Increase, besides Potatoes and Peas of various Kinds, that are very wholesome and nourishing. Then you may have Fruit in great plenty of every Sort, and every thing that grows in a Garden as good as the world affords. Then there is Water as clear as Crystal and as sweet as milk, and pleasant Streams for any Kind of Mills. Besides all these advantages above Ground, there are many promising Shews of Mines . . . Quarrys of Marble upon the Hills. In one word there is nothing . . . deserves the name I have given it of the Land of Eden . . . .. est People of Europe did not Know, what a Blessed Retreat they . . . in this Upper Country, they woud come over to it in great Flocks, as Wild Pigeons fly over it, which some times darken the Sky. If you can give .. edit to the Account (which is by no means Romantick) I hope you will not defer bringing your little Colony over in the Fall to take possession of So fine a Place.

I had much rather have to do with the honest Industrious Switzers, than the mixt People that come from Pennsylvania, especially when they are to be conducted by so prudent a Person as yourself. I shall wait for your answer, (if any thing shoud retard your comeing,) till the Spring, before I will make any Steps towards disposeing of this Land, which I have offerd preferably to you, and if you hold your

Resolution of bringing over your People, whether you think fit to embrace my Offer or not, you may depend upon all the good Offices in the world from your etc.

P. S.

You need not trouble your Self to bring Mill Stones, there being Stone very proper to make them. You must therefore only have men that understand how to work them out of the Stone. At first the People need have no other than Hand mills, which will be made with little trouble. In short bring as few cumbersome Things as you can, because of the Land Carriage, and nothing that your men can make here upon the Spot. Only they must bring Tools, and Arms and Ammunition besides their necessary cloaths.

To Mr Ochs.

VIRGINIA the 10th of Octo^b 1735

If my Dear Cousen Taylor be not a little Indulgent, She will be apt to think me a troublesome Correspondent this year. It's now the fourth time I have broke in upon her meditation, which is pretty fair for one who lives quite out of the Latitude of news, nor can pick up one dash of Scandal to season a letter withall. Tis a mighty misfortune for an Epistolizer not to live near some great city like London or Paris, where people play the fool in a well bred way, & furnish their neighbours with discourse. In such Places storys rowle about like Snow balls, and gather variety of pretty circumstances in their way, till at last they tell very well, & serve as a good entertainment for a country Cousen.

But alas what can we poor Hermits do who know of no Intrigues, but such as are carryd on by the Amorous Turtles, or some such innocent Lovers? Our vices & disorders want all that wit & refinement, which make them palatable to the fine world. We are unskild in the Arts of making our follys agreable, nor can we dress up the D—— so much to advantage, as to make him pass for an Angel of light. Therefore without a little invention, it would not be pos-

sible for one of us anchorites to carry on a tolerable correspondence, but like French Historians, where we dont meet
with pretty incidents, we must e'en make them, and lard a
little truth with a great deal of Fiction.

Perhaps you will think the story I am going to tell you
of this poetical Sort. We have here an Italian Bona Roba,
whose whole study is to make her Person Charming, which
to be sure will sound very Strangely in the Ears of our
English Lady. Those who understand Physognomy suspect
this Dear Creature has been a Venetian Cortezan, because
her whole mein & every motion prove she has been traind
up in the art of pleaseing. She does not only practice
Graces at her glass, but by her skill in opticks, has instructed her Eyes to reflect their Rays in a very mischievous manner. In a word she knows how to make the most
of every part that composes her Lovely Frame, as you will
see by the harmless adventure that follows.

You must know the two little Hillocks in her Bosome
have lost a pretty deal of their natural firmness & elasticity,
this is reacond a disadvantage to a fine Neck, but she has an
invention to brace them up again to a maiden Protuberancy.
She has a Silver Pipe made so exceedingly small at one end,
that 'twill enter the narrow orifice of the nipple. At the
other end of the Tube her Fille de Chambre blows with all
her might, til the Breast swells & struts like any blown
Bladder. This is no sooner performed, but a composition
of Wax Rosin and Spanish brown is nimbly applyd to hinder
the imprisond wind from escaping. Thus she preserves all
the Charms of the Horizontal chest, without the German
artifice of bolstering it up with a dozen of Napkins, that if
any of the monsters with eight legs and no eyelids should
presume to stray that way, she may fairly crack them
upon it.

But as no human Skil is ever so perfect, as to be secure
from misadventure, so you will be sorry for what befel this
Gentlewoman one day at a Ball. It happend that she had
deckt herself with all her artificial ornaments, but the

warmth of the weather, joind with the agility of her motion, occasiond so copious a perspiration that it softend and dissolvd the cement smeared upon her Mammels. By this accident the doors being set open, the wind unluckily rusht forth, as fast as it well coud do, thro' so narrow a channel & produced a sound that was a little unseemly, and that too not in seperate notes, but with a long winded Blast, which a genius to musick might have modulated into a Tune. It is not easy to tell you, whether the Company was more diverted, or the Signora more confounded at this accident : but so much is certain, that we were all Surprized at the unusual length of the noise, and the quarter from whence it Sallyd out. We vertuosos took her immediately for one of those Belly-speakers whose gift it is to make a voice seem to rise out of any part of the Body. The religious part of the company, which consisted chiefly of old women, concluded her to be a Demonaique, in the power of some evil spirit, who chose to play his Gambols in so fair an Habitation. While we were taken up in debating upon this uncommon event, the unfortunate Person slunk away thro' the crowd, & has never appeard out of her Doors since.

[To Mrs. Taylor.[1]]

LONDON the 29th of July 1723.

DEAR MAJ'R.

You must surely be mistaken when you reproach me with haveing receivd no more than one letter from me this year. I have you so frequently in my thoughts, that tis impossible but they must have had vent oftener than you mention. I can assure you Love has no more such violent operation upon me, as to engage all my thoughts ; there is room left for a Friend, especially for one I have so much regard and affection for as Yourself. Our dear Country inclines you

---

[1] This Mrs. Taylor seems to have been the widow of a brother of Byrd's second wife. Although his letters to her are in a free and easy tone, one of hers to him, which is preserved with his letter at Brandon, is a remarkably prudent and finely interesting communication.

all so much to that tender Passion, that you fancy we who
are in a colder clymate are as universally heated with it
as your selves.   For my part I can wash my hands in Innocence, and assure you that my Reason begins at last to get
the better of my Inclination.   I can figure to my self now,
that I see you put on a Sardinian Smile, and tell me, that
I am more indebted to my age for this deliverance, than to
my understanding.   But you are deluded my Dear major,
if you fancy this, and I have the pleasure to tell you very
feelingly, that my fancy was more vigorous formerly, but
not my constitution.   I find by blessed Experience, that
age ought not to be computed by the number of our years,
but by the decay of our Persons, as a Building is not properly old that has stood a great while, unless it be grown
ruinous & out of Repair.   Indeed time will wear out every
thing at last, but some antidiluvian constitutions with the
help of Temperance & Regularity will hold out a long time.
Nobody would have had the confidence to call one of the
Patriarchs old at 500, because at that age he was in truth
hardly the worse for wearing : but was in the bloom of his
beauty, and full vigour of his Strength.   A man was in
those happy days reacond at the years of discretion at a
hundred, and a Woman at about 150.   It was then Felony
by the Law, to have carnal knowledge whether lawfull or
unlawfull with a Miss under Fourscore, which was then the
time of Puberty, when her Breasts began to swell, and her
Fancy to be inflamed.   Then it was that Boys went into
Breeches about 40, Girles continued in hanging sleeves til
50, and plaid with their Babys til Threescore.   Age should
therefore be dated from the Declension of our vigour, &
the impairing of our Facultys, rather than from the time
we have livd in the world.   Otherwise a batterd Debouchée,
(like some of our dear countrymen) that is worn out at 40,
would be as young, as an orderly Heart of oak, who long
after that retains all the strength & gaity of youth, and is
able to render to the Ladys very handsome Justice.   After
the weddings you mention, I shan't be surprizd if I hear

that the Comissary is marryd, whose Heart I suppose is now at rest, and now the facultys of his mind have more leizure, the facultys of his body will want to be employd.   But the match in the world that woud most delight me, woud be that betwixt you and some charming nymph, that might by her fine Qualitys reconcile you to the Sex.

The man of War in which I am to come over is built, and launched, and will be fitted, and sail early in the Spring. But Sir my inclination to see you is so very Strong, that I believe I shall hardly have the patience to tarry so long. I am deliberating whether I shall come over in capt. Randolph's ship, which has so much the ayr of a man of War, that no modest Pyrate will venture to attaque Her.

I suppose your Tobacco debt from me is long since satisfyed, which makes me wonder I receive no Tobacco from those Tenants.   I must intreat the favour of you to let Mr. Banister know, how much is due from them, that they not [sic] run more in arrear than they will ever be able to pay.

Mr. Perry charges to my account several articles of money paid for things which have accrued since the death of Colonel Park.   I herewith send you a copy of them, that you may be convinced they belong not to me to pay, as you will find by reading over the last Paragraph of my articles with you.   By that I am obliged to pay all debts due at Colonel Parkes death, and not any that have accrued since.   I have let Mr. Perry know I will by no means allow them, but he must apply himself to those who by the will are obliged to pay the Debts.   So that I suppose you will hear from him upon that Subject.   For my part I have paid more by £1000 than appeard in the list of debts which was sent me before I contracted with you : but as I had obliged my self thereto I submitted.   But for proveing the will, & other matters that happend Several months after colonel Parks death I must desire to be excusd.   The thing is so evident that I am confident you will at first sight perceive they belong not to me to discharge, and therefore I will trouble you no farther about it; but wish you & my Cousens everything that is happy.   I am most assuredly

Dear Brother
Your most affectionate
humble servant,
W. BYRD.

[To John Custis.]

NOVEMBER the 18th, 1740.

MOST HYPOCONDRIACK SIR,

I had your list of complaints last night which you drew up in the form of a letter, I suppose, to save Blushing.   As to your first grievance of often wanting a Fire, I have this to say, that it was never my Intent that you should want one in cold weather.   And if amongst so many idle Servants, none would make it for you upon the first complaint to me, that Hardship should have been remedy'd, and you might be convinct of this, by my finding fault with your having no Fire on Sunday last, and giveing directions to kindle one immediately, and for fear of future neglects, charged Tom and Joe to take care you had a Fire every night.   I can do no more than this, unless you expected I should make your Fire myself.

Then as to your being often forc't like mad People, to sit in the dark without a candle, I have this to say, that orders have been given from the beginning, to furnish you with one every night, and if these orders have at any time been disobeyed, upon the least complaint from you, that Grievance too would have been redresst.   But I understand the Candles are not big enough for you.   I am sorry we have not wax, or at least mould candles to light you in your Lucubrations.   Had your Dear Friend Mr. Stevens supply'd us with more Tallow, perhaps we might have been better able to light up the white House with bigger candles.   In the mean time, if such as you have, by the Judgment of two good men would burn an hour and a half, that is full long enough to read by Candle light, wch is not good for the

Eyes, and after that Meditation and Devotion might fill up the rest of winter's evening. Then as to the Calamity of your wanting those usefull Implements of Tongs and Poker, that I must own is a very compassionate Case. One might divert ones self most usefully with them, and be no hindrance at all to contemplation. But I can clear myself of this Impeachment too, for I remember I ordered the smyth to make a Pair of Tongs on purpose for You, and if you or your chamberfellow unluckily destroyed them it was by no means the fault of   Yours &c.

   Mr. Procter.[1]

[1] William Procter was Byrd's secretary and librarian. A number of his letters have been preserved. By the side of the above letter to him I am able, through the kindness of Mrs. W. G. Stannard, of Richmond, to place the following from him to relatives in Europe:

" WESTOVER, 1739.

"I serve a very honorable and virtuous Master . . . For the time being I live as happily, if not it is my own fault, as my worthy master himself. He is very communicative in conversation, and lets me enjoy that of Strangers as much as may well be. I am library keeper, and have all genteel conveniences, moreover to save me a risk he gives me a draught upon his London factor, and orders my clothes with his own goods at the English price . . . besides the kindness of the family in having my linen made and mended. . . . For my future advantage . . . Col. Byrd will certainly procure me a parish, with £100 sterling a year, if I can like it, or help me to commence as a husbandman upon land of my own. . . . My good master, indeed, frequently is pleasant with me, and says wh'nt I be at once a parson and a planter."

REPORT OF THE COMMISSIONERS TO LAY OUT THE BOUNDS OF THE NORTHERN NECK [1]

To the Honble William Gooch Esq, His Majestys Lieutenant Governor and Commander in Chief of the Colony and Dominion of Virginia

The Underwritten Commissioners appointed by your Honour in Obedience to the Orders of his Majesty in his Privy Council of the 29th of November 1733 for Surveying and settling the Boundaries of that Tract or Territory of Land granted by the Crown to the Ancestors of the Right Honourable Thomas Lord Fairfax and under whom his Lordship now claims, Do humbly beg Leave to lay before your Honour the following· Report of their Proceedings and the Reasons why they have not been able finally to determine the said Boundaries according to his Majestys royal Intentions.

After we had the Honour to be named Commissioners on the part of His Majesty, the Lord Fairfax by Mr Barradall his Agent signified to your Honour in Council, that if the King's Commissioners were Members of the Council, His Lordship was contented that the same Commissioners shou'd likewise Act in his behalf, without appointing any distinct Commissioners of his Own. This induced us to

[1] This Report is the only considerable part of the " Proceedings of the Commissioners appointed to Lay Out the Bounds of the Northern Neck, lying between the Rivers Potomack and Rappahanock, Anno, 1736," which Byrd wrote. The rest of that article is omitted because it consists chiefly of commissions, depositions, and protests relating to the affair.

wait on his Lordship with our Commission from your Honour, to know whether his Lordship wou'd be pleased to give us powers to Act for him conformable to his Majesty's Order,   But we soon found His Lordship had alter'd his mind and now declar'd that he would not Submit the Determination of his right to any person in this Country, nor give any other Powers than barely to Survey the several Boundaries claim'd by him, and to report the Facts and circumstances examined into, to be laid before his Majesty, and soon after tender'd us his Commission for that purpose ; This being contrary to his Lordships Petition and the King's Order thereupon, We judged it unbecoming us to receive any Powers so different to those from His Majesty : and for that Reason return'd it to Him

His Lordship therefore thought fit to appoint three Commissioners on his own part, namely Charles Carter, William Beverly & William Fairfax Esquires

These Gentlemen we met at Fredericks burg near the Head of Rappahannock River on the 25th of September 1736 And after the Commissions on each Side had been produc'd and read, We observed that his Lordships Commissioners had no Authority given them to determine any thing concerning his Lordship's Bounds.   We made the proper Objections thereto as being inconsistent with his Majesty's Order.   But were answer'd that His Lordship wou'd by no means leave the Decision of the Controversy to any Commissioners whatsoever : When we understood this, we found Ourselves under a Necessity either to return Home without doing any thing, whereby His Majesty's gracious purpose would have been wholly disappointed, or else by the Latitude which our Commission gave us to drive the Nail that wou'd go, and join with them in obtaining a full and faithfull State of the Facts in Order to be laid before His Majesty,   Thus far we yielded to Act in Conjunction with the Lord Fairfaxes Commissioners, altho' they were not required by their Commissions to act in Conjunction with us.

After this, We desired to know of my Lords Commissioners what they demanded in his Lordships Name as the Bounds of his grant? To which they answer'd, that he claimed all the Land contain'd within the South Branch of Rappahannock River, and the main branch of Potowmack as high as the head Springs thereof. This extensive demand we apprehended would include many of the King's Loyal Subjects, who at a great Expence have seated themselves within those Bounds under Grants from His Majesty and his Royal Predecessors.

However, that the matter might be fully and fairly Stated, and his Lordship no longer delayed, It was agreed upon our Proposal, that the whole Territory claimed by his Lordship should be Survey'd, that so, the extent of his claim might the more fully appear. And that in performing this Service, and in executing the other parts of our Commission, his Lordship should bear one moiety of the Expence.

Then in Conjunction with my Lords Commissioners We directed the main Branch of Powtomack River called Cohaungorooton to be Survey'd to the head Spring thereof, and appointed Mr Mayo and Mr Brookes whom we thought Equal to the difficult Service on the part of His Majesty; To these were join'd Mr Winslow and Mr Savage for the Lord Fairfax These being all first sworn, were order'd by their Several Warrants to begin at the Confluence of that River with Sharando, and from thence to run the Courses, and Measure the Distances thereof to its first Spring; and of all this to return an Exact Plat, shewing all the Streams runing into the same on either side, together with a fair Copy of their Field-Notes. We also directed them to take the Latitude, and observe particularly where the said River intersects the 40th Degree

And to enable them to perform this arduous Work, We allotted them a Suffecient Number of Men for their Assistance and Defence, and a Competent Quantity of Provisions for their Subsistence

When these Surveyors were dispatch't, who had the
most difficult Service to preform, We appointed Mr Graeme
to survey and measure the South Branch of Rappahannock,
now call'd the Rappidan from the fork to the Head Spring
And, Mr Wood to survey and Measure the North Branch,
call'd Rappahannock, in like manner, requiring them severally to return us an exact plat describing all the Streams
or Water Courses falling into each River, together with a
fair Copy of their field-Notes : and also to take an Observation of the Latitude at the head Springs of each River.
My Lord Fairfaxes Commissioners appointed Mr Thomas
the elder to proceed with Mr Graeme and Thomas the
Younger with Mr Wood.   We at the same time made out
Powers to the Surveyors of the Several Countys in the
Northern Neck, requiring them to survey and measure the
boundaries of the Several Countys joining on the Rivers
Rappannock & Potowmack & the Bay of Cheasepeak

After these matters were dispatch't, the Commissioners
on both Sides proceeded with the four Surveyors up the
Fork of Rappahannock River & causing each Branch to
be measured, they found the North Branch to be widest
by three Poles and Nine Links ; but indeed the South
Branch may be allow'd to be one Pole broader than our
Measure made it, by reason that a small Stream of that
breadth issued from it at some distance above, and form'd
an Island on the South Shoar

The Depositions of John Talliaferro, Francis Thornton,
and William Russel were taken in the presence of the
Commissioners on both Sides ; And then having directed
the several Surveyors to proceed with all Diligence upon
the Services appointed them.   We parted with the Lord
Fairfaxes Commissioners, it being agreed on both Sides,
that until the Surveyors shou'd have made their returns,
nothing farther cou'd be done in this Affair

In pursuance of the Orders aforemention'd the Several
Surveyors proceeded to survey the several Rivers, And
after encountering many difficultys have returned to us

exact Plats of their Work, with Copys of their Field Notes
whereby to prove the truth of their performances, All
which we immediately directed Mr Mayo to join in one
General Map, and the same being now compleated in a
Masterly Manner, We beg Leave to make our Observations
upon it : And moreover to State all the Evidence we have
been able to procure relating to the Bounds in Dispute

All this, We think ourselves oblig'd to do Seperately,
and not in Conjunction with his Lordships Commissioners
for the following Reasons,

1st Because his Lordships Commissioners are not directed
by their Commission to make their Report in Conjunction
with those of his Majesty And therefore as those Gentlemen are at Liberty to make their Report Seperately there
is great Reason we shou'd be so likewise

2nd Because when we desired them to join with us in
naming a fit person to form the general Map, they refused,
and declared they wou'd have a distinct Map drawn by
their own Surveyors : If then we cou'd not agree in forming the Map which was to be the foundation of the Report,
we cou'd have little hopes to agree in the Report itself.

As the Lord Fairfax's claim of all the Lands lying between the Northern and Southern Branches of Rappahannock River has greatly alarmed the Inhabitants of the
Fork, and may very much Affect their property, We shall
in the first place State all the Facts and Evidence relating
to that Affair

We cannot find any Evidence that the Fork of Rappahannock River had been at all discover'd at the time that
the Lord CoLepepper obtained his Grant, But on the
contrary from the Evidence of John Talliaferro, Francis
Thornton, & William Russell it appears that in the year
1707, there were no Inhabitants on either side the River
so high up as the falls thereof, which is about fourteen
miles below the Fork. William Russell, who is an Old
Man, and was produc't by the Lord Fairfax, says, he discover'd the Fork about thirty five Years ago, as he was

hunting, and Mr Thornton about twenty Seven Years ago, But these circumstances are much posterior to his Lordship's Grant.

From the Surveys return'd to us, We cannot say which of these Branches is the Largest, only by the measure we made the North Branch was found to be widest at the mouth; But from the Face of the Map, it evidently appears, that the North Branch has more & Larger Streams falling into it which must occasion a greater Run of Water, That it lyes in a more direct Course with the main River: And that its head Spring lyes farther from the Fork than any Spring belonging to the South Branch

As the Lord Fairfax has produc'd to us no Evidence to support his pretension to the Southern Branch; We shall humbly offer the proofs in behalf of His Majesty for restraining his Bounds to the North Branch in case it shall be allowed that his Lordship has a right to go beyond the Fork of the River

The North Branch has from the first discovery of it, been called by the name of Rappahannock in all publick Writings; Whereas the South Branch about 20 years ago, by way of distinction, obtained the names of Rapidan; It has been a settled Boundary to the Countys in the Northern Neck, and if the sentiments of the Legislature of this Colony ought to have any upweight it is Evident, the General Assembly were of Opinion, that the North Branch was the true boundary of the Proprietors Grant, For in the year 1720, An Act of Assembly passed for erecting the County of Spotsilvania, which County is particularly bounded on the North by the River Rappahannock, That is by the branch which before was made the boundary of the County of King George, and is the North Branch: And for the encouragement of settling that Frontier, the General Assembly the same Year did address his Late Majesty to exempt the Persons coming to settle there, from the purchasing Rights, and payment, of Quit-Rents for all the Lands which shou'd be taken in that County: Which

Priviledges and advantages His said late Majesty was graciously pleas'd to grant under some Restrictions, And upon
this Encouragement it was, that all that Tract of Land between the River Rappidan, and that call'd Rappahannock
have been seated, cultivated and improved, to the great
Benefit and general Security of the Colony, as well as the
Encouragement of People to seat and Cultivate the Lands
lying contiguous on the North side Rappahannock River
to the encrease of his Lordship's Quit rents

The Lord CoLepepper who was the Original Patentee,
made a Grant to Brent and others dated the tenth day of
January 1686 of a large Tract of Land to be laid off in such
a Manner as not to come within six miles of the Rivers
Rappahannock or Potowmack, accordingly that Distance
was observ'd from the North Branch, which seems to be a
Concession that it was taken by the Patentee himself from
the beginning to be the main Branch of Rappahannock

The first Patent in the Fork of Rappahannock was
granted by Governor Nott in the year 1705 and altho' in
the year 1706 Robert Carter Esqr who was then Agent for
the Proprietors of the Northern Neck, began to contest the
right to the Lands in the Fork of Rappahannock, Yet
some Years afterwards he himself was so far convinc'd,
that the Proprietors could claim no further than the North
Branch, that he took Patents from the Crown for two
Tracts of Land in that very Fork which the Lord Fairfax
wou'd now claim as his,   And in the Several Grants of the
Proprietors Lands made by him which bounded on the
North Branch, he calls it the main Run of Rappahannock
River as will appear by two Grants made to Philip Ludwell Esqr

These last mention'd Grants, we must observe, were
passed in the Proprietors Office, where the Grantor cou'd
have call'd that Branch by what name he pleased, and no
doubt, he took care to call it by the right Name.   The last
instance We shall give, is, that when the aforesaid Robert
Carter Esqr had the Honour to be Commander in Cheif of

this Colony, upon the Death of Governor Drysdale he granted Land in the King's Name in the Little Fork as will appear by the Copy of Willis's Patent

Thus, Sir, having stated the Facts relating to the River Rappahannock, We shall go on to those which relate to the River Potowmack, by the Deposition of Mr Thomas Harrison, it appears, that about fifty Years ago, which is pretty near the time the Lord CoLepper obtained his Grant from King James the Second, there were no settlements made upon that River higher than Hunting Creek : And that at that time he knew nothing of the Falls of the River himself, But he beleives he might have heard of them from the Hunters about that time

The Lands at and near the Falls, were not granted till about the year 1709, nor can we find by any Evidence, that it was so much as known that the River ran thro' the great Ridge of Mountains till several Years after that

By the Map, you may please to observe, that the River Potowmack divides itself into two Branches, just beyond the blue Mountains, there the main River loses its name, and the North Branch, which is much the larger, is call'd by the Indians Cohungorooton, and the other Sharando, as therefore the name of Potowmack ceases at this Confluence, and the Branches into which its Waters are divided have quite other Names, The Fork may not improperly be called the head thereof.

In the Year 1730 a Good Number of foreign Protestants were encouraged by the Government to settle beyond the Mountains, in order to strengthen our Frontiers on that Side ; And they discover'd some distance up each of the aforemention'd branches, But none of these discoverys very far, till the Surveyor sent out by us the last Fall, trac'd the River Cohungorootun quite up to the Head Spring, which the found according to the Meanders thereof to be above two hundred Miles from its confluence with Sharando

It is evident from the Map, that the whole distance of

this River stretches beyond the great Ridge whereas the head Springs of Rappahannock reaches no higher than those Mountains, We therefore humbly conceive it cou'd never be the Intention of the late King James the Second to bound the Territory granted to the Lord CoLepepper by two Streams, one of which runs more than two hundred Miles higher than the other.

This, Sir, is a full and fair State of the Case, and the Observations we have made thereupon, we hope will be thought very just, and as the Grant to the Lord CoLepepper seems to have been made much in the dark, it required to have all the Facts Stated as distinctly as possible ; that those whose Province it may be to decide the dispute, may pronounce such Sentence thereupon as will be most agreeable to Justice and Reason All we shall presume to say farther is, that if it shall be thought just to bound the Lord Fairfax's claim by a Line drawn from the Fork of Rappahannock to the Fork of Potowmack, his Territory will then contain at least one Million four hundred and seventy thousand Acres of Land

If the line be drawn from the head of Hedgman River to the Fork of Potowmack his Lordship will then possess two Millions and thirty three thousand Acres.

And in case his Boundary shall be allow'd to run from the Head of Hedgman River to the head Spring of Cohungorootun, then his Grant will contain three Millions eight hundred seventy two thousand Acres

But if his Lordship be allow'd to extend his Boundary from the head of Conway River to the Head Spring of Cohungorootun, including the great and little Fork of Rappahannock, he will then have at least five Millions two hundred eighty two thousand Acres within his Grant, which is about as much Land as at present pays Quit rents to his Majesty in all the rest of Virginia

But if his Lordship shou'd after all be so fortunate as to have these extensive bounds adjudg'd to him, We humbly beg that your Honour will be pleased to recommend to

His Majesty the Case of all those persons who by Patents from His Majesty and his Royal Predecessors, are Possessed of Lands within those Bounds

Thus, Sir, We have proceeded with all Diligence and Fidelity, as far as we have been able, by reason the Lord Fairfax wou'd not empower his Commissioners to join with us in deciding and settling his Bounds But we shall be always ready to obey such further command as your Honour shall hereafter receive from his Majesty relating to this Affair

All which is most humbly submitted by

     Sir   Your Honours most humble Servants

          W. BYRD

          JOHN ROBINSON

          JOHN GRYMES

WILLIAMSBURGH
   August 10th 1737

APPENDICES
A and B

APPENDIX A

A CATALOGUE OF THE BOOKS IN THE LIBRARY AT WESTOVER BELONGING TO WILLIAM BYRD ESQR.[1]

HISTORY, VOYAGES, TRAVELS, &C.

Case No. 1, Lower Shelf, folio. Mexias Emperors, Mathews History of New England, Burnets History of ye Reformation—2 vols., Bradys Introduction, [do.] History of England, Bakers Chronicle, Bloomes Britannia, Histoire des Juifs par Joseph, Lloydii Dictionarium, Hacket's Life of Arch Bishop Williams, Burchetts Naval History, Bohuns' Geographical Dictionary, Bailii Opera Historica, Br. Browns Travels, Harrington's Oceana, The Dial of Princes.

Second Shelf, folio. Camdens Britannia, Clarendons History of ye Rebellion—3 vols., History of England—3 vols., Dewess Journal, Dugdales Baronage—2 vols., Memoirs of Castleman, Vesserii Annales, Heylius' Cosmography, Sam-

[1] The original of this catalogue was bought by William Mackenzie, Esq., from N. G. Dufief, bookseller, and bequeathed by him as one of five hundred books to the Library Company of Philadelphia. The present copy is itself a copy of a copy which was made for the late T. H. Wynne, and now owned by Mr. R. A. Brock, of Richmond, through whose kindness I am able to make this reprint. On the title-page of the original appear these words: *J. Stretch fecit.* It was probably made in 1777 just before the library was sold. It was the work, evidently, of a man not familiar with the contents of the books, for some of the titles are inexplicably distorted. It has been thought advisable to print these distortions literally. The catalogue was once printed, as the following advertisement in the Virginia Gazette, December 19, 1777, will show:

413

mes Britannia, Stanleys Lives, Theatrun Terra Sancta, Dugdales History of St. Pauls, Chauneys Antiquities of Hertfordshire.

Third Shelf, octavo. Davenant on Trade, [do.] on the Revenues—2 vols., [do.] on Grants, Ludlows Memoirs— 3 vols., State of Poland, Description of the Isle of Orkney, State of Moscovy, English Worthies, Dion Cassius—2 vols., History of the Times, Welwoods Memoirs, Account of Denmark, Vindication of Darien, Neals History of New England—2 vols., History of Venice, Wafers Voyages, Temple's Memoirs, History of Whitehall—2 vols., Rye Conspiracy, Evelyn on Navigation, Temple's Introduction, Miltons History of England, Temple's Miscellanea—3 vols.—2nd wanting, Connors History of Poland—2 vols.—1st wanting.

Fourth Shelf, octavo. Journey to Paris, Dampiers Voyages —3 vols., Haikes [do.], Miscellanea Aulica, Burridgii Historia, Nicholson's Historical Library—3 vols., Philip's Life of Arch Bishop Williams, Drakes Historia Anglo-Scotiae, Description of Formosa, History of the Bucaniers, [do.] of Portugal, Fryers Voyages, Narborough's [do.], LeComptes China, Temple's Letters—2 vols., Dutch East India——, Ray's Travels, Durchetts Memoirs, Ogilby's Roads, Geographia Classica.

Fifth Shelf, folio. Collection of Voyages & Travels—6 vols., Chronologia Funicii, Grimestones History of Spain, Forbosii Instructis Historico Theologica, Purchas Pilgrim-

" *This Day is Published* a Catalogue of the valuable Library, the Property of the Estate of the late Hon. William Byrd, Esq.; consisting of near 4000 volumes, in all Languages and Faculties, contained in twenty three double presses of black Walnut, and also a valuable Assortment of philosophical Instruments, and capital Engravings, the whole in excellent order. Great part of the Books in elegant Bindings, and of the best Editions, and a considerable Number of them very scarce. Catalogues may be seen at Messrs. Dixon & Hunter's in Williamsburg, and at most of the Book Sellers upon the Continent, and also at Westover, where the Library may be viewed, and the Executrix will treat with those who are inclined to purchase the Whole."

age, Rycants Commentaries of Peru, Camm de Rebus Turcici's, Rerum Anglicarum Scriptorei, History of Guiceland, Davila's History of France.

Case No. 2, Lowest Shelf, folio. L Vau Aietzenia von volg der Historien—2 vols., [do.] Historien—7 vols., Antiquitates Christianae, Iconologie par Baudoin, Wilkin's real Characters, Burnetts Theory of the Earth.

Second Shelf, folio. Leicesters Antiquities of Cheshire, Varenius Cosmography, E Van Metere Nederlanie Historien, Observator—2 vols., Imagines Philosophica &c., Theveriots Travels, Strype's Life of Arch-Bishop Cranmer, Sleidans History of the Reformation, Thuani Historia—5 vols., Index Thuania.

Third Shelf, octavo. Cockburns Travels, Critical History of England, Medulla Historia Anglicanae, Messons Voyages —4 vols., Trade in India, Description of Guinea, Woolseys Memoirs, State of Russia, Ditto—3 vols., Eachards History of the Revolution, Walkers Expedition to Canada, History of Virginia, Ward's History of the Reformation, Legreats Voyages, Picture of a favorite, Survey of Trade, State of Virginia, Journey to Jerusalem, Cookes Voyages—2 vols., Hispania Illustrata, Voyage to Abyssina, State of the Cape of Good Hope—2 vols., History of Persia, Travels of the jesuits, Salmon's Chronological Historian.

Fourth Shelf, octavo. Potters Antiquities of Greece— 2 vols., Kennets Lives of the Greek Poets, [do.] Antiquities of Rome, History of England—2 vols.—2nd wanting, Supplement to Clarendon, Woodward's History, Voyage to Cartesius's World, Raii Clavis Philosophica, [do.] Synopsis, British Empire in America—2 vols. Sales's Voyages, Stevens's History of Spain, Hennepins Travels, Trogei's Voyages, Temples Introduction, Accounts of Livonia, [do.] of Poland, Discoveries in South America, Magaillans China, History of Wales, Gage's Survey of the West Indies, Epitome of Josephus, Vertots Revolution of Sweden, New State of England—1703, Life of William the third, Strangers Account of Switzerland, Wallaces Account of the Isles of

Orkney, Account of Macasar, La Hontans Voyages—2 vols.

Fifth Shelf, folio.   History of England—3 vols., Burnetts History of the Reformation—2 vols., Ludol Historia Aethiopica, Nelsons Collection—2 vols., Rushworths [do.]—7 vols.

Second & Third Shelves, quarto.   Acta Eruditorum—Anno 1682 ad 1722—40 vols., [do.] Supplementum, [do.] Index—2 Tom., State of the Protestants, Voyage de Moscovie, Demoivre de Chanai, New York Conspiracy.

Fourth & Fifth Shelves, quarto.—Philosophical Transactions from 1669 to 1719—21 vols., [do.] Vol. 1 to 8 inclusive—8 vols., [do.] 6–7–8 ; 3 vols., [do.] 1669 to 1685 inclusive—8 vols.

Sixth Shelf, octavo.   Schefferii Lapponia, Onuphrii Reipublicae Romanae Commentaria, Scioppii Verisimielia, Loccenii Historia Rerum Suessicarum, Matthii Systema politicum, East India Trade, Lowndes [on] Coins, Account of Sweden, Howells Letters, Lives of the Twelve Caesars, History of Pennsylvania.

Case No. 3, Lowest Shelf, folio.   Father Pauls History of the Council of Trent, Foulis's History of Popish Treasons, Examen Veritatis, Cabala—Part 1st & 2nd, Chardins Travels, Daniel & Trussel, Drayton's Polyolbion, Dr. Fryers Travels, Lord Bacons resuscitations, New Body of Geography, History of the Caribee Islands, [do.] of Edward the Second, [do.] of the civil wars in England, Herbert's Life of Henry the Eighth, History of Scanderoon, [do.] of the wars of Italy, Smiths History of Virginia, Slaytegers History of Great Britain, Life of Appollonius Tyranneus, Ligai's History of Barbadoes—2 copies, Oleareus's Travels, Montames Gesautschapen van Japan, Temple's Netherlands—2 copies, Busquieus's Epistles, Ladies Travels into Spain, Account of [J]ersey, Addisons Remarks, Child on Trade, Rogers Travels, State of Persia, [do.] of Morocco, Modest Critick, Jovii Descriptiones, Bisselii Argonanticon Americanam, Herstelde Leuco, Morum Exemplar, Smiths Angliae Descriptio, Temples Memoirs.

The Uppermost Shelf of this Case. Universal History—20 vols. 8vo.

Fourth Case, Upper Part, Lowest Shelf, octavo. State of Germany, Roman History—4 vols. 1st wanting, Salts Breviarium Chronologicum, Memoirs of Philip de Comines—2 vols. Ditto—one volume, Boyse's Historical Review, Funnels Voyages, Rycants History of Turkey, Lassels Voyage to Italy, Voyage to North America, History of Portugueze Asia—2 vols., Salmons Polygraphia, Goedart de Insectis, Essay on Fire & Salt, Reflections on Learning, Woodwards Essays, Whishtons Account of a remarkable Meteor, Howels Letters, Memoirs of Cardinal Woolsey, Political Arithmetick, Webster on Metals, Voyage to St. Kilda, Cluverii Geographia, [do.] Epitome Historia, Segritidi State de i principi d ell Europa, State of the United Provinces, Stoical Philosophy, Art of Memory, Eachards Compendium of Geography, History of Martha Taylor, State of Italy, Account of New England, Hornii Historica Ecclesiastica, Voyages to the Canary Islands.

Third Shelf &c. octavo. Le Grand Miroir du Monde, Answer rejoined, Academie of Armorie, Remains of Britain, Lancashire Plot, Horrid Conspiracy, Essay on Ways and Means, State Poems, Rolt's History of the late war, History of Bucaniers, Geography [for] Children, Roman History—2 copies, Chamberlaynes present State, Art of Wheedling, Life of Des Cartes.

LAW, TRYALS &c.

Fourth Case, under Part Lowest Shelf, folio. Cokes First 2nd 3rd & 4th Institute, [do.] on Littleton, Bridgman's Conveyancing, Moores Reports, Leonards [do.], Keilways [do.], Littletons [do.], Saunders [do.], Rolles [do.], Palmers [do.], Rushworths Tryal of Steafford, Tryal of Arch-Bishop Laud, Blounts Law Dictionary, Bishops Tryals.

Second Shelf, folio. Ashes Tables—2 vols., Acta Gulielmi 7mo. 8vo. et 9mo., [do.] 9mo. et 10mo., Andersons Reports, Bridgman's [do.], Cokes [do.] Parts 1 to 12—4 vols., Dyers [do.], Crooks [do.]—3 vols., Brookes Abridgment, Sheppard's Epitome, Finch on the Law, Laws of Virginia.

Third Shelf, octavo. Journal of the House of Commons, Atterbury's Rights of an English Convocation, De Privilegiis Pacis, Style's Practical Register, Bates Elenchas Motuum in Anglia, Tyrals per pair, Fenwicks Tryal, Barron & Femme, Reports in Chancery, Modern Conveyances, Stanfords Pleas of the Crown, Plaidoyers de Monsr Patru, Kitchin of Courts, Heraldes de rebus Judicatis, Propugnaculum Catholicum, Instructor Clericalis, Greenwood of Courts, Brown of Fines, Summa Juris Canonici, Cromptons Jurisdiction of Courts, Blounts Tenures, Fitz Herbert's Natura Brevium, Wingates Abridgment, Browns Modus intrandi, Hale's Pleas of the Crown, Clerk of Assize, Faithful Register, Washington's Abridgment, Government of the Plantations.

Case No. 5, Lowest Shelf, folio. Cokes Entries, [do.] Reports, Rolles Abridgment—6 vols., Ditto—one volume, Clavini Lexicon Juridicum, Virginia Laws—1752.

Second Shelf, folio. Loix Civiles, New Statutes—2 vols., Laws of Barbadoes, [do.] of Scotland, Plowdens Commentaries, Suarez de Legibus, Maynards Edward the 2nd, Assizes of Edward the 3rd, Year Book Edward the 3rd, [do.] Edward the 4th, [do.] Henry the 4th & 5th, [do.] Henry the 6th—2 vols., [do.] Edward 5th Richard 3rd & Henry 7th & 8th, Bastells Entries.

Third Shelf, quarto. Fitzherberts Abridgment, Corpus Juris Civilis—2 vols., Haranques, Lex Parliamentaria, Scobell's [Remembrancer ?], La Droite Romaine, Praxis utries Banci, Puffendorf de Officio Hominis, Duck de Authoritate Romanorum, Kilburns Precidents, Bassetts Catalogue, Finch's Law, Neville on Government, Fortescaris [?] Laws of England, Wingates Briton, Cokes Copyhold, Doctor and Student, Office of Executions, Cowels Institutes, Mereton on Wills, Gray's Reports, Perkins Laws of England, Magna Charta, Jenkins Works, Glanville de Legibus Angliae, Phillips Directions, March's actions of Slanders,

Mirror of Justice, Brook's Reading, Dalthasii Decaelogia, Accursii Institutiones, Swinburn on Wills, Decretales Gregorii, Corpus Juris Canonica, Bracton de Legibus, Godolphins Abridgment, Orphans Legacy, Seldeni Fleta, Vinii Commentarii, Hughes' Abridgment—3 vols.

Fourth Shelf, octavo & duodecimo. Compleat Sollicitor, Compleat Attorney Sollicitor, Terms of the Law, Case of Ireland, Answer to Molyneux, Areana Clericalia, Natura Brevium, Clerk of Assize, Regula Placetandi, Lex Londinensis, Debates of Abdication, Guide to Surveyors, Navales Media Historia.

Fifth Shelf, folio. State Tryals—6 vols., State Tryals, Layers Tryals of the Whole Plot of 1722, Jones's Reports, Dugdale Orignes, Dyers Reports, Lambard de Legibus priscis Anglorum, Registrum Breviarum, Townsends Collection, Pophams Reports, Officiana Brevium, Siderfin's Reports, Spencerus de Legibus, Seldens Janus.

Case No. 6, Lowest Shelf, folio. Coke upon Littleton, Pultons Collection, Virginia Laws Manuscript, Cabala of State, Puffendorf's Law of Nature, Waterhouse's Fortescue, Tryals since 1682, [do.] 1696, Collection of Tryals &c, Ditto, Ditto, Meal Tub Plot, Narrative &c, Dawsons Origo Legum, Earl Danby's Case, Informations &c, Oates Tryal &c, Dr. Sacherverells Tryal, Plea in quo Warranto, Selden on Government, Blounts Law Dictionary, Hobarts Reports.

Second Shelf, folio. Noye's Reports, Winch's [do.], Hulton's [do.], Yelverton's [do.], Hobarts [do.], Cokes [do.] —13 parts in 6 vols., Table to Ditto, Benloes [do.], Laws of Jamaica, Continuation of Ditto, Cases in Parliament, Grotius on War and Peace, Scobell's Statutes.

Third Shelf, quarto & octavo. Puffendorf de Jure Naturae, Brownlow & Goldsborough's Reports, West's Symboleographie, Molloy de Jure Maritimo—2 copies, Virginia Laws Abridged—2 vols., Gentlemans Law, Cokes detection—3 vols., Table to the Statutes, Hale's Common Law, Bacon's Elements, Constitution of England, Anglia Liberia, Paterson on Funds, Hale on Parliament, Fenwicks Attainder for

High Treason, Ashby and White, Vinii Jus Civile, Pacci Analysis Institutonum imperatorum, [do.] Isagogica, Grotius de Bello ac Pace, Cassidori Opera.

Fourth & Fifth Shelves, octavo &c. Wingates Abridgment, Viris de officio Mariti, Speculum Politicum, Volcmarus de Pene Principum, Perkins's Art of Witchcraft, Tribunal Reformation, Seldeni Mare Clausum, Hobbes de Cive, Perezi institutiones imperiales, Debates of the House of Commons, Political Anatomy, Beverley's Abridgment, Cokes detection —2 vols., Arts of Empire, English Liberty—2 copies, Compleat Sollicitor, Office of a Sheriff, Law Maxims, Study of the Law, Institutiones juris Romani ac Gallici, Instructor Clericalis, De Comitiis imperatoris, Lawyers Recreation, Heaths Speech, Book of Rates, Shephards Corporations, Scobell on Parliaments, Dyers Abridgment, Tractatus Aureus, Littletons Tenures, Zouchaei Elementa Jurisprudentiae, Jus Sigilli, Justiniani Institutiones, Prerogative of English Parliaments, Terms of the Law, Clerks Tutor, Davenports Abridgment.

PHYSICK &c.

Seventh Case, Lowest Shelf, folio. Bibliotheca Anatomica —2 vols., Mayemii Opera Medica, Reverii [do.], Francisci Baconi Opera, Chornels Family Dictionary—2 vols., Andrea Matthioli Opera, Dodonaei Stirpium Historia, Hofman in Galen, Dr. Willis's Physical Works, Wisemans Chirurgical Treatises, Riverius's Practice of Physick, Sennert Opera —3 vols.

Second Shelf, folio & quarto. James's Medicinal Dictionary—1st vol., Vessalius de Humano Corpore, Hippocrates Foesii—3 vols., Collinin's Anatomy—2 vols., Glaubers Works, Femelli Medecina, Van Helmenti Opera, Brown on the Muscles, Culpepper's Dispensatory, Dictionan de Drogeus, Boerhaves Chymistry, Hermanus Paradisus Batavius, Rankins Theatrum Britanicum, Kemperii Amonitates Exotico, Pomets History of Drugs, Fabricius ab Aqua peridente.

Third Shelf, quarto & octavo. Weidenfield de Secretis Adeptorum, Linden de Scriptis Medicis, Februe's Chemistry, Tancredi de Fame et Siti, Hadriani Opera Medica, Tractatus de Organis, Willis de Cerebri Anatomia, Friends Emmenologia, Mead on the Plague, Dionis's Anatomy—2 copies, Bate's Dispensatory, Sanctorini Apharismi, Quinneys Lexicon, Theory of Physick, Friend's History of Physick, Treatise on the Plague—2 vols., Cheyne on Health, Cockburn's Gonorhea, Aureliani de Morbus Acutis, Hippocrates Aphorismi, Tryons Way to Health, Gibsons Anatomy —2 copies.

Fourth Shelf, octavo. Turner on diseases of the Skin, Friends Hippocrates, Scuterii Chirurgia, Treatise on Non Naturals, Regueri de Graef Opera, Radcliffe's Dispensatory, Andry on Worms, Van Helmonti Artres Medecina—2 vols, Regii Medicina, Dr. Sydenhams Works, Blair's Botannic Essays, Virtues of Water, Drake's Anatomy—2 vols., Shaws Practice of Physick, Lotichii Medecina, Practice of Surgery, Tanvry on Medicines, Zwelferi Pharmacopia, Hortus Academicus, Willis's Practice of Physick, Bartholini Anatomica.

Fifth Shelf, octavo. Pitcairns Works, Mead on Poisons, Lemery's Chemistry, Slares Experiments, Purcell on Vapours, Poor Planters Physician interleaved, Eustachii Opuscula Anatomica, Diseases of the Head Brain & Nerves, Willis's Physick, Salmon's Dispensatory, [do.] English Physician, Fourneau de Glauber, Oeuvres de Glauber, Culpepers English Physician, Physical Dictionary, Course of Chemistry, Curiosities in Art and Nature, Sydenham's Opera, Colbatches Treatises, Tennent's Epistle to Mead, Somnius de Febribus, Boyles Physical Experiments, Recherches des Cancers, Castelli Lexicon, Collutius de Calculo, Boerhaivii Institutiones, Arcana Microcosmi, Sea Diseases, Hortus Regius, Ray's Synopsis Medicinae, [do.] Catalogue of Plants, Art of Glass.

Sixth Shelf, octavo & duodecimo. Culpeper's Dispensatory, Theory of Fevers, Tolets Treatise of Lithotomy, Corncelsi Medecina, Cockburns Profluvia Ventris, Ray's Methodus

Plantarum, Hospital Surgeon, Lower de Corde, La Chymie
des Dames, Pinax rerum Naturalium, Keils Anatomy, Pharmacopia Extemporeanei, Conclave of Physicians, Parkers
Astrology, Harvey on the Pox, Medicamentorium Thesaurus, Pechey's Herbal, Farriers approved Guide, Shiptons
Pharmacopaeia, Cure by Expectoration, Hippocrates Coaca
prosagia, Family Physician, Officina Chyneia, Sanctora
Commentarii, London Distiller, Digsby's Cure of Wounds by
Sympathy, Starkey's Protechney, New Theory of Fevers,
Aphorismi Urbigerani, Hygiasticon, Riveti Antidorum con-
tra Pestem, Rhyne Meditationes in Hippocratem, Bayle's
Problemata—3 vols., Beverovicius de Calculo—2 vols., Fir-
cinus de Vita, Tracastorius, Hippocratis Aphorismi.

ENTERTAINMENT, POETRY, TRANSLATIONS &C.

Eighth Case, Lowest Shelf, folio.   Morrison's Historia Plan-
tarum, Willughbaei Historia Piscium, Raii Historia Planta-
rum, Plott's History of Staffordshire, Pettus on Metals,
Pisonis Historia India, Willoughby on Birds, Gerrard's
Herbal—2 copies, Bion's Mathematical Instruments, Top-
sel's History of Beasts, Ferrarii Hesperides, Hook's Works,
Blackmore's King Arthur, [do.] Prince Arthur, Cowley's
Works, Gadbury's Doctrine of Nativities.

Second Shelf, folio.   Ovids Metamorphoses, Langley's
Pomona, Beaumont & Fletcher's Works, Shakespeares
Works, Ben Jonsons Works, Drydens Virgil, [do.] Works—
3 vols., Chaucers Works, Spencer's Works, Brown's Works,
Compleat Gardiner, Bacon's Natural History, Cowleys
Works.

Third Shelf, octavo. Shaftesbury's Characteristicks—3 vols.,
Landsdown's Plays, Duke of Buckingham's Works—2 vols.,
Collier's View of the Stage, Answers to Ditto, Colliers de-
fence, Drake against Collier, Bentley v. Boyle, Miltons Life,
Terences Comedies, Life of Homer, Bruyeres Characters,
Colliers Essays, King's Works—2 vols., Erasmus's Collo-
quies, Boyle's Answer to Bentley, Etherege's Plays, Lucre-
tius, Life of Alexander, Ovid's Epistles, Marquis of Halifax's

Miscellanies, Cottons Poems, Tate's Poems, Locke on Education, Echard's Works, Satires of Petronius Arbites, Phalares Epistles, Hudibras, Tullys Oratory.

Fourth Shelf, octavo & duodecimo. Oldham's Works, Osbornes Works, Montaignes Essays—3 vols., Diogenes's Lives —2 vols., Dryden's Poems, Horaces Odes, Ogilby's Virgil, Pooles Parnassus, Rymer's Tragedies, Wallers Poems, Cleveland's Works, Bacon's Essays, Quevedo's Visions, Spencers Works—6 vols., Trappe's Virgil—3 vols., Demosthenes Orations, Rabelais's Works—5 vols. bound in 4.

Fifth Shelf, duodecimo. Otway's Plays—2 vols., Tacitus— 3 vols., Atlantis—2 vols., Gilden's Art of Poetry, Lover and Reader, Guardian—2 vols., Freeholder, Englishman, Spectator—9 vols., Tragedies—2 vols., Comedies—5 vols.—3rd wanting, Tragedies and Comedies one volume, Dryden's Poems—6 vols., Blackmore on the Creation, [do.] on Job, Eachard's Terence.

Sixth Shelf, octavo & duodecimo. Titchins Poems, Garth's Dispensary, Poetical Miscellanies, Ovid Travesty, Secret History of White Hall—2 vols., Denham's Poems, Hudibras, Virgil Travesty—2 vols., Unheard of Curiosities, Poetical Exercises, Clarke on Education, Tully on old age and Friendship, Ray's Proverbs, Landsdowns Poems, Cases of Impotence—5 vols., Caesar's Commentaries Abridged, English Horace, Polite Gentleman, Wilkin's Swift Messenger, Treatise on Education, Heydens Harmony of the World, Courtiers Calling, Addison's Notes on Milton, Discourse on Reason, Guardian's Instructor, Disorders of Bassett, Description of Meteors, Phytologia Britanica, Philip's Apology —4 vols., Tom Jones—4 vols., Devil on two Sticks—2 vols.

Case No. 9, Lowest Shelf, folio. Ben Jonson's Works, Le Grand's Philosophy, Harris's Lexicon technicum—2 vols., Gregory's Euclid, Dryden's Juvenal and Persius, Sir William Davenant's Works, Parkinsons Herbal, Clusii Exotica, Leigh's Account of Cheshire, Plotts History of Oxfordshire & Staffordshire, Miscellaneous Tracts, Systema Agriculturae, Pitfield's Natural History of Animals, Theatrum Insectorum,

Bacon's Advancement, Lord Brooke's Works, Virtuosi of France.

Second Shelf, quarto. Frazier's Voyage to the South Sea, Newton's Chronology, De Sacrificiis, Mechanical Experiments, Campanella de sensu Rerum, Philosophie Naturelle, Circulus Pisanus Berigardi, Borniti de rerum Sufficientae, Boyle's Essays, [do.] Natural Philosophy, [do.] of Colds— 2 copies, [do.] of the Air, [do.] New Experiments, Sprats History of the Royal Society—2 copies, Le Grand's Historia Naturae, [do.] Institutio Philosophicae, Thomasus in Stoican Philosophiam, Gentleman's Journal—2 vols., Mechanism of Chimney fires, Kircher Iter extratiume [?], Des Cartes Philosophical Principles, Lister de Cochleis.

Third Shelf, octavo. Oldham's Works, Gay's Fables, True Briton—2 vols., Buckinghams Works, De Foe's Works, Miscellaneous Poems, Sedley's Works, Suckling's Works, Tale of a Tub, St. Evrements Works—2 vols. 1st wanting, Congreves Works—3 vols., Blackmore's Essays—2 vols., Lucian's Works—4 vols., Priors Poems, Flatmans Works, Court Intrigues, Dryden's Miscellanies—3 vols., Plutarch's Morals —5 vols. 1st wanting, Dacier's Plato—2 vols.

Fourth Shelf, quarto. Tournefort Historia Plantarum—3 vols., Comedies—2 vols., Plays—2 vols., Tragedies and Operas—one volume, Lee Plays, Art of the Stage, Vanburg's Plays, Otway's Works, Pastor Fido, Cibber's Plays, Pritti Questiones Physico Mathematica, Dryden's Poems, L'Atre del Secretaire, Original Poems, Bacon's Letters, Dryden's Plays—3 vols.

Fifth Shelf, duodecimo. Examiner—3 vols., Hudibras—2 vols. Character of a Trimmer, Wallers Poems, Randolph's Poems, Milton's Paradise Lost, Medleys, Tatler—4 vols. 2 copies, Butlers Works, Hudibras, Sprats observations on Sorbiere's Voyage, Cumming's Stenography.

Sixth Shelf, duodecimo. Swifts Miscellanies—4 vols., Dryden's Plays—6 vols., Pope's Dunciad, [do.] Works—vols. 5th & 6th, Harriott Steuart—2 vols., Bysshe's Art of Poetry —2 vols., Unfortunate Young Nobleman—3 vols., Newtons

Ladies Philosophy—2 vols., Telemachus—2 vols.—1st wanting, Letters from a Persian, Gray's Memoria Technica,
Rochesters Poems, Homer's Iliad & Odyssey, Amusements
of the Spaw—2 vols., Gil Blas—4 vols., Roderick Random
—2 vols., Pilkington's Memoirs—2 vols.

Seventh Shelf, octavo & duodecimo. Boyles Works—4 vols.,
[do.] Final Cause—2 vols., [do.] Free Enquiry, [do.] on
Specific Medicines, [do.] on Qualities, [do.] on Nature,
[do.] Sceptical Chymist, [do.] Occasional Reflections, [do.]
on Colours, [do.] on Local Motion, [do.] Tracts—4 vols.,
[do.] Seraphick Love, [do.] Martyrdom of Theodora &
Dydimus, [do.] Reasonableness of Religion, [do.] Holy
Scriptures, [do.] Christian Virtues, [do.] on Gems, [do.]
Hydrostatick Paradoxes, [do.] Experiments & Observations
in Physick—2 copies, [do.] Theology, History of Justin,
Tully's Morals, [do.] Offices, Turkish Spy—7 vols.—1st &
6th wanting, Proposals to the Ladies—Part 1st & 2nd,
Wotton's Lives.

Tenth Case, Upper part, Lowest Shelf, octavo. Jarvis's Don
Quixote—2 vols., Lawrence on Gardening, Miller's Gardener's Calendar, Manner of raising Fruit Trees, Bradley
on Husbandry & Gardening—3 vols., [do.] of Planting &
Gardening—3 vols. bound in 2, [do.] of Cattle, [do.] Country Housewife, Lady's Director, Paradise retrieved, Husbandry & Gardening, Solitary Gardener, Switzer on Gardening—3 vols—2nd wanting, Rapin on Gardening, Treatise
on Husbandry, Quintinye's Compleat Gardiner, Treatise on
Husbandry, Dictionarium Rusticum, Mortimer's Art of
Husbandry—2 copies, Dutch Gardiner, Clergyman's Recreations, Ellis's Practical Farmer, Platt's Subterranean Treasure, Curiosities in Gardening, World of Cyder, English
Gardiner, Hughe's Flower Garden & Vineyard, French
Gardner, Painting of the Ancients, Elsums Art of Painting,
History of Painting, Dodonas Grove, Carribbeana—2 vols.
—4to.

Second Shelf, octavo. Principles of Painting, Dryden's Art
of Painting, De Piles's [do.], Fresnoy's [do.], Dictionarium

Polyorgicon, Compleat Distiller, Mandey's Mechanical Powers, Digby's Tracts, Miscellanea Curiosa, Reflections on Learning, Wootten on [do.], Moxon's Mechanical Exercises, Derhams Physico Theology, Hawksby's Experiments, Cibber's Apology, Swift's Miscellanies, Athenian Oracles—3 vols., State Poems—3 vols., Letters of Wit & Politeness, Digby's Works, Compleat Horseman, Watts Logick, Whiston's Euclid, Kennets Antiquities.

Third Shelf, octavo. Buckinghams Works—2 vols., Ward's Young Mathematician's Guide, Terences Comedies, Temples Letters—3 vols., [do.] Miscellanies—2 vols., Boccaces Novels, Colliers Antiquities, Spencers Works, Turberville of Falconry, Lister de Animalibus Angliae, Telluris Theoria Sacra, Godfrey of Bulloigne, Remarks on Des Cartes, Mandey's Mechanical Powers, Albertus Magnus de Herbis, Leonardus on Stones, Stonehouse's Arithmetic, Richard's Palladio, Perigrene Pickle—4 vols.—1st wanting, Ray's Physical Discourses, Herbert against Burnett, Cruchs Lucretius, Plautus's Comedies, Petronius English, Miscellaneous Poems, Stanhop's Epictetus.

DIVINITY &c.

Case No. 10, Lower Part, Lowest Shelf, folio. Manhaim Chronicus Canon Aegyptiacus &c, Le Blanes Theses, Biblia Italiana Diodoti, Clericus in Libus historicus veteris testamenti, Chillingsworth's Works, Cambridge Concordance, Grew's Cosmologia Sacra, Bishop Hall's Works, Book of Homilies, Bishop Sanderson's Sermons, Roger's Treaties, Dr. Babington's Works, Ainsworth's Annotations.

Second Shelf, quarto & octavo. Hebrew Bible, Biblia Hebraica—2 vols., Stillingfleets Origines Sacra, Parker's Law of Nature, Gregory's Works, Whiston's Chronology, Summa Conciliorum per Caranza, Episcopacy of Divine Right, Burges's Answer rejoined, Hale's Contemplations, Mores Sermons, Papists represented & misrepresented, Condition of the Promises, Prestons Remains, Practical Christian, Nichols's Practical Discourses, Ideas of Beauty &c., Scattergood's Sermons, Wilkins's Sermons, [do.] Gift of Prayer, Sprat's Sermons, Testamentum Graecum, Sandys Psalms, Barrow's Sermon on Christ's Passion, Geminiamus de Exemplis.

Third Shelf, octavo. Antoninus's Meditations, Thomas a Kempis's Christ-Pattern, Knatchbulls Annotations, Ditton on the Resurection, Fleetwoods Sermons, Hoadley's Sermons, Bulls Life, [do.] Sermons—3 vols., Bently against Atheism, Burnet de Fide & Officiis, [do.] de Statu Mortuorum, Blackall's Sermons, Bates's Harmony, Beza's Testament Greek & Latin, English Bible & Testament, Biblia Hebraica et Testamentum Graecum, Clarkes Sermons at Boyle's Lectures, [do.] on the Trinity, Claggetts Sermons, Christian Hero, Charnock on Providence, New Testament Greek & English, Sprats Sermons, Italian Common Prayer, Latin Bible & Testament, Biblia Graeca, Treatise on Delighting in God, Man of Sorrow, Death & Life, Almost Christian Discovered, Knowledge of God.

Case No. 12, Lowest Shelf, folio. Huteri Biblia Hebraica, Hammond on the New Testament, Search after Truth, Charnocks Works, La Sainte Bible, Biblia Hebraica, Medes Works, Moir Opera Omnia—3 vols., Novum Testamentum Millii, Grotius in Vetu Testamentum, [do.] Evangelios, [do.] Epistolas.

Second Shelf, folio. Prideaux on the Old & New Testament—2 vols., Taylor's Life of Christ, Willett on Genesis and Exodus, Whitby on the New Testament—2 vols., Josephus's Works, Ursinus on the Christian Religion, Ricaud's Lives of the Popes, Stackhouse's History of the Bible—2 vols.

Third Shelf, octavo. Tillottson's Sermons—16 vols. different editions, Snake in the Grass, Tyrrel's Law of Nature, Taylor's Holy Living & Dying, Bishop of Worcester on the Trinity, Wake's Authority of Christian Princes, Wilkin's Natural Religion, Wilkin's Sermons, Scott's Christian Life —4 vols., Dr. More on divers Texts of Scriptures, Goodmans Conference, Hammond's Catechism, Burnet against Bentley.

Fourth Shelf, octavo.   Duty of Man's Works—4 vols., Atterbury's Sermons, [do.] Funeral Ditto, Gastrell's Christian
Revelation, Norris's Miscellanies, Parson's Christian Direc-
tory, Judgement against Unitarians, Kidder on the Pentateuch—2 vols., Locke's Letter and Worcester's Answer—2
copies, Locke against Worcester, South's Sermons—6 vols.,
Sherlock on Providence, [do.] Judgement, [do.] Death,
[do.] a future State, [do.] Sermons.

Fifth Shelf, octavo & duodecimo.   Hebrew Bible, Norris on
Love, Norris's discourses—third volume, Patrick on Gro-
tius, Blount on Reason, Essay on the Soul, Piscatoris Anal-
ysis, Bishop of London three Pastoral Letters, Lucas's
Practical Christianity, Liturgia Ecclesiae Anglicanae, Tate
& Brady's Psalms, Patricks ditto, Psalmist's Companion,
Devout Christian, Blessedness of the Righteous, Testa-
mentum Graecum, Hieronymous's Tears, Psalmi G Majoris,
Erasmi Testamentum, Greek Liturgy, Herbert's Temple,
Dutch Bible, Bertram's Sacrament, Bartwicks Flagellum
Pontificis, Grotius de Veritate Religionis Christianae, Con-
fession of Faith, Christian Divinity, Confessio Belgicarum,
Thomas a Kempis de imitatione christi—2 copies, Vade
Mecum, Psalterium, Buchannan Poemata, Sylvani de Gu-
bernatione Dei, Bellarmini de Septem Verbis, Eikon Ba-
silikee, Hebrew Bible—7 vols. on the 2nd Shelf, Hervey's
Meditations—2 vols.

FRENCH BOOKS CHIEFLY OF ENTERTAINMENT.

Case No. 12, *Lowest Shelf, duodecimo.*   Virgile de Scarron—
2 Tom., Contese de La fontaine, L'art de plaire, Avanture
de Gil Blas—2 Tom., Amour des Dames, [do.] d'Anne
D'Autriche, Berger fidele, Oeuvres de St. Real, Procez aux
Enfers, Reflections Morales, [do.] de ce qui peut plaire—2
Tom., La religieuse en Chemise, La Science de Medaille, Le
Theatre de la Grange, La France Galante, L'Introduction a
l'histoire de L'Europe—2 Tom., L'histoire de la Duchesse
de Portsmouth, Honnete Homme, Histoire Poetique, Instructions Politiques, Jesuite en bonne humeur, Le Jesuite

defroque, L'Esprit de Luxembourg, L'Apocalypse de Meli-
ton, Tombeau de la Pauvreté, Lettres Provinciales, Le
Moine Seculairise, Gil Blas—4 Tom.—1st wanting, Gom-
Gam ou l'homme prodigieux, Fables de Phaedre, Delices
d'Holland, Nouveau Testament, Entretiens familiares.

Second Shelf, duodecimo. La Sainte Bible, Description de
Versailles, Decouverte de L'Amerique, Don Quichote—5
Tom., Entretiens sur la Metaphysique—2 Tom., Ciceron—
12 Tom., Elat de L'Europe—4 Tom., Histoire de Gil Blas—
3me Tom., Avanture de Telamaque, L'Aminte de Tasse,
De l'Incredulite.

Third Shelf, duodecimo. Histoire de France—8 Tom., [do.]
de Thucydide—3 Tom., [do.] de Commerce, [do.] de deux
Triumvirs—4 Tom. relies en deux, [do.] des Ordres Mili-
taire—4 Tom., [do.] de la Reine Christine, [do.] de Timur
Bec—4 Tom., Histoire de Malthe—5 Tom., [do.] du Grand
Genghizcan.

Fourth Shelf, duodecimo. L'Iliade d'Homer—3 Tom.,
L'Odysse d'Homer—3 Tom., Le Maitre Italien, Antiquité de
France—2 Tom., Conquete de Mexique—2 Tom.,[do.] de la
Chine, Comedies de Terrence—3 Tom., Guerre des Romaines,
Histoire de Gusman—4 Tom., La Geographie Francaise,
Lettres de Pline—3 Tom., L'Invasion d'Espagne, Lucien par
D'Ablancourt, Memoires du Cardinal de Retz—4 Tom.,
Manlius Tragedie par Mr de la Fosse, Religion Chretienne.

Fifth Shelf, duodecimo. Boyer's French Grammar, Description de Paris—2 Tom., Voyage de Monsr de Gennes,
Oeuvres de S D***—2 Tom., Oeuvres de Moliere—4 Tom.,
[do.] d'Hardie—10 Tom., [do.] de Tacite, D'enfants d'au-
truy—2 Copies, La Maniere de bien penser.

Sixth Shelf, duodecimo. Plaute de Limieres—10 Tom.,
Virgile de Mallemans—3 Tom., Vie de Fenelon, Poems de
Corneille—5 Tom., Rhetorique d'Aristotle, [do.] de Cice-
ron, Retraite de dix Mille, Revolution d'Angleterre—3
Tom., [do.] de Swede—2 Tom. relies en un, [do.] de la
Republique Romaine—3 Tom.

Seventh Shelf, duodecimo. Le Roman consique de Mr

Scarron—2 Tom., Voyage d'Hennepin, [do.] de -France, [do.] de Damont—4 Tom., [do.] de Lucan, [do.] aux Indes, [do.] de Bemier, Tableaux de l'amour, Traduction de Retrone—2 Tom., Theatre de Corneille—5 Tom., Tacite— 2 Tom., Fables de le Fontaine—5 Tom., [do.] d'Aesope, Galanterie de Monseigneur le dauphin.

Eighth Shelf, duodecimo. Voyage aux Isles d'Amerique— 6 Tom., [do.] d'L'Europe—7 Tom., [do.] d'Italie, [do.] du Nord, Le Voyageurs de L'Europe—2 Tom., Nouvelles de Scarron—2 Tom., Oeuvres de [do.]—2 Tom., Derniers Oeuvres [do.]—2 Tom., Quinte Curce, Receuils des Traitez de Paix, Relation de l'Expedition de Carthegena, Vie de Richelieu—2 Tom., [do.] de Socrate.

Case No. 13, Lowest Shelf, duodecimo. Journal des Scavans—24 Tom.

Second Shelf, duodecimo. La Bibliotheque choisie—23 Tom., Histoire de L'Academie Francoise, Recherche de la Verite—3 Tom. relies en 2, Testament du Marquis de Louvois, [do.] de Richelieu, Femmes Illustres—2 Tom., L'histoire D' Hollande par Aubery, La Politique de France, Amusemens Serieux, L'Art de parler, Interets des Princes, Oeuvres [de] du Bartas, Abrigé des Trois Etats.

Third Shelf, duodecimo. La Bibliotheque Universalle— 25 Tom. relie en 22, Rabelais reforme, Arliquiniana, Les Essais de Montaigne—2 Tom., Lettres de Voiture, [do.] dune Religieuse Portugaise, Oeuvres de Rabelais—2 Tom., Lettres Choisie du Sieur de Balzac, Histoire de la Bible, Traduction des odes d'Anacreon.

Fourth Shelf, octavo & duodecimo. Methode Latine, [do.] Greque, Lettres sur les Anglois, L'Homme Universalle, L'Etat et Succes de France, Traité de la Com [?], Remarques sur la Langue francaise par Vuagelais, 2 Tom., Contes des Contes—2 Tom., Conversations de Morale—2 Tom., Diversitez Curieuses—7 Tom., Oeuvres de Rapin—3 Tom., Lettres de Compte de Bussy—4 Tom., [do.] du Cardinal Mazarin—2 Tom., Dialogues des Morts—2 Tom., Amours de Cleanthe, Traite du Feu.

Fifth Shelf, duodecimo. Le Grand Miroir du Monde, Menagiana—2 Tom., Pieces Galantes—4 Tom., Tableau de L'Amour, Traite de la Civilite Francoise, Etat de France —3 Tom., Du Ble Esprit, L'Art heraldique, Des Bons Mots &c, Lettres Gallantes—7 Tom., [do.] de Lorcedani, Testament de Louvois, Oeuvres de St Evrement—7 Tom. relies en 4, Dissertation sur Monde St Evrement, Testament de Colbert, Les Agreemens & les chagrin du marriage—4 Tom.

Sixth Shelf, duodecimo. Cartes Nouveaux—2 Tom., Parfait Courtisan, Lettres de Boursault, Histoire de la Monarchie Francoise—3 Tom., L'Art de Plaire, Memoires de Duc de Guise, [do.] de Beaujeu, Parrhariana, Les Malades de Belles Humein, Reflections sur la Ridicule, Modiles des Conversations, Logique de Crousaz—3 Tom., Reflections et Bons Mots &c—2 copies, La Rhetorique par Lainy, De l'incredulite, Theatre Philosophique, L'Homme de Coeur, Pensier ingenieuses, Entretiens d'Ariste & d'Eugnie.

CLASSICKS & OTHER LATIN & GREEK AUTHORS.

Case No. 13, *the Two Uppermost Shelves, octavo & duodecimo.* Clerici Logica, Schefferus de Style, Terentius Fabri, Academia Orbis Christiani, Terentius Christianus— 2 vols., Vigerus de idiotismis Graecae dictionis, Elzevir Livy, Miltoni Logica, Phodri Fabula, Thesaurus Poeticus, Baronii Metaphysica, Buxtorfs Hebrew Grammar, Dyche's Vocabulary, Burgersdicii Logica, Juvenalis Latyrae [?], Terentii Comedie, Lucianni Dialogi, Manitowompae Pomantamoonk, Greek Testament, Justini Historia, Lusus Poeticus, Caesari Commentarii, De Institutione Grammatico, Cicero de Officiis, Farbri Lucretius, Sandersoni Logica, Thesaurus Poeticus, Institutio Graecie Grammatices, Juvenalis et Persiivatyra, Erasmi Adagiorum Epitome, Novum Testamentum Antiquum, Leusden's Greek Testament, Testamentum Graecum—2 vols., Van Sand historie der Nederlanden—2 vols., Ciceronis Opera Philosophica, Erasmi Opera—2 vols., Commenii Physica, Polydor Vergil, Dutch Eupues, Senae Tragedio, Sumerti Naturalis Scientiae

Epitome, Semnius de Miraculis, Savilius in Tacitum, Tobaccologia, Erasmus de Copia Verbum, Pausophiae Podronus, Apthonii Progymnasmata, Thesauri Caesares, Hortulas Genialis, Macovii Metaphysica, Hores Poctarum, Textoris Dialogi, Animalium Historia, Fostneri Notae in Tacitum, Erasmi Vita, [do.] Colloquia, Barclayii Sabyricon, Horatii Poemata Notis I Bond, Dyche's Phoedras, Grancis's Horace —4 vols., Davidson's [do.]—3 vols., [do.] Virgil—2 vols., 1st wanting, Clarkes Suetonius—2 copies, [do.] Justin, [do.] Nepos, Sterlings Terrence, Terentius Delphini—2 copies, Holmes Greek Grammar, Homeri Opera, Cato's Disticks, Sallust Minelii, Aesopi Fabula gr. & lat., Cicero de Officiis, Lilly's Grammar—2 copies, Isocrates Orationes et Epistolae, Nova Via docendi graecci, Porta Linguarum, Clarkes Introduction—2 copies, Gradus a Parnassum, Caesaris Commentarii, De Signo Filii Hominis, Turners Grammatical Exercises, Ovidii Opera, Clarke's Oesop, Virgilii Opera, Sententia Pueriles—2 copies, Disputationes Pueriles.

Case No. 14, Lower Shelf, folio. Ammianus Marcellanus, Appiano Opera Graeco Latina, Aristophanis Comediae— Lat., Budoei Commentarii Linguie, Graecae, Luciani Opera—Lat., Lexicon Pentaglotton, Zenophontis Opera Gr Lat, Stephani Dictionarium, Rhodigiani Sectionis Antiquie, Heroditi Historia, Erasmi Adagia—2 copies, Josephi Opera Gr Lat.

Second Shelf, folio & quarto. Scaligeri Poetices, Skinneris' Lexicon, Isocratis Opera, Fabulae Hygini, Censura Celebriorum Authorum, Barnes's Euripides, Caesaris Commentaries, Virgilii Opera, Hobbes's Thucydides, Pindari Opera, Alfieri's Italian & English Dictionary—2 vols., Dictionnaire de Richelet, Littleton's Dictionary, Rhemnir Grammatica, Suetonii Opera, Danets Classical Dictionary.

Third Shelf, duodecimo. Livii Orationes, Virgilius Minelii, Roma Pertitula, Lucanus, Petrarcha de remediis utrius Fortunae, Aldus Minutius, Justina Historia, Historia Romana, Cornelius Tacitus, Valerius Maximus, Plauti Commediae, Martialis Epigrammata, Quintus Curtius, Lemnius de Constitutione Corporis, Pindari Opera—2 vols., Terentii Comediae, Zenophon de Cyri institutione, Homeri Odysses —3 vols., Homeri Ilias—3 vols., Terentius, Sleidan de Monarchiis, Florus, Lipsi Monita—2 copies, Lipsi Politica, Ovidii Opera—3 vols., Prudentii Opera, Homeri Epitheta, Sallust, Horace, Bibliotheca Botanica.

Fourth Shelf, quarto. Le Tresor de Ouidin, Gouldman's Latin Dictionary, Robartsoni Thesaurus Linguae Janetae, Homeri Ilias, Littleton's Dictionary, Dictionnaire Francoise et Latine, Biblia Hebraica, Hexham's English & Dutch Dictionary, Devarius de Graecae linguae Particulis, Robartsoni thesaurius linguae Graecae, Sewell's English & Dutch Dictionary, Dictionnaire de Vineroni, Des Cartes Philosophia.

Fifth Shelf, octavo. Buxtorfi Lexicon, Isocrates Opera Gr Lat, Luciani Opera Gr Lat, Ciceronis Orationes—3 vols., [do.] Epistola—2 vols., [do.] Opuscula, Homeri Ilias, Smetii Prosodia, Walkers Idioms, Popma de differentia verborum, Gradus ad Parnassum, Commenii Jamea Linguarum, Anacreon Teius, Donati Terentius, English Epictetus, Zenophon, Budeus de Studio, Petronius Arbiter, Art of thinking.

Sixth Shelf, duodecimo. Ciceronis Opera Foulis — 20 Tom., Portae Magia Naturalis, Terentii Comediae, Aphorismi Hieroglyphici, Commenii Sebrola Ludus, Sandersoni Logica, Epigrammatum Delectus, Dutch Grammar, Horatii Opera, Virgillius, Cornelius Nepos, Valerius Maximus, Aliani Historia Faberi, Schenckelius detectus.

Seventh Shelf, octavo. Jensii Sectiones Lucianae, Caesaris Commentarius Delphini, Terentiae Comediae [do.], Virgilii Opera [do.], Horatii [do.]—2 copies, Johnsoni Sophocles Tragedies—2 vols., Polyacni Stratagemata, Grammaire Generale, Waesburgae Poematrum Periphrasis, Cardamus de rerum Varietate, Gazophylucium Anglicanum, Torriano's Italian Grammar, Wall's Logica, New Gefunden EDEN, Examen Philosophiae Platonis, Keckenni

Systema Logica, Theophrasti Characteres, Sertorius de Notis Romanorum, Janua Quatuor Linguarum, Bontekoe Tractatjes, Clerici Ars Critica, Aschami Epistolae.

Case No. 15, Lowest Shelf, folio. Demosthenes & Eschini Opera—3 vols., Platonis Opera Serrani—3 vols., Minshey's Guide to tongues, Etimologia Lingua Graeca, Dyonissii Halicarnassi Hist Rom—2 vols., Holyokes Dictionary, Gyraldi Opera, Dictionaire de Miege, Polybius—gr & Lat, Petiti Leges Atticae, Scapulae Lexicon.

Second Shelf, folio. Stephani Thesaurus Linguae Latinae —2 vols., Senecae Opera, Josephi Opera per Hudson—2 vols., Constantini Lexicon, Thucydides—gr & Lat., Thesaurus Graecae Linguae, Deonis et Ziphilini Opera.

Third Shelf, octavo. Dei Hominis Elogia, Boeti de Consolatio Philosophiae, Cardanus de Subtile fate [?], Scaliger ——, Scoti Grammatica, Bulialdus de Natura Lucis, Questiones ex Tacito, Seneca Opera, Observationes in Val Max & Vell Patere, Capello Satyricon, Vivis de anima et Vita, Cassandri Natura loqua, Toxius de Natura Philosophia, Sciopii Grammatica Philosophica, Petravii Rationarum Temporum, Macrafioti Ars Memoriae, Stephani Colloquia, Gretseri Institutiones Linguae [?], Janua Linguarum, Erasmi Apothegmata, Adamantii Phisiognomonicon, Antonius de Coloribus, Terentii Comediae.

Fourth Shelf, octavo. Luciani Opera—10 vols., Notae in Lucianum—2 Tom., Homeri Ilias—4 Tom., [do.] Odysses —4 Tom., Dounaei Praelictiones, Terentiae Comediae, Schenckelii Methodus, Buxtorfi Thesaurus Grammaticus, Gellii Noctes Atticae, Plutarchi Opera—6 Tom., [do.]—7 Tom.

Fifth Shelf, duodecimo. Phaedri Fabulas, Latin Testament—2 copies, English Epictetus, Mella Patrum, Synonimorum Sylva, Institutiones Philosophicae, Hooles Nomenclature, Sleidan de quatuor imperus, Westminster Greek Grammar—2 copies, Valerius Maximus, Ars Cogitandi, Enchiridion Ethicum, Seneca Tragediae, [do.] Opera, Walkers English Particles, Erasmi Colloquiae,

Ovidii Opera, Compendium Trium Linguarum, Socini
Opera, Chronicon Carionis, Columella de Re Rustica, Cae-
saris Commentarii, Cicero de Officiis, Sinetii Prosodia, Lin-
guae Graecae Institutiones Grammaticae, Juvenal Delphini,
Quintilian [do.], Sallust [do.], Cornelius Nepos, Herodia-
mus—Gr & Lat., Phalaris Epistolae, Schrevelii Lexicon,
Theocritas Greek [?], Florus Delphini, Turicus Propho-
cies, Italian Grammar, Scepsis Scientifica, Des Cartes de
Prima Philosophia, Isocrates Gr & Lat, Commentaria in
Syntaxisartis Mirabilis—4 Tom. in 3, Alstedii Thesaurus
Chronologiae—2 copies, Josephi Opera, Senecae Tragediae,
Symbolum Pythagoricum, Olizarovius de politica Homi-
num-Societate, Mela de Situ Orbis.

[Here ends the list of the classics, the rest being unclas-
sified.]

Case No. A, Lowest Shelf, folio. Pole Synopsis—4th &
5th vols., Laws of Virginia, Chambers Dictionary—2 vols.,
Dictionnaire Oeconomique—2 vols., Willugbai Ornithologia,
Lediards Naval History, Dictionary of all Religions, Mil-
lers Dictionary, —— Gardiners Dictionary, Architecture
di Scamozi, Herberts Travels.

Second Shelf, folio. Albert Durer's Drawings, Dilenii
Historia Muscovum, Biblia Junii et Tremelli, Coopers
Latin Dictionary, Buchannani Opera—2 vols., Flower
Garden Displayed, Stanley's History of Philosophy, Addi-
son's Works—4 vols., Cudworth's Intellectual System—2
vols., Histoire des Papes—5 vols.

Third Shelf, octavo. Ray's Wisdom of God, Operas
Italian & English—5 vols., Janua Linguarum, Spencer
de Urim et Thummim, Toyson d'Or, Collection of old
Plays—10 vols., History of Robbers—3 vols., Classical Geo-
graphical Dictionary, Rettrato di Roma Antica, Triomphe
Hermetique, Dictionaire Hermetique, Le Filet d'Ariadne,
Le Text d'Alchymie, Philosophie inconnue, Lumiere des
Tenebres, Clavis Homerica, Plays—2 vols., Planters Physi-
cian, Gentleman's Magazine, Baxter on the Soul—2 vols.,
—— Matho—2 vols., Ciceroni Orationes—3 vols., Boswell's

Method of Study—2 vols., Duke of Berwick's Life, Walpoles
Administration, Life of the Duke of Marlborough—2 vols.,
[do.] Lewis the 14th—3 vols., [do.] of the Czar of Muscovy,
Fielding's Miscellanies—3 vols., Collection of Tryals—2
vols., Miscellanies—3 vols., Travels of Cyrus, Discours
Philosophique.

Fourth Shelf, octavo.   Grey on Learning Hebrew, Middle-
ton's Cicero's Epistles, Shuckford's Connexion—3 vols.,
Conduct of the Duchess of Marlborough, Other Side of the
Question, Turnbull on Education, Rollins Roman History
—9 vols., Watson's Horace—2 vols., Francis's [do.]—2 vols.,
Atterbury's Sermons—2 vols., Life of King Alfred, Memoirs
of Earl of [Orrery], Dissertation upon Parties, Blair's
Sermons—4 vols.

Fifth Shelf, duodecimo.   Nature delineated—4 vols., Roma
Illustrate, Rollins des Belle Lettres—4 vols., [do.] Ancient
History—10 vols., Terence Comedia—3 vols., Life of Prince
Eugene, [do.] Marlborough, History of Joseph Andrews—
2 vols., Newton's Philosophy explained—2 vols., Antoninus's
Meditations, Moral Essays—2 vols.

Case No. B, Lowest Shelf, folio.   Kircheri Arca Noàe,
Stevens' Spanish Dictionary, The Common Prayer, Miege's
Dictionary, The Alcoran, Gwillims Heraldry, Raii Historia
Plantarum—2 vols., Stanley's Philosophers, Vocabulaire
dell Crusca, Gruterii Florilegii—Tom. 2nd, Clericus in
Pentateuch, Lock's Works—3 vols., The Art of Sound
Building.

Second Shelf, folio.   Salisbury's Mathematical Collections,
Lex Mercatorum, Jenkes Arithmetick, Browns Vulgar
Errors, Grotius on War and Peace, L'Estrange's Aesop—2
vols., Kersey's Mathematical Elements, Cambridge Con-
cordance, Hobbes Leviathan, Moxon's Perspective, The
Jesuit Morals, Advice from Parnassus, Popes Odyssey—5
vols., [do.] Iliad—6 vols. in 3, Euclid's Elements, Bacon's
Natural History, Tyson's Anatomy of a Pigmy, Rathbone's
Surveying.

Third Shelf, folio.   Boyle's Works—5 vols., Emblems of

Love, Figures de Versailles, Icones diversae, N Regionum delinatio, Amours de Cupid & Psyche, Gemme Antiche, Albius History of English Insects, Habits delineated, Figures de Sadler, Antiquitez de Perrier, [Views] of Versailles, Maison de France, Palazzi di Roma, Segment Marmor Romanorum, Tableau de Cabin du Roy, Festiva ad Capita Annulumque Decursio, Wells's Ancient & Modern Maps.

Fourth Shelf, folio. Ovid delineated, Maps of Great Britain, Bidloe's Anatomy, Catesby's Natural History of Carolina, [do.] of Plants, New General Atlas, Two large Books of Maps, Sellers Sea Atlas, Atlas Celestis.

Case No. C, Lowest Shelf, folio. Vitruvius Britannicus—3 vols., Atlas Gerardi—2 vols., Rowe's Lucan, Speeds History of Great Britain, [do.] Maps, Seats in Great Britain, Records of the Virginia Company—2 vols., Palladio's Architecture, Albertis Architecture—2 vols., History of the Bible with Cutts—2 vols.

Second Shelf, folio. Historie de L'Academie—3 vols., [do.] des Inscriptiones—4 Tom., Voyage du Frezier, [do.] de Feuillee—2 vols., [do.] de Tournefort, Ouvrages des Peintres —2 vols., Principes L'Architecture, Moeurs des Sauvages— 2 vols., I Cats Werken, Oeconomie de la Campagne, Traité d'Architecture, Medall Hist Van Hollande.

Third Shelf, folio. Merceri Thesaurus linguae Sanctae, Curiositez de la Mer des Indes, Histoire de France—3 vols., Dictionaire des Arts et Sciences, [do.] de L'Academie, Collier's Dictionary, Raleigh's History of the World, Dictionaire de Bayle—4 vols., Supplement de Bayle.

Fourth Shelf. Histoire de l'Academie from 1692 to 1718 —23 vols.

Case No. D, Lowest Shelf, folio. Prior's Poems, Antiquities Expliquies Par Montfaucon—10 vols., Pandectae Canoni Gr. & Lat.—2 vols., Gentleman's Recreation, Blank Books —2 vols.

Second Shelf, folio. Acts of William the 3rd, Nili Epistolae, N Tertum de le Clerc, Religion of Nature delineated, Travels from Moscow to China, Epitome Annalium Ecclesiae, Ushur's Body of Divinity, Private Directions for Travels in England—MS, Donati Roma vetus et Recens, History of the Bible, Critical History of the Old Testament, [do.] New Testament, Canons of the Church of England, Dinothi Bellum civile Galliae, Lyra Prophetica, Vidman's History of the Universe—2 vols., Prgim [?] of Parliament, Riccii Expeditio Christiana ad Linas, Guicciard Historia Itineraria, Machiavelii Opera, Tablau du Muses.

Third Shelf, folio. Ogilby's Africa, [do.] America, Embassy to China, Supplement to Josephus, Collection of Voyages—2 vols., Histoire de France—3 vols., [do.] de Louis Le Grand, Howells History of the World—3 vols.

Fourth Shelf, quarto. Bradley's Work of Nature, Daniel's History of France—7 vols., Histoire d'Angleterre—10 Tom., Quintilien de L'Orateur.

Case No. E, Lowest Shelf, folio. Spelman's Glossarium, Pisonis Indiarum Historia, Phillip's Dictionary, The Royal Commentary, Laws and Government of England, Chronicle of Britain, Livy's Roman History, Dr. Dees Relations, Algernon Sidney on Government, Harrington's Works, Robert's Map of Commerce, History of Scotland, Heylin's History of the Reformation, Cox's History of Ireland, Bacon's Natural History, The State of Europe, Cantera's Dooms, Tryal of Arch-bishop Laud, Caxton's History of Troy, Lydgates [do.].

Second Shelf, octavo. De Rebus Sicilae, Caesarea or an account of Jersey, The London Spy, The German Spy, Annals of Europe—4 vols., State of England, History of Europe—4 vols., Complete History of Europe, History of the King of Sweden, [do.] Apparitions, [do.] Pirates, [do.] Robberies, [do.] Portugal, [do.] The Saracens—2 vols., Descripto Italiae, Well's Sacred Geography—4 vols., Philips Conferences, New Essays on Trade, Robinson Crusoe's Life.

Third Shelf, duodecimo. Craftsman—14 vols., Busbequais's Epistles, De Rebus et Factis Memorabilibus, Guiccardi de iidem, Life of Gustavus Adolphus, Description of Paris, Secret History of Charles 2nd & James 2nd, Valuation of Ecclesiastical Preferments, Illustrious Actions of William Henry P of Wales, Second History of D'Alancour & Q Elizabeth, State of London, Life of the Bishop of Munster, Burnet's Letters on Italy &c., State of France, The Turkish Spy—8 vols., History of Lewis the 13th.

Fourth Shelf, octavo. Bucaniers of America, Ortelii, thesaurus Geographicus, Mieretii Syntagma Subsisivarum, Varii Tractatus, Polytecks & Maxims van Hollande, Memoirs of Queen Anne, Polinitz's Memoirs—4 vols., Collection of Histories, Terence in usum Delphini, Life of Lord Bacon, Ritteri Cosmographia Proro-Met [?], Grotii Annales Belgici, Echard's Ecclesiastical History—2 vols., History of the Magicians.

Fifth Shelf, octavo. Breviarum Chronologicum, History of Schah Nadir, Chamberlayne's Present State, Oldcastle's Remarks, College Character, Marlborough's Conduct, Life of William the third, History of the Turks—2 vols., Janthesius de Gubernaculo, Locke's Remains, History of Germany—2 vols., Life of Pythagoras, Voyage of the Dutch, State of Virginia, History of the World—4 vols., [do.] Virginia, Echard's Roman History—5 vols., Welwood's Memoirs.

Sixth Shelf, octavo. Puffendorf Alliance 'twixt Sweden & France, Revolution in Sweden, Prideaux Life of Mahomet, Philip de Comines, Systema Ecclesiastica Sclavonia, Adam's Veto Theolog Germanicorum—4 vols., Historia Exertorum, Glanville on Witchcraft, Bacon's Remains, History of the League, Cluverii Historia, Grafferi Itinerarium, Benjamin, Coke's detection—2 vols., Life of Van Tromp, Le Clercs, Compendium of History, Caesurum Vitae, Admiranda Nili, Deliciae Variorum Itinerariorum, Schroteri Historia Geographica, Britains Remembrancer, Debates of Lords & Commons.

Case No. F, Lowest Shelf, octavo. Monthly Mercury from 1688 to 1722.

Second Shelf, octavo.   Monthly Mercury continued to 1742 —4 vols., State of Europe—2 vols., History of [do.] 1703, Gentleman's Magazine — 8 vols., Works of the Learned— 8 vols.

Third Shelf, octavo.   Works of the Learned continued— 4 vols., Debates in Parliament—22 vols.

Fourth Shelf, octavo.   Political State—26 vols.

Fifth Shelf, octavo.   Political State continued—13 vols., Goodwin's Antiquities, Use of the Fathers, Pamphlets—14 vols., Miscellanies.

Sixth Shelf, duodecimo.   Tilomanni Discursus philosophicus, Essay on Preaching, Biblia Graeca—2 vols., Human Prudence, Al Mondo, Baudi Epistola, Hornii Ulysses per, [do.] Historia Ecclesiastica, [do.] Arca Noe, [do.] Orbis Politicus, Barclaii Argenis, Bronchorsti Aphorismi Politici, Symbola Politica, Valentini Epistolae, Ens Epidorfi, Ernstii Philosophia, Vitae humanae Proscenium, Aphorismi politici & Martiales, Newhusii Epistolae, Leusdeni Compendium Novi testamenti, Bartholemus de Mundo, Diodorus Siculus, Historicum Compendium Belgicum, Thomas a Kempis, · Helenae Raptus, Castaign's Interest Book, Meibon de usu flagorum in re vene rea.

Seventh Shelf, duodecimo.   Nanfa's Essays, Beverly on Fornication, Kormanni Templum Naturae, Lomeie de Bibliothecis, Eben Calendium historicum, De obligatione Conscientae, Pamphlets, Gronovius de Sertertius, [do.] de centerimis usuris, Pedagogus divitum, Art of Swimming, of Oeconomy, Christian Virtuoso, Historica Franciae, Pontani Discursus Historicus, Epictetus, Cases of Conscience, Method with the Deists, Conjugium Conjurgicum, Staera Appenra &c, Art of Metals, Articuli Lambethiani, Men before Adam, Flores Intellectuales, Rabelais Works—4 vols., Elenchus Motuum, Campiani Rationes, Chytraeus de lectione Historiae, Echard's Geographical Compendium.

Case No. G, Lowest Shelf, quarto.   Saunderson's Algebra —2 vols., Newhouse's Navigation, Hatton's Arithmetick, Jee Vaart van Gietermaker, Pritle Questiones Physico

Mathematicae, Argoli Ephemerides—3 vols., Cluverii Geographia, Art of Accounts, Travaux du Mars—3 vols., Sturmins's Mathematicks, Ship Building, Clavis Commercii, Moxon on the Globes, Wards Mathematicks, Woolthius's Algebra, Palladio's Architecture, Geometrical Key, Vade Mecum, Newton's Opticks, [do.] Mathematical Philosophy, [do.] Recreations, Derham's Astro Theology, Beverigii Chronologia.

Second Shelf, octavo. Debtor & Creditor, Rowes Navigation, Bucholeri Index Chronologicus, L de Linda Orbis descriptio, Flavel's Tables of Interest, Constructions of Maps & Globes, Cours de Mathematique par Organum—5 Tom., Watson's Astronomy, Whiston's Astronomical Lectures, Practice of Arithmetick, Whiston's Astronomy, [do.] Euclid, Longitude found, De Cometis [?], Des Cartes's Musick, Lamy de Perspective, Norwoods Trigonometry, Coley's Astrology, Gunter's Works, Blaeu de Usu Globocum &c, Wharton's Works, Grammaticae Libri Tres, Celestial Worlds discovered, World in the Moon.

Third Shelf, duodecimo. Treculphi Chronica, Gassendi Astronomica, Leyborn's Guide, Cocke's Decimal Algebra, Panarithmologia, Wingate's Arithmetick, Epitome of Geography, Moore's Arithmetick, Oughtred's Clavis Mathematica, Practical Architecture, Gravesande's Philosophical Institutions, Practique d'arithmetique, Galilaei Systema Cosmicum, Wilkin's Mathematical Magick, Playford's Musick, Haynes Trigonometry, Elemens de Geometrie, Euclid's Geometry—vol. 2nd, Chales's Euclid, Recreations Mathematique, Harris's Algebra, Jacquets Geometry, [do.] Arithmetick, Leeks Gnomonicks, Abregé de Vitruve, Hedraei Astrolabium, Sphaera Jonnes de Sacrobosco, Euclidis Elementa, Compendium Mathematicum, Barrow's Euclid Elements of Geometry, Sellers Geography, [do.] Atlas Celestis, [do.] Atlas Maritimus, [do.] Pocket Collections, Carionis institutiones Mathematica, [do.] Chronicon, Varenii Geographia.

Fourth Shelf, octavo. Doctrine of the Catholic Church,

Boyers Dictionary, Cole's [do.], Bailey's [do.], Quesnal on
the New Testament, Clarendon's Review of the Leviathan,
Schrivelii Lexicon, Beverley's History of Virginia, Varii
Tractatus—2 vols., Seneca's Morals, Richteri Axiomata
oeconomica, [do. do.] Politica, Timothy on Philatheus—3
vols., Elliott's Indian Bible, Cockburn on Duels, Trials of
Wits, Palmer's Essays, Law of Subordination, Eme's Deist,
Mottos of the Wanderers.

Fifth Shelf, octavo. Apology for Parson Alberoni, Whis-
ton's Primitive Christianity—5 vols., Hobbes's Tripos,
Aristotle's Art of Poetry, Colloquium Ethicum, Book of
Martyrs—2 vols., Royal Politician—2 vols., Rights of the
Christian Church, Bruyiere's Characters, Mahomets Alco-
ran, Reformation Abridges, Hickeringills Works—3 vols.,
Heiders philos: politic: Systema, Consolation of Philoso-
phy, Lux Orientalis, More's Account of Virtue, Loyd's
Popery, Stanhope's Epictetus, Scripture Chronology,
Saints Reign upon Earth, Military Discipline, Of Frugality.

Sixth Shelf, duodecimo. Argyle's Instruction to a Son,
Carter's Passions, [do.] Proverbs, Allington's Grand Conspiracy, Christian Policy, Raleigh's Mahomet, Polit: et
Milit: Haut-bock, Historia Bataviae, [do.] Britannien,
[do.] De Spectrés, Politike Discoursen, Frontinus, Historien de Russen, Spanhemii introductio ad Historiam, Military Dictionary, Galdene Annotatien, Naerdere unie,
Wheari Reflectiones historicae, De Conscientia, Valsche
Kaerspaeldus, British Compendium, Larger British Compendium, Irish [do.], Scottish [do.], English Baronetts—3
vols., Comenii Historia, Raleighs Remains, De Republica
Hebraeorum.

Seventh Shelf, duodecimo. Rosos's View of all Religions,
Petri Rami de Militia, Julii Caesaris Opera, Emblemes
divers—2 vols., Alciati Emblemata, Biblia sacra Junii et
Trimelli, Gildon's Letters, Memoirs of the navy, Eure-
mont's Essays, Sibelline Oracles, Montaigne's Essays—3
vols., Art of Speaking, Spanish Decameron, More's Utopia,
History of Medals & Coins, Locke on Government, [do.]
Reasonableness of Christianity, Mistresses of France, Eikon

Basilikee, Thompson's adversas Lipfiune, History of Mo-
nastical Orders, Frauds of the Monks, Dissertatio Le
Divities, Heinsii Orationes, Mythologia Naturalis Comitis,
History of Oracles, Sea Dialogues, Scots fencing Master,
Solomon's Ethicks &c.

Case No. H, Lowest Shelf, Quarto. Aulus Gellius Delphini Paris Edition, Justinius [do.], Florus [do.], Sallustius [do.], Dictis Cretensis [do.], Tacitus [do.]—4 vols.,
Quintus Curtius [do.], Caesaris Commentarii [do.], Valerius Maximus [do.], Cornelius Nepos [do.], Titus Livius
[do.]—6 vols., Suetonius [do.].

Second Shelf, quarto. Statius Delphini—2 vols., Plautus
[do.]—2 vols., Prudentius [do.], Catullus Propertius [do.]
—2 vols., Martialis [do.], Virgilius [do.], Claudianus [do.],
Ovidus [do.]—4 vols., Juvenalis [do.], Horatius [do.],—2
vols., Lucretius [do.], Manilius [do.], Phoedri Fabulae.

Third Shelf. Wasse's Sallust, Pomponius Mela Vossii—2
vols., Suetonius Causabon, Ausonicus Variorum, Lucanus
[do.], Marcobius [do.], Tacitus [do.], Ovidi Opera [do.]
—3 vols., Tullius de Oratore [do.], Statius [do.], Lucretius
[do.], Historia Augustorum Scriptorum, Casteus Blancardi,
Sallustius Gruterii.

Fourth Shelf, folio & quarto. Vergilii Opera, Horatii
[do.], Catulli Propertii, Terentii Comediae, Diogenes Laer-
tius—2 vols., Phoedri Fabulae, Horatius Bentlei, Plautus
Delphini—2 vols., Petronius Burmanni—2 vols., Silius
Italicus Drakenborchi, Barnes's Homer—2 vols., Quin-
tiliani Institutiones, [do.] Declamationes, Polydor Virgil.

Fifth Shelf, octavo. Vellius Paterculus Delphini, Eutro-
pius [do.], Panygeric Vetus [do.], Pomponius Festus [do.],
Apuleius [do.]—2 vols., Terentius [do.], Boetius [do.],
Cicero de Oratore [do.]—2 vols., [do.] Orationes [do.]—3
vols., [do.] Epistola [do.], Plinius [do.]—5 vols., Ciceronis
Opera, Marcellini res Gestae.

Sixth Shelf, duodecimo. Cicero Gronovii—11 vols., Titius
Livius Clerici—10 vols., Seneca Elzevir—3 vols., Notae ad
Senecam, Caesaris Commentarii, Plini Epistolae, [do.]
Historia—3 vols., Senecae Opera, Sallustius.

APPENDIX B

GENEALOGY*

THE BYRDS IN ENGLAND

1. HUGH LE BIRD, younger son of the family of Charlton, *m.* Werburga, daughter of Roger Dombvel, and had issue: 2. John², *m.* Isabel ——, and had a son, Hugh le Bird³, who d. s. p.; 3. *Richard²*; 4. William², *m.*, and had a son, John le Bird³, who d. s. p.

3. Richard², *m.* Mary, daughter of Henry Brentishall, and had a son,

5. David³, *m.* Elizabeth, daughter of John Fitzhugh, of Lithrogg, and had a son,

6. Hugh⁴, *m.* Roose, daughter of Albaney Cheyney, and had a son,

7. David⁵, *m.* Mabel, sister and heir of Henry de Broxton, and had issue: 8. *Richard⁶*; 9. *Hugh⁶*; and 10. William⁶, about whom there is no data.

8. Richard⁶ le Bird, of Broxton, *m.* Mabel Codogan, and had a son, 11. *Hugh⁷.*

---

* This Genealogy was prepared by Mr. W. G. Stannard and published in the "Beau Monde," a Richmond periodical which is not now published, April 7 and 14, 1894. Through the kindness of Mr. Stannard the editor has been able to add to it some facts not embraced in the original articles. The English portion of the Genealogy was taken by Mr. Stannard from Holms's "Heraldic Collections for Chester" (Harleian MSS., No. 2119), and from a pedigree prepared at the Heralds' College, London, in 1702, for William Byrd II. For some of the facts relating to the children of Richard C. Byrd, of "Whitehall," the editor is indebted to the kindness of Mrs. Sally Nelson Robins, assistant secretary and librarian of the Virginia Historical Society. —EDITOR.

9. Hugh[6] le Bird, *m.* Agnes, daughter of William de Bick-erton, and had issue: 12. *David*[7] *of Broxton;* 13. Ughtred[7], who left two sons, Thomas[8] and David[8]; 14. John[7], of Broxton.

11. Hugh[7] le Bird, *m.* ——, and had a son, John le Bird[8] of Broxton, whose daughter and heiress was Margaret[9], who in 1379 was wife of Roger Bulkeley.

12. David[7] le Bird, of Broxton, *m.* Mawde, daughter of David de Edge, of Edge, and had a son,

15. John[8] Bird, *m.* Alice, daughter and heiress of Peter Bulkeley, of Broxton (by his wife Nicola, daughter of Thomas[8] Bird), and had issue: 16. John[9] (who witnessed a deed in 1440 and had a son, John le Bird, of Tilston, who was living in 1467); 17. *Tomalyn*[9].

17. Tomalyn[9] Bird, of Bostock, living in 1440, *m.* Phillippa, daughter of Hugh Broxton, of Henhall, and had a son,

18. Henry[10] Bird, of Broxton, *m.* Winifred, daughter and heiress of Adam de Raley, and had a son,

19. John[11] le Bird, of Broxton, *m.* Ciceley, daughter of John Dutton, of Hatton, and had issue: 20. *Peter*[12]; 21. *Thomas*[12]; 22. John[12].

20. Peter[12] le Bird, of Broxton, *m.* Anne, daughter of Rich-ard Clive, of Clive, and had a son, George[13] le Bird, of Broxton, who *m.* Elizabeth, daughter of David Dodd, of Edge, and in turn had a son, Thomas[14], who *m.* Jane, daughter of Ralph Bulkeley, of Haughton. (Here in Holms's pedigree this branch of the family ends.)

21. Thomas[12] le Bird, *m.* Margaret, daughter of William Dodd, of Broxton, and had a son,

23. Henry[13] le Bird, of Broxton, *m.* Anne, daughter of John Phelkin, of Tattenhall, and had issue: 24. *John*[14]; 25. *Thomas*[14]; 26. Hughe[14] (d. s. p.); 27. *Robert*[14]; 28. Roger[14]; 29. Anne[14], *m.* John Carden, of Calcott; 30. Elizabeth[14], *m.* Hugh Williamson, of Chalkley; 31.

Mary[14], m. Richard Davenport, of Locroff; 32. Katherine[14]; 33. Robert[14], m. Elizabeth, daughter of Francis Lolland (or Callorne), of Aymount.*

24. John[14] le Bird, of London, m. Elizabeth, daughter of Oliver Burgh als Copparsmith, and had issue: (a) William[15]; (b) John[15]; (c) Henry[15]; (d) Elizabeth[15]; (e) Anne[15].

25. Thomas[14] le Bird, m. Ales Palyn, and had issue: (f) Anne[15]; (g) Raphe[15]; (h) Margery[15]; (i) Peter[15]; (j) Jane[15]; (k) Thomas[15].

27. Robert[14] Bird, m. Elizabeth Holland, and had a son,

34. John[15] Bird, m. Elizabeth Bine, and had a son,

35. Thomas[16] Bird, m. Elizabeth Bud, and had a son,

36. John[17] Bird, or Byrd, of London. He was a goldsmith of London, m. Grace, daughter of Thomas Stegg, or Stegge, of London (and for a time of Virginia, where he held important office), and had issue: 37. William[18], eldest son, and founder of the family in Virginia; 38. Thomas[18], who was perhaps the youngest child; and four daughters: Elizabeth[18] (who perhaps m. Rand), Mary[18] (who perhaps m. Guy), and Sarah[18] and Grace[18] (one of whom perhaps m. Robinson).†

THE BYRDS IN VIRGINIA

1. William[1] Byrd arrived in Virginia before 1677 (perhaps as early as 1670), and inherited the estate of his uncle, Thomas Stegg, Jr. He lived first at "Belvidere," in the bounds of the present city of Richmond, but about 1691 moved to the estate of Westover, twenty miles below his former home, on the

---

* The English genealogists have perhaps made some error in regard to 27 Robert[14], and 33 Robert[14], le Bird. It is hardly probable that a man would have two sons named Robert, one of whom married Elizabeth Holland and the other Elizabeth Lolland.

† See the letters of William Byrd[1] in the possession of the Virginia Historical Society.

James River, which became the famous seat of his family. He *m*. Mary, daughter of Colonel Warham Horsemanden, then of Charles City County, in Virginia, but who shortly returned to England, where he settled at Purleigh, in Essex. William[1] Byrd was *b*. in London in 1652, and *d*. Dec. 4, 1704, at Westover. His wife had *d*. in her forty-seventh year at the same place, Nov. 9, 1699. He had issue : 2. *William*[2] ; 3. Susan[2], who *m*. John Brayne, merchant, of London ; 4. Ursula[2], *b*. Nov. 29, 1681, *m*. Robert Beverley, the historian, *d*. Oct. 31, 1698, had one son, William[3] Beverley ; 5. Mary[2], about whose life nothing is known ; 6. Warham[2], *b*. 1685, and *d*. in childhood.

2. William[2] Byrd, *b*. March 28, 1674, *d*. at Westover, Aug. 26, 1744 ; *m*. :—

(1) Lucy, daughter of Colonel Daniel Parke, who died in 1710 as governor of the Leeward Islands, and had issue : 7. Evelyn[3], *b*. July 16, 1707, *d*., unmarried, Nov. 13, 1737 ; 8. Parke[3], *b*. Sept. 6, 1709, *d*. June 3, 1710 ; 9. Philips William[3], *b*. Feb. 23, and *d*. Dec. 9, 1712 ; 10. Wilhelmina[3], *b*. Nov. 6, 1715, *m*. Thomas Chamberlayne, of King William County, Virginia, from whom there is descended a prominent line ;*

(2) Maria, daughter and co-heiress of Thomas Taylor, of Kensington, England, and had issue : 11. *Anne*[3] ; 12. *Maria*[3] ; 13. *William*[3] ; 14. *Jane*[3].

11. Anne[3], *b*. in London, Feb. 5, 1725, *m*. Charles Carter, of "Hamstead" (afterward of "Cleve"), *d*. Sept. 11, 1757. From this marriage is descended a numerous line.

12. Maria[3], *b*. Jan. 6, 1727, *m*. Landon Carter, of "Sabine Hall," *d*. Nov. 29, 1744. From this marriage is descended a numerous line.

* For the Chamberlayne pedigree see an article by Mr. W. G. Stannard in the "Beau Monde," March 31, 1894. A bound file of this valuable little periodical is in the possession of the Virginia Historical Society.

13. William[3] Byrd, *b.* at Westover, Sept. 6, 1728,* *d.* Jan. 1, 1777, *m.* :—

(1) April 14, 1748, Elizabeth Hill, only daughter of John Carter, of "Shirley," and had issue : 15. William[4], *b.* Aug. 2, 1749, who became a lieutenant in the 17th British Regiment, and was killed at Caen, France, July, 1771, by being thrown from a carriage (d. s. p.) ; 16. John Carter[4], *b.* Jan. 27, 1751, *m.* widow of William Randolph, of "Wilton," and d. s. p. ; 17. *Thomas Taylor[4]* ; 18. Elizabeth Hill[4], *b.* Nov. 29, 1754, *m.* (1) James Parke Farley, (2) Rev. John Dunbar, (3) Colonel Henry Skipwith ; 19. *Francis Otway[4].* On July 5, 1760, Elizabeth Hill Carter Byrd died, and within six months William[3] Byrd was married to

(2) Mary,† daughter of Charles Willing, of Philadelphia, by whom he had issue : 20. Maria Horsemanden[4], *b.* Nov. 26, 1761, *m.* John Page, of "Pagebrook" ; 21. Anne Willing[4], *b.* March 25, 1763 ; 22. Charles Willing[4], *b.* April 8, 1765, *d.* Aug., 1766 ; 23. Evelyn Taylor[4], *b.* Oct. 13, 1766, *m.* Benjamin Harrison, of "Brandon" ; 24. Abby[4], *b.* Nov. 4, 1767, *m.* Judge William Nelson ; 25. Dorothy[4], *b.* Feb. 17, 1769, *d.* the 24th of the same month ; 26. Charles Willing[4], *b.* July 22, 1770, United States district judge for

* The pedigree in the "Beau Monde" has it 1729, which cannot be right. The Byrd family bible gives 1728, which has here been adopted.

† Mary Willing was first cousin of Peggy Shippen, the famous Philadelphia beauty who married Benedict Arnold. Her sympathies during the Revolution were with the British, and Arnold's invasion of Virginia brought a number of their officers to her house. She was accused of treasonable correspondence with them, but on investigation was acquitted. She ruled her house and plantations with great success, and was known far and near for the courtesy and elegance of her hospitality. The Count Chastellux was struck with her "agreeable countenance, and great good sense." Her will, with most of the facts relating to her life, is published in the Virginia Historical Magazine, Vol. VI. p. 346. The will contains a list of the Byrd portraits.

Ohio, *m.* Sarah Meade; 27. Jane[4], *b.* Jan. 17, 1773, *m.* Carter H. Harrison;* 28. *Richard Willing*[4]; 29. *William*[4].

14. Jane[3], *b.* Oct. 13, 1729, *m.* John Page, of "North End," by whom comes a numerous descent. Her portrait, showing a fine face, is now at William and Mary College.

17. Thomas Taylor[4] Byrd, *b.* Jan. 17, 1752, became a captain in the British army, where he served under Colonel Fanning, *m.* Mary, daughter of William Armistead, of "Hesse," Gloucester County, had issue : 30. John[5], killed in the battle of North Point; 31. William B.[5]; 32. *Francis Otway*[5]; 33. Elizabeth[5], *m.* in 1827 General Elisha Boyd, member of the State Senate; 34. Maria Carter[5], *m.* Philip Norborne Nicholas, of Richmond, judge of the General Court and attorney-general of Virginia, and had issue : (*a*) Cary, (*b*) Sidney, (*c*) Elizabeth Byrd, of Washington, D. C.; 35. *Charles Carter*[5]; 36. Thomas[5]; 37. *Richard E.*[5]

19. Francis Otway[4] Byrd, *b.* May 8, 1756, was officer in the British navy and resigned at the beginning of the Revolution to offer his services to America; in 1775 he was appointed an aide to General Lincoln; in Jan., 1777, he was made lieutenant-colonel of the 3d Virginia Dragoons and served through the war; afterward he was sheriff of Charles City County, and *d.* Sept. 2, 1800; *m.* Anne, daughter of Robert Munford, of "Richland," Mecklenburg County, and had issue : 38. Maria[5], *m.* Davidson Bradfute; 39. Lelia[5]; 40. Eliza[5], *m.* Alexander Tompkins; 41. Evelyn[5], *m.* Roger A. Tompkins; 42. Anne[5], *m.* —— Wright; 43. William O.[5], *d.* unmarried; 44. Abigail[5], *m.* in 1825 Dr. H. Davis.

28. Richard Willing[4] Byrd, of Smithfield, Isle of Wight County, *b.* Oct., 1774, *d.* Oct., 1815, member of the House of Delegates, 1804-6, *m.* (1) Lucy, daughter

* Carter H. Harrison moved to Kentucky, and from him comes the prominent Chicago family of the same name.

of Benjamin Harrison, of "Brandon," (2) Emily
Wilson, and by his first marriage had issue: 45.
Addison[5], *m.* —— Custis; 46. Otway[5]; 47. Mary
Anne[5], *m.* in 1825 Dr. Richard Kennon, U. S. N.

29. William[4] Byrd, *m.* Susan, daughter of Addison Lewis,
     had issue: 48 Addison[5], *m.* Susan Coke; 49. Mary[5],
     m. Richard C. Coke, M.C.; 50. Jane O.[5], *m.* G. W.
     McCandlish; 51. *Dr. Samuel Powell[5].*

32. Francis Otway[5] Byrd, served with distinction at
     Tripoli in 1805 under General Eaton, and as an
     officer of the War of 1812 with such eminent gal-
     lantry that the Virginia legislature presented him
     with a sword and a vote of thanks. He removed from
     Clarke County, Virginia, to Baltimore in 1855, and
     died there May 2, 1860, aged 72 years; *m.* Eliza
     Pleasants and had issue: 52. Mary[6], *m.* Samuel G.
     Wyman; 53. Anne[6].

35. Charles Carter[5] Byrd, *m.* Jane Turner and had issue:
     54. Lucy[6]; 55. Thomas[6].

37. Richard E[5]. Byrd, of Frederick County, *m.* in 1826 Anne,
     daughter of Benjamin Harrison, of "Brandon." He
     was a distinguished lawyer, member of the House of
     Delegates in 1839, 1840, 1842, etc., and of the Con-
     vention of 1850–51, served on the staff of General
     Gorse, C. S. A., and *d.* Jan. 1, 1872, aged 72 years;
     had issue: 56. *George H.*[9]; 57. *William[6].*

51. Dr. Samuel Powers[5] Byrd, of "Whitehall," Gloucester
     County, *m.* (1) Catherine C. Corbin, widow of ——
     Fauntleroy, and (2) Mary L., daughter of Dr. Mat-
     thew Brooke; by his first marriage had a son, 58.
     Richard E.[6]

56. George H.[6] Byrd, of New York, *m.* Lucy C., daughter of
     Edmund Wickham and his wife Lucy, daughter of
     Dr. Robert Carter; has issue: 59. Anne[7]; 60. Ed-
     mund Wickham[7]; 61. Mary Wyman[7]; 62. Alfred[7];
     63. George H.[7]; 64. Samuel W.[7]; 65. Lucy C.[7]; 66.
     William[7]; 67. Francis[7].

57. William[6] Byrd, *m.* Jennie Rivers, had issue : 68. Mary[7] ;
69. Richard[7] ; 70. Otway[7] ; 71. Margaret[7].

58. Richard C.[6] Byrd, of "Whitehall," *b.* Sept. 9, 1837, *m.*
Agnes Gordon Marshall, had issue : 72. Samuel P.[7],
b. June 23, 1861 ; 73. Richard C.[7], *m.* —— Walke ;
74. Lewis W.[7] ; 75. Mary B.[7] ; 76. Fannie M.[7], *m.* Cor-
bin Waller ; 77. Anne G.[7], *m.* —— Clark of New
York.

INDEX

INDEX

455